Chips On My Shoulders

by

Joe Robinson

Copyright: Joe Robinson 1999

Printed and published by TUPS Books, 30 Lime Street,
Newcastle upon Tyne, NE1 2PQ
Tel: 0191 233 0990 Fax: 0191 233 0578
ISBN 1 901237 13 3

*to the memory of my dear brother Michael
who left too soon*

Acknowledgements

I wish to thank my wife Judy for her support and encouragement as well as for her careful and patient editing throughout the various stages, as well for her invaluable advice.

I wish to thank my daughter Hannah for her proof reading and for her criticism which always comes so willingly.

My gratitude goes to Geoff Phillips of GP Electronic Services for supplying the background photograph for the cover.

And I wish to thank my publisher, Dave Temple of TUPS BOOKS for his encouragement, advice and kind help.

Also by Joe Robinson:

The Life and Times of Francie Nichol of South Shields
(George Allen & Unwin, 1975, Futura, edition 1977)
Adapted as a drama for the stage by Live Theatre, Newcastle upon Tyne, and subsequently for BBC Radio 4.

Claret & Cross-buttock, *(George Allen & Unwin, 1976)*

Tommy Turnbull - a miners' life, *(TUPS Books, 1996)*

Francie *(TUPS Books, 1997)* Adapted by Tom Kelly as a musical for The Customs House, South Shields

Poms & Pahehas — A Geordie in New Zealand, to be published by TUPS BOOKS in 2000

PREFACE

The first time I ever heard the phrase, 'chip on your shoulder', it was being used with regard to me. It always seemed such a silly phrase yet it was applied to me many times by various people over the years. I believe I understand what it means: basically it's a rebuke to anybody who protests and is used when no satisfactory rebuttal comes to mind. I worked this out for myself when Mr Jamieson, the commerce teacher, said it to me after I'd handed in my punishment essay. I had committed some trifling misdemeanour, the kind of thing fifteen-year-old boys do in class and even though we [he] were behind with the syllabus for the school-leaving examination, he made me write a 500 word essay. I'd rather have had the belt but he was a liberal and as such the only master that eschewed corporal punishment - certainly neither of the scripture teachers did. He was so contemptuous of the essay's worth even before I'd put pen to paper, that he couldn't be bothered to think of a title or a subject, saying it could be on anything that mattered to me.

'Injustices Perpetrated in the Name of Education' was a big, big title, I know, but I thought his curiosity would guarantee that some of his time would be wasted also. It did and quickly. He called me out in front of the class the next day, professed deep disappointment with the essay's sentiments and claimed he was hurt by it. 'You have a chip on your shoulder, Joseph,' was his rationalisation.

Before letting the episode slip back into its nearly fifty-year-old past, maybe I should say a little more about the essay. Without naming anybody, I had discoursed on victimisation by certain schoolteachers and how such a thing could adversely affect the developing personality of the pupil, perhaps turning him into a brute. Jamieson wasn't really a victimiser, he was a decent sort of a bloke; I was the victimiser in this instance. But I was really angry. And I think that is what saved my bacon.

The Veterinary Investigation Centre

1

Sleety snowflakes laden with grime were coming out of a grey green sky that had descended as far as the sagging trolley wires, and as they scudded onto the oily black road with its piles of slush and onto the sheer ice of the pavement, they decomposed in an instant.

I was standing at the bus stop on Stephenson Road, near the bottom of Heaton Road, across from Dr Grieve's, behind me the Corner House silent and in withdrawal after all the recent festivities. Out of the gloom of Newton Road came the raucous sound of the No 19 Walker Circle bus as it crossed over and headed up Heaton Road with its load of workmen, clerks, shop assistants and subdued pupils bound for Middle Street and the grimmest term of the year. My heart stopped momentarily, the way it had on the few occasions when I'd missed it and been lashed on both hands, front and back if there had been a lot of us and Headmaster Jarrold's wrath had been unassuagable.

One of Dr Grieve's cockerels gave out a strangled crow as though its testy master's huge hands were around its neck, the traffic lights changed, cars and vans raced across the junction towards Jesmond Road and all of us waiting for the trolley bus to take us into town, nimble and not so, leapt back, slipping and sliding and desperately trying to remain upright as the bow-waves of heavy slush surged the length of the queue, splattering coats and nylon stockings and filling the turn-ups of neatly-pressed trousers. With a skating motion everybody returned grumbling and moaning to their place on the edge of the kerb; where one stood determined whether one would get upstairs, downstairs or possibly not on at all.

I was well placed and today couldn't afford to spend time helping old ladies with ankles like steam-puddings, only to be barred entry myself by an elbow-patched navy blue arm whilst to the left and right of me opportunists from way back piled on.

Today was the 4th January, 1954 and I wasn't merely standing on a bleak pavement in a safe Conservative constituency of dirty old Newcastle-on-Tyne, I was on the brink of a new world. Today was the first day of my working life and I was starting at the Veterinary Investigation Centre [VIC] of the Ministry of Agriculture and Fisheries.

My father wanted me to be a civil servant like himself mainly because of the cast-iron security, doing work you were interested in was irresponsible self-indulgence as far as he was concerned. But I wanted to be a vet and because my family couldn't afford for me to take the long university course, I was hoping I might get in by a back door.

Mr Jarrold, five-tailed leather belt notwithstanding, had been dismayed when he received a request from my prospective employers for a reference; I had been top boy in his school and as close as any small wretch could get to being a favourite. The position of 'laboratory attendant' sounded so close to 'lavatory attendant' that neither he nor my father would trifle with subtle distinctions. So I had made a pact with them that I would take the Civil Service Home and Foreign Service Open Examination when it came around in March and I think they thought the allure of being one of Her Majesty's clerks punctiliously filling in forms in London or the Sudan would ultimately prove irresistible.

When the bus came I bolted straight upstairs before the conductor could shout 'Hey, you..! Downstairs..!' Downstairs was where the lame old men, women and kids went. Upstairs, with its windows streaming with condensation and air like a fire in a tobacco factory, its terminal coughing and cynical laughter, was the domain of the Working Man.

2

The veterinary department, along with various other Ministry of Agriculture divisions, was located in Elswick House, Elswick Park, in the west end of Newcastle. Like other grand houses occupied by government departments, the absolute minimum of changes and installations had been made and sufficient of the architecture and trappings left untouched, presumably to allow restoration to former glory should the Earl of Elswick ever ride in on horseback with a handful of retainers, swords drawn, to reclaim his property. High ceilings with ornate plasterwork served art rather than science, and the substantial doors, picture rails and skirting boards were probably magnificent under the hard gloss of utility paint. The most obvious concession to the vulgarity of the workplace was the huge radiators and pipes which kept the temperature of the building a degree or two above lukewarm and remaindered the massive sullen fireplaces whose gobs were covered over with hardboard.

When I had attended for the interview I'd been briefly shown around so knew the department comprised a large room with a partition that divided it into two laboratories, a tiny annex for the cleaning of glassware, an even smaller cloakroom-cum toilet, an outbuilding used as an animal house, and a shed for post-mortems.

I got off the bus at the first stop along Elswick Road, walked the short distance through the very basic park to Elswick House and its firmly closed front door and was looking around to see if there was another entrance, when a strange individual came up and introduced himself as Oliver, senior scientific assistant in the veterinary department and my immediate boss. I put my hand out and he seemed to think it very funny but took it all the same and his chins and whole buttoned-up and belted mackintoshed body shook as he chortled with delight. He was small boned and fat, rendering him almost shapeless; neither his face, his body or his hands having any recognisable structure. He had a boy's haircut, a boyish face sparsely covered with fine downy hairs, round wire NHS spectacles and a voice that didn't seem to have broken. He was like a fifty-year-old Billy Bunter and whenever I said anything his eyes lit up and rolled around in his head as though I were a big cream cake. I could see he thought I was going to need taking under his wing and that he was going to enjoy it.

When he had opened the door with a huge key on a huge ring that he pulled, puffing and panting, from under several layers of clothing, he led me along the passage into the veterinary department, unlocked that door also and took me to a cupboard containing a variety of coloured laboratory coats folded like new shirts. He handed me a pale brown one that had obviously done valiant service and took a white one for himself with 'O.N. Atherley' written in biro on the inside collar, his lips moving as he silently read it with a smile of satisfaction. Then he painstakingly transferred the contents of another white coat hanging on the back of the door, to the new one: pens, pencils, forceps, scissors, scalpels and other surgical instruments, the key ring and three or four battered boxes of matches. I felt almost naked in mine with its empty frayed pockets and small acid-burn holes where the tiny squares of the pattern on my shirt showed through. My predecessor must have been nearly six feet tall, so that didn't help either; maybe brown only came in a single size, that for the laboratory attendant ideal, a big but manageable fellow with a brain so small he couldn't be trusted with handling any fluid stronger than tea. Tomorrow I'd bring a few pens and things of my own in the way of accessories and see if I could make myself look a little less like a laboratory animal and a little more like a laboratory attendant.

By the time Oliver had shown me around and explained my duties, the rest of the staff had arrived and I was paraded in front of them and introduced. It was soon plain that right down to Bella, the washer-upper and Albert, the animal man, Oliver wasn't taken seriously by anybody, yet he accepted it with good grace, winking at me after one particularly humiliating crack, as much as to say there was an ongoing joke between him and the rest of them and this time it was their turn to get a dig in. He never once retaliated and I suspected his weakness was that he didn't want to hurt anybody.

When he gave me my chores for the morning he made them sound vital to the functioning of the department and explained everything in terms of the dangers of not doing it properly, which were mainly that various members of staff would get into a state of what sounded like uncontrollable fury.

My first job was autoclaving. The autoclaves were formidable vertical cylinders made of gunmetal, which sterilised their contents by steam under pressure at a rate of 15lbs per square inch. There were two of them side by side: one for sterilising 'dirty stuff' consisting of bacterial cultures in petri dishes, bottles and tubes, and the other for sterilising 'clean stuff', such as newly-prepared culture media, glassware and instruments. The clean one had a rather savoury smell with its broths made of best beef heart and a variety of sugars, the other stank of hydrogen sulphide and other waste products of bacterial metabolism. They were like good and bad angels.

Each autoclave was loaded with square baskets so it was necessary to utilise as much space as possible and pack things carefully down the sides. When it was full, the lid was secured with eight large ring fastenings which were tightened with an iron bar, the gas ring underneath was fired up, the valve closed when the steam was continuously blowing off and the timer set when the steam had reached sufficient pressure. The actual sterilising process took fifteen minutes. Apparently this was the most efficient way of killing all micro-organisms.

Oliver had managed to put the fear of God into me about the necessity of getting everything sterile and of the danger of steam under pressure, and I stood by those two autoclaves for the full hour and a half, prepared to protect the thoroughness of the process and the safety of the whole laboratory with my life if necessary. 'There's no need to stand and watch them,' Steve and Lawrence, the two scientific assistants, kept saying as they passed by. 'They're like kettles, man. You know what happens to kettles if you watch them, don't you?' But I wouldn't be seduced from my post by either of them; they had already grudgingly conceded that Oliver was senior to both of them, however absurd that might seem to them.

My next job was to 'nail out' a dozen hens ready for post-mortem. It was a kind of crucifixion except that they were poultry and already dead, and it was done by placing them on their backs on wooden boards about 18" x 18", driving a large nail through each spread wing and each spread foot, and then drenching them with Lysol from an aspirator on a shelf above the small sink next to the bench on which they lay in a row.

After that I was given some pipettes to plug with non-absorbent cotton wool. Almost all pipetting was done with the mouth rather than a teat, and because highly infective material was frequently pipetted, the plug was intended to prevent the contents entering the mouth. If the plugs were too tight, Oliver warned, all the staff would curse me as they sucked and sucked until their dentures dropped down and the plug suddenly gave way and they got a mouthful of some very bad stuff; too slack, and the plugs either fell inside the pipettes where they acted as an immovable obstruction, or shot into the mouth followed by everything else.

Next I was sent out to clean the pig pen in the yard and the one I had to appease this time was Albert. For this I had to climb into a galvanised cubicle, six feet square and five feet high, and do the necessary with a yard broom, a can of disinfectant, a pail of soapy water, and a two-hundred-weight boar still inside because there was nowhere else for it to go. In no time the two of us were slithering around the floor and the boar was grunting and squealing nonstop. I think it was concerned with its dignity more than anything else but the metal walls acted like amplifiers and the noise was awful. However I emerged soaking and reeking but unharmed, leaving the boar with what couldn't have been any more than a glancing blow to its pride.

'Pooh! I hope you're not intending to go home by bus tonight, lad,' Lawrence said. 'Or you've got a long walk ahead of you.'

'Who won?' Steve said with a grin.

One of the vets screwed up his face when he came by but Oliver's eyes gleamed when I went to him to report mission accomplished. I felt rather pleased I was exuding something malevolently protective, a bit like a skunk presumably does. Wasn't this what work was supposed to be: getting stuck in and letting everybody know it?

At long last lunch-time came and I was so proud to have completed half of a working man's day. My mother had packed some date and apple sandwiches and a quarter pint bottle of orange squash into the small ex-army gasmask bag I had used for school and balked against bringing in case it would be recognised as such. 'Don't be so daft! They know you're just a lad,' my mother had said. But I hadn't been entirely convinced.

I cleared a little space on one of the benches and started into the sandwiches. I had never been given anything as grown-up or lavish as date and apple at school, so there had been some recognition at home of my position. I was really hungry and they tasted great.

Everybody else had gone out: Mr Atkinson, the huge Experimental Officer, in his Ford Prefect, Mr Standish, one of the assistant veterinary officers, in his Ford Popular, Mr Hunter, the other, in his, Oliver in his Austin 30, Lawrence on his Vespa scooter, and last of all Steve on his motor-bike with his county cap pulled right down, RAF goggles, engine roaring and scarf flying as he tore around the front of the building and shot off into the depths of Elswick.

After lunch I was sent to the animal house to help Albert clean out the rabbits, guinea pigs and mice. As soon as I opened the door, the clamour and the fumes met me like a wall and my new gaffer chuckled as he limped past; there was no greeting, I just followed him from room to room until he was cornered and had to acknowledge my presence. We were two brown coats together, though his was in decidedly better condition and you could see where his wife had made alterations to allow for his short arms.

I wanted to know as much as I could about the place I'd come to work in, particularly about the people I'd be working with, and as I scraped, brushed and wiped, I asked him all kinds of questions; I thought he'd be a walking glossary of trenchant phrases, one for every member of staff, the way tradesmen usually were. But Albert was neither an initiator or developer of interesting conversations - he was a terminator - and after an afternoon with him I'd have to say that if you could have something more complex than a chip on your shoulder, something that indicated a grudge against the whole of mankind, Albert had a big one; I knew about misanthropists but thought they were dead writers.

He was smaller than me, looked as though his hair had been destroyed by radiation and had a lantern jaw with a deep cleft in it which traversed his upper lip and divided his nose into two parts. He wore a huge speckled cap to conceal as much of his head as possible and kept it on even when we went into the laboratory for our tea-break. His breath smelled of a compound of cigarette tar, sawdust and guinea pig pee, and I don't see how it could have smelt any other way given the atmosphere he spent so much of his life in.

No wonder he was a man of few words; what was the point of being garrulous if your society comprised hundreds of small laboratory animals, all doomed. I could imagine the combination of acrid smell, wittering guinea pigs, squealing mice, and Albert, would be a powerful repellent and that nobody would come into the animal house unless they absolutely had to, especially when all tests on animals were done in the laboratory.

The animals didn't seem to be bothered by Albert's mindless whistling which, like their squeaking and squealing, went on incessantly, but a whole day of it, all of it, would just about drive you crazy. I don't think it represented communion with the animals so much as an attempt to convey unflappability and preoccupation with the abstract, for the benefit of the rest of the staff.

He was one of those people who refer to things as 'your' this and 'your' that; not in a magnanimous way so much as to imply that if anything went wrong you were the one who would get it in the neck. 'Your thingy's jammed,' he would say, identifying a problem with a water bottle I might have in my hand, which was fastened to the side of one of his cages containing one of his rabbits. Really of course it belonged to the Ministry, it certainly didn't belong to me and I wasn't responsible for it either; I'd just started, I didn't even own the tatty brown coat I was wearing.

While I cleaned out their cages Albert disposed of dozens of 'used' mice with dabs of different coloured dyes on their backs, by taking them by the tails and whacking their heads on the side of a large refuse bin before dropping them inside where they twitched in a variegated heap. He never said 'Want to have a go?' or anything, he just whistled his way through the whole lot, hoisted the bin on his back and limped out on his bandy legs to the incinerator next door.

Despite the ancient premises, dim light, claustrophobia, lack of ventilation and sheer soullessness of breeding, feeding and cleaning up after hundreds of little beasts, all of which were destined for a more-or-less painful end, the place couldn't have been kept tidier or cleaner if Albert had had an army helping him.

After I'd finished the things he had given me to do, by which time he probably couldn't cope with my youthful enthusiasm and cheerfulness for another minute, he packed me off back to Oliver who sent me to assist Mr Hunter in the post-mortem house. Mr Hunter was about twenty-seven years old, very tall with a shock of black hair, and when I went in he was talking to himself rapidly and loudly, singing, rushing about and clashing things around. He pointed to a large sack on the floor. 'Right, Joseph! You can start by emptying that out.'

While I was untying the knots in the twine, he was looking on, barely able to contain himself as he fastened his apron, drew on his gloves and briskly sharpened a knife; and when I'd got the sack open, tipped it up and out came seven live piglets to tear around the room squealing their heads off, I got such a shock he guffawed and slapped his thigh with the side of his knife.

Picking up the weakest one by the legs, he swung it onto the table and swiftly cut its throat, the blood squirting up his arm and spattering his face.

'You might as well start learning the terms,' he said, pointing to a record book. 'Pick up the pen and start writing... Number 219. Landrace. One of seven. Spleen enlarged and friable. Lungs congested with some consolidation in the left lower lobe. Pericardium contains some petechial haemorrhages... Got that..?'

Without waiting for an answer he loudly and quickly spelled out 'friable' and 'petechial'.

'Watch,' he said, flinging a piece of liver on the floor. Immediately the other piglets started gobbling it up. 'So much for animal consciousness, eh..? Do you believe animals have consciences, Joseph..? Because if you believe in consciousness, it's the same thing. That's the reality down there.' He indicated the piglets with his knife. 'Here, little piggies. Have another bit of your brother.'

He threw another piece down and the piglets gobbled it up. Seeing the look on my face he laughed and cut off a piece of lung and flung that down. Then, joke over, he turned back to the carcase. Working fast whilst amusing himself with ditties and silly comments that he laughed uproariously at, he never paused with knife or banter for a single moment.

After he had finished dissecting the carcase and taking various samples of tissue which he put on an enamel tray, he killed five of the other piglets with a sharp blow of a hammer on the skull and quickly post-mortemed them also. Then he washed his hands, picked up the post-mortem book, quickly looked at what I'd written, stuck out his lower lip and nodded.

'We'll tell Albert he can look after the other one. That'll please him, hee hee! You can clean up here now.'

Off he went with the book and the trays of samples, singing a rugby song at the top of his voice. The place was immediately quiet and when I looked under the table, the piglet was standing still and looking up at me like a little dog; conscience it mightn't have had but there was something in its eyes not unlike what would have been in mine had I been in its place.

When I had cleaned up the post-mortem house to Oliver's satisfaction he told me I could end the day helping Bella in the wash-up. She was a little woman in her late forties and 'dead canny', as we say on Tyneside, the nicest person I'd met all day. She was cheerful but in an ironic way and when she laughed, her teeth, which had a greenish coating of food and saliva, clattered. Her husband was called Ronny and he worked in a factory. They had no children but they had a motor-bike and sidecar and they were their life.

I felt at ease in here, safe from sarcasm and the need to be constantly on my mettle. It was a dingy little room reeking of Teepol and gas, full of steam and so much upturned glassware dripping on the piled up benches that the floor was running with water and that was why Bella worked in wellingtons. This must be the very bottom of the veterinary division of the Ministry of Agriculture and Fisheries, I thought. There was no ladder leading anywhere from here and nobody could make conditions any worse or better. Whether Bella was jaundiced and emaciated before she came here, or whether it went with the job, I had no way of knowing. I supposed it was a cleaner's fate to handle with blissful ignorance the refuse of her employers.

It had been the longest day of my life and I didn't know if I was any closer to becoming a veterinary surgeon than I was when I left home that morning.

'Well, lad?' my father said at tea-time. 'How did you get on?'

'Good, thanks. It seems an interesting place. I learned quite a lot.'

'Hmmph!'

3

The afternoon of my second day at work saw only Steve and me in the lab. Lawrence had gone out with Mr Hunter and Mr Standish had gone off on his own somewhere. Oliver had gone to the General Hospital to scrounge some chemicals, Mr Dougal-McKay, the head of department was still away, nobody knew where, Bella had gone home and Albert was probably dashing mice brains out or maybe it was the day for throttling guinea pigs.

Steve was about twenty-four, not handsome but certainly attractive to women I would imagine with his dark hair sleeked straight back; he wasn't big but he was strong and even quicker in his movements than Hunter. Like Hunter, he was supremely confident in his ability and of all the people in the place he least fitted the image of a laboratory worker. In the short time I'd known him and from the laconic things he said about himself and the cynical things he said about life and everybody else, I realised he was somebody to look up to. He had done eighteen months' National Service in Kenya, had had a front tooth knocked out in a fight with a gang of thugs on Scotswood Road and had it replaced with a tiny denture that he could flick in and out on his tongue, had a Norton 500cc, was a sprinter who competed at White City, and had a married woman for a girlfriend.

Tuesday apparently being the least busy day of the week, we had cleared everything up by three o'clock.

'Right! Time to weigh the girls!'

Time to do what..?

Above the doorway between the two labs he had already hung the big spring balance I'd seen used to weigh carcases the day before, and to the bottom hook he was attaching a rope sling which he slickly tied with a sheepshank or some such marvellous knot. Then he telephoned the typist pool. Within three or four minutes, highly-scented giggling young women in their twenties started tripping into the lab, one at a time.

Steve lifted each one into the sling with considerable horseplay and they were hanging on to him, shrieking with laughter. When he was satisfied they were properly in, he would hold their ankles to steady them but keep them sufficiently apart so we could see the insides of their thighs and the colour of their knickers. He would then call out a figure and pass a comment both funny and sufficiently flattering to have them squealing with delight as they went out to send the next one down. 'Send Noreen next!' he would shout after them. 'Or I'm coming up to get her and carry her down over my shoulder, tell her!'

A few minutes later somebody else would come capering in on her high heels. 'Ooh, Steve! You're such a naughty man! I hope you're not going to do to me what you did to poor Nancy?'

Seven he did in all and you could tell they loved it, every one of them. Just as the last one was getting off, a very aristocratic Scotsman with ginger hair tufting out of his nose and ears came in dressed as though he had just come off the grouse moors.

I thought 'This is it! All three of us are going to get the sack.'

But I don't think he even noticed. 'Hullo..! Anybody about?' he called.

'Mr Hunter is at Ushaw Moor this afternoon, sir... Can I help?' Steve asked, leaving the girl and following the man who was obviously Dougal-McKay into the corridor. A couple of minutes later he was back, whistling, with a small package in his hand which he threw nonchalantly onto the bench. He winked, patted the typist on the bottom and out she went, flushed and trembling. The whole thing would have me fantasising for weeks; I was becoming increasingly attracted to increasingly mature women and calculated that if it didn't tail off soon, by the time I was twenty I was going to be aroused by women in their late eighties.

Suddenly the door burst open and in came Oliver with a few faeces samples in a wet and disintegrating cardboard box.

'Give me a hand, will you, Steve..? The Old Man wants these given the once-over for Johne's Disease... I haven't even been to the General yet.'

He hung up his coat and it fell straight down, and as he bent to pick it up all his pens and things clattered out of his top pocket.

But Steve was around the corner loudly sharpening knives and whistling 'Hold My Hand, I'm a Stranger in Paradise'.

'Can I not do them?' I asked Oliver.

He shook his cheeks and grumbled 'Grrrrrr' in Steve's direction. 'Come on, then. I suppose you've got to learn sometime.'

He had shown me how to prepare the samples and was about to show me how to examine them under the microscope when the back door burst open and Mr Standish came in with a tray of blood samples, followed by Lawrence carrying a sack with something kicking inside.

'All hands on deck..! Oliver, get these centrifuged as quick as possible and properly packed to catch the post for Weybridge. And I mean properly..! If I get one more letter about a broken bottle, somebody's for the high jump.'

'I'm just - '

'Now! I don't care what you're doing..! Steve, can you get started on these lambs?'

But Steve didn't want to be yelled at, he already had the sack in one hand, knife in the other, and was halfway out the door.

'Lawrence, before you empty the van, tell Albert I want a dozen mice. Then set up the anaerobic jar... And pour some more blood agars. I've got to ring Lewis before he leaves.'

Space was so limited that as soon as one job was done, the bench would be cleared and something else done immediately after.

On my third day I was sitting eating my lunch when somebody came in with a sackful of hens and dumped them on the floor. As soon as I finished, to show how conscientious I was I shook the hens out of the sack and nailed all six of them out on boards, hosed them down with Lysol and left them ready for Mr Hunter to do when he came back from lunch. Hens were done on the bench by the sink in the lab, only large animals were done in the 'P.M.'.

When Oliver came in, quarter of an hour early as usual, to try to please Mr Hunter he began to open up the hens with knife, scalpel and bone cutters and proceeded to remove the heart, lungs, liver and gizzard and lay them out by the side of the carcase. Then he slit the oesophagus, trachea and small intestine along their length and scraped away the flesh over the main nerves of the wings and legs. He had done three and was just setting about the fourth when Mr Hunter came in. Oliver turned around, apron on, big red face shining with pride, hands covered in blood and motioning towards the carcase with the knife as much as to say 'See what a good boy am I?'

Mr Hunter took one look at the carcases and then roared at him. 'What do you think you're doing..! They're still alive, you bloody imbecile!'

Sure enough two of the three nailed out and waiting for the knife were twitching and poor Oliver was horrified when he realised what he'd done. Obviously he had assumed that whoever nailed them out, which he would have known to be me, would have made sure they were dead; the time to check wasn't after they were nailed out and doused with Lysol. From what he had already told me about the Hancock Museum, the RSPCA and the various ornithological and naturalist societies he belonged to and was trying to get me to join, nobody could have cared more for animals than him. But he could hardly have told Mr Hunter it was my fault, especially not with me standing there, so I owned up.

'Never mind,' said Mr Hunter, dismissing me with a wave of a hand that was holding a small chopper. 'It's your responsibility!' he shouted at Oliver. 'You're the one who's opening them up!'

From then on he harangued Oliver in the most awful way, calling him every kind of sadist and idiot under the sun and Oliver got so upset his spectacles fell off into the carcase. Mr Hunter yelled at him louder than ever and Oliver picked them up and put them back on; they were covered in blood and bits of tissue and he could hardly see through them but Mr Hunter wouldn't let him take them off to clean them. He was bawling at him all the time, telling him to do this and that and poor Oliver was making one mistake after another. Then Mr Hunter started pushing and shoving him until his spectacles came off one ear and dangled down his face and when he reached up to put them back, Hunter roared 'Never mind that! Where's the proventriculus..? Go on! Show me! Where is it..? You've lost it, haven't you, you bloody fool! You've mixed it up with that one's!'

There was a sickening thud and Oliver fell to the ground, clutching his leg. 'Oh, my leg..! You've kicked me in my bad leg!'

'Get up, you useless lump! Get up this minute or I'll kick you so hard you won't be able to!'

Oliver struggled to his feet and as he was putting his dirty spectacles back on he whimpered 'I could report this to the union.'
'You what..! Your union..? This is what I think of your damned union!'

With that he swung back his arm and fetched Oliver such a smack across the face that his spectacles were knocked flying onto the floor and tears were streaming down his cheeks. I think he knew that if he said another word Hunter was likely to stick one of the knives in him.

'Get out! Get out of my sight!' Hunter roared.

Oliver needed no further urging and hurried out to the cloakroom to wash his spectacles and bathe his face.

With a big grin on him Hunter then came into the main lab where Steve, Lawrence and I were pretending we hadn't heard a thing. He ran his fingers through his long hair.

'I think we need a bit more of that sort of thing around here. It might sharpen a few ideas up.'

'I hope I'm not included in that statement,' Steve said quietly.

Hunter just chuckled and went out.

For the rest of the afternoon Oliver sat at his bench working at his microtome and trying to hide the side of his face which was so red you could almost feel the heat coming off it. Hunter seemed to have expected applause for what he'd done, instead he had created an atmosphere of such intense hostility that whenever he came in all he got was the barest of responses from anybody.

I don't know what Lawrence would have done if Hunter had clouted him, maybe he would have had an attack of his asthma. But I haven't the slightest doubt Steve would have returned the same blow without compunction, only harder. And I would have done the same. All kinds of people were able to hit you with impunity when I was a kid: adult relatives, school teachers, policemen, park-keepers, any official and almost any adult who was aggrieved. But now I'd left school, I wouldn't put up with it from anybody except my mother and father and even from them I resented it. I didn't doubt that Mr Hunter wouldn't hesitate to strike me if he had already struck a colleague twice his age and got away with it.

From the day I started I had to make the tea and take it into the main lab on a tray. Every mug was a different shade of brown and they were all crazed, chipped and deeply stained on the inside, yet every member of staff would be ready to kill if somebody else used their mug. No fellow staff member would do such a thing because all the blood, guts, pus and tumours in the world wouldn't have been as repulsive as a colleague's mug, so the mistake could only be made by a stranger. If a visitor, such as a vet in private practice, had brought in a specimen around tea-time and picked up somebody's mug instead of the vile 'visitor's mug' - which had long since been tacitly condemned for staff use - whoever it belonged to would be almost apoplectic until the plunderer had finished and gone, when if the owner were Steve or Lawrence he would take the said mug into wash-up and tell Bella to be sure to thoroughly scald it out and leave it soaking in disinfectant until next tea-time.

The other thing which keenly exercised the opprobrium of the two of them and Albert even more so, was that although we all paid the same amount into the tea club, guests, none of whom ever came to see anyone beneath the rank of VO (veterinary officer), never paid a soss.

'Bloody Blackett drives around in an MG yet always gets here dead on five minutes before tea-break. The money he's got, why doesn't he go into a bloody cafe!'

After I'd been there a few weeks I decided I wasn't going to make the tea any more. I didn't mind scraping up the remains of post-mortems and getting down on my hands and knees and scrubbing out the pig pen, but I balked at waiting on anybody. Most of all I disliked waiting on Lawrence who would keep me waiting while he drained every last drop before plonking his mug down on the tray with a little snort. I was the only person in the place that Lawrence could bully; not even Bella, and certainly not Albert, would take any of his haughty talk. So I knew when the news got out that I was refusing to make tea any more, he would launch the most strident protest.

Even my father who frowned on insubordination anywhere said nothing when he heard about it. He still hoped that something would make me change my mind about continuing to work at the 'vet lab', as they all so disparagingly referred to it at home. I never realised that a veterinary laboratory could have any bad connotation until I heard it from the mouths of my own family. 'Vet lab..! Urgh..!' It was as though I'd got myself a job at the sewage works. By now I had taken the civil service examination thus fulfilling my part of the compact with my father and my headmaster, been successful and offered a 'post', as they called it, but had declined in favour of the 'vet lab', so whatever contempt was poured on me by my brothers was considered well deserved.

When I told Oliver of my decision to stop making the 'departmental tea', he was shocked.

'You're the junior..! It's your job... You've always done it.'

'I know but I never liked doing it.'

'"Like" doesn't come into it. You drink tea along with everybody else. You're surely not expecting anybody to make tea for you, are you?'

'I'm not drinking tea any more. I'm bringing orange juice from now on.'

'Well, I don't know what Mr Hunter and Mr Standish are going to say about this... Or Mr Dougal-McKay. He might go mad.'

But I stood there in the tiny cloakroom which was part of the small corridor on the way out to the animal and post-mortem houses, the place where all confidential conversations took place, and shrugged. He glared at me and his chins were quivering.

'This could affect your prospects,' he said. 'You've done quite well so far, I might tell you. But I think you've got a bit of a chip on your shoulder and you're going to have to work hard to get rid of it. Otherwise...'

'How's that..? I just don't want to make the tea...that's all. I'm not refusing to do anything else. Tea-making isn't part of a laboratory technician's work, is it?'

'It is and it isn't. You could put it like that.'

'Well I'm not having tea any more after Friday, so I won't be in the tea club any more.'

He went out and then came back into the doorway and stood in it sideways. 'Don't you think you're being just a wee bit selfish not making tea for everybody else just because you've decided not to have it any more..? If I were you, I'd give this matter more thought. It's quite serious.'

But I wouldn't give in once I'd made up my mind and when Lawrence came to me later on almost snarling and said 'What's this we hear about you not making tea any more? Who do you think you are, you little pipsqueak?' it just made me that bit more determined.

'Not making the tea any more, you cheeky little bugger, eh?' said Steve who thought it was a huge joke. Whatever happened, he certainly wouldn't be making it. They could drag Albert in kicking and squealing like one of his rabbits but if Steve was thirsty he'd drink sulphuric acid before he would make tea for anybody. As far as Mr Hunter was concerned I don't think he could have cared less whether he got his tea or not, he never had time to finish it. And Mr Standish was hardly ever in. As for Dougal-McKay, he was virtually never in and never paid anyway.

Later on I went into the wash-up when Bella was getting ready to go home, to find her making a pact with Albert that neither of them would do it and declaring it was a disgrace because wherever you went the youngest one always made the tea. But I knew Bella would agree with whatever anybody said just to keep the peace and that eventually she'd almost certainly be the one making it.

The following Monday I came in with a half pint of orange juice in my haversack and discreetly drank it on my own in the toilet, making sure to get it down damned quick and get back to my work. The whole place was tense until a few minutes before eleven o'clock when a livid Lawrence came in with the tray, exhaling through his nostrils rather like a dragon would if it had been made to carry a tea tray. I pretended not to notice but saw him looking at me and knew he felt the whole department should drag me off my stool and lynch me, and that when they had finished and I was lying on the floor unconscious, he should be invited to take a good long run and endeavour to score a try even though he had never been on a rugby field in his life.

Making tea wasn't really a big deal and I think I had just come to the point where I had to make it clear that although I was the youngest, I wasn't necessarily the most inferior being in the place. I suppose it was a little challenge thrown out, more woollen mitten than iron gauntlet, and it was interesting to see how predictably it had been picked up.

After the first few days when everybody treated me with some coolness and Lawrence pretended I didn't exist, no more was said and Bella made it from then on. One time when she was off Oliver asked me if I would make it and I said no and Lawrence made it with no more good grace than before.

You could identify anybody in the lab from the back or from a distance by their clothes because everybody in the lab wore the same clothes every day: the same patched jacket and trousers, the same tie and down-at-heel shoes; only the shirts and darned socks were occasionally changed for something of a different colour, though the same kind. Dougal-McKay, 'the Sherlock Holmes of the Scottish grouse moors', as everybody at Elswick Hall referred to him, was the only one in the place with anything decent on his back or out in the yard, he had a Wolsely with a walnut dashboard, leather seats and a heater.

You could always tell Ministry vets from ones in private practice by their everlasting clothes, old utilitarian cars and long intervals between haircuts, yet they had an unmistakable air of superiority about them and most of the private vets seemed quite happy to go along with it; all three vets at Elswick thought they were quite dashing.

Miss Bell, one of the shorthand typists, would come down at eleven o'clock every morning flushed with excitement, and sit on a high stool directly in front of Mr Hunter with her very long legs locked together, while he sat in a low chair, legs spread, an ancient urine stain in the crotch of his pale blue trousers that Steve reckoned was a perfect map of Italy, and sent her into fits of giggles with his innuendoes as he dictated the lab reports at breakneck speed. No matter what he said to anybody, she still adored him.

I had learned from Mr Standish that there was no way I could become a veterinary surgeon without going to university full-time for six or more years, there were no part-time, evening-class or correspondence courses. I could work for about ten years, maybe save enough money and go in as a mature student but he had never heard of anybody doing it without considerable financial support from somewhere.

'You have to be able to live as well as work and study,' he said. 'Why not do the technician course that Steve and Lawrence are doing and make a success of that? They'll be able to tell you all about it.'

I was so disappointed. I had asked him so many times and he had been very understanding but this time I knew from the way he said it that he had reached the limit of his patience and that if I asked him again I was probably going to hear something I wouldn't like.

What I found out from Steve and Lawrence was that there were no technician courses for veterinary technicians, only for medical technicians and it was the medical course they were taking, they didn't make it sound easy either.

First you had to apply for student membership of the IMLT [Institute of Medical Laboratory Technology] and before you could enrol for their course you had to have biology and chemistry. If they then accepted you, you had to do their three-year night-class course for the Intermediate

Examination which was equivalent in standard to an intermediate BSc. You then elected to study for the Final Examination by specialising in one medical laboratory subject which took two more years. If you were successful you were made an Associate member of the Institute and entitled to put the letters A.I.M.L.T. after your name. If you were prepared to study another medical laboratory subject for a further two years and were successful you were made a Fellow of the Institute and could put F.I.M.L.T. after your name, the highest qualification any technician, veterinary or medical, could achieve anywhere in the world. It would thus take a minimum of seven years' continuous study at night classes to gain Fellow membership.

The intermediate course required proficiency in medical bacteriology, medical biochemistry, medical histology, medical haematology and medical blood transfusion. Here in the veterinary centre we did no haematology, no blood transfusion and no biochemistry of any kind; we only did veterinary bacteriology and histology. However, a career in veterinary surgery was out so I enrolled at Rutherford College to do three nights chemistry and biology; Oliver at over fifty was still trying to pass his first final in bacteriology and Steve and Lawrence had just matriculated and were embarked on the I.M.L.T. intermediate course.

Being young and fit and keen to make a name for himself in the area and a few pence per mile subsistence from his old black Ford, Mr Standish was the vet who most often went out to take blood, milk or faeces samples from herds of cattle or flocks of sheep on farms as far away as Berwick-on-Tweed or the Cheviot Hills. And I was invariably the one he chose to take with him. On the way he would tell me what we were going to be doing and why: maybe it was to take milk from a herd of cows suspected of having TB or blood tests from a herd of sheep suspected of copper deficiency, but whatever it was he explained it lucidly and articulately, never hesitating on any word no matter how complex.

When we got there I would help with herding the animals into somewhere we could better come to grips with them, such as a byre, a steel cattle-crush or a wicker sheepfold, and I would pass Mr Standish the syringes and needles and label the bottles for him. Afterwards on the way back he would question me on what I had learned in the lab and at night classes and would answer any questions I had. He was no crawler as far as Mr Dougal-McKay or any of the titled landowners were concerned, intelligence was the thing he judged everybody by; if they had something between the ears he respected them and would talk and joke with them, if they hadn't, he wouldn't give them the time of day, he would just go in, do what he had to do, and out, and they'd hardly get a word out of him.

For most of my childhood I'd had a broken tooth in the upper front of my mouth which I eventually pulled out myself but was left with a permanent abscess at the base of the new tooth. Every now and again something would trigger it off and my whole face would swell up overnight, my nose flatten across my face, my right eye close and my whole head throb with pain; it always happened overnight and would last about three days before responding to penicillin. The pain affected my eye, my head, my right ear and the glands in my neck and there was nothing I could do but rest until the antibiotic had done its work, I could neither eat nor drink and couldn't talk properly.

One morning I was due to meet Mr Standish at the corner of Newton and Stephenson Road to go with him to sample sheep, he could easily have come past the house and picked me up at the door but that wasn't the kind of thing he would do. I awoke with a face like a balloon and when my mother saw it she immediately rang work to let Mr Standish know that I wasn't fit to go. He said it was too late to get anybody to go in my place at this late stage - which wasn't true - and that we were expected at the farm in two hours. Why hadn't I said anything about it yesterday? Surely I must have known then?

He was right, I hadn't felt too good the previous afternoon when I'd been getting all the sampling gear ready and packing the baskets into the back of his car. But if I'd told him I didn't think I'd be well enough to go out to work on a farm in the cold wet Cheviots the following day, he'd have said something sarcastic. Like my father he tended to see illness as a weakness, especially among people he worked with. He'd have said 'Don't go out tonight. Get yourself to bed early. You'll feel better in the morning.'

In the finish I got up and told my mother to ring him again to say I was going. We had a hard day of it as it turned out: the farm help was hopeless, the cows were stubborn and a whole batch of needles hadn't been sharpened properly. Mr Standish never said a word about my face, he pretended he hadn't noticed it and behaved as though there had never been any phone calls. He probably went home thinking he'd done me a favour, that he'd helped make a man of me. He'd have made a perfect First World War artillery officer.

One day when he was going out Mr Hunter tossed a veterinary book down on the bench and told me to read the section on poultry diseases because he was going to test me on it when he came back. It was an old book written in archaic scientific language with all the illustrations in the form of fine line drawings and the content was interesting and easy enough to absorb. As soon as he came through the door an hour and a half later he began testing me on it. I'd learned it practically off by heart and he seemed satisfied.

'I'll bet the lad knows more about lymphomatosis than you do,' he said to Oliver who was sitting opposite counting sheep worms in a bowl of formalin. 'I think it's time we gave you a little test. You've heard young Joseph here, so you must have learned something.'

Oliver chortled nervously. 'I'll give it a go but it's a while since I had the old text book out.' He began to compose himself, packing his pipe, tucking his coat underneath him and nearly falling of the stool and twittering as though it was going to be a kind of game.

'Put that filthy thing down!' Mr Hunter snapped. Oliver immediately took his pipe, his main prop, out of his mouth and put it to one side. He wasn't chortling now, he knew this wasn't going to be funny at all. He suddenly turned on his stool and yelped and his head went down beneath the bench.

'Come back up, you ninny! What's the matter with you?'

'Yow..! I've twisted my gammy knee!' His face was contorted as though in agony.

'Don't be such a damn cissy..! Get ready.'

The rest of us were either in the main lab or the small lab beyond the partition, so everybody could hear everything. When the test was over and Oliver had scored only two out of ten, to add to the humiliation Hunter had already dished out he told Oliver that a mere lad like me knew more about veterinary pathology after only a few months than he had learned in thirty years. He insulted and railed at him until he had reduced him to a quivering wreck, stammering and incoherent and saying the stupidest things. Then he hurled the book at him, almost knocking him off his chair, and told him to study it during his lunch break because he was going to be tested again straight after, and if he didn't get every question right he would be taking it home and studying it every night until he did.

One of Oliver's jobs was to inoculate white mice which he did by inserting a syringe needle into their tail vein. In order to dilate the vein, which was tiny, he would put half a dozen mice in a little wooden box with a glass lid and stand it on a tripod over a bunsen burner adjusted to pilot flame; by the time the glass lid was steamed over so that the mice could no longer be seen, the veins would be prominent enough.

Oliver was in such a state on this particular day, knowing Mr Hunter would crucify him if he didn't fare better in the test that afternoon, that he took the book with him when he went out at lunch-time and completely forgot about the mice. I was back from lunch first and could smell the roasting flesh right along the corridor. When I came in the wood was on fire and the mice were like sticks of charcoal. I had just doused them with water and put them aside when the door opened and Oliver came in, lips twittering like a child memorising a poem, fists clenched with the effort, old textbook under his arm. The instant he saw me with the box he began to shake and his eyes rolled around in his head as though he were going to throw a fit. He dropped the book, picked up the still-smoking, still-steaming box and peered into it.

'Mr Hunter'll go mad when he finds out about this!' he wailed but stopped short of begging me not to tell anybody.

God only knows what Mr Hunter would have done to him if he'd found out, he might well have had him sacked. Luckily he was called away for the rest of the day and by the following morning had other things to occupy his mind than a bit of sport at Oliver's expense.

4

Being the eldest of five brothers isn't as easy as it sounds. At sixteen there are many frontiers to be pushed back without the added burden of having to serve as a good example to four human beings who know all your faults and vehemently deny you have any virtues. I seemed to have been born into the Age of Discipline, what with the Second World War breaking out when I was two and then going to a Catholic school when I was four. It seemed all stick and no carrot. There were bombs, sweet rationing and blackouts on the one hand; canes, martyrdom and hell on the other, and dental clinics in between. Even religious processions at St Teresa's had been like martial events with the wearing of sashes, marching in ranks and intense blowing of pea whistles.

When our father was demobbed and came back he seemed to have the idea that my brother Johnny and I must have ran amok during his five-year absence, when the truth was quite the contrary, our mother also had very definite ideas about good behaviour and the shine on the black leather belt in the top drawer in the kitchen testified to that. His own father was a professional boxer who had died at twenty-four, leaving my grandmother to bring up their family on her own, and as the eldest child my father had shouldered a lot of responsibility; because of it I think he saw the duties of a father as primarily breadwinning and character-building. Whether he would have been less of a stickler for security if his own childhood had had more of it, I don't know, but I could see why the security of the Civil Service had so much appeal.

My family lived in Plessey Terrace, High Heaton, but my father and mother originally came from South Shields and that is where I was born. My brothers, Johnny and Peter, younger by fifteen months and ten years respectively, were born in Newcastle, and Michael, seven years younger than me, was born in Gilsland during the Second World War. Anthony still a toddler was also born in Newcastle. All my father's people and all of my mother's, and there was quite a few of them, remained in South Shields; an aunt, my father's sister, had emigrated to Australia but even she came back to Shields. Although I grew up in Newcastle, when I heard that my great-great uncle, Johnny Robinson, the lightweight barefist champion of England was called a 'Shieldsman', I decided the designation was good enough for me too. My father's family had been boxers long before coming from Ireland in the early part of the Nineteenth Century.

My father and mother met at Tyne Dock Cycling Club and when my father was made a Relieving Officer for the National Assistance Board in Newcastle, they married and came to live in Heaton.

My mother's side, the Smithwhites, were plumbers from as far back as anybody could go. My mother had to change her religion to marry my father and several of her sisters had to do likewise to meet the uncompromising requirements of the Catholic Church, but Grandfather and Grandmother Smithwhite remained Protestant and unable to ever enter the Kingdom of Heaven, so said our teachers at St Peter & Paul's in South Shields and St Teresa's in Newcastle, the two primary schools Johnny and I attended.

In every generation of Robinsons there had always been a Johnny who happened to be the second son, and right down from the great Johnny who beat Dick Burge before he became world champion, they were tough, they were quick and they were outstanding fighters. My father and my brother Johnny were just the same with the same determination and the same stubbornness and never complaining about anything or anybody.

I was different. I was determined but not stubborn and I wasn't as fearless or tough, nor as tolerant. I would argue and resist when I thought things weren't right, I wouldn't care about standing alone or making myself unpopular with the wrong people; from an early age I disliked abuse of authority and hated any kind of privilege and it seemed to me they were everywhere.

I couldn't understand how my father put up with the young priest who came uninvited to our home to berate him and my mother for sending us kids to Protestant schools, while supping our tea and munching our biscuits. I couldn't understand why we had a picture of the Queen in our hallway either; the day George VI died we had all been sent home from school, all cinemas and places of entertainment were closed and the BBC broadcast only sombre, gently jingoistic programmes and ecclesiastical muzak. I thought 'My cousin was killed a few months ago on his twenty-first birthday while doing his National Service in the RAF and there was none of this; those that wanted to, mourned, those who didn't know him, didn't have to. Yet Arnold Smithwhite had meant something to me, George Windsor meant nothing.

A few months after I got my G.C.E. results I was promoted to Temporary Scientific Assistant and given my first white coat. Although it was frayed and had holes in it, at least when visitors came into the lab and I was the only one in they didn't automatically say 'Nobody here?' and walk straight through. I think brown coats made you invisible to a lot of people.

I was now eligible to attend the annual Technicians Conference at Weybridge, as one of the two delegates from Newcastle branch, and because Mr Standish liked me and wanted to push me on, he recommended I should go. There was no way Steve would go to Weybridge, the great bonus of which was a day and a night in London, with a little squirt like me tagging along. The last time he went he'd gone to a show in Soho where customers went into a dark room with a thick glass ceiling, the light went on up above and a huge Egyptian woman came in, squatted on the glass and opened her bowels - although those weren't the words Steve used. It was the most awesome thing I had ever heard.

Oliver couldn't go to the conference because he was studying for his final examination again, so when it was announced that Lawrence and I were going, Lawrence fulminated and fumed, though not so much as to put his own place in serious jeopardy and certainly not to Mr Standish. He told me he regarded my accompanying him as an enormous favour on his part and warned me not to give him any trouble; I think he meant I had better not get homesick or anything, I couldn't think what else he might have had in mind, unless he meant ratting on him for some show he was planning to go to. But I'd never been further from home than a week's camping in Edinburgh, so whether Egyptian ladies going to the toilet was on the menu or anything remotely like it, I wasn't going to be breathing a word to nobody.

Lawrence came from Seaton Sluice. He was the same age as Steve, had the same qualifications and the same rank - full strength Scientific Assistant - but was nothing like him. He had wavy hair which grew out from his head like a corrugated iron roof; if I'd had hair like his I'd have had a crewcut and it would have looked great.

He was interested in all kinds of living things, including insects and cacti and especially aquaria, and kept guppies which were small multicoloured tropical fish that the books said were such good breeders it was almost impossible to stop them, dozens at a time apparently dropping perfectly formed from the females. I was dying to get a male and two females but they cost a shilling each from pet stores and although I had a 12" x 10" x 8" aquarium waiting, I was still paying for the heater, thermostat and thermometer. I only earned £2 5s a week and half of that went into the house. 'Why don't you ask Lawrence?' Steve suggested. 'His have just bred again and he needs to get rid of them because he's got too many and the pet shop won't take any more.'

But Lawrence wanted to charge the same price as the pet shops. 'He'd rather flush them down the lavvy than give them away,' Steve said. However he did give me a spare greater-crested newt that he'd got from Benton quarry. 'You should stick with the cold water stuff till you gain more experience,' he said ponderously. 'I might take your heater and thermostat off you if they're any good...if they're at the right price for secondhand equipment, that is.'

'I haven't had a chance to use them because I haven't any fish yet,' I protested.

'They're still classed as secondhand, chum. Once you take them out of the shop, they're secondhand. That's the law.'

The conference caused nearly as much excitement at home as at work.

'Conference..? What are they letting you go to a conference for..? It can't be a proper one. You know nowt. You're still just a kid,' was the unanimous opinion of my brothers. But even my father was a wee bit impressed.

Before the time came to go I was told as much about the itinerary Lawrence had planned, as Lawrence decided I needed to know and no more. 'God help you,' Steve said. 'At least your mother won't need to have the police out looking for you. With him you'll be in bed by nine o'clock every night.'

We were booked into a small guest house in Weybridge and for the first time in my life somebody called me 'Mister'. Lawrence, always and in every way in Steve's shadow in the lab, now sought to show off to me. He had obviously made up his mind that for the next few days he was the one going to be lionised and the main way he sought to do it was by speaking axiomatically and I learned that 'as the bishop said to the actress' and the converse could be applied to almost any statement on any subject.

Our itinerary included a visit to Earl's Court for the motor show, Lawrence and Steve always fantasised about new cars and coming away with a brochure from the Aston Martin stand was the next best thing to having the car itself. But the highlight of our trip was to be a visit to Piccadilly Circus to see a new kind of film called 'cinerama'. I wasn't consulted about it, nor about any other matter connected with the trip, and wasn't going to be given the option of waiting outside and saving my money - an unbelievable twelve shillings - in case 'something happened' to me and Lawrence got the blame for not looking after me properly; no doubt Oliver had impressed on him the gravity of this responsibility.

Lawrence had read about cinerama in some magazine and decided he was going to be one of the first, perhaps the only one, from the North of England to see it even though he had to share that honour with a whipper-snapper with insufficient savvy to appreciate it. He had talked about nothing else in the days leading up to our trip and every time Steve had got bored and gone out, leaving Lawrence and me together, I would ask if he was sure he couldn't possibly get cheaper seats than twelve-shilling ones.

'You have to be in the front of the upper balcony to see it properly, or there's no point in going. So shut up about it! I've already written away and booked the tickets.'

The most I had ever paid to go to the pictures was two shillings and threepence and I'd only done that once with a girl who had insisted on it and was subsequently never taken anywhere again.

Lawrence wasn't what you could call 'scintillating company', preferring to read his portable library of pocket Observer books both on the train and in bed: The Observer's Book of British Wasps, the Observer's Book of British Trains, The Observer's Book of German Bombers. And the conference was unbelievably boring, so all we had was the cinerama.

While we were waiting in the ticket-holders-only queue, membership of which had Lawrence almost snorting with pride, he was so excited whenever we passed a poster that he was making sounds like one of Albert's small animals mating. As for me, I couldn't help thinking about how many female Egyptian bowel movements we might have seen for twelve shillings.

Cinerama was 3-D without glasses and the show consisted of a series of short films exploring the possibilities. Most memorable were a ride on a rollercoaster and one on a Harley Davidson in the undulating streets of

San Fransisco. The screen wrapped halfway around the walls of the cinema, to the left and the right and three different projectors were used to produce the effect. But surely we hadn't come all this way and spent all this money just to go 'Oooh! and Aaah!' like everybody else. If this was their reaction at a film show, however slick, imagine what they'd be saying if when the lights dipped, instead of the curtains drawing back, the ceiling was revealed to be of glass and...

'Well, what do you think now?' Lawrence demanded, his breath smelling of the mints he'd been surreptitiously snaffling in the dark; his excuse for eating sweets at work or when you were going out with him in the van and not offering you any, was that they were only for catarrh.

It had been interesting enough 'if you like that sort of thing', as Lawrence himself might have put it. But it had been twelve shillings for forty minutes. Surely no pleasure on earth that only lasted forty minutes could be worth that much.

'Well..?' He was waiting for an answer.

'I still think twelve shillings was far too much.'

We were going down the stairs into the Underground yet he turned on me with unbridled fury, almost screeching 'For God's sake, stop bleating, you mean little bugger! The Ministry's paying for this. It's not as though it was coming out of your own pocket!'

Up until the Saturday before I started work I had been a newspaper boy, I had been one since I was ten, delivering papers every morning before I went to school and delivering them as soon as I got back, Saturdays and Sundays as well. My brother Johnny and I had collected orange boxes from the greengrocers, chopped them into sticks and bundled them up with wire from the scrapyard and sold them door to door for fire-lighters. Half of all my earnings from that, the paper round, the carol-singing and anything else had always gone into the house, so I knew the value of money all right. The image of going up and down those hills in San Francisco at breakneck speed before crashing into a huge van that suddenly pulled out of a side road would be with me a long time. But nowhere near as long as the dirty fundament of a large Egyptian woman.

By the spring of 1955 several billets at the old RAF camp on Whitley Road, Longbenton, had been converted into a suite of laboratories and offices and the VIC moved there.

It was much nearer to where I lived. A few weeks after starting at Elswick I'd made up a bike from a frame I'd found on a scrap heap and two odd secondhand wheels I bought cheap. It had no gears or brakes, the saddle was like the blade of an axe and getting up Corporation Street hadn't been easy on the fixed wheel I'd got to save buying brakes, but I went on it in all weathers and saved quite a bit on bus fares. Now we were at Benton I could get to work in quarter of an hour and that was taking it easy. Sometimes I went there and back for a whole week and never touched the saddle once, I'd had piles since I was fourteen so it was a real boon. Plus I could carry half a side of lamb tied to the crossbar and a dozen pork chops in my gasmask case.

My father would never touch anything I brought from the lab. He allowed my mother to cook it and the rest of us to eat it but he was convinced there must be something not right about it. Sometimes I was sure I could see his mouth watering at the sight and savour of the meat, the likes of which had never graced our table before, certainly never in this quantity. But he would just get stuck into his bit of sausage or whatever my mother had brought from the 'proper' butchers and say something like 'This is good, Evelyn. Really good. Storey's, you say..? You want to keep going to him.'

At Longbenton we all had our own laboratories in the form of small rooms off one or the other side of the central corridor that ran the length of the building, and when things were quiet you could sometimes imagine the ghosts of the Boys in Blue lying in their beds thinking about their sorties into the Fatherland. The adjacent building housed all the animals, their food and equipment, the laboratory stores, and at the front end, the PM house. We also had several acres of decent pasture for grazing a dozen experimental sheep.

My laboratory was Parasitology and my main duties were connected with that. Faeces samples could come from any animal from a horse to a cat and often from a whole flock of sheep, and I did them all, extracting the worm and fluke eggs, identifying the species and counting them. But I was too junior to be called a 'parasitologist': 'Faeces Lad' was more like it.

Steve did most of the post-mortems which were a very large part of the work at the centre, as well as the bacteriology. Lawrence made up the culture media and reagents and Oliver did the histology and counting of adult intestinal worms. Histology was the processing of tissue for microscopy and involved impregnating it with wax so it could be cut into very thin slices on a microtome which was like a small bacon-slicer, and staining it with various dyes; it was even more boring than counting worm eggs. But the counting of adult worms was stultifying and nobody in the department except Oliver would have done it; whoever devised the method could only have devised it for someone else to carry out, a lesser, more disposable being.

He had to wash out the intestinal contents of a sheep into a large bowl, add formaldehyde, stir it round and around and then peer into it for hours under a light, with a needle in one hand and a counter in the other, while he picked out minute grey nematode worms from among the debris of partly digested vegetable stalks and the mucoid detritus of intestinal lining. The smell of formalin was so overwhelming that nobody could bear being in the room with him, and so noxious he had to keep his door closed because of the complaints.

Mr Standish was in charge of research and particularly interested in Nematodirus, a parasitic worm which infested the small intestine of sheep. He chose me to work with him, promising me that when the work was complete and he published a scientific paper in the British Veterinary Journal, my name would go on it; and even though according to Steve that would only mean under acknowledgements at the end, it meant a lot to me.

He was seeking to find out how quickly and at what age sheep became infested with Nematodirus and my part in the research was to regularly sample the pasture to determine how long the infective larvae, which hatched on the ground from the eggs in excreted faeces, survived.

Somebody at Weybridge called Pollock had developed a method of sampling the grass and Mr Standish arranged for me to go down for a week to learn it.

Full board had been arranged for me at the house of a MAF employee who had an Ariel motor-bike and sidecar and I was taken to headquarters in it every day which was a great thrill. One of Mr Pollock's technicians had been delegated to show me what was what and it wasn't very much, but the lab had a pet kestrel which excited me and there was a girl in the animal house who'd had a screen test at Ealing Studios the week before and she excited me even more. I had a girlfriend in the biology class back in Newcastle but I was forever on the lookout; she was always on about a friend of hers who used to 'sleep' with her boyfriend - it seemed so odd to me, I couldn't understand the point or the practicability of it.

The first time I had dinner in the house I was staying at, the father of the employee, the landlord if I can call him that, told me how his stomach and half his oesophagus had been removed because of cancer and that he could only eat mush. I supposed he was only trying to be chatty and put me at my ease but it put me right off my dinner and I wondered if his wife's cooking had anything to do with his problem; it was nothing like my mother's, that was for sure.

The pasture-sampling method was so simple you could have committed the entire contents of Pollock's scientific paper to memory in twenty minutes and I was surprised at the flurry of excitement publication of his article was supposed to have caused. The technique, which Mr Standish had me doing the day after I got back even though it was raining, was to take a pair of scissors and a bucket, and along an imaginary diagonal line drawn from one corner of a field to the opposite one, cut off the tops of the grass and put them in the bucket and then do the same between the other two corners. The clippings were then brought back to the laboratory and the larvae, which couldn't be seen with the naked eye, hosed off into a measuring cylinder through a sieve, a sample centrifuged to concentrate them, a measured drop put under the microscope, and the larvae identified and counted. Pollock's real achievement it seemed to me was to put that into scientific language and make it sound brilliant.

To justify the expense of my trip Mr Standish had me out every day in every paddock until I'd blunted every pair of scissors in the place and Oliver had to order more. It was so daunting setting out in a field, whatever its size, to cut one's way back and forwards on one's knees by the longest route, and so profoundly tedious that curling one's finger up the sheep's recta to collect their faeces, which one always had to do immediately afterwards, was almost a treat. On top of that the RAF camp still functioned as a records branch and there was always somebody walking past who had something to say when they saw some idiot cutting the grass with a pair of scissors. 'Will ye come and do our lawn when you're finished, hà-ha-ha?' 'Is it bob-a-job you're doin', son, heh-heh-heh?'

It went on for months and if I was off work for any reason, nobody did it; Oliver wasn't mobile enough to crawl for what amounted to several miles on his knees with a pair of scissors, and Steve and Lawrence claimed they weren't sufficiently trained in such a demanding technique and in any case always managed to have such a lot of other work on.

5

By the middle of my second year in the veterinary service I had become sick of the sight of sheep faeces. The highlight of the day was when I finished counting worm eggs and joined Steve in the PM. This was where I heard so much about life's underbelly, this was where I heard the inside story about the Mau Mau in Kenya where Steve had done his National Service, and this was where I learned how Africans stretched their penises by wearing stone weights. And when there was a clunking of lead as I got off my stool in the library at the end of a tea-break, Steve was the only one who grinned as we were going out the door and said 'The cord's too long, man. You're walking around as though you've got a pendulum in your pants.'

He could sharpen a knife with a couple of strokes of the long steel and then send both knife and steel flying through the air to stick in a poultry board we'd put up as a target. He could chat with any of the private vets who came in and make them grin, or have all the senior staff that came up from Weybridge gravely nodding assent. He seemed to know exactly what to say to anybody, always stopping short of pandering but managing to ingratiate himself all the same. I am sure it was because his competence in the laboratory never failed him; he knew how to do everything, knew where everything was kept and knew something useful about everybody. Nothing fazed him: no amount of carcases that came in just before closing time, no accident, examination, or woman so big and brassy - and more than a few of these worked in the RAF camp, ones he said that would have sucked me in and blown me out again.

His mother had died tragically when he was very young and his father had been terminally ill for some time but I imagined such things would have been accommodated by mere adjustments in his philosophy which was an optimistic though sceptical one. He was very cautious with his praise, always first seeing the disadvantages and flaws in anything or anybody, and he was intelligently curious about anything or anybody new. He was also a very successful loner and I think it was this last quality that

I admired more than anything else. Coming from a big family as I did, where there were always brothers to accompany you everywhere whether you wanted it or not, nothing was ever undertaken alone or without support. Somebody therefore who did everything without reference to any other mortal seemed to me to possess a powerful strength. The fact that Steve seemed to have no close friends and very few relatives didn't seem a drawback at all to someone like me living in the land of plenty.

No wonder I modelled myself on him. I talked like him when I was out at night with my pals and they were amazed at my progress. I talked impassively about the most terrible diseases and afflictions of mankind and womankind and they thought I verily knew how many beans made five, my ability for such calculations being daily augmented with every hour spent in the VIC PM house.

Things at home weren't very good. My father wasn't happy about some of my mates and my mother thought I had too many 'different' girlfriends. My father especially didn't like my anti-establishment attitude and both he and my mother thought I was a bad influence on my younger brothers. They didn't know about my daily exposure to Steve's atheistic and amoral views over the last eighteen months and blamed my 'attitude' on my pals, Jim and Tod.

Jim was well over six strapping feet and considered himself breathtaking, though his short blond hair and glasses let his image down somewhat. He was inches taller than Tod but didn't look it. Tod was broad and hard and had the most frightening face of anybody I had ever had met, he was one of those human beings one can never imagine having once been a baby or even a child. He had won a scholarship to the Royal Grammar School, the most exclusive school in the North of England but nobody would ever have called him a fag. His mother was a Labour councillor and a 'scourge' who would sit down in the wrong places and jump up at the wrong time. She was like no other friend's mother I had known. She was provocative, articulate and rough and Tod was just the same, nobody said anything out of line when either of them were around. We were all only seventeen and Tod had been an atheist, anarchist, a drinker and gambler for years. Steve and Tod were the only two people I had ever met who dared say there was no God and that the vast majority of mankind was rotten to the core.

When Tod, Jim and I went out to 'get dames', I was the one who would do the chatting up and Tod and Jim would bring up the rear with Tod staying out of sight like a vulture until I'd made the kill; 'Tash' was what Tod collectively called them because of their surmised pubic hair. They usually went around in twos so I'd get the best one and either Jim or Tod, or both of them, would get the other, the one they called 'The Dog'. Even a mediocre girl looked okay when she was teamed up with a shocker and she was positively stunning beside Tod. To his credit he wasn't particular as long as he got something and if he'd been listening to my patter and didn't fancy his chances of getting anything at all, he'd come out of the shadows, reveal himself like Frankenstein and say something unbelievably crude that would 'put the bubble in' for all three of us. 'If I'm not getting one, you shitheads aren't,' he'd say and he'd be right.

On a Saturday night we would to go to the Stoll on Westgate Road, the picture house that showed all the X movies, though by 'X' was meant things like 'The Creature From The Black Lagoon'. Tod was always more forthcoming in the dark and would cheer on the monster, shouting 'Grabba, ye useless nowt! Givva somethin' to think about!'

At the end of every performance as soon as the National Anthem started Tod always stood up, slammed his seat back and walked up the aisle whistling a Lionel Hampton arrangement or singing something like 'I don' wan' your greenback dollar, babe, I don' wan' your silver chain...' Jim and I had no choice but to follow amidst the boos and hisses even from a roundhead audience like the Stoll's.

How he managed it nobody knew but Tod once got himself a girlfriend down in Tynemouth and on Sunday nights before her mother put a stop to it, he used to invite all his pals down to her house to watch her taking a bath.

On a Tuesday night we used to go to the jazz club in the Royal Arcade down Pilgrim Street to see the Newcastle City Jazzmen or Mighty Joe Young, and there was a really rough pub up a lane opposite, called the 'Golden Tiger'. If I had gone into the 'Tiger' on my own I'd have instantly been 'nutted' by blokes with Neanderthal foreheads who would butt you between the eyes for no reason other than the gratification of bursting your nose. Sometimes if Tod had gone for a 'slash' and I'd gone to get the drinks in, even with Jim beside me they'd be moving in, the edges of razor blades showing in the lapels of their jackets; the reason for the razors was so that anybody crazy enough to grab them to 'stick the nut' on them would have their hands cut to ribbons. But when Tod, still fastening his fly, came wandering over to the table with a face on him like Beelzebub, they would very soon disperse, lapels and all.

I never deliberately initiated trouble and only fought when my back was up against the wall but Tod always did things that were calculated to upset people, friends as well as foes. No matter who or what you praised, he always had a rejoinder. Even if he didn't know what you were talking about, he still criticised it, it was instinctive with him. He was the most excoriating critic I have ever met and best of all he was totally sincere, he had faith in nothing and in nobody and he couldn't believe anybody ever did anything out of the 'goodness of their heart'. 'What a load of crap!' was his definitive comment on practically everything. Above all he hated sentimentality. Steve could be charming, considerate even when it suited him; Tod never.

When he and Jim came around to the house one Sunday afternoon and caught me drying the dishes, he never let me forget it. Yet my father was as tough a proposition in his own way as Tod's mother, and when I came in late I'd be locked out, something Tod with his own key never was. Sometimes I'd go to Tod's where he would still be up listening to 'The Hamp' on his tape recorder. But Tod wasn't the kind who gave up his bed or even any of his blankets or pillows for a mate, you just slept as you were on the floor amongst his sweaty underwear and stinking socks. His mother would never get up to make a bed for the son of anybody, let alone the son of a civil servant.

Steve and Tod were heretics, not rebels, but if they were an influence on me I suppose I was ready for it.

Two years National Service was compulsory for all men over the age of eighteen, though in careers like mine deferment for three years until they had completed their studies was the usual thing. By now I think my father had given up all hope of my becoming a civil servant and just wanted me to complete my studies and be somebody or something. But being a veterinary technician with the Ministry of Agriculture and ending up like Oliver instead of Standish had less and less appeal with every day that went by and Longbenton seemed to me to be at the far edge of an outer galaxy.

The British Army was always advertising for men who wanted to 'See the world!' and I reckoned it must apply to National Servicemen as well so I decided to waive deferment and take my chances. I knew it had bases in Hong Kong, Kuala Lumpur, Cypress, Aden, Colombo, Germany, Gibraltar and Northern Ireland, and any of them would do me.

Mr Dougal-McKay had retired to the Isle of Wight though I don't think anybody noticed and his replacement was a different species of chief veterinary officer. Not only was he a chain cigarette smoker instead of a pipe man, he was introverted, ordinarily dressed, hardly ever away and knew a lot more about veterinary science.

'Are you sure that's what you want to do, Joe?' Mr Bailey asked in his strong Edinburgh accent with a troubled look on his face. 'Two years is a long time out of a body's life, you know. You could wait and get your diploma and then go in at a higher rank if you wanted to. An officer maybe.'

'No, thanks, Mr Bailey. I've decided to go in now.'

He was reluctant to write the necessary letter cancelling the deferment papers he had already sent in as a matter of course, and hung back for a few days in case I'd just had a bad day dealing with too many sheep with diarrhoea, or something. And when he next came in to see me to make sure I really wanted to go in, he was shaking his head sorrowfully when he walked back along the corridor. Even if he thought it he was too polite to suggest there might be a chip on a body's shoulder.

My father was furious when I told him, he said I was a bloody fool and the Army wasn't going to be anything like what I seemed to think. I didn't think it was going to be a holiday necessarily but I did think it would be a bit of a laugh getting kitted out in uniform and all that yelling and marching about and everything, especially if I got to go to a place like Hong Kong. He was more upset with me than I could ever remember at any time of my life and anything I said only made things worse.

Although I had definite opinions and was capable of expressing myself well, I could never do so at home; not just because my views were sometimes diametrically opposed to my father's but because there were too many other pairs of ears listening, ears attached to heads opposed to anything I said as a matter of principle. I wanted to question everything: no longer how things were, but why. I wanted to find out if any doctrines or traditions could justify their existence. And I wasn't going to find out in Simonside Terrace or at Longbenton. At home, at work, in the newspapers or on the radio, it seemed to me nobody wanted to question anything. Whereas in the Army I reckoned everybody would be more or less the same age as me and have the same outlook.

In the end it got so that neither my father nor I could say more than two words to each other without there was a row, with my brothers all siding with him and my mother in tears. So I went into work one morning, telephoned the recruitment office and requested a call-up as early as possible. I was sackless enough to tell my father as soon as he came home from work that night because I wanted to punish him. 'That's it then,' he said and there was never another word about it.

Jim said if I went in, he was going into the Northumberland Fusiliers. Tod snarled his contempt. 'You stupid twats! With those khaki cretins..? Fuck that for a laugh!'

In less than a week I got my call-up papers. I wasn't jubilant but I was exhilarated...exhilarated and just a wee bit apprehensive. Now that my father had stopped objecting, there wasn't the same need for indecent haste. But he and my mother had resigned themselves to it and I think my mother hoped it might do me good.

When I left Central Station at eight o'clock on the morning of the 11th November 1955 with a railway ticket I'd been given at the ticket office in exchange for the travel warrant to Fleet in Hampshire, that the RAMC [Royal Army Medical Corps] had sent me, the figure in the well-worn brown trilby and mackintosh seeing me off was my father. 'Take care of yourself, son,' he said as he shook my hand. The whistle blew, I boarded the train, we waved to each other through the window and a couple of minutes later I was crossing the Tyne Bridge knowing he would already be making his way out of the station to catch the bus to Blaydon where his office was.

The Royal Army Medical Corps

6

A fair-haired fellow whose face between the acne was deeply pitted had got on the train at York and although we had both got off at King's Cross, here he was again in my compartment balefully heading west with me. This time we were alone so I spoke to him.

His name was Lenny Crampton, he was a coalminer and like me was bound for Queen Elizabeth Barracks in Crookham and two years in the RAMC, and like me he was already farther away from home than he had ever been in his life.

I was happy to be doing my National Service in the Medical Corps because hopefully I'd be able to continue my training as a laboratory technician and get some valuable experience on the medical side. Lenny however was not at all pleased to be allocated to a 'poofter regiment', he wanted to be in the Tank Corps or at the very least an artillery regiment. 'I want to be making big holes in something,' he said, opening the window and spitting out.

As we drew nearer to our destination there were more and more young men like ourselves carrying a single case and less and less of the rest of humanity. When the train stopped we all got off. It was an austere little station called Fleet and there was only one place to go, one exit, and we all tentatively went through. Outside were four army lorries and a dozen or more soldiers with one or two stripes rushing about with sticks under their arms and angry little faces, shouting and yelling as though there was an emergency and they had to evacuate the station in a hurry.

'Everybody for Crookham Barracks, get on those lorries! You there..! Yes, you! Get up! Last man on board gets my boot up his arse!'

All their bawling and fleeing about amused and baffled us, nobody was in a hurry except them; we far outnumbered them and there were some big blokes amongst us prepared to do no more than a slow shuffle.

'Who do they think they're kidding?' somebody next to me said.

I just shrugged, I didn't know what to make of it. They were so young, silly-looking and agitated it was hard to believe they weren't putting on an act; if there was anybody over twenty in the RAMC they certainly weren't here.

Suddenly there was a lot more shouting and three of them rushed into the station. When they came out there was a stocky lad in front of them with a familiar face and his shirt hanging out of his trousers. A little sergeant with a thick baton under his arm and the peak of his red cap pulled so far down over his eyes that he had to put his head right back to see in front, quickly capered up so close I thought he was going to bump into him.

'Where've you been!' he yelled.

'What's it to you?' came the broad Yorkshire voice.

'Where've you been!!'

'For a pee. There's no law against that down here, is the?'

'What's your name, soldier!'

'I'm not a soldier yet.'

'You're a soldier all right! As of 0900 hours today!'

'What the fuck's that supposed to be in English?'

'Say "San't" when you speak to me!'

'Say what?'

'What's your name!'

'Lenny Crampton... What's yours?'

'What's your number!'

'What number?'

'Your call-up number!'

'Buggered if I know... You mean that bloody long thing on the form..? I could never remember that.'

'Where have you come from!'

'Barnsley.'

'Right, Private Crampton from Barnsley,' the sergeant said, mimicking the Yorkshire dialect, 'I am never going to forget you. And believe me, you're never going to forget me... Now get on that lorry right now, or I'll have you picked up and thrown on!'

Lenny looked at him and for a moment I thought he was going to hit him but he clambered aboard instead, muttering 'Just you try it, mate.'

The lorries drove us to an army camp that was part wire-fenced and part brick-walled, past a sign saying 'Royal Army Medical Corps, Queen Elizabeth Barracks, Crookham' and in through gates where soldiers in peaked caps were standing guard. Inside there were rows and rows of long wooden buildings all exactly the same with small grassed areas in between, large flat concrete squares with different groups of men marching on them, and individuals and small groups walking along various narrow paths, every one of them in uniform. It was like being on another planet.

'This is it, lads,' somebody at the back said cheerfully. 'You're in the bloody Army now!'

The lorries stopped in front of a large wooden building, the NCOs [non-commissioned officers] who had met us at the station quickly jumped out, pulled down their peaks, straightened their tunics, stamped their boots to let their trousers hang over their gaiters, and the shouting started all over again, this time decidedly more vulgarly now we were on territory evidently sanctified for the purpose; hence when we were told to alight and enter the building, it was put rather more colourfully. They kept shouting 'You there!' as they had done at the station and everybody thought they were being shouted at. I suspected it was a ruse.

Inside the very large hall were draped all kinds of military flags, pennants hanging up and huge pictures of people like Montgomery and the Queen on the walls. A long line of narrow tables ran along three sides with soldiers of various ranks sitting at them with their hats off. A notice on a blackboard and easel stated this was the 1600hrs induction for C-Company.

For the next two hours we walked past every desk, answering questions about schools attended, exams passed, religious denomination, professional qualifications or trade skills, health and vaccinations, army cadet experience, relatives who had served in the Army, hobbies and interests, and most exhaustively of all about sporting prowess.

'Surely you're good at something?' they would say. 'What about cricket or basketball..? You mean you've never won anything in the whole of your life? Have you never been on a winning team?' And when you shook your head, their faces displayed withering contempt and you could see they thought you were absolutely useless and were going to be nothing but a dead weight in their army.

From what I could see, anybody who had boxed or played football or rugby produced the only smiles and animation. In their case an officer standing back keeping an eye on things with his peaked cap on would be called over and he would address them with the kind of bonhomie newly-transferred star players in the First Division of the Football League would have got.

Like the majority however I aroused no interest whatsoever as I went from table to table trying to justify my life on earth up to this point, which was transcribed into a series of ticks and crosses on big forms and rarely merited a single written word. The lucky few who had had a trial for Leeds United, or been North Wales Schools under-16s boxing champion, came through smiling smugly, assured they were going to be well looked after.

At the end of it we were given our KFS [knife, fork and spoon] and an enamel mug - 'KFSM' would have made more sense - and then moved into another hall with huge tea urns that had milk and sugar already added, and black trays with hard scones whose raisins were encrusted with carbon. 'Refreshments over there! Quick about it! You there, get a move on! You're not in Forte's Restaurant now!'

While we were consuming our first army victuals, a number of very smart fresh-faced soldiers with a single stripe on their arm one by one read out a list of names and numbers. They were lance-corporals and we were assigned to whichever one read out our name, which meant we were in his squad and had to follow him to his billet. If you hadn't started or finished your tea, tough luck.

Our lance-corporal was a rather podgy fellow with a pleasant face and he herded my thirty-one companions and me to C-7 billet. It was among rows and rows of the same creosoted huts, outside all of which were two lines of sixteen men, some in disarray and in civvies like us, others in fatigues and in some semblance of order, yet others in full uniform responding like a single soldier to every command. Each group was being shouted at by a spruce lance-corporal who was strutting up and down in front of them. As far as you could hear into the distance in every direction it was the same thing.

The billet was as spartan inside as it was outside. A row of sixteen iron beds two feet apart ran down each long wall, separated in the middle by a strip of lino six feet wide. Between each bed was a wooden locker which we were told we'd have to buy padlocks for. On each bed was a mattress with a grey green coverlet, two blankets, a pillow, a pillowcase and two sheets, all of them very basic and resembling those in prisoners' cells in movies. The lance-corporal showed us how to make up our beds with 'hospital corners' and we followed suit, some doing it quickly and well, others taking ages and making a hash of it; Lenny was one of the latter.

Next, while standing by our beds we were told how to recognise and address different ranks - lance-corporals were 'Corp'l' - told to consult the barrack-room [the inside of a large standard billet] rules and duties that were on the notice-board and to memorise our army number and camp address. Most important of all, we were told, 'Don't think'; for the next two years our thinking would be done for us: we would be told when to get up and when to go to bed, when to stand up and when to sit down, when to eat and when to sleep. There would be a 'sick parade' at 0800hrs every morning where anybody who was ill could report, but anybody thinking of going had better be really sick because the doctor was an army officer and would sharp sort the skivers out and from then on their lives wouldn't be worth living.

We were then told to assemble in two ranks outside and were shamble-marched from there to the barber's. This was essentially a shearing shed containing three soldiers with electric shears but neither scissors nor combs, and three wooden chairs. An elite of corporals was standing at the back, laughing like senators at the Roman Games, while in batches of three we had our hair shaved off beneath an imaginary line drawn around the head one inch above the ear and everything above it left untouched. I had a crewcut so my hair was short anyway but they still shaved it according to army pudding-basin regulations which reputedly stated 'No hair must be seen below the beret'.

Quite a few of the lads had DAs [duck's arse hairstyles] so called because of the way the hair was combed into a parting which ran down from crown to collar and was quintessential for Teds [mock Edwardians] who now looked hideous. As the lance-corporals spluttered and whinnied at the mess the barbers were making, the emasculated Samsons, pride shorn off and lying on the floor with their brylcreamed swathes, rose from the chairs stunned and white-faced; all it had taken to subdue them was a bad haircut that took about fifteen seconds.

The next event in the process of becoming a soldier was a visit to the canteen which would eliminate any remaining doubts about the British Army being a funny place. It was another big wooden hut and when its bolts clashed back we all jostled in to file past a row of huge steaming stainless-steel bins, behind which stood a line of men dressed in white jackets and eccentrically shaped chef hats who seemed to think they belonged to the Praetorian Guard rather than the Catering Corps. They stood poised with ladles in each hand as though they were used to playing the vibraphone or perhaps a set of drums and deftly flung food from their bins on to the edges of our plates while making sarcastic comments and laughing to each other as they forecast our individual fate.

There was burnt fried stuff, cold and stodgy stuff, and tea which everybody said contained barium to suppress our sex-drive, and whether it did or it didn't, it tasted like it did. I couldn't eat anything except a bit of one of the scone-things we'd had earlier in the induction hall; even the tea I rolled around in my mouth trying to do some kind of chemical analysis before swallowing.

Lenny Crampton and I sat by ourselves. I think most of the others were avoiding him so as not to be included in the wrath of the sergeant at the railway station, when it descended. He told me he was going to do his two years, do the very least he could get away with and come out of it no more a soldier than the day he went in. He was a miner and no twat in a uniform was going to make him into anything different.

'They'll be bloody sorry they put me with this lot. Can ye imagine me stickin' a needle in somebody's arse..? What do you do, anyway?'

'I work in a veterinary laboratory.'

'A vetinary laboratory..? And they put you in the medical corps..? Bloody typical, that is... You want to tell them you want to be in the vetinary corps where they have all the horses and dogs.'

'If you tell them you want to be transferred, they'll keep you where you are just for the sake of it,' said a fellow in fatigues across the table from us. 'They always do the opposite to what you want. They think it's good for discipline. The only time they take any notice is if you're volunteering for something. And if you're daft enough to volunteer for anything in the British Army,' he said as he stood up, 'you deserve all you bloody get.'

When we returned to the billet most of the others were already back. Some of them were sitting on their beds writing letters and some were combing their hair in front of tiny mirrors, trying to salvage a little self-respect. Others were joking and messing about, smoking or eating something they had brought with them. A few were lying on their beds staring upwards as though in a coma. Two were drawing up charts with little squares for the days.

'Only 729 days to go, lads!' one announced.

'Jesus wept! This one's not over yet.'

'Fuck! Fuck! Fuck!'

'What's up?'

'Next year's a leap year so we have to do an extra day.'

There were groans from one end of the room to the other.

'Shitttttt!'

'Lights out at 2230hrs! I want every man up and fresh tomorrow morning!' It was the corporal at the top of the barrack-room but he quickly turned on his heels, disappeared into his little room and closed the door.

Opposite me was a fellow from Leicester called Harvey Otley. He had round gold-wire spectacles and a semi-crewcut and was in his vest all the time so everybody could see he was well made; like several others he had just qualified as a pharmacist and had an air of self assurance about him. On his left was a tall nervous Jewish-looking fellow from London, with slightly hunched shoulders and what looked like a trace of a hare-lip hiding under a black moustache; he was another pharmacist. They were both at least twenty-two and because of their qualifications would expect to be promoted to sergeant as soon as the eight weeks' basic training was over.

On Otley's right was the first Welshman I had ever seen and the most self-contained fellow in the whole barrack-room. His hair had been shaved higher up his head than anybody else's, right up to his crown and around at the sides a good three inches above his thin ears; I hadn't had a good look at him before we went to the barber's so maybe it was already like that. His skin was very white, he had prominent cheekbones and a tiny pencil moustache, and he wasn't speaking to anybody. It was the business-like look on his face and the way he went about everything that so impressed me; he never asked anybody to repeat what had been said or joined in any of the discussions which followed, and he never hesitated or looked to see what anybody else was doing. It was hard to believe this was his first day.

Others talked incessantly and a friendly fellow from Liverpool with no bone in his nose was going from bed to bed asking everybody where they came from and what they did, and everybody else was listening. There were people from all over, many with accents I had never heard before. It was a good way to find out something about everybody. In just a few words the way they answered told you something about their confidence, their education, their attitude towards National Service and if they were friendly or not.

Apart from the pharmacists, there were two medical lab technicians, a chiropodist, an optician, a couple of physiotherapists, an x-ray technician, a health inspector, an ambulance driver, a prosthetic-limb maker, a few others with some vague connection to health, a butcher, an undertaker's apprentice and a number of others like Lenny with no connection whatsoever.

I was on the left-hand side about halfway down the room, which I later found was the worst place to be because during inspections this position was where whoever was inspecting would be most likely to exercise his talent. On my right was a big good-natured fellow who worked in the shipyards at Middlesborough, and on my left a quiet fellow who kept his locker door open all the time as a kind of screen, so much so that I hardly knew what he looked like.

We were all shapes and sizes and as varied in looks and, it seemed, personalities, as in places of origin and occupation. Some of the older ones like Harvey were cheerful and stoic, others were acting on like kids at a school camp, while others fulminated nonstop. A few looked dumbstruck as though they couldn't believe where they were.

I waited until the lights were switched off before getting into my pyjamas, never having fully undressed before anybody in my life except my mother and brother and I hadn't done that for a long time now. Some of them had dropped their trousers and underpants as though born to it and wandered around looking in their case for something or speaking to somebody, and you could see everything they had. I never realised how hairy some men could be at eighteen or nineteen, some I was amazed to see had hair growing out of their behinds. Even when the lights were off a ray of moonlight was coming through the window, so I wrapped my towel around me as I'd do when changing into my trunks at the beach but I did it quickly because I saw a couple of them nodding their heads towards me and grinning.

'Geordie's got something worth hiding there, by the looks of it,' one of them said.

That was the first time I had ever been called 'Geordie' and I felt quite proud, it was as though I was representing Tyneside.

Some were still at the ablutions and had been away for ages and I wondered if they were going to come back. There was one fellow at the bottom of the room who was turned away with his blankets drawn right up over him like a cocoon as though he had withdrawn from everything.

This was the first time I had ever experienced the phenomenon of pungent comments delivered from a bed in the dark, I had certainly never experienced anything like it at home. It was as they were getting into their beds that most of those who had something to say, said it, rather like a parting shot to the day. Some of the comments were defiant and most of them funny. Several expressed the philosophy of capitulation, 'If you can't beat 'em, you might as well join 'em,' a sentiment I detested, even at eighteen.

Finally, from those who had contributed little in the way of wit, came the farting and this was far more ferocious than anything I had ever heard in the dressing room of the gym at school. At first every fart drew a comment from somebody but after about twenty minutes of it when the depths of near-depravity had been plumbed, the novelty began to wear off.

This was the first time since I got off the train that I'd had any time to myself, the first time I didn't feel the need to watch out for myself. I thought of home, of the bed I'd slept in with my seventeen-year-old brother Johnny even as recently as last night at Plessey Terrace, High Heaton, and it seemed such a long, long time ago. I had slept in that bed for as long as I could remember, right through the Second World War with the exception of short periods of evacuation, through mumps and measles and chicken pox and bad colds, and never alone, always with the best pal in the world. I had dropped him as somebody to go out with of course, he'd been far too young for that for a long time and now had his own young mates.

I wondered if those on either side or opposite me had somebody who never hesitated to get into anything to help them out, somebody who would have risked their life for them. I had never known anybody else like that, no matter how estimable they were with their hand-to-hand battles with the Kikuyu or clashes of Neanderthal nut against Neanderthal nut in downtown Newcastle. Already I was sorry I had taken him for granted, sorry even that I'd given my father such a hard time. In fact I was very penitent indeed and wasn't sure whether I was more sorry for them or myself.

But loud snores invaded the penitence before it could become unmanageable and I could hear mumbling, though whether it was somebody saying his prayers or talking to somebody in the next bed, I wasn't sure. I now said my own including a new 'Army one' I made up - Mam had always composed new prayers to cater for a change in circumstance or situation.

Somebody called out 'Nighty, nighty. No more wanky!' and a few laughed.

'Night!' I called out, expecting a flurry of responses echoing around the barrack-room and instantly regretting it. But there wasn't a sound. Were they asleep or were they lying there grinding their teeth and biting their lips, I wondered.

7

I was deep asleep when the barrack-room door burst open simultaneous with the harsh sound of marching boots and a voice shouting 'Wakey, wakey! Hands off cocks! On socks! Up, you idle shower!'

As he clomped down the middle of the floor whacking his stick against the metal frames of the bed, every bed, it was like an electric shock; I had never experienced anything like it, not the jolt, the vibration or the sheer brutality.

I looked at my watch. It was half past four in the morning, the middle of the night at this time of year. All around me heads were raised and there were moans and groans and bewildered faces.

'What about reveille or whatever you call it? I thought we were supposed to be woke up by some fucker blowing a bugle...outside?' It was Lenny.

'That was only in Beau Geste.'

'Some fuckin' jest!'

Five minutes later the orderly sergeant was back and this time he made everybody get out of bed. The light in the room was yellow and dim, it was pitch black outside the windows and it was freezing cold. It was like a bad dream, like being under an anaesthetic at the dentist's.

People were already going out with their towels over their shoulders and toothbrushes and razors rattling in their mugs.

The ablutions consisted of rows of sinks on one side and a row of lavatories on the other. They were old, cold, dark, absolutely miserable and again I was reminded of a prison. Pathetic graffiti was scratched on the walls dating back to 1940, as it was on the inside of the lockers in the barrack-room. It was clear that nothing anywhere was post-war: we were living in the same accommodation and using the same taps and sinks and lavatories, the same knives, forks and spoons that soldiers in the Second World War would have used and there was something grisly about it.

By 5.50am I was in a queue outside the canteen which was closed and seemed devoid of life inside. It was still dark, the ground was hard with frost and there was a stupefying noise of knives forks and spoons being rattled in metal mugs. Some of the men seemed to be enjoying themselves, laughing and pushing each other, others were talking in earnest tones, many were morosely silent.

Although rumours about all kinds of things had been rife the previous night, now we were mixing with the intake from other billets there were many more, such as that starting with our intake, National Service was being extended indefinitely because trouble was brewing in Cyprus and the Suez Canal and we were going to be sent there as soon as training was over; another was that the RAMC was just a ruse and we were going to be parachuted in with the Black Watch, the Pioneers and all the rest of them, machine guns, grenades, bayonets, the lot; the Black Watch were all murderers from Glasgow jails and every officer had killed at least three people; anybody with a medical qualification would be promoted to sergeant, the rest would be emptying bedpans for two years; the Catering Corps were a bunch of slimy bastards who were rougher than the Black Watch and kept all the best food for themselves; the cooks peed and spat into the dixies of porridge and stew out of sheer malice. All this I heard before the door opened.

Breakfast consisted of cornflakes and milk, bacon and egg, and bread and jam. The cornflakes came out of a huge bin but otherwise looked normal and the milk was ladled out of a huge dixie but also seemed okay. Mind I was hungry now and maybe Harvey, the newly qualified pharmacist, was right when he said edibility was inversely proportional to hunger.

After breakfast we went back to the billet to make our beds and see what was going to happen to us next. Quite a different corporal was addressing us now; yesterday he was like a senior prefect, today he was a martinet.

'Anybody not read barrack-room regulations?'

There was a mumble, it wasn't the kind of question that seriously expected an answer.

'Right! Everybody by their beds! Feet together! Arms by your sides! Shoulders back! Hands clenched like this!' He showed us how to make the kind of pointed fist where the index knuckle extended down the outside of the leg.

'Eyes front! Mouths closed! Chest out! Stomach in!

'Now, when I ask a question, you will not think! You will respond immediately and automatically! And you will say 'corporal' whenever you are referring to me! When you speak to me...and you will only do that when you are spoken to...you will say "Yes, Corp'l!".

'If on a matter of great importance you need to speak to me, you will only do so at certain times and never during drill or training! You will come to attention and you will call out your number, your name after the word "Private", and then, "Corp'l! Permission to speak!". Then you will wait! And if you are not given permission, you will take one step back, turn to the right, and march away..! Got that!' he yelled.

'Yes, Corp'l!'

'What did you say!!'

'Yes, Corp'l!!'

'Right! When I come into this room, no matter what you're doing...whether you're cleaning your boots or saying your prayers...and whether I say anything or not...you will all jump to attention! If another NCO comes in, you will jump to attention! And if an officer comes in, you will jump to attention, you will salute, and you will practically shit yourselves..! Got that!'

'Yes, Corp'l!!'

'Some of you might be under the illusion that a lance-corporal is just one step up from you... Well, let me tell them this. It is easier for a camel to get through the eye of a needle, than for somebody like you to get to be a lance-corporal! The difference between a lance-corporal and a field marshall in this man's Army, is less than that between a private and a lance-corporal! Nothing in the whole British Army is lower than you! Nothing is more worthless..! No rifle, no mess-can, webbing strap or bootlace..! And why is that..? It is because they are all of some use. Whereas you are utterly useless! You are costing this Army money and time and other valuable resources!

'But this unsatisfactory state of affairs will not continue for very long. Up until you came to this barracks, you were nothing! Your life had no meaning. Now that will change. For I am going to make soldiers of every one of you! Do as you are told and become good soldiers and you might make somebody somewhere proud of you someday!

'If, however, any of you give the slightest bother...if you fail to become the perfect soldier, you will let your squad down. And if you let your squad down, you will let your company down. If you let your company down, you will let your corps down. And if you let your corps down, you will let the British Army down. And if you let the British Army down, you will let your Queen and Country down... And if you let all those people down, you had better believe it that you will have let me down... But let me assure you that long before you get that far, I will have dealt with you and you will wish you had never have been born!! You will see two years last the rest of your life..!! Any questions!!'

'No, Corp'l!'

'Any questions!!'

'No, Corp'l!!'

'Now that you know how to address me, you might wonder how the Army and the uncountable numbers of your superiors in the Army are going to address you... In here you will be addressed as "Barrack Room!". Outside, you will be addressed as "Squad!" or "C Company!". As individuals, you will be addressed according to what your superior thinks of you..! Got that!!'

'Yes, Corp'l!!'

'When I say "Barrack Room, tow!" [tau] you will come to attention as you are now. "Atten-shun!" is what they say in the Girl Guides... When I say "Stand at ease!" you will move your left leg a pace to the left and clasp your hands behind your back.

'Ready!!' he roared.

'Yes, Corp'l!!' we all shouted back.

But instead of saying what he'd said he was going to say, he shouted 'Bagoom..! Ba-goooom-Tow!', giving a short funny little screech on the word 'tow'. And instead of saying 'Stand at ease!', he shouted 'Standaaaa-Tease!' with the same little screech on the last syllable. He repeated both commands half a dozen times and eventually we responded with something approximating what he wanted. Then we were marched off to the QMS [Quartermaster's Stores] to get kitted out, though we didn't know where we were going till we got there.

The QMS was another wooden utility building, this one with shelves upon shelves of military apparel and accoutrements, and we proceeded by shuffling in a long line along a very long counter, at the other side of which were soldiers in fatigues [loose-fitting khaki denim jerkin and trousers] each one handing out a different item of clothing. No measurements were given or taken, they merely glanced at us and plonked something on the counter as we went past and we added it to the pile we were already carrying.

We each came out with two sets of battledress and fatigues, two pairs of boots, gaiters, socks, drawers (unwearable green underpants), two berets and a brass badge, two shirts, towels and ties, one pair of gloves and braces, one kitbag, greatcoat, jumper, steel helmet, webbing belt and buckles, gas-mask, large haversack, small haversack and their webbing, two yellow dusters, one tin of boot polish, Brasso and Blanco, and a medium and small brush. Everything was recorded in quasi-legal language like *'cellular drawers, green, prs 2'*, and everybody signed for what they had in their hands and to say they understood that anything damaged or lost would be deducted from their pay; expendable items like the cleaning materials would be deducted from our first pay-packet in any case.

There was no toothpaste, facecloths, toothbrushes, handkerchiefs, combs or vests, notebooks, pens, washing powder, nor any weapons of any kind, but we were given two little booklets, the size of passports: a brown one called an *AB 64 PART 1* and a white one called an *AB 64 PART 2*. The first was an identity card that included information about things like vaccinations and had to be guarded with our lives in case someone got their hands on it and tried to impersonate a British soldier, a heinous crime which could seriously damage national security. The second was what we would need if we wanted to be paid in a fortnight's time and every fortnight thereafter, and although nothing was said we presumed the same strictures applied. Like everything else, both documents would remain Army property.

Even those who had cursed the British Army ever since they had arrived could hardly wait to get back to the billet to get out of their civilian clothes and see what they looked like in a soldier's uniform. Already we were sensitive about going around the camp the way we were. 'Get some in, sprogs!' was shouted at us without fail every time we passed anybody in uniform. Already we had learned that the longer a National Serviceman had been in the Army - no matter what his rank or regiment - the greater the respect due to him by every other National Serviceman.

Consequently, 'How long have you got to do?' was the most trenchant and frequent question anybody could and would be asked in two whole years. Somebody who had been in eight weeks, completed basic training and shed all awkwardness of dress and manner, was what was meant by the term, 'old soldier'. He won all arguments because he knew all that mattered and he had achieved a status that couldn't be appreciated by anybody except a sprog, a sprog being the lowest form of uniformed life in the known universe.

As we got into khaki battledress, boots and gaiters, constantly referring to the model of our corporal who stood there posing unselfconsciously, differences were being revealed between us that had not been so apparent in civilian clothes. At a glance you could now see whose mother had straightened his tie before he had gone off to work, you could see who would very soon make a soldier and who never would, you could see the extrovert and introvert, the Anglo Saxon and the Celt, the compliant and the defiant.

When half an hour later we were marched out of the barrack-room and into the big martial world outside, 'marching' had a whole new meaning. Gone the rubbers, suedes, crepes and fancy slip-ons, all feet were now theoretically capable of making the same sound and in concert. I think at this point all of us were enthusiastic and tried to march the way we had seen so many soldiers doing it through the streets of our childhood; I know I could clearly remember many times seeing all kinds of servicemen and women proudly marching along Barras Bridge and up to the Memorial in the Haymarket, bands playing, people cheering and more than a few tears being shed.

But this was quite different. We were conducted - half led, half bullied - to the parade ground which was one of the concrete squares we had seen on the previous day, across which the damp icy November wind cut like a knife while we stood in silence in two rows and waited. Eventually a lone tailor surprisingly dressed in civvies took rough and rapid measurements whilst we tried to calculate his rank, and we were then marched back to the billet, covered in chalk marks. We changed into our fatigues and handed in the items the tailor had marked. Alterations were confined to the BD [battledress] and greatcoat; everything else, from beret to boots we had to make do with, and my boots were too tight.

After that we were each given a piece of brown paper and a length of string, told to wrap up all our civilian clothes and belongings into a single parcel and write our home address on the outside. We were then ordered outside into two rows, told to put the parcel under our left arms, and conducted in the usual way to the camp post office where we handed in our parcels in the manner directed. Although I never heard any mention of it afterwards, I suspect a few hearts must have sank when they saw their last few pieces of connection with civilian life, the real world outside, disappear; I know mine did.

We were then given our first drill and introduced to words most of us had never heard before.

First we had to 'dress from the right', which meant sorting ourselves so that the tallest man was at the extreme right, the end that would lead off, and the smallest man at the extreme left. For some reason this was accomplished not from reading out from a list, nor by our calling out our heights, not even with a tape measure; but by short shuffling movements like in a penguin colony where the heads are constantly flicking from left to right. Then we had to individually 'number from the right' which meant shouting out the number of our position in the line, starting from the tall guy on the end. It was a futile exercise if ever there was because one lapse of concentration or misunderstanding of a strange dialect and the mistake was compounded all the way to the end, or until the corporal's ranting managed to stop it. But that's the way it had been done since time immemorial and we were now ready to be formally initiated into the mysteries of marching, the mode of locomotion by which conquests from the most ancient times had been facilitated, the way of conveying ourselves in public that would make old men weep and young women swoon.

'Left arm, right foot! By the right! Qui-iiick mach!'

In response to unintelligibly compressed command words, we were bullied and ridiculed into learning how to swing our arms to shoulder height, lift our feet straight up off the ground and stamp them down to produce a crunch rather than a scrape, and how to turn around when necessary. 'By the left! Abbow-tan!'

Right from the start there was no patience shown to anybody and no such thing as extenuating circumstances. Those that were able and willing to learn regimentation were clearly going to get on all right; those that weren't, weren't. The optician, who was poorly co-ordinated in terms of his arms and legs doing what the corporal's brain wanted, was obviously intelligent, timid and close to breaking down, yet he was bawled at and called an idiot so many times everybody believed it.

Other corporals had their squads out perhaps no more than ten or fifteen yards away and it was clear they were trying to outdo each other in wit and volume of scorn for the men in their charge. All around, for what seemed like miles, people were being insulted in the most offensive and public manner. 'Get your bloody finger out!' they were shouting. I had no idea what its origins were, only that it sounded vulgar and meant 'Hurry up, for goodness sake'.

Why were so many men putting up with so much abuse from so few? And already. We'd only been here for less than twenty-four hours.

At quarter past one we were given three quarters of an hour to get to the canteen and back to the billet by two o'clock - rather, 1400hrs. Every soldier in the camp seemed to be there and the noise of clomping and grating boots, KFS rattling in mugs, ladles clashing against dixies and plates, plates banging on tables, cutlery scraping on plates or clunking in the communal sink, and the conversation of hundreds of men, was terrific.

Suddenly all went quiet. We knew by now that a peaked cap meant trouble - officers, sergeant-majors and MPs [military police] all wore them - and two had just appeared. One was an officer and the other was a sergeant-major and they were strolling about, every now and then stopping at a table to ask the men what they thought of the fare. Nobody called it what they called it to everybody else, which was 'utter shite' or a regional variation of it. He glanced at me but didn't stop to ask and I noticed he seemed to concentrate on big strong-looking men, as though their needs were more important; maybe he was making sure they were being satisfactorily nourished before they took to the RAMC rugby field; maybe he knew they were the kind with coarse palates that would eat shite and like it, there is always somebody like that in any company.

Apart from distinct items like sausages or carrots, much of the stuff on our plate could have been almost anything and was so repulsive I couldn't bear to look at it and was very relieved to see nobody being forced. Everybody said the cooks just took the leftovers from the previous meal, mixed them up and served it as either stew or pudding, depending on how it came out.

After 'lunch' we were marched to various places to be scrutinised, such as the DO's [Dental Officer's] and MO's [Medical Officer's] and for various selection interviews. Never were we told where, when or why we were going. We were just marched there, waited, dealt with and marched back. It reminded me of school during the war.

Sometimes a 'cockup' - my first but by no means last acquaintance with this word - occurred and we would be marched somewhere only to find there were several squads already waiting. We would then be marched somewhere else, find the same thing and be marched back to the first place to find there were two more squads than there were before and then we'd just have to wait. At one period it rained so hard we were marched back 'at the double', which was a kind of trot, to get our groundsheets which were grey-green plastic things that also served as cloaks. But by the time we got back it had stopped raining and there were more squads than ever, some like us with groundsheets around their necks.

After that we were marched into a smallish darkened building which, judging by the screen at one end and projector at the other, was some kind of theatre; it was already packed with seated soldiers and the back and sides were lined with NCOs who could observe reactions and see the show at the same time. We were ordered to sit down and the lights went out.

There was no preamble, the film just started. It stopped a few times before it got properly going and we were treated to vast silhouettes of peaked-capped men with sticks that looked like cannons under immense arms, flickering across the screen.

It was made by a US pharmaceutical firm in 'luri-colour', if there was such a trademark, and the narrator and cast were all mid-west American. No faces were revealed except the bespectacled and crew-cutted American MO who looked like Aldo Ray, everybody else being shown only from the neck down. Without any semblance of a story line we were shown American soldiers being drilled so far into the distance that none of them could be recognised. This was then cut to a street of neon-lit bars somewhere in the Orient and we were suddenly plunged into what appeared to be Aladdin's cave, until the camera drew back and the first gasps of recognition went up. We were looking into an enormously magnified very black, badly-shaved vagina complete with what must have been hand-tinted bright red innards oozing yellow and green pus. The organ was so huge and the camera so close that the lens would have had to have been disinfected immediately afterwards. Still reeling, an enormous Caucasian penis with ulcers and sores was then thrust at us, followed by thick undergrowth which turned out to be a pubis infested with mites.

I was surprised by the number - there were at least half a dozen - who had to leave the theatre to throw up, to the sniggers of the NCOs, and I wondered if it would go into their records, perhaps their *AB64 Part 1*.

The film ended with a strong verbal message delivered full frontal by the doctor-major in his white coat, not about morality and certainly not about abstinence, but about the health of the regiment. We were told how to recognise lesions and the importance of reporting to the medical orderly room after every dubious encounter but condoms weren't mentioned, no doubt out of respect for Catholic soldiers. As we stood up and began to vacate the theatre in compliance with our corporals' instructions, we weren't supposed to talk of course but a lot were complaining about being shown something like this just before tea-time. For myself, I must say I found the whole thing stimulating and wouldn't have complained if every day ended in this way, preferably in cinerama.

Until yesterday I thought the word 'bullshit' was simply a rude noun that meant 'an exaggerated claim'. Now I found 'bull', or a conjugation of it, was a very descriptive word. 'To bull' or 'not to bull' were transitive verbs, 'bulling' and 'bulled' were present and past participles. Apparently it was impossible to comprehend or survive Army life without it, although its practice was illegal and the corporal would never refer to it because it involved the abuse of Army property, so we would have to find out how to do it from somebody else.

Of the two pairs of black boots we had been issued with, one pair was coarser than the other but both were quite ordinary except that they were covered in pimples. Whether the pimples had been added by some process or whether they were a leather hallmark for inelegance, nobody seemed to know; all we knew was that the toe and heel caps had to be transformed into glossy black carapaces with a surface that was both transparent and brittle and only thousandths of an inch thick.

To achieve this we had to buy a candle from the NAAFI [Navy, Army and Airforce Institute] canteen, stick it in the inside lid of the Cherry Blossom boot-polish tin, heat the back of our KFS spoon with it and use the spoon to iron out the pimples on the toe and heel caps. Then we had to put a finger in the duster, dip it in the polish, spit on the depimpled area of the boot and rub it in tiny circles for hours. First it took on a frosted look, then a patent leather look and finally that of glass. Nobody could claim the transformation of leather, polish and spittle was a miracle because although the Lord sometimes performs in strange ways, not in a barrack-room he doesn't. This was alchemy, pure and simple but it wasn't achieved in a night, it only happened after many nights because there were other things to be bulled apart from boots.

The battledress blouse [jerkin] had to be ironed in such a way that the pleats at the back were like blades - something that maybe the Teds could understand but which was lost on the rest of us. The trousers had to have a ring of lead made to go inside and around the bottom of each leg to make the trouser hang over the gaiter like an inverted stove pipe. The beret had to be converted from a schoolgirl's hat into the kind of thing the 'paras' wore; this was done by soaking it in water, wringing it out, pulling the right side down to the ear, tying it with string or a pair of braces and keeping it on for as long as possible, such as while bulling other items, and then very carefully taking it off and putting it on the radiator to dry overnight.

The cap badge, which was an unchased brass moulding, had to be nail-filed to its proper contours and then polished with Brasso to look like gold. There was a shortcut but it was tricky: you heated it with a candle to ever so slightly melt the surface first, but a second too long and the badge instantly melted into a blob in the Cherry Blossom tin and you would have to buy a new one from the store.

Belt, gaiters, haversack and webbing had to be blancoed and then brushed so they had the merest hint of a shine. Buckles were pitted and misshapen and had to be straightened before being rendered, as all brass, like gold.

The best item of Army issue, which in the unforeseeable flower-power period ten years hence would be adorned with both swastika and crucifix and associated with anarchy, was the greatcoat. It was a wonderfully warm and protective garment that hid many of nature's handicaps and gave the illusion of making the wearer invincible to bayonet, shrapnel or bullet. But for some reason it was issued with plastic buttons that had to be cut off and replaced with bullable brass ones which had to be purchased and sewn into place before being burnished.

The worst item, which was only properly used by lads who must have come from homes where underpants were a luxury, was the 'drawers, cellular, green'. These incongruous articles which looked as though they had been designed to allow the end products of dysentery to cascade unimpeded during Far East campaigns, were used by the rest of us as dusters for the primary bulling of cap badge, belt buckle and coat button; they were nowhere near delicate enough for boots.

While we bulled, we joked, swapped tales and rumours we'd heard, laughed at melted badges and boots that wouldn't yield to spit or polish, and ogled those that had achieved nirvana. Most of all we agreed that regular soldiers [career soldiers], especially National Servicemen who had signed on for an extra nine months to get higher pay, more holidays, better prospects and a dress uniform, must be thicker than pigshit.

8

The second morning began exactly like the first: a violent awakening at an unconscionable hour, followed by grunting, groaning and farting, ablutions, breakfast and bulling the barrack-room.

The parade ground seemed to be primarily a place of harassment, its purpose being to subvert human personality; individuality, which I had been brought up to cherish, was clearly despised, and shouting, bullying, humiliation and robotic movements used to annihilate it.

I had never in my life seen any group of people abused with sustained personal and collective sarcasm, let alone a large body of chauvinistic young men, many of them physically powerful and some of them used to brawling. To see grown men stand still and allow other men of comparable age and peerage, in many cases of considerable physical and mental inferiority, to scream into their faces from a distance of two or three inches so that globules of spittle spattered their eyes and cheeks and lips, and not utter one word or make any retaliatory movement whatsoever, was mesmerising. I couldn't believe it would have happened had they still been wearing their own clothes. Perhaps the novelty of the situation and the unabashed vaudeville had something to do with how all of this was being perceived. One thing was for certain and that was that the longer retaliation was delayed, the more difficult it would be.

The square was a stage for NCOs to audition on. Apart from lance-corporals like our own, there were full corporals, sergeants and sergeant-majors and they all wanted to have a go. Lance-corporals were first and would canter up shrieking to ridicule somebody's appearance and intelligence, demand a verbal response and then deride the way he spoke and the place he came from. When they had spent their puerile wrath they would withdraw and the full corporals would prance up to cap their performance. Then would come the sergeant-major to add his briefer and marginally less brash but more lethal sardonicism to the damage wreaked by his inferiors. The picadors and banderilleros had had their turn with lance and dart, running up, striking and then running off, and now came the matador, needing to make only a few passes before giving the coup de grace that would bring the quarry to its knees.

And then it would begin all over again with somebody else, seemingly randomly, while the rest of us stood trying not to draw the slightest attention to ourselves.

A sergeant strode up to the chiropodist in our squad.

'And what's your name, laddie!' he snarled, thrusting his Norman-Conqueror-like peaked cap into his face.

'Jonathan Purvis, Sergeant.'

'Jonathan..? Oooh!' the sergeant smirked, turning to the two lance-corporals flanking him. 'We have a Jonathan in the Company, do we..? And, for good measure, we have a Purv-vis..? Well I don't know about the rest of C Company but I'm not sure I'm altogether happy about that.'

'From now on, article!' he yelled, 'your first name is "Private"..! Got it..!'

'Yes, Sergeant.'

'San't!'

'Yes, San't.'

'And you are pathetic..! Got that!'

'Yes, Sergeant...I mean, San't.'

'You are pathetic and you are detestable..! Got that?'

'Yes, San't.'

'What are you?'

'Pathetic and detestable, San't.'

There was some sniggering from among the ranks. One of the lance-corporals scurried along the lines. 'Are there some cretins amongst you who think that being pathetic and detestable is funny?'

The sergeant returned to the chiropodist and swiped his beret off with his stick.

'Wipe that grin off your face, Private Pervert! It seems I underestimated you. You are not only pathetic and detestable...you are stupid into the bargain! You are pathetic and detestable and stupid! And you are like a badly-filled bag of guano!!'

'Now, what are you!'

The chiropodist repeated every word like a lamb.

Although the amount of abuse was incessant and humiliating, it always stopped short of sacrilege. Out here on the parade ground there were no obscenities or profanities; synonyms and euphemisms like 'fornicating', 'haemorrhaging' and 'paternally problematical' were used instead. And there was no direct physical contact. A baton would flick a pocket flap or tie, or a boot grind a painstakingly wrought glass toecap, but never a hand or finger touched the skin of any victim. Just as in the barrack-room when one of them wok you by whacking your bed with a stick and shouting every obscenity imaginable into your ear, they never committed a 'violation', not one recognised in Queen's Regulations, that is.

Maybe it was because of things like this that even though most of my comrades were intelligent men, no serious topics were discussed and they joined in inanities like,

> *Mr Lavatory Seat*
> *Did it all on the floor,*
> *Wiped it up with my toothbrush*
> *Don't clean my teeth much anymore*

and when a particularly obnoxious NCO came into the canteen they would softly sing,

> *Happy little fellow*
> *Everybody knows,*
> *Face just like an arsehole*
> *But he thinks it's like a rose.*

On the notice-board at the top of the barrack-room was a plan of what had to go where in the lockers and how they and the beds had to be presented. Every item of clothing and equipment had to be stored in a certain place on a certain shelf and had to conform to precise measurements. So if socks were to be stored at say, 4" x 3" x 2" and an empty haversack had to measure 18" x 8" x 10", the only way this could be achieved was by buying or begging cardboard and cutting it to these dimensions less the thickness of whatever they were to be the template for. But putting the cardboard inside the exactly folded socks would not render a perfect rectangle, so the cardboard had to be sewn into the socks. After morning inspection whatever was to be used that day would have the thread unpicked and the cardboard carefully withdrawn and put away. It would then be put on, used, dirtied, washed and dried that night and the cardboard sewed back in place the following morning.

Every morning we had to present our lockers, kit, beds, barrack-room and the area outside, for inspection at 0800 hours.

Blankets and sheets had to be folded into squares and all kit laid out on the bed in an exactly specified manner. All sixteen beds down each side of the barrack-room, and everything on them, had to be aligned with the same items on every other bed. So when we had everything cleaned and laid out, one person would kneel at the top bed, close one eye and get each person by their bed to move an item a fraction this way or that so the lines were all true.

Apart from dusting, washing windows and polishing all the woodwork and metal fittings of the barrack-room, the grass outside had to be cut with scissors - I think this is where Pollock of Weybridge must have got the idea - and the lino on the floor had to look as though it had been shellacked. First, large quantities of polish were rubbed in, then it was buffed by hand with rags, then with a broom covered in rags, and finally a man wrapped in a blanket was hauled up and down the length of the floor half a dozen times. Between then and Inspection, nobody was allowed to step on the lino; if you absolutely needed to cross it, you had to skate over it with one of your own blankets tied around each foot.

In addition, the sinks, washbasins, baths and lavatories in the ablutions and latrines had to be vimmed, woodwork and floors scrubbed, taps and metal fittings polished and buckets of fire-sand cleaned and filtered.

Finally all brooms had to have their handles and the wood between the bristles scraped with a razor blade to remove every fingerprint so that every day they looked brand new, albeit ever so slightly smaller.

At eight o'clock we would have been standing by our beds for at least five minutes, all chores completed, breakfasted, washed, shaved, fully dressed, beds laid out, locker doors open.

'Bagoom! Bagoo-oom Tow!'

Everybody would come to attention and wait, standing to the left of his bed, while the Corporal came down, examined every man, every item, poked things with his stick, shouted abuse at the man, and then on to the next, rarely allowing anybody to escape some form of criticism, and always totally demolishing somebody. Safe from the relative civility required in a public place like the parade square, our leader, teacher and exemplar would criticise, humiliate, intimidate and insult his way down one side of the barrack-room and back up the other, threatening terrible but undefined punishments.

Inspection over, he would give his second order of the day which would be for us to dress in the way he stipulated and bring whatever equipment he specified. We were then dismissed - 'Diiiss-miss!' - and would scramble to our beds and lockers, some of which would have been overturned scattering all over the floor the kit we had spent half the night cleaning and polishing. And as we picked things up, wiped them and put them away, pride as flat as the beret with a crushed badge and boot imprint in the middle of it, we would sometimes feel we were no more than he said we were, namely 'pimples in the arsehole of humanity'.

We had been profoundly insulted in front of our comrades and unable to salvage anything by laughing, by pretending it was all a big joke. Only they had laughed. Drawing on every ounce of character, it was sometimes all you could do to control the anger and fight back the tears.

From now on it was the same routine every day: bull, drill, inspections, lectures, PT, canteen; shoulders back, chest out, stomach in even for those standing in the queue outside the MO's office with appendicitis or a slipped disc.

Breakfast was the most edible of Army fare and I learned to tank up on cornflakes and milk, fried egg and bacon, and wash it down with a bromide suspension called 'tea'. Dinner was always revolting. Sometimes I would go to the camp shop and buy a pork pie or a chocolate biscuit but it meant skimping on Brasso or boot polish, both of which were greater necessities.

My boots, which were like glass on the outside but a full size too small on the inside, had chafed all the skin from my heels and most of my toes and at the end of every day my socks were caked with blood. I was very reluctant to exchange them for a new pair at this stage but was getting so much stick for marching gingerly that I went to the QM, not realising that changing a pair of boots in the British Army was a difficult operation.

'Who says they're the wrong size?' demanded the clerk.

The staff-sergeant came out.

'What's wrong with these boots?' he said, turning them over. 'They look perfectly all right to me.'

'They're too small, Staff.'

'Who says?'

'Me, Staff.'

'How do you make that out?'

'They hurt my feet, Staff.'

'You'll have to get a chitty from the MO if you want them changed.'

'How, Staff?'

'Go on sick parade.'

Rather than go through the ridiculous and humiliating process of reporting sick, I cut a piece out of each inner heel and wore a big elastoplast on each ankle, which I washed each day. It was astonishing how everybody in the Medical Corps believed anybody reporting sick was a skiver; that was another new word for me and it was a word that needed no explanation; 'skivers' were referred to with contempt mingled with envy - a job that was a 'good skive' was one nobody in their right mind would pass up.

By the time I'd been in the Army three weeks I felt as though I'd been in a lifetime and knew all there was to know, barrack-room lawyers were fully qualified in three days. The novelty of being in the Army had long since evaporated and I would have given anything to be out of it. It was an incredibly stupid place, it was crude, it was heartless and the only highlight was when the mail was handed out at 1100hrs - that's if your name was called out.

One night I came in from the canteen to find my mattress cover had been taken and in its place was another with a cigarette-burn hole; it was in the worst place, in the thick black line that bordered the coverlet. I would have to buy a new one if it was discovered, so I rubbed the brown cigarette burn off with a florin, bought a shade of Blanco that matched the green of the coverlet and every morning blancoed the white mattress under the hole to match the coverlet; then with a match I drew a line along it with boot polish. I would do the same thing every day until the time came to hand in my bedding at which time I would make sure it was carefully folded.

The boots however weren't a mere cosmetic problem and my feet were getting worse. I was determined not to buy another pair because as far as I was concerned it was the Army's fault, not mine and because I sent more than a third of my pay home I'd have nothing left for weeks. So I persevered.

One Saturday afternoon after I'd been in the Army a month and the squad was allowed out of camp, Harvey, Taff and I went to Aldershot which was reputed to have the Ritz of NAAFIs: a canteen with different menus, a dancehall with a band, a good shop and a lounge with a licence.

Part of the way we hitched but most of the way we walked and by the time I had walked ten miles my boots were soaked with blood and I had to walk the rest of the way in stockinged feet. My companions offered to help carry me back to camp but I was damned if I was going to let their day out and mine be spoiled for the sake of a pair of lousy boots. When we got to Aldershot I bought some cheap elastic bandage from the NAAFI, soaked it in cold water and wrapped both ankles, had a plate of gorgeous fish and chips in the restaurant and then sat in one of the armchairs in the lounge with my boots slackened off for the rest of the day, apart from a couple of dances in stockinged feet; it was like being in heaven.

We had come more than halfway and were counting the days to 'passing out parade' when our basic training would be finished and we'd be gone from Crookham Barracks hopefully for ever, and I was cleaning my kit on my bed one night, when Harvey called out that my name was up on Company Orders. We were all supposed to read the notice-board every time we came into the barrack-room but the same ones always read them and could be counted on to shout out if there was anything of interest.

There was only one item and that was that 23194576 Pte Robinson had to report in full kit - everything on your back except your bed and locker - at the Orderly Office at 0800hrs the following morning. That meant only one thing, I was being posted somewhere. And if I was being transferred to another regiment, I'd have to start all over again... What about my comrades? Was nobody else going with me? I knew the strengths and weaknesses of everybody in the squad and they knew mine, we even knew each other's girlfriend's names.

I stared at it until my eyes began to sting and still I stood, aware that all was quiet behind me. I didn't want to turn and face them, they all knew what it meant. After tonight we'd probably never see each other again.

'Thank God it's not me,' somebody groaned.

Maybe I was being sent as a late addition on the Officers' Training Course, Harvey suggested; somebody had noticed the way I stepped daintily because of my boots, and not heavily like a trooper, and they were accepting Geordie accents at Sandhurst now.

We all laughed.

'Maybe you're goin' into the vetinary corps,' Lenny barked in his gruff Yorkshire voice. 'That's where you belong. And you'll get to ride horses and train dogs, what you like doing.'

'Tough shit.' Taff patted my shoulder and then walked away, he was the only one in the squad who wouldn't have cared one way or the other as long as the two years were served.

Worst of all maybe I was being discharged. Suddenly Crookham Barracks and C7 weren't so bad. I had coped with everything that had happened to me up to now with good humour but this seemed so bloody-minded. I didn't want to join another regiment. I didn't want to be a prick at Sandhurst. And most of all I didn't want to be discharged, to be kicked out of the British Army would be the worst thing that could happen to anybody.

I walked back to my bed with my head averted and got on with cleaning my kit. Raymond, the lad from Middlesborough who was always carrying on with me, put his arm around my waist in a friendly daft way.

'Come on. Gis a kiss afore ye go.'

'Piss off, Raymond.'

He and I often wrestled in fun but now we did it savagely and I buried all of my emotion in it as I flung him against the radiator and we fell heavily to the floor. He was hurt and taken aback and when I let him up he wasn't very pleased.

'Fuck you, Geordie,' he said, and I was sorry immediately.

It was with a very heavy heart that at 0745hrs the following morning I shook hands with everybody in the barrack-room and left them to return to flaying broom handles and dragging each other over the floor in blankets.

With two others I didn't know from other squads I was being sent to the Army Physical Training Centre at Salisbury in Wiltshire. At 9st. 1lb I was apparently two and a half pounds lighter than the Army allowed a person of my height to be and so my basic training was being interrupted so that I could undergo the rigours of a six weeks' PT instructor's course. Had the British Army never heard the word 'wiry'...or 'lean'...or 'slim', even?

RAMC, Salisbury

9

Life at Salisbury was entirely different to Crookham. There were no NCOs below the rank of staff-sergeant, there was very little drill, hardly any bull and the barest minimum of parades and inspections. Physical prowess was all that mattered here.

Every morning we ran at least five miles, not round and around a concrete square dressed like pack-mules but along country lanes and across moorland looking like a boxing team; the rest of the day was spent in the gym doing weight-lifting, gymnastics and judo. I revelled in it, I loved the feeling of freedom outside the camp, loved the trials of strength and unarmed combat. Never in my life had I reached such a peak of health, never known how it was to feel invincible and capable of doing anything, beating anybody. It was a complete change of body and mind, like being in love without any intermissions of doubt or tribulation; an hour after the most exhausting feat I would feel incandescent and so bursting with energy that I wanted to leap into the air.

We blacked our brown plimsolls with boot polish, something that would have amounted to a crime at Crookham, and wore the black-and-red-ringed jerseys that distinguished the PT instructors from the rest of the Army as surely as red berets did the 'paras'. I even managed to get the worst pair of my boots changed at the QM; when one of the staff-sergeants had noticed me limping and I told him the problem, he had just signed a chitty and that was that.

I liked the instructors, they were like the staff of a physical training college and we the students and there was no 'them and us'. They paid mere lip service to regimentation although their discipline on matters physical was strict. They admired strength, they gave credit for pluck and effort, they were always encouraging and they were good-humoured.

Worldly without arrogance or affectation, they were devoid of the personality disorders that had afflicted the lot at Crookham.

The youngest instructor, Staff-sergeant Whipple, who was a Welsh Methodist minister and less of a chauvinist than the others, took a liking to me and it showed; I was sure there was nothing 'contrary to Army Regulations' about it but it embarrassed me. One Saturday afternoon he came into a barber's in Salisbury where I was having my crew-cut shortened to a stubble, and tried to pay the barber on my behalf. I refused to accept it and he was very hurt.

He was a body-builder and good looking and there was a photograph of his back on the cover of the current issue of *Health & Strength*, of which he was very proud. Everybody but the middle-aged ex-boxers who were his colleagues, thought he was like a Greek god, but it just didn't feel right having a staff-sergeant talking to you like an ordinary human being and a friendly one at that.

One day I won a judo competition and the prize was a wrapped copy of Health & Strength. Staff-sergeant Whipple was delighted to present it to me, which he did in front of everybody in the changing room, and I knew by the look on their faces what they were thinking so I said, 'This isn't the one with your back on the front, is it?'

'Yes,' he said, blushing.

'Give it to somebody else, then.'

'Why?'

'Because it's full of show-offs with a lot of muscle and no brain.'

'Is that what you think?'

He stood there with the magazine in his hand and I turned away.

When he went out my companions said 'You're in the shit now, Geordie. You've fuckin' had it, mate.'

Later on Whipple came to me on my own and asked if I'd changed my mind and I said no.

'You've got a chip on your shoulder about something... What is it?'

'You're a preacher, aren't you?'

'I'm a Methodist and that's part of my religious duties, if that's what you mean.'

'Yet you signed on to be a full-time soldier?'

'What's wrong with that?'

'It's hypocritical.'

'How do you mean?'

'The two don't go together. War and God. We can't have him on our side while the Germans or whoever else has him on theirs, can we?'

'It's not as simple as that... Anyway, God isn't on their side and never has been... You're a Catholic, aren't you? So you believe nobody else has access to God or heaven..? Well, if that's what you want to believe, carry on believing it. But I happen to believe there are other ways...

I come from a poor family and I've always been interested in physical training. The Army could give me that. That's why I joined up... And my religion's my business. If you want to come along to a prayer meeting, you'll be as welcome as anybody else. Otherwise, watch it, soldier!'

And that was the last time we spoke to each other.

Because of the nature of the place and there were men from every corps and regiment in the British Army, there was far more macho behaviour here than among what Lenny called 'The Poofters of Crookham', certainly among the men themselves. There was little incentive to form friendships because we knew we were only here for a short time but there was clannishness among members of the same regiment and there was considerable barrack-room bullying, solitary figures in particular were regarded as outsiders and punished for it.

In the barrack-room I was in there were five men including me. In the next there were thirty and some of them were from heavy armour regiments and very aggressive towards anybody from a poofter regiment.

A gang of about twenty led by a guy called Brennan who never did anything himself but just told them who to get and what to do to them, would turn somebody's bed over in the middle of the night, drag him away and dump him in a bath of cold water. Worst and most humiliating of all, was when they rived somebody's trousers off and scrubbed his genitals with boot polish while clamping his mouth and nearly stopping him from breathing, let alone yelling; it was called 'ball-blacking' and I often wondered if it had anything to do with the blackballing that was supposed to go on in 'gentlemen's' clubs.

They always did it to ones who had never done them any harm and I was sure it wasn't the pain they inflicted that fulfilled them so much as the humiliation. It seemed to me that anybody who could do that could just as easily rape or lynch and maybe kill somebody. I didn't like any of them but it wasn't the ones who initially went in and grappled to overcome the victim that I despised most: it was the ones who from a safe distance 'put the boot in' and looked as though they were going to come with excitement. I felt anybody who had had that done to him would never again be able to raise his head and look anybody else in the eye; not then, not ever, and I made up my mind that I would fight to the death if anybody ever tried to do it to me.

One night they came clashing into our barrack-room drunk and yelling and flinging every bed over. Although I hung onto mine, they picked it up with me on it and turned it over, burying me beneath. As I scrambled out I heard Brennan calling 'Eeny, meeny, miny mo, catch a nigger by the toe... If he squeals, let him go, eeny meeny miny mo'.

He pointed at a dark-skinned man, the tallest man in the camp, whose bed was right opposite mine. Immediately four or five of his gang sprang at the fellow and overpowered him and the rest then clustered around to help pull his pants off. Taking his Cherry Blossom black boot polish and brush from his locker, they brushed the polish all over his private parts, front and back, even though every time a hand slipped off his mouth he screamed in agony; polish and blood were spattered all over him, his pyjamas and his sheets.

'We'll be in to see you shortly,' I called to Brennan as he swaggered out with his men.

He turned around. 'Take one step inside my barrack-room, any of you, and you'll wish you'd never been born.'

When they had gone, I asked who was coming next door with me.

'What? You must be mad! There's thirty of them in there!'

'I'm not getting my bollocks blacked!'

'You can count me out!'

'And me!'

'We could at least get some of their beds over, if we rushed in,' I said. 'Two of us could take the top two on the left and two take the ones on the right.'

'Brenny'd bloody kill you!'

I could never stand the way some people could hate somebody yet were so afraid of them they would always refer to them by their buddy-buddy name, as if they were an intimate, in the hope the little tribute might get back and do them some good.

I argued with them for nearly quarter of an hour but couldn't persuade them, so I went on my own. As I went out the door, one of them shouted 'You'd better not get us into trouble! We don't want any bother on account of you!'

I opened the door of Brennan's barrack-room and walked straight to his bed about three-quarters of the way down, he was sitting on it reading *Titbits*.

I asked him if his bed was ready.

'Ready for what, you Geordie twat?'

'You know...ready for bed?'

'What's it to you..? Get to fuck out of here!'

Before he had a chance to move, I grabbed his bed and heaved it over with him still on it. Nobody said a word, they just looked on in astonishment and a couple of them laughed.

I was walking back up the aisle when Brennan came flying onto my back. We fell to the floor and fought hard and rough for nearly ten minutes. In the finish I left him there and walked out and nobody made any attempt to stop me. The next day he came up to me in the gym and although he didn't offer to shake my hand or say he was sorry or anything, he told me if anybody in the camp ever gave me any bother I only had to say the word. I told him I was deeply touched.

I didn't know whether it was due to a shortage of bromide, whether it was because of the extra physical fitness or whether there was something in the Wiltshire air, but the promiscuity here was something neither school nor anything else had prepared me for. I had never used a four-letter word in my life, not even in my sleep. In our house, 'backside' was considered a swearword and only my father was allowed to say 'bloody' if the occasion warranted it. I was still the male equivalent of a virgin, a Catholic who had been brought up to 'save' himself for marriage. I had never even broken wind in the presence of another human being, including any of my brothers; nor in front of a cat or a dog, not even a canary.

So I was totally unprepared for the 'better-out-than-in brigade' of farters, for beat-the-clock toss-off competitions between contestants sitting opposite each other on beds, practically riving their penises off in a frenzy, egged on by a dozen or more of their mates. And I was totally unprepared for NAAFI girls climbing out of one bed and straight into the next, right in front of my eyes while I was trying to play patience or writing a letter that began 'Dear Mam and Dad...'

10

My first leave was for five days, it began at 1200hrs on the day before Christmas Eve and I was given a travel warrant to the nearest mainline station to my home, which was the Central Station at Newcastle. I was dying to get back and see all their faces when they saw me in uniform.

I hadn't finished basic training yet of course, far from it, but I'd been in the Army long enough to know how to look like a soldier and to most people my uniform meant I was doing my bit for the country. I shaved every day now as well, not because I needed to but because everybody said the way to get whiskers was to shave first thing every morning and last thing at night, the way you got a lawn to grow. Although I wouldn't be old enough to vote for another three years, I was old enough to be hanged if I killed anybody and that made me feel quite grown up as well.

I had to change trains three times and stand all the way from King's Cross to York but quite a few people got off there and I managed to get a seat. York was so obviously the beginning of the North, after places like Peterborough and Grantham that seemed part of a world I had never belonged to, and everything seemed to open up and become more friendly. The station was thronged with soldiers and airmen, many being met by girlfriends and families and it was great to feel part of it, I imagined it would have been the very same during the war.

The final haul from Darlington to Newcastle was the longest and we had a delay for nearly an hour in the snow, but eventually we came through Gateshead and on to the High Level Bridge and it was like opening the doors to Sesame.

Crossing over the Tyne in the dark and seeing the lights of the city ahead and of ships anchored in the river and the quayside below, meant I was coming home in a way nothing else had. Nothing could stop me now, no nasty lance-corporal who came from a place I'd never heard of and didn't want to know about, no ugly MP with the peak of his red cap pulled down so far over his eyes all he could see was his own bulled boots.

This was my territory, this was where my army was. This was Newcastle and Tyneside where I was born and grew up in. This was my city and that Keep down there was where we put the bad buggers. At the mouth of the river was South Shields, my birthplace; Marsden where we went for our holidays and played in the sand and caught crabs on the rocks; North Shields across the river from it by ferry; Cullercoats and Tynemouth where the winkles were; White City and Whitley Bay which were until a few months ago hunting grounds for Jim, Tod and me; Jesmond Dene and the Vale where Johnny and I used to go for conkers when we were kids; Leazes Park where the sticklebacks were easy to catch because they all had white-spot; St James's where United played and my father used to go to watch the wrestling on a Saturday night before it became a sham; the Exhibition Park where the wonderful Hoppins (travelling fair) came every June; Paddy Freeman's where we played football; Heaton Park where we went birdnesting, the Spinney where we went sledging in winter; Gosforth Park and Plessey Woods where we went for blackberries; Morpeth where we went camping with the school; and so many, many other wonderful places. They would all be there in the dark, waiting as they always waited, waiting for their season when they would be visited and appreciated by so many Tynesiders, young and old, rough and genteel, robust and frail.

Now I was a man and proud soldier coming back to reassure his kith and kin that he was ready to defend them like his father and uncles before him. And as I got up, put on my belt and fastened my buckles as straight and smart as for any drill parade, I made sure my trousers were hanging equally all around the top of my boots and stamped my feet to give them that bit extra hang. After checking my buttons were all fastened and my beret pulled down rakishly over my right ear, badge facing dead centre, I hauled on my greatcoat and gloves like a soldier posted to the Ukraine and turned around drawing myself up to my full height, aware of the huge khaki fighting machine that was me.

A little old man with several fingers missing and an elastoplast holding the middle of his glasses together was sitting in the corner of the compartment and I realised he must have been watching me. He smiled and raised his hand in a gesture of a salute.

'Merry Christmas!' I said to him.

'Merry Christmas, son,' he said. 'May you have many of them.'

Central Station was decked out with the huge 'live' illuminated Christmas tree it was sent every year as a gift from the Norwegian people, underneath it the marvellous model railway any kid would have given his right arm for. But this time I wasn't stopping to look at it. There were soldiers, airmen and sailors everywhere, smoking cigarettes and shouting advice about the dangers of various excesses to mates getting trains to Sunderland or Shields; others, kitbags plonked down, were embracing girl friends. There were shouts, shrieks of laughter, whistles and blasts of steam and somewhere in the background the Salvation Army was playing carols. Every now and then there was a strong whiff of brown ale as somebody came staggering by, leering into your face as much as to say 'Wha' d'ye think you're lookin' at..?' Then the lovely tones of a female Tyneside voice came over the loudspeaker to announce that the train from King's Cross was now standing at the platform. 'Why aye, pet! I know! Haven't I just come up on it?' I wanted to call back. 'I've been living down there and I've come home for Christmas. Look..! I'm in the Army!'

It was wonderful to be back... Wonderful...

I went out the main arcade past the taxi ranks and across the road to get the double-decker Midnight Circle. I had to wait nearly ten minutes for the conductor to get on and then another five for the driver and I could have strangled the two of them for messing about, but by half-past eleven I was trudging through the slush up Newton Road, along Horsley Road and then to the corner house of Plessey Terrace with the big triangular garden that would never grow anything but indestructible grass. Then, marching up the path to the front door, I knocked, only a couple of times but hard. My mother would still be baking, my father would have been back from the pub long since and have the cards and decorations up and the wireless on, and my brothers would be wrapping up their presents and squabbling over somebody using too much paper. There'd be one mad pelt for the door when they heard my military knock.

I waited...and I waited. I noticed there didn't seem to be any light on. At last the door opened and a middle-aged man I had never seen before was standing in the passage in the kind of pyjamas never worn by any member of our family, neither on my father's side or my mother's.

'Who's that?' he said.

And I realised. I'd come to the wrong house. The family had moved and were living a mile away in Simonside Terrace now. I felt such an idiot, I'd already moved into the anticipated embrace position.

I quickly made my apology, picked up my gear and practically ran all the way up Heaton road and down Simonside towards 'Chilly' Road. I didn't know the door because I'd never been there before but No 41 turned out to be the dark green one, second from the bottom.

I pressed the doorbell and almost instantaneously a light went on behind a frosted glass door. The door opened and my mother's lovely face was beaming through the clear glass of the front door. I grinned and it opened and I could feel the warmth of good coal burning, smell the mince-pies and hear the excited chatter of my younger brothers.

'It's Joe! It's our Joe!' my mother called back over her shoulder. She had a flour-stained pinny on. 'Eeeh! Come on in, son. Come on.'

My father was behind her, sleeves rolled up, scissors and coloured paper chain in his left hand, his right held out for mine.

'Hello, son! How are you? Come on in then and let's have a look at you.'

It was a great Christmas and different from any I'd ever known. When I went out sometimes I had my uniform on, sometimes not, no MP was going to accost me here. The rule I made was to let them all - friends, relatives, neighbours and local shopkeepers - see me in uniform at least once and I think I can honestly say everybody was impressed except my brothers.

'Urgh! Our Joe! Big man! Thinks he's great because he's in the Army... Where's your stripe? Have you not got any stripes yet?'

'Are you the one that polishes all the boots?'

'Why no! He's not good enough for that job. He's the one they send to the beach to fill the sandbags.'

'He couldn't lift a sandbag. He couldn't even lift one if it was empty!'

And of course not Tod who insisted Jim and I had to always be in civvies when we were with him because he wouldn't be seen dead in the company of a couple of 'thickies'. Jim was stationed in Northern Ireland with the Northumberland Fusiliers and had a little plume in his hat. 'You prick!' Tod said when he saw it and I had no doubt Jim never forgot it every time he put it on after that, whether back in Northern Ireland or anywhere.

On New Year's Eve, as at Christmas, traditions were strictly observed in our house. No matter if it was snowing, raining, or bombs were dropping, my father would put on his hat and coat and leave the house at ten to twelve with a bit of coal in one pocket and a bit of salt in the other, and wait outside in the cold and dark, quietly greeting the heads of other households who were standing likewise outside their own houses. Old and young, tall and short, fat, ginger or bald, they were all ready to play the role of Dark Stranger, sometimes expanded to 'Tall Dark Handsome Stranger', who would be the first to cross the threshold of their homes and bring good luck throughout the new year to all inside.

At dead on midnight, when the Westminster chimes could be heard on every radio as every front door opened and illuminated the path outside and cheering could be heard from every direction, my father would come in, take off his hat, wish my mother 'Happy New Year!' and she him and they would embrace. Then each and every one of us, every brother for a few hours setting aside his individual scorn, would do the same. After that, standing around a beautifully laid out table of ham sandwiches and salad sandwiches, coconut haystacks, mince pies and the New Year fruitcake iced and decorated, a small glass of home-made ginger wine in every hand, the speeches would begin. First my father with immaculately chosen words would wish all our friends, relatives and the world at large, a happy, healthy and prosperous new year. Then my mother would be invited to speak and she would say 'Same goes for me, as for your Dad'. Then all of us sons, from me the eldest, down, would have to say a few words which would be articulate and humane, even a little bit funny as long as we didn't 'go too far'.

After that we would all sing Auld Lang Syne and shed a few tears except Dad who would smile benignly. We would then fall upon the feast while listening to the BBC Hogmanay party with the likes of Andy Stewart, Kenneth McKellar and Moira Anderson.

When we had eaten our fill, the table would be cleared away and banjo, fiddle and mouth organ produced. Dad played the two stringed instruments, the rest of us were the wind section. A kazoo for the less gifted could be quickly assembled by doubling a piece of 'Izal', the hard glossy lavatory paper that 'went a long way', over a comb. From then until about 3am we drank either beer or Tizer, depending on age, and sang every song we knew and a good few we thought we did.

New Year's Day being the Feast of the Circumcision and we all being good circumcised Catholic males, except for Mam, went to Mass. It was one of the most bizarre reasons for going to Mass in the Tridentine calendar, quite embarrassing and never talked about; in our house we just called it New Year's Mass. On the way there and back everybody we met would say 'Happy New Year!' and we would smile and say the same back and it wouldn't matter if we didn't know them.

When we came home we would have dinner, this time with pork instead of chicken, and the meal would be every bit as splendid as Christmas Day's, with the rest of the crackers and virtually the same jollity. At some time or other one of the younger brothers would start up with a couple of carols in order to keep Christmas going and not let it deteriorate into something less bountiful, or too soon, and we would all laugh and join in singing 'God Rest Ye Merry Gentlemen!', leaving others of our creed to more sombrely celebrate the anniversary of a quite painful and rather pointless divine event.

The only time my father had ever missed first-footing the house was during the war when he was in Belgium and Mam had got young Alan Feltoe from next door to do the job. This year I was back in my barrack-room at Salisbury while my father would have been preparing to go outside with his coat buttoned, collar up, hat brim down and a little packet in each pocket. First-footing was more a primeval urge than a piffling tradition where I came from, so at five to midnight, sitting on my bunk in the bottom corner of the barrack-room, facing the opposite direction to my five fellow occupants, the wall, I took out the little medicine bottle containing ginger wine that my mother had carefully packed for me, removed the slice of Christmas cake from its greaseproof paper wrapping, and silently toasted them at home the way they would be doing at exactly the same moment to me and to all our relatives and friends.

One very cold night towards the end of January when I was waiting for orders that would send me back to Crookham Barracks I was so lonely I did a terrible thing: I telephoned home 'reverse charge'. I heard my father's curt acceptance of the call when asked by the operator and then I knew for certain that I shouldn't have done it, the chances of Mam making such a momentous decision having been minuscule.

'Hello, Dad. It's me...Joe.'
'Yes? What's the matter?'
'I just thought I'd ring up to see how are things.'
'What things?'

He would know I'd have received his letter giving all the news that morning, he wrote without fail every week and so did I.

'I'll be going back to Crookham soon.'

'Yes, we know. You said so in your letter. Let's know your new address as soon as you get it.'

'Don't worry, I will...as soon as I get it.'

I could almost hear a few pennies dropping every second.

'Is that all, then..? Is there anything else?'

'Er, no, not really. I er...'ll be seeing you, then.'

'Right. Take care of yourself, lad. Your mother says to tell you she sends her love.'

'Me to her as well...and the boys.'

'Cheerio, then.'

'Cheerio, Dad.'

As I came out of the freezing kiosk into the blizzard outside, I wished I hadn't done it. I knew he'd think it was weak. I was the one who had thought I was the 'big man', the one who wanted to join the Army. Well, this is what it was like and I should be 'making the best of it' by now.

RAMC, Crookham

11

Three days later I was back in Crookham to begin the most depressing and humiliating six weeks of my young life. I gathered from rumour and one thing and another that I was going to have to wait for the next intake of conscripts before continuing my basic training, my old squad was passing out the following week and the intake that had followed them were already halfway through their eight-weeks training. In the meantime I was being put in the relegation billet, a barrack-room of misfits awaiting their various fate: some to be dishonourably discharged, some to be discharged on medical or mental grounds, others to be transferred or posted for some less than satisfactory reason, and various odds and sods who were victims of tragically absurd errors who should never have been in any army.

I had never met anybody like these people, not so many altogether in the same place. They were disgruntled, some of them totally bewildered, and they were suspicious and resentful. Two or three were uncontrollably violent, beyond the 'therapy' of prison, and being rejected for that reason. Those awaiting discharge on medical grounds, and they were mainly congenitally deformed people, were shocking; it was beyond belief that they had passed a medical in civvy street, passed another one in the Army and been issued with uniform, boots, helmet and all the rest of it. Among the 'loonies' - as those being discharged on mental grounds were called - were some who were so depressed they could hardly move, some who were such a bag of nerves they couldn't keep still for a moment, schizophrenics and, supposedly, a few genuine skivers.

All of them were waiting for a little piece of paper with an orderly sergeant's stamp and the CO's [Commanding Officer's] signature on it that would be their passport to somewhere else, preferably civvy street, and some had been waiting many months.

There was no discipline in the barrack-room because nobody in the world outside cared and nobody inside seemed to know anything. The one who had assumed charge was a brute who had been busted [demoted] from corporal for attempting to kill somebody. He had been here for longer than anybody knew and the general opinion was that he was waiting for the Army to decide whether he was invaluable or ungovernable and then what to do with him. He was swarthy, powerful with a thick neck and a bullet head, and had hair growing on his nose. He was the first person I'd ever met that I thought was evil, I didn't know much about astrology but could easily have believed he was conceived when Mars was aligned with Hell or something like it.

He never did anything to me and hardly ever spoke to me but to some of the others he was a swine. The first time I saw him he was drilling four or five of what were surely the most pathetic physical and mental specimens ever to be conscripted into any army, creatures who would have needed a chaperone to see them safely back to their homes when their discharge eventually came through. He was shouting and yelling at them and they were shouldering brooms and marching up and down the barrack-room in bare feet but otherwise in full kit, saluting lockers and reporting to fire-buckets. I thought they were playing some kind of game and that it was meant to be funny. But the next time was in the middle of the night and they were nearly crying.

He had a garotte that he had got from Singapore when he had been stationed there and was always twisting it between his hands and making a snapping noise. He would wake certain ones up with the garotte around their neck - especially one poor wretch who suffered from terrible headaches and walked around all day holding his head and emitting a low whine - and they would nearly die of fright.

He would laugh and make out everything was just a big joke but after a while it became obvious that all of them in the barrack-room were terrified and most were completely subjugated by him. I appealed to him to leave them alone but he said they liked it. 'Don't you!' he roared at them and they nodded with sheepish grins. Sometimes he would come in drunk in the middle of the night, get them out of their beds and have them marching up and down in their pyjamas in the freezing cold. He seemed to have a mania for drilling. They had neither the savvy nor the courage to resist or complain; in any case, nobody would have listened to military lepers, not at Crookham; the whole environment encouraged bullying: in the barrack-room, on the parade ground, in the lecture hall, the canteen, everywhere.

Most of the NCOs on the depot came to this swine to have their uniforms pressed, not because he was outstanding with an iron but because the high rates he charged represented some kind of protection money. He could quite easily have gone berserk one night, hacked half a dozen people to pieces in their sleep with his illegal Malayan dagger and then merely been sentenced to a life-time of valiumised tranquillity in the nutters' hospital at Netley. And nobody would have wanted that, somebody like him you wanted only dead.

The same martinets who yelled and swore all day at thirty-two mostly reasonable men, were scared shitless by this one so on Friday nights they took him their BDs and King's shillings. 'How's it going, Gus? Got another pair for you, mate...if that's okay. Thanks, Gus, mate. I'll pay you now if that's okay? Thanks, mate. See you. Thanks a million.'

This fellow wasn't even in the medical corps, he belonged to REME, so God knows what he was doing here at all; mind, 'cock-ups' were the one thing the Army was consistently good at.

'Relegation' wasn't just a convenient sobriquet for a barrack-room, the place where we were all housed; it was the official title of a squad. We were 'Relegation Squad' and as such disdained by everybody in the camp. There could not have been a more ignominious address to have to give your family, girlfriends and pals back home. I hated the word and hated the epithet and hated that my father had to address his letters to me in this way.

Our duties were those of GDO [General Duties Orderly] and we did the lowliest jobs in the camp, cleaning the latrines was about the only useful one. We ran around after everybody including privates with little more service than we had. We were sent from one place to another carrying silly messages and illegible chitties, we painted coal white, cut grass by snapping the blades with our fingers, cleaned out stoves with our bare hands and shovelled coke with bits of cardboard. All day every day was spent scheming and jockeying for the best chores, ones like sorting out misprinted forms in the Orderly Office where they at least had a stove going, or outside in the sleet looking for 'nice-shaped' stones to go around the Commanding Officer's wife's garden.

We were the victims of stupid mistakes and nobody knew what to do with us, whether to despise us or feel sorry for us. We were convenient scapegoats however and were verbally abused for anything that went wrong anywhere near to where we were or had been within living memory. In Relegation Squad there was no honour, no decency, no ethics of any kind. Like anybody with an iota of sensitivity I had to fight the feelings of despair and desolation which were all around and constantly crowding in, especially in the long dark nights which began at half past six after coming from the canteen.

Sometimes I would bump into Harvey or Taff in the canteen, or somebody else from my old squad, but we had little to say to each other. They were now vastly superior beings, immaculately turned out and drilled to perfection. They hardly seemed to remember me as they swaggered about, heads high, chests out, stomachs in, totally engrossed in military business. They would avoid me if they could when they saw me sitting at the table in fatigues, black with coke dust and, as Harvey warned, with what looked suspiciously like a chip on my shoulder. It was as though their minds and bodies had been taken over by some kind of military Triffid. They thought they were in the real world and sometimes I thought I was. Yet I'd have given anything to have joined them, no matter how much catching up I had to do.

I felt I had to do something about what was going on in Relegation Squad, I couldn't accept that it was a legitimate part of the British Army, so I tried to get an interview at the Orderly Office to see the CO. But in the Army you couldn't get to see anybody unless everybody in between him and you knew what you wanted to see him about and were prepared to let it go any further than themselves. I was told I'd get myself in serious trouble if I got as far as the Orderly Sergeant, let alone anybody with 'pips', because each and every one would see it as a criticism of himself and of how he ordered the daily duties of the Company. A complaint from a 'bloody sprog' was like a squeak from a mouse, it only drew the wrong kind of attention.

It wasn't until now that I realised how many people there must be in the world who were quite beyond any appeal to justice or human decency because of where they had placed themselves and they must have been well aware of the tiers of zealous insulation that protected them from the need for any benevolent nod.

The friendliest response I got, and it was from an old private who must have been in the Army when my father was in, was 'Just do as you're told in this man's Army, son. And don't ask anybody anything. That's the way to survive. Say the wrong thing and you'll end up in Clink [Colchester Military Prison] and time in Clink doesn't count. You have it all to do when you get out, if you get out. You could come in for two years and spend the rest of your life here.'

Eventually the new intake came in and I was put in Squad C-2. Apart from being kitted out again - though I went through the rigmarole of being marched in and out of the QMS like everybody else - I did everything I had done before in my first four weeks. It was like re-living an old nightmare.

The corporal in charge of my new squad was called Devine and I knew from my first spell in Crookham that he was the most feared and hated NCO in the camp. He was tall, thin, slightly bucktoothed and sickly-looking; the two or three long hairs in each of his nostrils failed to conceal their pink mouse-ear transparency, the irises of his protruding eyes were black and he wore an angry little frown as though to stitch up the fear and weakness from leaking out all over his face. But he had a powerfully shrill voice and enough malice to subdue thirty-two men at a time.

On the first hearing, his wit, though in every instance sarcastic and demeaning, was funny. He could master longer quotations and deliver them to greater purpose than anybody I had ever met inside or outside the Army. But if anybody laughed it infuriated him, this being because his intention was to entertain himself, not us. He would stand with his silly contorted face no more than six inches away from your own, which was presumably the minimum distance laid down in 'Queen's Regs', and scream: 'Is your hymen still intact, laddie! Is that why your legs won't open..! Or is your anal sphincter jammed! In which case it maybe needs that broom up it..! Which is it..! I want an answer!' It was absurd and if you were to take it seriously, you couldn't have put up with it, so you tried to give him the benefit of the doubt, pretending it was part of the game of playing soldiers and there was nothing personal in it.

But Devine not only insulted you, he spattered globules of his filthy spittle all over you because of the shape of his mouth and teeth; he flicked out your tie with his little whiplike baton; he poked your beret so it slid slowly off your head; he dragged the coverlet off your bed so everything was flung on the floor; he pulled stuff out of your locker and kicked your letters and private things all over the floor. And when, after you had stood there and taken it all in front of thirty-one of your peers, some of them pals, some not, and he had finally gone, you had to get down on your hands and knees and pick up all your things while wiping his cold spittle off your face with the back of your hand. But this was the second time around for me and the shock of the primary experience had been replaced by one of stupefying indifference; at least that was the intention.

One night when we were sitting on our beds doing our bulling and moaning about the Army and Devine in particular, I suggested we refuse to take any more and get up a deputation or petition to protest to some authority outside the Army; after all, we weren't really soldiers, we were civilians doing the country a favour by giving our time to help the Army out.

'That's mutiny!' screamed Devine, suddenly stepping out from behind a locker. 'One man complains and it goes down on his record! Two men complain and they're up for mutiny! And don't let any smartarse try to kid you you can write to the papers or your MP..! It'll never get there! Any such letter sent by anybody in the armed forces is referred back to his commanding officer..! Do that on this camp and I give you my word your life won't be worth living!

'You belong to the Army now! You have got no rights! You're supposed to be soldiers but you're no more use than the lumps that drop out of a dog's anus!'

It was a sobering thought.

In the Army, like everywhere else, it was the weaker men who were victimised, the ones who tried so hard but could never get things right, never get their blankets square, never get enough gloss on their toecaps and never march in step, creatures nature hadn't created for this kind of activity; if they were in the Army a hundred years they still wouldn't look like soldiers; these were the ones the Army sought to break, not the tough ones.

As the weeks of bulling, drilling, inspections, parades, rifle-training, PT, and lectures carried out in the manner of a primary school class, went on, I saw this barrack-room of thirty-two men one by one buckle down. Those who at first had howled loudest, sworn resistance and threatened reprisals - though never in the presence of Devine or anybody like him - were among the first to give in. 'Crawlers' was another indispensable word I had never heard until I came into the Army, and it was amazing how many of them there were and what they would do to please Devine, including bulling his boots and kit - something they were not required to do because lance-corporals weren't entitled to batmen.

They would preach that the only way to survive was to submit, remonstrate with me for not having any 'esprit de corps' and complain they were suffering because of it. But I instinctively hated team spirit. To me it meant combining with others to effect something they could not achieve by themselves, something determined by less than unanimity to be an ideal and I imagined a lynch mob would be the best example of it. Here it meant the subjection of thirty-two individuals to the whim of one man whom they all hated, even though some would joke with him at the doorway of his little room at the top of the barrack-room and say flattering little things to ingratiate themselves; they would then come back and tell the rest of us, 'He isn't such a bad bloke when you get to know him. He has to be firm. It's his job.' And they would make sure it was said loud enough to be heard where it would hopefully count most.

We were all obsessive about bulling yet with the exception of the squad instructors, no kit was as highly bulled as any sprog's, not even the Regimental or Company Sergeant-major's, and certainly none of the officers'. Theirs was clean and polished but that was all.

Some of my companions' only pride seemed to reside in the shine on their brass buckles and the gloss on their boots and they bulled compulsively every spare minute they got. They were pharmacists, opticians and health inspectors with a shine fetish and they would put their kit away in their lockers afterwards and treat them like crown jewels; to knock against their heel or toecaps or touch their brasses with your ungloved hand - many never handled their kit without wearing their khaki gloves - incurred a wrath close to psychosis. On the drill square the same ones marched more stiffly, shouted out louder when dressing from the right and slammed down rifles and boots with even greater precision than the NCOs. They might have made good soldiers in this sense, which was the only criterion that seemed to matter to the Army, but I suspected they'd make poor comrades in a trench or POW [prisoner of war] camp.

In wartime this kind of bulling could never have existed, apart from anything else there wouldn't have been the time. It had to be a peace-time convention, the British Army's way of deploying the energy, time and talent of men who could have been doing something useful in the world. It made me wonder what it would be like being in the British Army in a war when drastic things happened quickly and effective communication was critical. Any communication I had seen always took the form of bullying.

In peacetime it should have been a model army, conditions were arguably perfect for it. Yet it was nothing like it. It couldn't arrange a visit to the dental clinic without making a hash of it. Its philosophy was blind to reason, its NCOs deaf to appeal and its officers inaccessible.

The men I was with had only been in the Army a matter of weeks but I had been in so long it seemed forever and I had long since decided I would do no more than I was required to do. This meant I would never be doing anything as a favour for Devine or anyone like him. In return he did everything he could to break my spirit.

The day we went for our TABT injection, which was an inoculation against Typhoid and Tetanus, we had to march to the medical centre in beret, greatcoat, pyjamas and boots. The reason for this was that if anybody reacted badly to the injection, a common event, the rest of us could pick him up and carry him back to the barrack-room, and if he needed to be put to bed nobody would have the bother of undressing him and putting his pyjamas on for him. The alternative would have been to have the medical officer go to each barrack-room and do the injections there, but that would have been too complicated for the Army, the RAMC, to have organised.

The injections were carried out using the same needle until it was so blunt it wouldn't have penetrated the skin without a hammer. Four out of our squad collapsed and the rest of us had to carry them back to the barrack-room and into their beds. They didn't have time to suffer the 'flu' effects of the injection, and it wasn't anaphylactic shock; it was fear. So much rumour had gone around, fortified by the order to prepare for imminent collapse, that as soon as the needle point touched their arm they had keeled over. The injections were given at 1600hrs on a Friday so we could recover in our own time over the weekend.

When we got back to the barrack-room I was one of the few with no reaction at all but we were all confined for the weekend. I was lying on my bed with my arms behind my head when Devine strolled in, slapping his thighs with his stick as he surveyed the casualties.

'Have you been done?'

'Yes, Corporal,' I said.

He stood there for some time, obviously weighing up how far he could go and then said 'See that beam above your head?'

I looked up.

'The last man in your bed tried to hang himself from that beam.'

I just looked at him.

'You know why?'

I shook my head.

'He couldn't take it any more. He knew a man had hanged himself from it six months previous and succeeded and he couldn't get it out of his head.'

'Must be an unlucky bed, is it?'

He stood there glaring at me. I hadn't got to my feet because we were now supposed to be on sick leave and like the rest I was still in my pyjamas and bare feet. I wasn't going to stand to attention, I wasn't even going to get off the bed.

'You'll be sorry,' he said. 'Mark my words.'

Whether he meant sorry for not hanging myself or sorry for not regarding him with awe every time he stuck his pasty face into the barrack-room, I didn't know.

Apart from learning to respond like an automaton rather than a normal eighteen-year-old male human being and learning to shoot the non-combatant's rifle, a Lee Enfield .303, medical training consisted of basic nursing, first aid and stretcher drill. Everybody, no matter what their civilian qualifications, had to pass the NO III [Nursing Orderly III] exam to qualify as a ward labourer, the bullock of a military hospital. The first aid was to the level of St John's Ambulance III, third class being the lowest recognisable grade of anything in the Army, less than that and you were nothing at all.

Of the three disciplines, if that isn't too grandiloquent a term, stretcher-drill was the most demanding.

I don't know where I'd got the idea that there was always a man at each of the four corners of a stretcher, because there were only three men to a stretcher here and that counted the one lying on it.

Devine determined who would be the bearers and the borne and to make it more challenging would put tall bearers with short ones. The drill was carried out among ruined buildings surrounded by hedges, streams and other obstacles, with barbed wire, loose stones and mud everywhere.

Invariably I was designated a 'casualty', one of the wounded who had to deploy themselves on roofs, in ditches and in other awkward places selected by Devine, and wait for the stretcher men to come. We weren't allowed to move, wave, call out or give any indication as to our position; we just had to lie there in a frozen February ditch or on a roof in an icy wind until we were discovered. Devine would be out of sight but moving around with binoculars to see if anybody cheated. To be lowered from a roof bound to a stretcher with leather straps, by two men who hadn't the strength or skill to control it, wasn't a laugh for very long. On one occasion my bearers slipped on the ice on a corrugated roof and the stretcher and I were let go. The stretcher went over the edge and stuck into the ground, leaving me perpendicular and upside down until they clambered down in a panic and came to get me.

But it wasn't a simple matter of locate and retrieve, nor was it as altruistic as I had always thought. Devine had a wooden Tommy gun, the kind of toy we had as kids during the war, and he would wind the ratchet to make a rata-tat-tat sound. Whenever the stretcher bearers heard it they had to preserve their own lives by immediately dropping the stretcher, no matter where it was or who was on it with whatever injury.

The whole thing was a game to Devine. He would wait until you were being carried across a stream or over a patch of nettles or pile of bricks and then pop up from behind a hedge or wall and screech 'Enemy! Every man down!' He would blow his whistle and furiously rata-tat-tat his gun, saliva frothing from the corners of his little mouth. The fellows carrying you would say 'Sorry, mate!' and drop you, and if it was into a really mucky place you'd have all your clothes to wash and dry that night. The only place to dry anything was over a few precious radiators and you would have to stand guard and fight for every inch or it would end up dirty on the floor if you were lucky, or vanish altogether if you weren't. Nobody had anything as luxurious as soapflakes, we just used the same bar of soap we washed ourselves and hair with.

Because both camps I had been in had been used during wartime, I had often come across graffiti on a lavatory wall or among the ruins we used for stretcher drill, but instead of expressing disaffection with the Army, they were mainly touching sentiments - farewell messages from individuals who usually identified themselves with their initials and the date - perhaps the Army had erased any that were critical of it. One weekend we were doing a field hospital drill on the plains and I was one of the casualties made up with blood and protruding bones to mimic multiple compound fractures - wishful thinking as far as Devine was concerned - and I had lain out in the snow for hours. The tent we were in that night had the words, 'GOD HELP THE POOR BUGGERS WHO SLEEP IN THIS TENT' carved into the canvas top and icy water dripped from them all night.

Opposite me in the barrack-room was a massive public health inspector called Ian Mablethorpe who every day received parcels of food from his mother and letters from a fiancée whose photograph he was careful never to let anybody see. At night after lights out he would wait about ten minutes, during which time he no doubt fervently whispered his prayers, and then his locker door would be heard slowly creaking open. There would be the squeaking of the springs of his 'cot' and the wheeze of his laboured breathing as he stretched and twisted himself, the crackle of brown paper and then a gobbling and whimpering sound, the kind the boar we had at the VIC used to make. Then we would have to listen to the low moans of surfeit followed by the creaking of the slowly closing locker door. Finally there would be the restless sounds of a human body with tender skin and a thick layer of subcutaneous fat lying amidst crumbs of apple tart, chocolate cake and buttered scones.

One night somebody shouted 'You greedy bastard, Mablethorpe!' and the lights were flung on. But the unedifying sight of the eighteen-stone health inspector with his crude basin-haircut and his startled bloated eyes wasn't worth repeating and for the rest of the eight weeks we just let him get on with it.

As the biggest man in the squad and the biggest crawler, whenever Mablethorpe heard Devine coming out of his room in the morning he would take it upon himself to shriek 'Bagoom! Bagoo-oom tow!'

I, however, a senior soldier with two months more service under my belt, would never jump to his command and even Devine could find nothing in Queen's Regulations to deal with this. I would wait until thirty-one boots had hit the wooden floor in unison, wait a second, and then stamp my own.

'Why don't you take responsibility for it, then?' he would whine, 'instead of being such a blooming bolshie! There are some of us just want to do as we are told and do things right and not make any trouble for ourselves.'

It completely stymied his oblation to Devine and several others complained it would spoil our chances of winning the Best Squad Award but most of them just laughed.

Eventually I forgot about my old squad; they were now long gone from Crookham, split up and posted to goodness knows where and I would probably never see any of them again. This squad was now my squad and this was where I now made my pals; there was the same mix of personalities, origins and occupations, the same small number of short-lived anarchists and the same number of decent ordinary human beings getting on with their training and trying not to think too deeply about anything - Army life has a way of deterring the intellect from soaring too high.

The programme was identical to the previous one: tedium, humiliation and banality, and incidental revelations about the petty selfishness and crudity of human existence. I reckoned eight weeks was probably the maximum period that normal young men could be subjected to the rigours of basic military training before something vital in them was destroyed, and no doubt it had been proved.

If this was the hub of the Royal Army Medical Corps and represented the ideology of the British Army, and every corps and regiment's depot was the same, then God help those who depended on it. I had seen nothing in it that showed any regard for morality, let alone humanity; no evidence of political or social conscience, no magnanimity or sensitivity of any kind. Whilst recording the history of every button and exploiting the latent qualities of a boot, its capacity for wasting human resources was profligate.

On Sundays unless you obtained a sick certificate from the MO you were marched to a church billet, Catholics to Mass and everybody else to the 'C of E'. This was as close as the Medical Corps at Crookham Barracks came to recognising there might be such a thing as a soul and that it might need some kind of nourishment.

RAMC, Chester

12

In April my association with Crookham Barracks at last came to an end and the day after the 'passing out' parade, at which Mablethorpe's parents and fiancée wearing a big hat were present but very few others, I was given a posting to the Pathology Laboratory, Western Command Hospital, Moston, Chester, a 48hr pass and a travel warrant.

I had survived twelve weeks basic training, seven weeks physical training and six weeks in a barrack-room with nutcases, comparative privation and considerable verbal abuse, more than a hundred and fifty terrible dinners, exposure to some very carnal appetites and to toy machine-gunning. Chester had to be like a holiday camp after that.

After my brief respite at home I reported to the Orderly Sergeant at Chester and was put in Monty Billets which were sheds divided in the middle, with four beds in one half and four in the other. There was no heating but they were considered to be the best billets in the camp and the one I was in had x-ray technicians and theatre technicians, some of them corporals.

Meals were better than at Crookham, discipline more relaxed and apart from weekly parades and morning inspections, drill was minimal. I would be working as a lab technician from now on and studying medical laboratory technology to Lab III level. When off duty we could go into Chester which was a charming old town and now that I was no longer a sprog I was allowed to wear civvies. (Nobody was 'entitled' to wear civvies, be given leave or anything, because a soldier was entitled to nothing; it was a 'privilege' and privileges could and would be revoked, they were the first line of punishment).

I had never been anywhere like Chester. The older people were modish though quite reserved but the young ones were very outgoing. There were 'olde worlde' pubs and coffee rooms - I had never tasted coffee before - classy shops, a jazz club, and down by the river there was a regatta-like atmosphere, something I had never experienced although I had lived only a few miles from a major river all my life. Chester fathers apparently tried to keep their daughters well hidden but the lovely working-class girls from Birkenhead and Liverpool poured down at weekends to mine the rich ore of we eighteen-to-twenty-year-old males out for a good time, and there were QARANCs [Queen Anne's Royal Army Nursing Corps nurses] from the hospital.

There were eleven of us in the lab, including a staff-sergeant and a full corporal. The pathologist CO was a Maltese colonel with chronic dysentery and it showed on his lugubrious face. He had no buttocks and obviously no tailor had been called on to compensate for it even though a continent man with trousers like his would have looked as though he had just shat himself. The distance from his office in the corridor to his house across the road from the laboratory was almost too much for him and he would sometimes break into a trot, fingers crossed, anxiously glancing from side to side. He never smiled and I think he was self conscious about not being Anglo-Saxon, though it could have been the other thing, but he never gave anybody a hard time, I doubt if he knew any of our names apart from Staff-sergeant Kipling's.

Lieutenant Rose, the deputy pathologist, was shaped like an egg and contrary to the Colonel had a sense of humour he found difficult to suppress. He was responsible for training the technicians; he gave all the lectures and Staff-sergeant Kipling gave the practicals. We were taught haematology and blood transfusion, biochemistry, histology and bacteriology, none of which I had ever done before.

Kipling was the chief technician and the only regular soldier in the lab apart from the Colonel. He wasn't big but had large features and a high forehead which despite its acute slope he considered proof of high intelligence. He was very pretentious, which seemed an odd quirk for somebody who had chosen the British Army for a career, and I think he was embarrassed about having done so, he certainly never seemed to know quite where to pitch himself with us.

Underneath him was Corporal Sam Heworth from the Isle of Man, a tough little fellow with spectacles and spiky fair hair; Sam was very dry and if you could impress him, you could impress anybody

Apart from me there were three other student technicians who had been posted here at the same time: one from Leeds, one from Wales and one from Devon, none of whom I had ever seen before.

After morning parade where we were inspected by the Company Sergeant-major, we worked in the lab from half-past eight in the morning until half-past five at night on weekdays, and half day Saturday; in addition we did on-call duties at nights and weekends on a roster basis. Although the nature of the work and the methodology was the same as in any civilian hospital - everybody except me had worked in a hospital before coming into the Army - the laboratory, like the hospital, was very much a military entity and you could never forget it. Every Thursday there was a stiff inspection of the laboratory and all floors had to be bumped (polished like glass), all metal fittings gleaming - brass like gold, steel like silver - all of the large windows sparkling like crystal, and all woodwork and the leather upholstery in the Colonel's office polished like antiques.

The Colonel never spoke to us and we were never allowed to address him, although when he came in in the mornings and had to come through the lab to get to his office, having no doubt already yielded to the petty demands of nature in recoil, his jowls would shudder and his large brown eyes would occasionally dart to the side and this might be interpreted as 'Good morning'. I couldn't hazard a guess as to what his philosophy of life was, whether he was eloquent or not, or even whether he had a stammer; all I could presume was that in his scheme of things we were probably more useful than cockroaches.

Lieutenant Rose was very aware that he was an officer but he was approachable nevertheless.

One of the big differences between Chester and Crookham was that here - in the whole camp, not just the laboratory - we did more or less what we wanted in our own time and could follow our hobbies or interests to a degree: we could go to the pub, do physical training, go out with a girl, read, pray, fix a motorbike or play cards - and there was never a night when pontoon and poker wasn't played in the Duty Technician's room which was a tiny annexe to the lab but very cosy with a bed to sit on and a makeshift card table.

I soon learned to play pontoon and three-card brag and that you played them for real: no money, no game, and you never got your money back no matter how much you lost. Heworth had a record player and three records: a 78rpm of Michael Holliday singing 'Ten Thousand Miles', one of Lonnie Donnegan singing 'Rock Island Line', both of which we all sang along to, and an EP [extended play] of Chris Barber, a trombonist with a traditional Dixieland jazz band.

I was instantly hooked on trad jazz and in a matter of days could whistle, note perfect, every tune and riff on the record - Monty Sunshine's arrangement of 'Wild Cat Blues' for clarinet was something I'd do as a party-piece for years afterwards.

Everybody played cards except Bob Gibb from Devon and Geraint Taylor, a big soft Welshman who was too tight to risk a few coppers for a night's entertainment. 'No, thank you very much. I've a family to think about. You lot can go on and squander your own money if you want. But leave me out of it.'

'If fannies could talk,' Kipling observed, 'they'd sound just like Taylor.'

Kipling would sometimes drop in for a game and the fun would go right out of it the instant he put his half-crowns and florins next to everybody else's sixpences, threepenny bits and pennies.

'Right! Make way for a real poker player! Anybody with a yellow streak up his back had better leave the room right now.'

'Call me "Chris",' he would chide when we were sitting with our jerkins off and he was winning. 'We're all mates here, for Christ's sake!'

But there were limits to the levity and democracy when he was down a few bob. Then he would suck on his pipe as though it were a thumb and struggle to keep self control as he watched his money going into the kitty and not coming back out, and woe betide anybody who made a crack. Then it was 'Watch yourself, sonny boy! Don't think a pack of cards erases all barriers, or you'll find yourself cleaning latrines!'

If his wife was refusing him nooky and he was really riled up - he would always bleat about it to Eddie, the office clerk, and that's how we got to know - he would come into the card room, or washroom if it was during the day and we were having our tea-break, and interrupt any conversation we were having, whether about jazz, life after death, Jamaican nurses or anything else. As far as he was concerned he knew more about everything than anybody here, and his was the opinion that always silenced everybody else's. 'Only a complete and utter fool would say that,' was the way he dispensed with your point of view and you just had to stand there not saying a word until he had finished and then go to the sink to wash your mug, tea-break wasted.

A week after Bob Gibb had been called up his girlfriend had drowned while swimming in the sea and he was permanently depressed. He blamed the Army for her death, insisting that if he had been there, strong swimmer that he was, he would have saved her. He was an athlete and whenever he was off duty he went running, always alone; I think he was trying to run away from life. All day he worked in histology cutting up biopsies and looking for malignant cells and I didn't think it did him any good.

I was probably the closest anybody could get to being a friend and one night I persuaded him to let me go running with him so I could see where he went. He told me to bring my swimming trunks.

We ran a few miles until we came to a canal and Bob immediately peeled off and dived in.

I loved swimming and had swam in public swimming baths, in the sea, in rivers and in lakes but never in a canal.

'Come on!' Bob shouted. 'The water's great!'

But I waited, watching what looked like the remains of a Jack Russell freeing itself from a branch and floating on.

I would never do this again. I dived in and came up with something in my mouth. Whatever liquid was in the canal wasn't a bit like water: it was thick, it was stinking and it tasted vile. I practically leapt out onto the bank and ran all the way back to camp, my whole body covered in slime. I went straight to the ablutions, scrubbed myself all over with disinfectant until I was red raw and then went to the lab and autoclaved my trunks.

Bob came back later after completing whatever other mortifications of the flesh he carried out on himself on his Spartan excursions. When he saw me, he smiled; it was the first time I had ever seen him smiling, it was a smile of friendly genuine amusement.

One day the Colonel's wife came into the lab carrying a box and asking for Staff-sergeant Kipling. Almost tripping himself in his eagerness to please, Kipling came running out of his office.

'Good afternoon, Ma'am,' he said. 'Can I be of assistance?'

'Cosmo's in here,' she replied, nodding without looking down at the box in her arms. 'Can you geeve heem somtheen to make heem sleep?'

'Cosmo?'

'My pussycat. He's getteen too old.'

'Certainly, Ma'am. We'll do everything we can.'

When she went out Kipling thought she had meant something to help it make it through the night but the rest of us were sure she wanted something to send it into 'the long dark night' and leave it there.

'She wants you to do away with it, I reckon, Staff,' Eddie said.

Kipling was the kind of man who liked to give the impression he was quick on the uptake and rather than ask anybody to elaborate if he hadn't quite understood, he would go off half-cock and let somebody else ultimately take the blame.

But he was in a major dilemma here. If he put the cat to sleep forever and the Colonel's wife had only wanted it to get a good night's rest, he'd be in big trouble. So he went into his office, sat down and told Eddie to set the box on the table and close the door, lit his pipe and the two of them went through the conversation over and over again, reproducing and considering every inflexion, every gesture Mrs deSanta had made with her histrionic hands. Kipling now acknowledged it looked like she wanted 'curtains' for the cat but had to be dead certain or he could be sent into oblivion himself and with less time taken with the deliberations than he was giving the cat.

Suddenly he slammed his podgy little fist on the table and showed his bovine teeth, the way he did when he won a big hand in the card room. He had hit on a brilliant ploy. Eddie would go over to the Colonel's house and ask Mrs deSanta what she wanted doing with the cat 'afterwards'.

Five minutes later Eddie was back, beaming.

'"Just bury heem," she said,' and they both laughed and shook hands in congratulation.

'Shall I get Joe Robinson to do it?'

They all knew I worked in the veterinary service in civilian life.

'Like hell you will!' Kipling retorted, reaching for the laboratory handbook on small animals. 'Get the stinking thing out of my office while I look something up... Post mortems... Here we are. This'll do... Euthanasia of the guinea pig...'

'Drat it! The bloody thing's clawed me!' yelled Eddie, drawing up his sleeve to reveal a scratch the length of his forearm.

'Where is it?'

'It's escaped!'

'Don't be such an old woman! Go and get it and put it back.'

But cats aren't like guinea pigs and there was no way it was going back in the box, not after it had probably gathered what was going to happen to it, and there was a series of crashes as it knocked over jars of chemicals on its way out of the office and up the corridor.

'Quick! Quick!'

Eddie took off up the corridor but lost it as it disappeared through the space between the plastic at the bottom of the swing doors and the main corridor of the hospital.

'You imbecile!' shouted Kipling. 'You fucking useless, spineless nonny!'

'"Spineless"?'

'Yes, spineless.'

'If I was frightened of it I wouldn't have got close enough to get attacked... Look at my arm, Staff. Look how deep it is. Shouldn't I have something for rabies?'

'Shut your face, for God's sake, will you! If the Colonel finds out that his wife's cat's marauding the fucking hospital, he'll have my goolies for garters... And by God, if that happens, I'll bloody-well have yours on the end of a stick!'

'Shall I put some vaseline on it or something?'

'Come here, you bloody sap. I'll do it.'

'Bloody hell!' Eddie yelped as Kipling liberally dabbed his arm with iodine.

Kipling then detailed four of us to go on the wards armed with trays and syringes as though we had come to take samples from the patients. 'Start at each end and work your way through. I want every ward checked. If you see the thing, grab it by the scruff and bring it back. I don't care if it squawks, I don't care if it spits teeth. Any man that lets it go can consider himself on a charge... Now beat it!'

Three days later the cat turned up, it had been captured on the cardiac ward and Kipling was supervising its triumphant return in a sack well tied with string and carried by two of the lads from the lab.

'Shall we get Robinson to do it this time, Staff?'

'If anybody so much as mentions that private's name again with reference to this cat, I'll have him for breakfast! I'm going to superintend the whole operation from start to finish myself.'

He then ordered one of the spare incubators to be completely emptied except for one wire shelf. It was another brilliant idea, a miniature gas chamber.

Onto the shelf they bundled the cat, still in its sack, and into the bottom chamber he placed two open jars of ether. The inner glass door and the outer metal one were closed and the temperature turned up to maximum, which was 100°F, and Kipling padlocked the whole thing.

'Right! Everybody out!'

He was shoving us all out of the room. 'And nobody but nobody comes into this room without my express permission. Everything is to be left exactly as it is until after lunch.'

'Surely all that ether makes for a serious fire hazard?' warned Heworth. 'It'd be a pity if the whole hospital was turned into an incinerator for the sake of a bloody cat.'

'Mmmm...'

'Mmmm' was the closest Kipling ever got to admitting he was wrong. There were tiny beads of sweat on his forehead and his eyes bulged as he no doubt contemplated the smouldering remains of a military hospital and its ramifications.

'You'd better stay then, will you, Sam? Just to be on the safe side. You can go for lunch when I come back.'

'And if it leaks and I snuff it?'

Kipling laughed. 'I'll tell the duty technician to pop in every now and then to make sure you're awake.'

'You won't be putting a padlock on this door as well, then?'

'Ho! Ho! Ho! You're a real card, Sam. You're sure you won't think of signing on for another three years?' Heworth grimaced.

When Kipling returned from lunch he was in a state of high excitement. Followed by the entire staff except for Sam who just picked up his beret and walked out, Kipling very carefully removed the padlock on the incubator, opened the outer door and peered in through the glass.

'We've done it, Sam!' he shouted over his shoulder, obviously hoping Heworth hadn't left the building yet. 'It's a one-hundred-per-cent fait accompli..! One stiff and very dead moggy. And no mess.'

Kipling was playing to an almost full house and using every dramatic device.

'Stand back, all of you! I want nobody in front of this incubator except Corporal Heworth... You there, Private Robinson. Bring Corporal Heworth back!'

Heworth was going up the steps of the canteen when I caught up with him. 'What a prick!' was all he said. He deliberately sauntered back and I kept pace with him.

Kipling greeted him with what can only be described as a beatific smile. 'Come in, Sam. Come in, old chap.'

'Not with the fuse lit, I'm not.' Heworth motioned to the pipe in Kipling's mouth.

Kipling snatched it out of his mouth and thrust the wet dripping end into the hand of the ever-attendant Eddie. 'Here, put it in my office.'

'Hadn't you better ventilate? Otherwise we're all going to be anaesthetised the instant you open the incubator door.'

'I was coming to that, Sam... Privates Winters and Robinson! Up on that bench and open all windows!'

When we had done as we were ordered, we retreated to the doorway where everybody else was and watched the heavily-breathing Kipling, ample brow glistening, cautiously opening the glass door of the incubator before stepping back with a flourish.

'What a pong!' somebody groaned.

'Hah! Fat lot of good you sprogs would have been in the trenches. The old mustard gas would have seen you off like a lot of white mice.'

He gave one of his big patronising winks in Sam's direction to convey 'Childer, Sam. They be not veterans like thee and me.'

The cat had evidently made some attempt to escape before succumbing because the string was loose but the pathetic little bundle now lay very still.

'Gosh! Every drop of the ether has evaporated, Sam. Nearly a litre of the stuff!'

'A bullet would have been cheaper. You could have blindfolded it and taken it down to the range and let the artillery blast away at it. Even if they'd missed, they'd have scared it to death.'

'This is a clinical kill, Sam. This is the way we scientists do things.'

He was reaching out to remove the bundle when suddenly there was a flurry of grey fur and bright red mouth as the snarling cat shot out of the incubator, bounced off his shoulder and went straight through the window.

'You crazy fucking bastard!' shrieked Kipling. 'My face, Sam! It's got my face..! What's it like..? I think it's taken my eye!'

But he was all right, pretty badly scratched but all right.

'I'd better get a rabies shot for this, Sam. You'd better come with me. We're going to have to work something out before we get to the MO.'

'The swine!' Eddie complained, rolling up his sleeve after Kipling and Heworth had gone. 'He wouldn't let me go for one. Look at that..! I'll be carrying this scar for the rest of my life.'

When Kipling came back he told Sam to tell me to drop everything until I'd caught the cat and got rid of it and that he didn't give a damn how I did it as long as it was done as soon as possible.

I passed my Laboratory III examination and having done well in bacteriology was put to work on that bench. It suited me very well because I'd decided I wanted to make my career in microbiology which also included the new science of virology although it was only done in specialised laboratories and not here.

It was my job to examine exudates and excretions from patients suspected of having a bacterial infection, identify all bacteria present and carry out antibiotic sensitivity tests on any pathogens; thus I would examine specimens of pus, mucous, blood, faeces, urine and cerebrospinal fluid. Not a few specimens came from the venereal clinic and the incidence of gonorrhoea was quite high now everybody knew there was a cure for it. The bacteriology bench was also responsible for mycology which was the science of yeasts and fungi and I had to collect these specimens myself; it required the scraping of unhealthy skin with a scalpel and the removal of a few hairs but was less painful than it looked. Collection of most bacteriological specimens was also quite painless, though the sampling of cerebrospinal fluid, which required a lumbar puncture, was a different matter.

Most bacteriological results were obtained in two days, though tubercle bacilli and fungi sometimes took four or five weeks because of their slow growth rate.

13

One weekend when I was on duty my old tooth abscess recrudesced and I awoke on the Saturday with a swollen face and all the other symptoms. I persuaded the corporal from the dental lab which was adjacent to ours to let me have some penicillin lozenges but he would only do so on the condition I reported to their CO, Major McClure, the hospital dental surgeon, on the Monday morning.

By Monday the abscess had gone down so I didn't go to see him but was sent for. According to McClure the abscess was a cyst and would have to be removed along with the tooth it was under.

I said thanks all the same but I preferred to keep both tooth and cyst, the tooth was right in the front and perfectly sound and I'd look an idiot without it. McClure said one of his technicians would make me a false tooth with a tiny little palette and it would look every bit as good as the real thing, and that I'd have no more trouble with the abscess which he said the x-ray indicated was deep rooted.

I said I'd think about it but he said he'd already done so and it was coming out along with the tooth whether I liked it or not, and it was coming out the next week.

I felt betrayed by his corporal who was just standing there saying nothing. The abscess predated my entering the Army by many a year, I said, so it was a 'civilian cyst' and the Army had no right to commandeer it. 'You belong to the Army, never mind the cyst,' he smirked. 'Major McClure's the dentist here and you're the private with no choice in the matter.'

I got up and went out but I wasn't happy about it at all. Nobody - certainly no National Serviceman - regarded a regular army dentist, doctor, chaplain, or the likes, as a 'proper' - real - one. We were absolutely convinced they had either done badly in their exams in civvy street, or worked their way up through the ranks picking up a bit here and a bit there; after all, wasn't that what improvisation - the great army canon - was all about? It was unthinkable that anybody with any kind of talent or skill would enlist in the British Army in peacetime.

As for McClure, officers considered themselves so superior to ordinary soldiers that it was impossible to imagine him caring what kind of a mess he made of a private's teeth. There was currently a paper up on the noticeboard in the canteen advertising an all-ranks dance, which said 'The following are invited: Officers and their ladies, NCOs and their wives, and ORs [soldiers with no rank] and their women.'

Ten days later I was on the surgical ward. The floor was covered with the same sticky thickly-polished tawny linoleum that covered every military floor I had ever been on, and walking barefoot on it was like having the soles of your feet licked by a council-house cat; yet at the bare edges the old dry floorboards delivered spelks like shrapnel.

The ward was spartan and cheerless but spotless. If my heart and lungs survived what I was sure would be a very amateurishly administered anaesthetic, and massive haemorrhaging didn't follow the sloppy surgery, at least dust mites were hardly likely to be a problem.

There were seven others on the ward, all with the same old-soldier mentality that celebrates total capitulation; how the British Army ever won a battle beggared belief.

'It's no use getting yourself agitated, mate. The Army owns you and they can do anything they like with you. They'll cut your fuckin' balls off if they have a mind... Come and have a game of dominoes. It's only sixpence a game.'

If ever there was a game that got right under my skin, it was dominoes: the silly clacking noises they made as they were laid on their backs and the inane clatter as they were all turned over and shuffled about. I'd have defied anybody to watch a group of lunatics playing this game, and a group of any other people playing it, and detect the difference.

As I lay there, unable to escape the atrocious sound of the abominable dominoes, I got more and more incensed. I didn't want a perfectly good front tooth out. I didn't even want the abscess or cyst, or whatever it was, out. It was fine now: no swelling, no unpleasant taste, no pain, nothing. McClure must have been taught to regard teeth, the way most doctors regarded tonsils, adenoids, the foreskin and the vermiform appendix: the most damning argument against the theory of evolution.

I considered requesting permission to go and see McClure to point out that everything was all right now and suggest he invest his valuable time on some more deserving case. I was only eighteen and the way I was headed, my reasonably good looks were going to be shattered on the morrow and I'd never get a decent-looking girl ever again, I was going to be tagging along behind Tod from now on. Anybody with a front tooth missing automatically looks like an imbecile; cartoonists caricatured idiots, especially ones that came from the slums, by the simple device of blacking out one of their front teeth.

I awoke about 5pm the following day and licked around the inside of my mouth. Something was wrong, there was nothing there at the front, nothing except what felt like a piece of barbed wire buried in my gum. I got up and went into the bathroom to look in the mirror. All four of my upper front teeth had gone and a hole had been gouged out of my gum at the front that was big enough to put my thumb in; there were several pieces of thick black heavily-knotted thread drawing together swollen bloody flaps of gum. My nose and cheeks were swollen and bruised. I tried to smile, not because I felt like it but to see what it looked like...
'Yak!'

I was discharged the following morning and off duty for the weekend so I changed into civvies, walked out of the camp and hitched a lift to Liverpool Station. Normally I would never waste money on trains because lifts from lorry-drivers were always easy to get if you were in uniform, but anybody looking down and seeing me standing on the roadside was likely to drive on; anyway I didn't feel like chatting, my speech was so bad I couldn't make myself understood and had to write 'Newcastle-on-Tyne' on a piece of paper for the ticket clerk.

When I got home and grinned through the glass at my father as he came to answer the door, he hesitated for a moment as though he had mistaken me for somebody else.

'Hello, Ga.'

'Hello, son..! What happened?'

My mother then appeared behind him, most disconcerted.

'Hello, Ga.'

'Oh, me bairn..! Whatever's happened to you..! Your poor bit face!'

Over a plate of scrambled eggs I told them what had happened. My mother was upset but my father said 'What's done's done. If it puts an end to the trouble with the abscess, it'll be worth it.'

He never made a fuss about illness or pain and never liked anybody else to either, and when my mother kept going on about it he said 'For God's sake, woman...it's only a few teeth. It's not as though he's lost an arm or a leg.'

My brothers had a different view. 'Urgh! Look at our Joe! He's even uglier than he was! He's had it for the girls now. He won't even be able to get Maggie Bolton...and she's got a face like the back of a bus!'

I returned to Chester on the Sunday night and had the stitches out later in the week but had to wait some weeks until the gum had settled before they could make me a denture. I was good friends with the dental technician who was doing it and we went through a movie magazine he had of male pin-ups and I opted to look like Tab Hunter who was supposed to be Hollywood's number one sex symbol.

I'd been at Chester about six months when an oddball called Denholm Cranshawe was posted to the lab. He was an entomologist in civilian life so they put him in the medical corps, medicine being a subject he had no interest in whatsoever. He was a Buddhist, a lover of modern jazz, a blue belt in a martial art I'd never heard of, and most remarkable of all he was the only man I had met in the British Army who had no time for women. He was different to anybody in the lab and the whole camp and gave the impression he was grateful for it.

Most thought he was a 'bit funny'. He had tortoise-shell spectacles and long curly fair hair above the basin-line, was rather thin, very articulate and interested in all kinds of things; but I wasn't sure that was the definition of a queer. I was certainly the only friend he had and the rest of them in the lab were surprised.

I often tried to imagine Denholm going through basic training with somebody like Devine as squad corporal and could only conclude he was a living tribute to the will to survive, maybe he had put himself into some kind of trance for the eight weeks. His interests seemed inimical to soldiering and I suspect it was a triumph more of intellect than spirit, though that might not be altogether fair. He was probably the first person I met who genuinely had no regard for what the rest of the world might think of him, let alone his barrack-room companions; neither Steve nor

Tod was quite like that. I thought it could be a great vice as well as a great virtue.

He showed me the Buddhist literature he regularly received through the post and it started me questioning my own faith and the existence of the God I had been brought up with. To be born a Christian and then become a Buddhist seemed to me an act of reasoning, not faith; and to break with tradition for this reason, an act of courage rather than defiance.

Although he preferred modern music, including modern jazz, every week Denholm and I used to go to the traditional jazz club in Chester where we saw and heard greats like Ken Colyer, Cy Laurie and George Melly. Although he didn't drink, funnily enough he would get up and jive and jive the way you might expect a Buddhist entomologist would. Afterwards when we were walking back to camp he'd explain the origins and appeal of modern jazz as well as that of Bartok and Stravinsky.

We went to see Bill Hayley's film, 'Rock Around the Clock', when it came to town and there was nearly a riot when the 'Rockers' from Liverpool came down to dance in the aisles; it had been banned in their city because of the rumpus it had caused. The soldiers from the camp and these guys didn't see eye to eye at all but Denholm would have nothing to do with anything like that, not being what you could call a 'gang' man.

Denholm was one of a number of people I had met since coming into the Army who were very self-possessed and seemed mature far beyond their years; I could never imagine their feelings getting the better of them, as mine sometimes would me. They didn't seem to have much in common, physically or mentally, only intelligence. I suspected it had nothing to do with the size of the families they came from, though families and background weren't topics for conversation in the Army - maybe it was different with those in overseas postings.

I would have liked to know whether they consciously exercised self control in the face of provocation or whether they were immune to it. Perhaps what they had was essential to survival under extremely adverse conditions, like two years in the Antarctic or a Japanese POW camp; perhaps it was essential to agreeing to undergo an operation with less than a fifty-percent chance of success, or being a professional poker player. Maybe it was the quintessence of ruthlessness, certainly their smiles were a little cold, though I hadn't carried out a survey. What I do know is that it was a loss to me when they got rid of him; he hadn't fitted in so they posted him to Netley, the Army's dreaded mental hospital.

Nonetheless I enjoyed life at Chester. A couple of nights a week I would go into town with some of the lads from the lab and we would go looking for girls. And if we couldn't be bothered or it was wet, there was always a card game on the go and the crack that went with it.

My father wouldn't have agreed but I thought playing cards for money was character-building in some ways, leaving aside the platitudes about gambling. The rules, which were always rigorously enforced, were rational and egalitarian in marked contrast to the absurd ordinances of the organisation that controlled our lives, and none of the discipline was gratuitous. Success or failure depended more on fate than anything else and although luck sometimes seemed capricious, it was never malign and I wasn't sure that life was any different. Poker required stoicism rather than deceit, I thought, and any card game played for however low a stake revealed things about the character of the participants more clearly than most sports.

We had rented a radio for the lab so the duty-technician wouldn't get too bored on his own in the middle of the night. 'Oh-oh-oh yes, I'm the Great Pre-te-e-nder,' we would sing along as we cross-matched two pints of blood for transfusion in the operating theatre, or 'Bee-boppa-loola, she's my baby, Beeboppaloola, I don' mean maybe,' as we tested a urine for oxalates. We also listened to the 'Top Twenty' on Radio Luxembourg every Sunday night and learned the top twenty off by heart. There were so many great songs, like, Pat Boone's 'Love Letters in the Sand', Tommy Steele's 'Singing the Blues', Guy Mitchell's 'Yellow Rose of Texas', Elvis Presley's 'Love me Tender', Frankie Vaughan's 'Green Door', Sammy Davis Jnr's 'Ain't that a shame' and Fats Domino's 'Blue Monday'. Every couple of weeks a new one would come out, instrumentals as well as vocals, piano as well as guitar. And many a night we would be walking the five miles back to camp after a few pints of black velvet, singing 'Di-anna, I am but a foo-oo-ol,' or 'Se-ven lonely nights make one lonely week,' as with arms around each others' shoulders we would console ourselves for having failed to score and having to return to camp with more or less the same companions we had set off with in such high hopes earlier that night.

Back home in Newcastle we had a HMV cabinet wireless that stood on the floor and the family all sat around but it only ever broadcast the Home Programme and sometimes the Light in our house, so I was used to being entertained only by what the BBC served up. Popular songs of the 1940s were considered acceptable fare but 1950s stuff was very dubious. It would have been a kind of blasphemy, an abuse of the set almost, to have tuned the radio into the salacious Radio Luxembourg and as far as I know it was never attempted; I certainly didn't so none of the others would have.

Whenever 'The News' came on there had to be dead silence throughout the house even though the war had been over long since and hangings and their rejected appeals had taken over the sombre spot. We even listened with respect at ten to eight every morning, to the Radio Doctor, a man whose tonsils and adenoids clearly hadn't been removed as ours all had.

Here in the lab at Chester we had an unbeautiful but robust and fairly-portable bakelite radio and while it was on we could move around, talk and carry on, have it on loud, have it on all night, and switch it off whenever Anthony Eden came on.

Whatever else life in the Army was, it was unremittingly crude. In Monty Billets, which we presumed were named after Field Marshall Montgomery and considered to be a more than ample memorial, was an x-ray technician called Tomkins who was always in bed by 8.30pm. National Service was such an ordeal for him that he coped by spending as much time as possible unconscious; otherwise it was military duties performed to the letter, quick meals and punishing exercise. 'Why not stick a few nails and broken glass in your mattress?' fellows would say to him.

Also in the billet at the far end were two regular old corporals who would be busted one week and made up again the next for offences arising from drunkenness. They would come in every night cursing and swearing, fall over Tomkins' bed which was the first inside the door and on several occasions they threw up over him. They just laughed their heads off and there was nothing Tomkins could do about it, he was very religious and I think he thought it was God's will; up he would get to clean his bed and give himself a thorough wash while the rest of us would be shouting at him to hurry up and put the light off.

In the next barrack-room was Fred Morris, a huge corporal who was forever blocking up the toilet and never would more than a few days pass without somebody waking you up to come and view the 'Unbelievable! Bigger than ever, I kid you not. This has to be seen before they call in the bomb disposal squad. You'll never forgive yourself if you miss this one. If he ever produces another like this, it'll kill him.'

When you went, crowded around a lavatory with astonished disgusted expressions on their faces, there could be as many as a dozen men in pyjamas, marvelling.

This was what it was like in the Medical Corps, supposedly an elite corps. God only knows what they got up to in the Pioneers. Right from my first day the poor Pioneers had been slandered: 'They're the ones they test the minefields with. They just send them in with instruments that are no good and worth nothing...with lead innersoles in their boots.'

14

Whenever I went home on leave, the first thing I would do after a meal and wash would be to go and find Johnny who would usually be out with his pals at a pub or dance and afterwards we'd always come home together.

He didn't have a girlfriend and didn't seem to have any idea how to go about getting one, so one Saturday night after I'd picked him up I said I'd demonstrate how to score with a couple of the many girls who walked about in pairs. He wasn't at all enthusiastic especially when I had explained the protocol: a good-looker would always choose a 'plain' one as a companion so you had to decide between you before you went up, who was going to get whom. In this instance, since I was going to be delivering the patter, I would be getting the best one.

Never mind, after we had scrutinised several pairs from a distance and Johnny hadn't fancied any of them, I decided to strike if only for instructive purposes.

The patter was inane but it worked and after half an hour of it I returned to Johnny having arranged for he and I to meet them next time I came home as it was too late for anything more tonight.

Johnny, who had been keeping a respectable distance as instructed, wasn't impressed at all, he was certain I had failed and nothing I could say would convince him.

The next morning being Sunday Johnny and I went to the eleven o'clock Mass at St. Teresa's, the 'Old Man's Mass', Father Ord called it, as though it wasn't geared to the needs of young men or females.

When we came out, Michael who was twelve and Peter who was nine, and had been to an earlier Mass, were waiting in a state of high excitement.

'You've to come quick, our Joe! Dad wants you! You've had it!'
'What's up?'
'There's a whole stack of horses at the door!'
'What!'
Johnny and I broke into a run while the other two raced on ahead, every

now and again looking back to make sure we were following.

We turned off Heaton Road into Simonside Terrace and before we'd got very far we could see three large horses saddled up with riders cavorting outside the door of our house and on to Chillingham Road.

'Shit and corruption! It must be those two from last night,' I wailed.

'Don't swear when we've just come out of church,' Johnny said. 'It's too late to go to another Mass.'

As we approached the house my father was standing in the porch with my mother behind him. Prancing on and off the three-feet-square patio were three highly-strung horses with their riders dressed in black hats, red jackets and jodhpurs as though on a foxhunt, and collecting the 'real manure' which was dropping in considerable quantities in front of the house, were neighbours with garden spades and coal shovels.

'Get yourself in here, Joe!' my father said.

I nodded to the girls as I went in. 'Hang on a minute.'

'What in God's name have you been telling these girls? They've been here for the past three quarters of an hour with some tale about you being a vet. We've told them you're nothing of the sort but they won't go away. Now get yourself out there and get rid of them and their flaming horses and tell them we don't ever want them back!'

'I didn't tell them to come,' I pleaded.

'It's just like you to put on a show like this. It's been all your mother and I could do to stop the damned things from coming into the house!'

When I went back outside the horses were very restless, especially with half a dozen women poking shovels at their back-ends.

'You said you could tell me if my horse was pregnant, remember?' said the main one I had been tapping up the previous night.

'He wouldn't know the front of a horse from the back, if it wasn't for them shovels,' Michael chirped.

'Shut up, you cheeky nowt..! Keep these lot out the way while I sort things out, will you, Mam?'

I nodded to the other horses. 'Johnny, keep those two back while I examine this one.' I had to try to retrieve some dignity, not only for myself but for the whole house.

'You realise I haven't any instruments with me here, Angela...so it'll only have to be a rough check?'

I went to her horse and put my ear against its belly and everybody went quiet.

'Not this one. It's a gelding. That's the one.' She pointed to the horse her sister was sitting on.

'I know that. I just thought I'd give them all a quick check now they're here.'

I then deliberately went to the third horse, another gelding, and did the same, this time tapping the belly with my finger a few times.

'Mmmm... Abdominal cavities well filled and peristalsis normal... Those two are fine,' I said, going over to the third. 'They're in pretty good condition, I must say.'

I was now at the one with nothing underneath. I listened carefully as I went through the finger-tapping routine and all went well until for some reason I grabbed its tail and yanked it up.

The horse reared up on its front legs and if I hadn't been quick it would have kicked the rest of my teeth out as it lashed out with both back legs.

'What are you doing!' Angela protested.

'Never mind that... My opinion is that it might be' - I glanced around at the transfixed neighbours - 'you know what... On the other hand, it might not... So just keep on doing what you're doing and keep an eye on it...and call in one of my colleagues if you have any further trouble.'

She wasn't a bit impressed and everybody could see it, and with a toss of her haughty head, she and her two haughty companions and their three haughty horses cantered off up Chillingham Road.

One morning early in November there was great excitement in the camp when lorries with hundreds of soldiers in full kit suddenly appeared. They were nearly all RAMC and at least a dozen of them came into the laboratory.

In true Army fashion nobody knew what was happening. For days we had been hearing on the radio that trouble was brewing between the British Tory Government and Colonel Nasser of Egypt because he was going to nationalise the Suez Canal. The British and French who controlled it had reneged on their promise to help finance the construction of a dam in the Nile that would have been of great benefit to the Egyptian people, even though the finance was to come from tolls exacted from ships passing through the Canal. Apparently they had gone back on their promise because they were incensed about the good relations between Egypt and Russia.

The Tories had always hated Nasser because he had the gall to stand up to them and it seemed the only good Arab was a dead Arab as far as they were concerned. But attacking Port Said to take control of the Canal was apparently against the wishes of most of the British people and the whole of the rest of the world except Israel. Nobody knew if the British Army had any say in the matter.

Those that came into the lab were lab technicians like us and some of them were very nervous; whether the British Government was right or not, it was the Army that would be organising things and that was enough to strike fear into any heart acquainted with it from the inside. They and their comrades stayed in camp for less than two days before being lorried away and then shipped or flown to their destinations.

The whole thing was a mess and the troops were back at their home bases before the smell of gunpowder had disappeared. It was called the 'Suez Crisis, 1956' but it was an absolute farce.

By the time my second military Christmas came around I had served thirteen months, more than half my allotted time, so unless the new prime minister Harold Macmillan declared war on anybody else and my time was extended, which was every National Serviceman's nightmare, I'd be out by the next one.

We were allowed to put up a few decorations in the lab but nobody was prepared to spend any money on them so we made them out of newspapers and pages torn from glossy magazines. Somebody had found a very old packet of Durex and was using them as balloons, though as a Catholic I could not in all conscience touch one, let alone put the end of it in my mouth and blow into it.

We had drawn lots to see who would do Christmas duty and who would do New Year but the three Scots lads had indicated they wanted New Year off so the odds were in my favour when I drew Christmas.

I had made a bet with everybody in the lab that on the Saturday before we went home I would go into Marks & Spencers at the busiest time, which was the middle of the afternoon, go to the lingerie counter, select the most outlandish pair of knickers, hold them up as though estimating something, buy them and ask for them to be gift-wrapped. Although we were a vulgar lot in the Army, something like this was considered an act of extreme valour, however warped.

Seven of us went in and the others took up positions where they could see exactly what went on while I went up to the counter, picked up a pair of pink transparent panties with tiny hearts embroidered along the edges, called over the sales assistant and with hands trembling and face on fire, held them up so that everybody in the store could see. It took her ages to give me my change, meanwhile I had to endure the appalled looks of nearby women customers who were temporarily paralysed. But the whole operation was carried out smoothly and efficiently, the way military operations should be carried out and typically it had been carried out by a group of National Servicemen, all of them privates.

As I left the shop and entered the main street I was greeted with a roar of cheers. In triumph I returned to camp where the parcel was unwrapped and rewrapped so many times, and the contents handled by so many people, that in all decency they should have been laundered before being finally wrapped to be given to Noreen, my girlfriend back in Newcastle.

Because it was Christmas we were given train rail warrants and I went home via Crewe and York. I no longer went home in uniform, that was something you only did once. All the mainline trains were full of young men the same age as me, many of them old-timers like me and strictly in civvies; out of uniform some soldiers behaved like gentlemen, others like louts but you could still tell. The bar was packed until closing time and many would be drunk at some stage during the long haul home but it would usually wear off before they reached their destination. Nearly everybody smoked and many played cards, so the character of 1950s British Rail plying from south to north and west to east probably wasn't that much different to that of the 1850s Mississippi riverboats, except for the mosquitoes, the accent and the glamour.

Those who went the whole hog were a tired, crumpled, headachy few. When I got off at Newcastle there were four jocks going on to Edinburgh, and one on to Inverness, but they were practically in a coma.

It was already the early hours of Christmas Eve when I arrived home but a few hours kip in a warm comfortable bed had me fully restored and ready for anything. That night I went out for a drink with Dad and Johnny and came back full of carry-on. In a moment of indiscretion I told them the knicker story. Johnny was shocked but Mam, who Dad immediately told for some reason, was mortified.

'You can't give a girl something like that for her Christmas box, our Joe! Whatever will her parents think?'

Sweet demure little Noreen who worked at the Co-op with my old pal Jim had a bit of a reputation, and it was largely on the strength of that that I'd asked him to fix us up. Though of course my mother didn't know that.

'It was just for a laugh, man.'

'Well, we don't think it's a laugh. Do we, Jack?'

My father shook his head.

'We call it indecent.'

I shrugged my shoulders. 'They're all wrapped up now.'

'Joe..! How could you..?' She began to cry. 'Where did we go wrong..? What mistake did we make that he should turn out like this?'

'Damned if I know, Evelyn,' my father answered.

I went over and put my arm around her. 'Come on, Mam. It's only a bit of fun. She'll take it in good part, I know she will.'

'She cannot be much of a girl if she does, that's all I can say.'

My father nodded but I knew he was amused.

'Where are they now?' my mother asked.

'In my case in the bedroom.'

'Right. Go and fetch them.' She had pulled herself together and was going to try to retrieve the situation.

'Oh, Mam...'

'Go on, get them! I want to see with my own eyes what kind of present our eldest son buys for his girlfriend.'

I fetched them but didn't hand them to her, I just put them on the table.

She began to remove the paper and now I began to get annoyed; apart from anything else I was sick of wrapping them up. 'Don't, Mam. Leave it alone. It's a Christmas present.'

'This is no Christmas present if it's what you say it is!'

'Right, then. Give's it back. I was only kidding.'

But by now she had it open and real tears were flowing down her cheeks. 'I'm keeping these!' she said, putting it in her lap and clasping her hands over it. 'You're not giving such a thing to anybody!'

'If you do, I'll have no alternative but to give her the present I've got for you. And yours cost a lot more than hers.'

'You wouldn't dare!' She got up and took away the parcel containing Noreen's panties and I never saw them again.

On Christmas morning when all the presents had been given out my mother looked so plaintively at me, as much as to say 'You've forgotten somebody, haven't you, our Joe?'

I shrugged and she burst into tears. Everybody looked at me as though I was a cad and I had to run across the road to the only tobacconist's that was open to buy her the biggest box of Black Magic in the shop, its cover bleached from being in the window for so long, wrap it up with torn gift paper salvaged from the bin, write a soppy inscription and give it to her. It wasn't the same as giving her her rightful present but I had never intended to hurt her; she thought I was out of line, and I thought she was.

The dental laboratory was adjacent to ours and there was always rivalry between us.

One night two of us were on duty in the medical lab and we'd opened a window in the wash-up to let the autoclave steam out. The dental lads noticed, got their huge fire hose and blasted water in. All my Scots supernumerary and I had to retaliate with was buckets of water slowly filled from the tap, and in no time we were absolutely drenched and the whole place flooded. There were four of them and the jets of water which hit us straight in the face when we went to the window to try to throw a bucket of water at them, had us breathless and hanging on to the benches to try to keep upright. Worst of all, the wash-up door behind us had been left open and jets of water went clear over our heads, across the corridor and into the Colonel's office. It was in a terrible mess and we pleaded with them to stop but every time we opened our mouths to say anything, we were practically drowned.

I knew there was no way we could win so I went into the main lab, got a bottle of carbol fuchsin which is an extremely powerful deep red dye used for staining bacteria, and poured the whole bottle into two buckets of water. My mate took one and I took the other and when the heads of the dentals next came to the window, we threw our buckets. The dental corporal, who had been hiding just beneath the window, copped the full load of my bucket. By this time it was almost dark but they knew something serious had happened and withdrew.

We had one hell of a job cleaning up that night and it was nearly dawn by the time we'd dried the Colonel's papers in the incubator and restored everything. But the dental corporal was apparently in a awful state: his clothes were ruined, his skin was bright red - particularly his face and head - and for the rest of the week he had to get up to all kinds of ruses to avoid parades. It was three days before the dye came out of his skin but it remained under his fingernails, in his ears, in his eyebrows and in his hair which had been fair and sparse and was now magenta and he was scared to wash it too much in case he lost any more of it. A month later he was demobbed, hair still bright red and he still couldn't forgive me. The night before he left they were having a party for him in the dental lab and I went to wish him well and say again that I was sorry. 'It were a right shit trick,' he said in his Manchester voice and refused to shake my hand.

It was so cold and draughty in Monty Billets that I had bought a tiny electric fire from home which balanced on the bed and plugged into the light socket. One night a fellow from the Pay Corps who had the bed opposite me, came in drunk, knocked my fire over, wrenched the cord out and pulled the socket off the ceiling. I got into trouble over using it and wasn't allowed to any more.

The next time I was in town I bought a little tin of fast-drying black enamel and a small paintbrush and that night, when the fellow from the Pay Corps was asleep, I painted an Adolf Hitler moustache on him by the light of a laryngeal pen torch borrowed from a ward. The next morning when he went to get washed and saw himself in the mirror, he was past himself. There was no way he could get the tash off and had to go on parade with it, mouth red raw from scrubbing.

As always in the Army, because it had no detective corps and no idea of justice, it was the victim that got punished. Anybody beaten up in a fight would be treated, perhaps hospitalised, and then charged with some violation of Queen's Regulations. In this case the victim was confined to barracks for a week and ordered to get the moustache off even if he had to use sandpaper.

He took it badly and asked if it had been me. I said yes and offered to let him get his own back in a paint fight and he agreed. That night we poured all of my black enamel on the bristles of an old six-inch paintbrush we had scrounged, stuck it in a bucket in the middle of the floor and retreated to opposite walls, standing on our own beds naked save for our underpants. All the lads from Monty Billets were packed in the room, well back. Bets were laid and some were yelling and shouting for him and some for me.

The rules were that when the signal was given we would both race for the brush and whoever got it would daub the other once and that would be it, there would be no fighting over the brush, no paint over anybody's bed or kit; and it would be done in the dark.

The lights were switched off and as soon as the shout to start was given, I leapt over my bed, dived at the paint tin, grabbed the brush and there was just sufficient light for me to see his figure leaping down. With one sweep of the brush I caught him in the crotch and the paint went right up his chest and he yelled out. The light went on and everybody including me, was horrified at the mess he was in. He was angrier than ever but he never reported it and never bothered me again.

Several of the dental lads had motor-bikes, as did several from our lab, and they used to park them between the two labs and work on them together at night, tuning them, cleaning them and eulogising them, and standing by watching and listening I fell in love with these wonderful machines.

I could get weekend passes to go home every three weeks but there were no travel warrants to go with them so I would have to hitchhike, usually through Warrington to Manchester and Leeds and then up the Great North Road. It was easy getting lifts on the main roads, the difficulty was coming back on a Sunday night once I'd left the GNR; and if I were late and missed parade on the Monday, not only could my next few passes be stopped but I could also receive punishment from the laboratory.

On one trip home Steve told me Mr Standish had a 197cc Ambassador for sale at £20, so I went up on the Saturday afternoon and took an old school friend who knew a bit about motor-bikes, with me. I spent a hair-raising quarter of an hour riding it around the RAF camp, bought it and went back to Chester on it on the Sunday.

After that, whenever I went home I always rode and would go via Alwinton and Hexham and come back through Barnard Castle, Brough and Kirby Stephen. It was a long and lonely haul and many a time the bike would break down through overheating and I would have to spend the night in a field among sheep or cows and then strip the carburettor and coax it back into life at dawn. The speedometer went up to 55mph but the engine never achieved more than 45mph and it always used to overheat going over the Pennines, they were merciless, especially in the snow.

I always forgave the Ambassador after I'd abused it and can only think it must have forgiven me also because we went everywhere together. It was an indescribable thrill to get on a motor-bike, bring your foot down on the kickstart, have the engine splutter into life and then open the throttle and make it roar so the whole neighbourhood would know you were once again mobile, getting ready to depart for who knows where: maybe just around the block to wake up everybody on nightshift, maybe to the ends of the earth, and because you were in the Army everybody made allowances.

I loved to pass it on my way between billet and lab, clean and shiny and fully lubricated, parked ready and waiting for me, as loyal a steed as any Roy Rogers' stallion or pitman's pony. Just to see it parked by the wall every time I came in or out was immensely reassuring and it was all I could do to refrain from nodding or waving. I was now one of the elite who had no use for British Rail, no need to depend on benevolent lorry-drivers, and many a night until dusk I could be seen among the bikemen in the pit between laboratories, hands covered in oil, disassembling and reassembling parts just for the sake of it, sharing spanners, hints and the most magnificent bullshit.

Chas Waites from the med lab looked like a First World-War pilot when he rode off on his belt-driven Brough and he was regarded by all as a master mechanic. That, plus the fact he was the longest serving National Serviceman, earned him immense respect among the whole fraternity.

When doing blood tests in the laboratory it was the practice to take blood samples from ourselves to act as controls for batches of specimens sent in from patients in the hospital, and Chas who worked in Haematology one day donated a sample for Biochemistry which was discovered to have a high serum bilirubin. Kipling told the Colonel and Chas was immediately diagnosed as suffering from infectious hepatitis. Chas was neurotic at the best of times and was terrified in case the diagnosis would affect his demob which was only six weeks away. He wasn't concerned about the hepatitis, convinced he'd be all right once he got back into civvy street, it was the thought of indefinitely remaining in the Army that nearly drove him round the bend.

'Never will I ever give another blood sample!' he yelled in his thin voice. 'So from now on, don't any of you dare ask..! You do something like this out of the goodness of your heart, and then this happens. I probably had it before I came into the bloomin' Army and it never stopped me getting in. So I'm damned if it's going to stop me getting out!'

But he knew the regulations. If any illness was diagnosed during National Service, it had to be cured before you could be discharged; so if it was terminal, you could end your days in khaki, the most horrific end conceivable to a National Serviceman.

One of the MOs had told him to drink plenty of water and he drank it by the gallon, even to the point of making himself sick. 'Either I'll flush it out or I'll dilute it so it cannot be traced!' he'd retort whenever any of us told him to take it easy. And if you asked him how he was feeling, he would nearly shriek at you. 'I'm as fit as anybody in this laboratory! The whole bloomin' lot of you should be tested. Then we'd see!'

But his bilirubin hardly dropped as the weeks went by and he became desperate. Then with only ten days to go, it was suddenly normal; but instead of being ecstatic at the news, he was more nervous than ever. His pal from Biochemistry who Chas had unfairly blamed all along was now substituting his own blood for every test on Chas, and Chas got out in time. The look on his face when the MO discharged him was something you could only expect to see on somebody walking on water.

One morning we were all in the wash-up in our nursing orderly gowns having our tea-break and chatting, when in came Kipling in his lab coat with the huge armband that showed he was a staff-sergeant - his wife had cunningly embroidered it a bit, especially the crown, so the whole thing looked more imperial than it was ever meant to be.

'It seems to me a lot of the privates on this camp need thoroughly sorting out', he said to the general company as he picked up his mug and started slurping from it.

I was sick of him disrupting any conversation however interesting or entertaining, fed up with the way he always overrode everything no matter who was saying what.

'It seems to me some of the staff-sergeants on this camp need sorting out as well,' I said.

There was dead silence.

'What did you say?' Kipling said, taking the mug from his mouth.

'No more nor less than what you said about the privates.'

'Do you know who you're talking to!' he shouted, slamming his mug down.

Somebody grabbed my arm. 'Shut up, Joe. You hear?'

'If you said what I think you said, you're in big trouble, laddie!'

I repeated what I'd said.

'You want to listen to your friends...! They know what's good for you. You've got a chip on your shoulder. That's what's wrong with you... Now you immediately withdraw what you just said and I might let it go at that because you're still a youngster.'

'Is that a command or a request?'

'Don't be funny with me, soldier! It's neither..! It's sound advice..! Withdraw it! Now!'

'Go on! Do it, Joe! Don't be so bloody daft!'

'You withdraw what you said about the privates, first.'

'I bloody-well will not!'

'Then neither bloody-well will I.'

'Who do you mean..? Do you mean me..?'

'Say no more,' urged Geraint. 'Just apologise.'

'Because if I thought it was personal, I'd break every bone in your body... So if it's me you're referring to, step outside into that corridor. But before you do, you'd better know I've done a lot of unarmed combat in my time...including boxing and ju-jitsu. And I'm not talking about the pansy stuff they teach you nowadays. I'm talking about the stuff the troops in Burma were taught before tackling the Japs.'

He was already slowly and ritualistically removing his white coat and handing it to Heworth. 'You hold it, Sam. You're my second and you'll be the referee. It's looks like I might need to give this young pup the hiding of his life.'

Sam obviously didn't want it and laid it on the bench. 'Give over, man,' he said to Kipling. 'He's just a lad. You know what he is.'

Kipling was now slowly undoing his battledress. 'He knows the alternative. He simply needs to apologise and then he can get on with his tea.'

'What if I come into the corridor and beat you?' I asked him.

'Ho! Ho! Ho! Fat chance of that..! Did you hear that, chaps? Ha ha..! Tell him, Sam. Tell him what he's in for... You come out there, chum, and I'll show you no mercy. It won't be your understanding laboratory chief you'll find out there. Not once you cross that line.'

'Don't go, Joe!' the others urged. 'You'll be up for striking a superior and you'll end in the Glasshouse for sure.'

'Rubbish!' yelled Kipling. 'I'm not that sort, and well you know it...all of you... Here!' He quickly finished undoing his jerkin and tossed it nonchalantly at the bench whereupon it fell on the floor. He was now in the corridor rolling his sleeves up and showing his teeth like a dog.

When I stepped into the corridor he adopted an old pugilist stance, both arms up, leaning back, feet wide apart.

I grabbed him by the neck and threw him straight to the floor, I had never known anyone go down so easily. I didn't hit him or hurt him in any way, I just sat on his chest and pinioned his arms, wondering where we went from there. Suddenly the door opened and the Colonel came in with a look of horror on his face.

I immediately let Kipling up and we both got to our feet, Kipling pushing back his hair and tucking his shirt into his trousers.

'Just showing the men a bit of unarmed combat, sir,' he said, forcing a smile. 'Right, all of you! That's enough! Back to work!'

The Colonel looked at me and then at Kipling, shook his head slowly and went into his office. A couple of minutes later he called out from behind his door. 'Keepleen!'

'Yes sir,' said Kipling, grabbing his jerkin and running into the Colonel's office.

'You've bloody had it now,' Heworth said to me.

A fortnight later I was posted to the military hospital at Colchester where the British Army prison was located.

'You'll have to bloody watch yourself there, soldier. There's no guardroom there. One step out of line and you're straight in the glasshouse. They'll sort you out all right.' It was the last piece of advice my understanding old chief ever gave me.

During the time I had been at Chester I had volunteered to go to Cyprus and to Suez when the 'crises' arose and had always asked to be considered for any overseas posting and been overlooked every time. It was the married men who wanted to stay in England that they sent, this was discipline made manifest, this is what turned opticians, chiropodists and laboratory technicians into real 'fighting men'.

The Army had bases in Hong Kong, Kuala Lumpur, Aden, Cypress, Germany, any one of which would have done me, and here I was, headed for Essex.

RAMC, Colchester

15

Sleepy Chester was to Colchester, what Scarborough was to Sodom, Great Yarmouth to Gomorrah.

Like Aldershot and unlike Chester it was a garrison town and there were soldiers everywhere, both in and out of uniform; most of the populace had some military connection and even the housewives kept their chests out and their stomachs in when they were downtown.

A month after I arrived the corporal in charge of the laboratory was demobbed and I being the longest serving technician was made up to lance-corporal. After a month to get used to the weight of the stripe and make sure I didn't go berserk with the power I was made up to full corporal and put in charge of running the laboratory and disciplining its five staff. The bacteriology I did myself.

I had now been in the Army so long that I could tell the pathologist, Captain Rose, another ex-Chester man, to 'get some in'. I did too but he didn't like it. I used to sign off with it every night when I made out my duty report. Here was a fellow from Hampstead, all of twenty-four years and with a medical degree, yet when it came down to it he was just the same as any other National Serviceman. He understood that any National Serviceman with a month's service more than himself was superior in all that really mattered and only demobilisation would eventually erase the difference, though it was never expressed in terms of how long you had been in but how long you still had to do, and no matter how the question was asked, that was how it was always answered.

A military prison in peacetime was a hard concept for me to assimilate; it seemed to me that criminals, violent or otherwise, should be dealt with by proper civilian courts. Everybody thought the Army's rules of conduct as given in Queen's Regulations, an authority never seen but forever deferred to, were derisory, and nobody could have any faith in a judicial system that was entirely punitive.

Venial offences like AWOL [absent without leave] or failing to carry out some order, were dealt with at the camp where they occurred; every camp had its regimental police and guardroom, its camp commandant who acted as judge and jury and could impose penalties ranging from suspension of privileges to CB [confined to barracks], the docking of pay and innumerable abjectly silly drills or tedious cleaning duties. But for an assault on a superior or some other such action which the Army regarded as dire, culprits would be sent to Colchester Prison, the 'Glasshouse', where the discipline was excruciating.

So unpleasant were conditions in the prison, that inmates frequently tried to commit suicide; and in hospital, apart from patients who had been badly injured by somebody else, there were those who had maimed themselves with their KFS, drank a tin of metal polish or swallowed wire wool between slices of bread, tried to hang themselves with their belts, jumped out of a window, or simply tried to bash their own brains out against a stone wall.

It seemed to me that if a man continually went absent without leave because his wife had run away from home and left their children behind and he had gone back to try and sort things out, or if he repeatedly tried to escape because he couldn't stand life in the Army, why not let him go..? What use was he to the Army..? What right had the Army to his life, especially in the case of a National Serviceman who had signed no contract with it..? He was surely nothing but a liability to the Army, and to send him to a place like Colchester was nothing if it wasn't futile. After all, a man could walk out of his job in the shipyards, factory or office, for whatever reason, and never be imprisoned for it.

Colchester had two kinds of prisoner: those who were incorrigible criminals, and those whose lives were severely disrupted or rendered impossible because they were in the Army - and that would include conscientious objectors who had committed an offence that didn't exist outside the Army, or at least the Armed Forces. I suspected conscription had always been a selective thing anyway, even more so in peacetime. I and countless other young men in the professions could easily have got deferment so that we could have done 'our bit' at a higher and more comfortable level and in many cases avoiding it altogether. But this wasn't the case for the bricklayer or carpenter serving a trade, they had no way of escaping the net.

About 2am one night I was called out to do a CSF [cerebrospinal fluid test] on a prisoner who had been brought into the hospital in a coma after apparently trying to kill himself.

When I went to the ward it was to find a nineteen-year-old lad - the same age as me - lying on a bed with the sheets stripped back, surrounded by a young MO, a nursing sister, a male charge nurse and a very young female nurse. They were convinced he was shamming because although his eyes were shut and he made no response to any questions, his eyeballs could be seen moving under their lids and he perceptibly reacted to the prick of a needle and other painful stimuli. The MO and charge nurse were insulting him when I went in, to see if they could raise him through his pride.

Cerebrospinal fluid is obtained by puncturing the spinal canal in the lumbar region with a syringe, and it isn't very pleasant even if done properly. Again and again, without giving him the benefit of any anaesthetic, the clumsy and irate MO plunged the long needle into the lad's back until the area was badly bruised.

'Come on, you bastard! We know you're just coming the game!' snarled the charge nurse.

If the patient wasn't in a deep coma, or not for some other reason insensible, he must have been desperate to put up with all this.

The charge nurse roughly pulled his hair and the young nurse began to sob.

'Get her out of here!' snapped the MO. 'Blubbering females are the last thing we need.'

The charge nurse then bent right over the patient's ear, pulled the lobe so the orifice was wide open and yelled into it, 'Get up, you lazy swine! I'll teach you to mess us about! If you think you've got yourself a smooth passage in here, you've got another think coming, matey..!

'Want me to give him the hot and cold water treatment, sir? I'm sure I can get him to say something.'

I suggested there was little chance of getting the clear sample, free from blood cells, that I would need, and we should settle for a blood sample from his arm.

'Who asked you..? Get back to your lab and await further orders.'

Coma or not, the poor blighter stuck it out until the next day; then he opened his eyes. We couldn't find anything physically wrong with him and he was discharged two days later. The day he left to go back to prison he sought out the charge nurse and told him he would never forget what was done to him the night he was brought in, and that when he was demobbed he would come back and 'get' him. The charge nurse had just laughed, threats of this sort were a constant feature of Army life and I never heard of anybody revenging themselves after they left; I think when the time came they were just too glad to get out and put as much distance between them and the Army as possible, plus the fact that they wouldn't be entirely free of the Army for at least another two years.

I couldn't affirm that cruelty was British Army policy, not even during basic training; I am sure you wouldn't have found it in Queen's Regulations if you could have got hold of a copy. But Army life certainly engendered it and nothing was done to suppress it. Heartlessness was one of the very first impressions of Army life and the *sine qua non* of its preceptors and prototypes, the corporals and lance-corporals at its training depots, and there is a point where heartlessness becomes stark cruelty.

If your own moral code wouldn't allow you to embrace or tolerate the practices of everyday Army life or if your intelligence balked at the petty observances of absurd regulations, there was absolutely nothing you could do about it. If you felt aggrieved, exasperated, frightened or appalled by the things that went on around you, there was nobody you could go to for comfort, help or counselling, let alone redress. There were no doctors, there were only medical officers; no priests, only chaplains; both were Army men - party men - before they were anything else. They might not have deemed themselves 'soldiers' in the sense of being handy with the bayonet but they both had crucial roles to play in executions for instance where they were unequivocally soldiers first and whatever else they claimed to be, way after. Although there were regiments and corps for everything else, including a veterinary corps for the dwindling horses, there was no psychotherapeutic corps, no provision for anybody with a troubled mind, a mind perhaps on the way to schizophrenia or nervous breakdown; 'shell-shock' was what they called it in wartime and the treatment was dispensed by a firing squad, and they still hadn't come up with an alternative diagnosis or more effective remedy.

A nineteen-year-old was a lad, not a man; and a seventeen-and-a half-year-old, the age of entry for a regular, was still a boy. Basic training, their introduction to their new life - and it was constantly ground into them that it was a 'life' and not a 'career' - was a brutalising experience. The incident with the CSF revealed the hospital was a military installation, ordnance, as wholly as any cannon gun or tank.

Now that I was a corporal I had duties outside the laboratory and they included responsibility for the billet I lived in. It was a brick building with small rooms that had at one time been married quarters and I had a little room with a bunk at the very top.

One morning when I was doing my round of inspection there was a new man, a fellow in his late thirties with colourless deep-set eyes that were so far apart in his square bony face, you couldn't look him in the eyes, you had to fix your gaze on one or the other. He was an 'old soldier', having seen service in Malaya, and could barely conceal his contempt for me and the other National Servicemen in the room.

I had to tell him to remove the obscene pictures he had stuck up on his locker door and he stood looking at me with cold hate, chewing the muscles in his jaw. I knew the others were waiting to see if I would back down so I snapped 'Now! Get them off or I'll pull them down myself.' I took a step towards him, sure he would either rip them to shreds or take a bite out of my face.

My heart was beating so hard I thought it might show through my jerkin but I daren't look down. He stared into my eyes for about ten seconds without once blinking and then slowly turned away, took the pictures down and handed them to me; they were of young women in bikinis with bigger than normal breasts and impudent expressions.

I shook my head. 'You can keep them. Just don't put them up.'

Looking at me with a faint smile - although it might have been an old scar - he slowly compressed the pictures into a tiny ball in his hand and I knew he was thinking what a mess he could make of my immature features if he butted his battering ram of a head into them.

'Stand at ease..! Dismiss!'

They turned to close their lockers and I came away.

'You'd better watch out for that crazy bastard,' somebody said to me later. 'You know what he did in Aden?'

'I heard.'

He had apparently been a sergeant on patrol with a young lieutenant and four other men in a jeep when it had been ambushed. The officer had stopped the jeep and ordered the men out, which was a mistake, and had then stood paralysed with fear while one by one they were killed except the one I now had in my billet. 'Get back in the jeep and let's go!' he had yelled at the officer but he had just stood there whimpering while the new man in my billet leapt into the driving seat. 'Get in! Get in!' the new man in my billet shouted at him. But the officer wouldn't or couldn't so the new man in my billet just shot him and drove off.

How he had got away with it if it was true, was beyond me, but that was the tale and one look at him and you knew he was capable of it.

The Officers Ward was the first along the corridor from the lab. It had the best beds and bedding set farther apart than in any other ward, a little light above each bed so the occupant could read or write, and an air of genteel Nineteenth-Century infirmity. It also had far and away the best-looking nursing sister but that might have been no more than coincidence.

The rest of the patients in the hospital were undifferentiated relative to their rank, sergeant-majors sharing wards with corporals and privates and being similarly allocated one small bottle of beer per day whilst their commissioned superiors tippled brandy or gin.

Even though the Army requisitioned everything and kept a running inventory of everything, a lot of trading went on and no matter where you were you always had something to barter and somebody else always had something you wanted.

One night I went into the Officers Ward to scrounge a drop of brandy and the two nursing orderlies on duty, one of them a steelworker in civilian life, the other a docker, were feeding the brigadier, an old man who had suffered a severe stroke and was paralysed. Although always in pyjamas, the brigadier was surrounded by insignia and paraphernalia appertaining to his rank and there was no way he could have been mistaken for an old corporal, not even in the bath.

When I went in they had him sitting up in his bed in a private room and were tormenting him mercilessly.

'Come on, Grandad. Slops time. Stop playing with your willy and open your gob.'

One of them slowly moved a spoon laden with food puree towards their patient's lips and then at the very last moment jerked it and half the contents went up his nose and the rest down his neck.

'Oops. Sorry, old boy!'

They both laughed.

The old man was making awful sounds that indicated to me he was not as far gone as they took him to be.

'Watch this,' the steelworker said. 'We're having to retrain him because his brain has turned to mush. Hasn't it, Willy..?' he shouted into the brigadier's ear. 'His proper name is Wilberforce but we just call him Willy. Don't we, Willy..?'

He then put the brigadier's gold-braided red hat on his own head, put a pair of underpants over the brigadier's and arranged the brigadier's arm so he was saluting him.

'They'll string the two of you up if they catch you,' I said.

'Willy doesn't mind. He likes a bit of fun. Don't you, old son?' They patted his head.

16

One of the hardest things about coming into the Army was leaving my brother Johnny behind. Although I had four brothers, the others were much younger than me. Johnny and I were born fifteen months apart not long before the war, evacuated and shunted from one place to another together, carried in and out of shelters one after the other, went everywhere together and played, fought and had the same illnesses together. Our personalities were different, our abilities, likes and dislikes different, but we totally understood each other.

When I was sixteen and working, Johnny was still only fourteen and going to school. I was then running with a different pack, bigger and harder and seeking a wholly different quarry from birds' eggs and frogspawn, and if I hadn't excluded him, at least outside of the house, I would have been excluded myself. But at home things were still the same and no matter how far I descended into the underworld between 8pm and 9.30pm, I had to ascend pretty quick before coming in the backdoor.

'Urgh! Our Joe thinks he's a big man because he's got five Woodbines in his pocket and a chatty lighter with the petrol always leaking out. Just a kid and talks about "women". Who does he think he is?'

When I came into the Army and was put in a barrack-room, a place without refuge if ever there was, with thirty-one other men, none of them remotely like any of my brothers, I realised my back wasn't protected any more; I was no longer with people who would forgive me no matter what I said or did to them and for the first time in my life I was wholly accountable. I realised that loss was the only way to evaluate some things and that it was going to be hard to find somebody I could trust absolutely, somebody who wouldn't take advantage of my weaknesses, somebody who wouldn't hesitate to give his life for me. Johnny had been modest, perversely stubborn, fearless, generous and, like a barnacle, always there.

And since then I hadn't met anybody with a brother who was that close, certainly none who had confessed it, and I never talked about mine either.

Johnny wasn't a subject for discussion, no more than my father or mother or any of my family were. I didn't want anybody twisting their face up or giving sarcastic little smiles and saying 'Huh!' or 'I know, mine's just the same', not about my family.

I hadn't been home on leave for a while because Colchester was too far for a bike with a maximum speed of 45mph, so Johnny hitched his way down to me and we had a great weekend together perpetrating a little coup that amused him and gave me no end of satisfaction. He travelled the last stage by train and I met him at the railway station in uniform.

We had discussed entering the camp through the 'back way', all camps had them, but ultimately settled for strolling in through the main gates, past MPs and RPs [regimental police], across the parade square, around the hospital and into the labyrinthine billet where I lived. It was a Saturday in summer so things were quiet, obviously this was the best time to invade the British Army. I gave him my spare uniform and he ate in the canteen, slept in the billet and we went in and out of the camp, sometimes on the bike, sometimes on foot, as we pleased, I an NCO in the Royal Army Medical Corps, he its unacknowledged guest. I had warned one or two mates who bunked in the billet that there would be a new 'postee' for a few days, but nobody else.

One of the funniest things that happened was when we went into a pub in Colchester and they wouldn't serve Johnny because they said he was too young, he was really peeved because he had been eighteen for some months and his indignation was threatening to blow everything. We were in civvies but I had my AB64 Part1 which stated the holder was a corporal in the RAMC and I gave it to him but he wouldn't deign to use it so I showed it to the barman to vouch for him on the premise that RAMC corporals never lie. But he didn't much care for that either and sat at the table glaring at the barman all night.

I doubt if he told the folks what he was going to do beyond saying he was going down to see me, because neither of them would have approved. It wasn't his idea, it was mine but there was nothing he dare not do. 'Are you sure you won't get into trouble if we get caught?' was the only question he had asked. After each successively more brazen act, the two of us would laugh like hell. We could have nearly gone up to the armoury, signed out a couple of .303s and gone rabbitting.

There was never any kind of intellectual stimulation, no discussion group, art exhibition, lecture, concert or even so much as a library provided at any of the four camps I had been at and neither Bob Hope nor anybody ever came to entertain. Nothing was done to maintain mentation above the most basal functioning level, let alone soothe the troubled breast. I am sure the British Army considered morale unnecessary during peacetime and intellect a burden at any time.

Rose held a discussion group in his office on a Friday night to which nobody in the laboratory was ever invited. Rank was unimportant and so was membership of the RAMC, several of his guests illegally came from outside both the hospital and the RAMC. However, they did have one thing in common - they were all Jews, where none of the laboratory staff were, though the word was never mentioned all of the time I was there. They would meet in Rose's office which was attached to the main lab, and whoever was on duty that night would hear them, they seemed like intense philosophical discussions and some of us would have gladly joined in had we been invited.

Rose and I had an odd relationship. He had an awful inferiority complex which sometimes came out as self-deprecating humour and you couldn't help but warm to him for it; at other times he was defensive, sarcastic and aloof. I think we both liked each other but circumstances made it impossible for us to be other than on opposite sides of several different fences.

He once arranged, like a great conspiracy, for histology to be carried out during the night on what the rest of us in the lab deduced to be an important relative of the hospital commandant. The patient had a cancerous growth on his testicle and the aim of the surgical team was to eradicate all malignant tissue at the one operation and not a morsel more. To do this they would need to have samples of the tissue examined in the histology laboratory to detect where the malignant tissue ended and healthy tissue began.

In order for biological tissue to be analysed in this way it has to be stiffened without distortion so that very thin slices can be cut, stained with various dyes and examined under the microscope. The usual way to do this - and the only way we ever did histology before or after this case - was to immerse a piece of the tissue in formalin to arrest natural deterioration and then impregnate it with wax by a series of graduated steps using various concentrations of different solvents, the whole process usually taking half a week.

This particular operation took place at a weekend and Tom Caudwell, the histologist, and Captain Rose and myself, were on duty well into the night. We used a new histological technique of stiffening the tissue by spraying it with compressed carbon dioxide to freeze it, thus avoiding the laborious time-taking wax procedure, while the patient was still under anaesthetic in the operating theatre. Rose would rush into the laboratory with a further, 'deeper' slice, Tom would prepare it for microscopy, Rose would examine it and then rush back to theatre. Half a dozen times this happened and while it was going on it was my job to attend to any other lab emergencies. We were all exhausted by the time it was finished mainly because of the stress and anxiety injected by Rose.

Throughout he had been as excited as a little boy keeping toot while his bigger companions were up a tree pinching the crop, and he was almost obsequious in his gratitude, especially to Tom. I could imagine the pride with which he would have finally announced to the theatre staff that he/they had come to the end of the malignant cells and the enemy was at last vanquished.

'Whew!' he would have exclaimed, mopping his brow and hoping for a round of applause.

There were two people I met at Colchester who broadened my mind. One of them was a heavy-drinking middle-aged corporal without a tooth in his head, who had a gramophone on which he played nothing but grand opera. I used to visit a friend in the Dental Corps who was teaching me judo and was quartered in the same barrack-room as the corporal and I would be on my back, hanging over a bed, with a thirteen-stone man who made dentures strangling me as I tried to dislocate his shoulder, whilst a chorus of Italian singers would be praising the Lord in the most glorious fashion.

I never spoke to the corporal because he was an ignorant bugger who never spoke to anybody unless he had to, but after a few months of his music I brought away something I never thought I would have brought away from the Army and that was a love of the human voice as a wonderful musical instrument.

The second was a private of about thirty who had done his National Service, entered university to study biochemistry, been thrown out for some mysterious reason, enlisted in the Army which he said he abhorred, and one day appeared in my billet. He was well-spoken, knowledgeable about literature and theatre and modelled himself on the hero of John Osborne's play, 'Look Back in Anger', which was currently a big hit.

Most of all he was passionate about politics and professed to be a Communist, though I'm sure he never professed it to the Army. He talked about Engels and Marx, Lenin and Trotsky, Joseph McCarthy and 'unAmerican activities', about movie heroes like John Wayne and Robert Taylor and the Black List they helped to support, and most of all about his hero, Paul Robeson and the sacrifices he made. He introduced me to the *Spectator* and *New Statesman* and made me think about politics the way Denholm Cranshawe had made me think about religion.

The more he talked, the less anybody could understand why he, who so derided the Army in every way, who fulminated against its ex-public-school General Staff whom he regarded as criminally incompetent misanthropists, should voluntarily come back in and still wear his uniform like a sprog.

'I guess I'm just a plain old-fashioned masochist,' he would say with a twisted smile.

He was certainly a plain old-fashioned cynic, and I think, in his own way, a snob.

'Forgive my ignorance,' he would lead off and automatically it would give him the advantage, and 'However, you must pay no heed to an ignorant peasant like myself,' would allow him to nicely sew things up.

At night when the rest of us were indulging less intellectual appetites, he would disappear, nobody knew where, presumably to renew himself. Then at morning tea-break when we were all gathered in the patients' waiting room to eat the Crunchies and flaky pastry sausage rolls that would sustain us until tea-time so we wouldn't have to resort to lunch in the canteen, he would sit with a frown on his face, waiting to dispense a devastating apophthegm that would totally demolish affection or respect for some public figure, living or dead. He was an iconoclast like Tod, though more subtle, and I was indebted to them both.

One night my motor-bike was stolen. The Colchester police eventually located it and found the thieves and several weeks later Tom Cauldwell and I had to go to the magistrates court in Colchester town to give evidence.

When we came out there were two MPs waiting for us, one a corporal, the other a lance-corporal, and right there in the middle of town they started berating us on the assumption we had committed some crime. After quite a commotion and the gathering of a small crowd probably hoping to see truncheons in action, I produced my AB64 Part 1 to show I had more service than the full corporal and was therefore senior to him and was delighted to see it mattered. However they then started into Tom, a private with less service than either of them.

'You, Private,' the lance-corporal said in tones too low for the crowd to hear, as both their peaks thrust into Tom's face like vultures beaks, 'you are like a disgusting heap of shit! You are a disgrace to your Queen and country! The RAMC must be taking in anything these days. I bet you don't even wipe your arse properly... Do you believe he wipes his arse properly, Corporal?'

'That I do not, Corporal,' snarled the full corporal. 'I think what we have here is strictly a non-arse wiper of the worst kind. A category-one, non-arse-wiper. I am prepared to bet this man has crabs living in the cracks around his dirty arse... Now, you listen to me, Private! You get out of here this minute! On the double! Get back to your hospital and get that dirty arse of yours wiped!'

'As for you, Corporal,' he said to me, 'if the court is finished with you, you had better get yourself back to your depot. Because if I see you in town five minutes from now I am going to arrest you for loitering.'

It would have been no more than a month at the most when I was working at the bench in Bacteriology and Tom came to me in a state of high excitement, tears of what could only be described as joy, in his eyes.

'You're not going to believe this! You're not going to fucking believe it!!' He was laughing hysterically. 'Guess who's in the waiting room?'

'No idea.'

'Who in the whole world would you most like to see in the waiting room...waiting to have his balls scraped..? Come on, man..! Who!' He was shaking my shoulders and trembling.

'I don't know. Who the hell is it?'

'Corporal Lynch..! Corporal fucking Lynch, MP..! And I'm not talking about a Member of fucking Parliament! I'm talking about those two bastards who gave us a hard time the day we went to court about your bike!'

'What..! I don't believe it..! Not..?'

'The very same!'

'Where is he?'

'He's out there waiting for you to heat up your scalpel and cut his fucking dick off!' He was almost shrieking.

'Hush, man..! Do you think he recognised you?'

'I don't think so.'

'You didn't burst out laughing?'

'Course not..! Do you think I'm a fuckin' idiot?' He then dissolved into laughter.

'Come on.'

'Not me! I'm not fucking coming..! Just make sure you give it to him good and proper... Make him crawl out of here on his hands and fucking knees!'

'Look, you're my assistant. I'm teaching you mycology. We're both going in.'

He was shaking with fear and delight but followed me in.

It was the MP corporal all right, and as soon as he saw the two of us he visibly wilted.

'Put that cigarette out at once!' I ordered. 'Don't you realise there're inflammable substances in here!'

It was already on the floor and he was stamping on it. 'I was a bit...on edge,' he said.

Just for a moment my heart went out to him but then it then came straight back.

'Where's your request form?'

He handed me a piece of paper which had been folded many times. It was a request for a skin scraping to identify a fungal lesion on his scrotum. I read it and without looking up said 'Drop your trousers.'

'Beg your pardon?'

'Drop your trousers...and your underpants, if you have any on. And don't sit down on anything. I'll be back in a few minutes.'

I strode out followed by Tom who was nearly choking.

'If you laugh, Tom...just one silly little giggle even...he could put a complaint in and we'd be in clag so deep we'd never get out. Me being busted would be the least of it.'

'Please don't make me go back in there.'

'Just think of something sad...think of somebody you once loved who has died.'

When I had loaded a tray with instruments and specimen bottles, we went back.

He was standing, trousers neatly folded over the chair, buckled belt in a perfect circle around his red cap, on top

'No need to take your cap off. Put it back on. I need to put the tray there. Put the rest of your things on the floor.'

As he put his cap on, its vertical peak pointing down to his diminutive genitals, his pathetic scrotum hanging so forlornly, his hairy legs disappearing into his highly bulled boots, I heard a spluttering sound from behind me as Tom rushed out.

I then lit the small spirit burner, turning the flame up as high as it would go, and proceeded to carefully select scalpel, needle, and forceps. With all the goodwill in the world, it would have been impossible to remove a decent-sized sample of skin from his scrotum without drawing a few specks of blood, nobody could.

'Will this affect my you know-what?' he yelped.

'Hmmph,' I answered.

I had scarified part of his left testicle and his rough khaki trousers would play havoc with it for days and I had discharged my duty to medicine and to Tom, there was no need to make the poor bugger commit suicide. Anyway, I was sure he had died in here several times already.

'Don't ever go into town unless you really have to,' I told Tom afterwards.

Whenever I was called in front of the camp commandant it was invariably due to some supposedly insubordinate remark I had made to Rose on one of his ultra-sensitive days, or because I had been discovered with 'civilian personnel' - a girl from town - in the duty bunk. My sentence would be something like a mind-numbing three-day fire-fighting course without any fire, or a week in the cookhouse - somewhere from whence I could be quickly recalled if a laboratory emergency arose. One day I offended Rose's pride and he never forgave me, even though it should have been the other way around.

Whenever a nice QARANC was posted to the hospital I would always introduce myself but this didn't mean I seduced her, a fact Rose considered beyond credibility. He liked to boast to his fellow officers that his corporal had carnal knowledge of every woman in the camp, and if it pleased him to think so, it was no great inconvenience to me.

A quite beautiful nursing sister had come to take charge of the Officers Ward and like all female SRNs [State Registered Nurses] she was an officer (male SRNs were given the rank of sergeant). She was tall with golden hair and had real 'class'. Of all the dress uniforms I had seen in the Army, that of the QARANC officer was without equal with its Dutch-nun high starched head-dress that swept over the shoulder to the gorgeous scarlet coat beneath. At twenty-seven years of age Vivien was everything a youth of nineteen could desire and I was deeply in love with her, though Rose wouldn't have called it that and I never told anybody but her.

Although we were discreet, Rose, who made it his business to learn any gossip around the camp, found out and one night when I had made up one of my methylated-spirits-absolute-alcohol-orange-juice-and-tinned-pears punch for one of his officers' parties in the laboratory, he and a couple of his tipsy companions came to ask me what she was like.

'What do you mean?' I said.

'Come on, Corporal Robinson..! Don't be a spoilsport! You know what I mean. We're all men here.'

'Is she really blond, or what, heh-heh-heh?' asked Captain Forbes, one of the surgeons.

'You're the doctors. If anybody could invent an excuse to find out, you could.'

'Leave him to me,' Rose assured them. 'You lot go on and see what old Tuttle's doing over there... He'll tell me all right.'

'Now, then,' he said, putting his arm around my shoulders. 'Help yourself to another drink. I only said for you not to get drunk...not that you had to be a total abstainer.'

'No, thanks. I've had enough. I've been drinking the stuff all day.'

'Come on, now. You can tell your commanding officer... What does the Lieutenant look like without any knickers on?'

'What does your wife look like without any on?'

'Why, you insolent..!!'

'I don't see why your wife's dignity should be any more precious than Vivien's.'

Just a little thing like that did it. He pointed a podgy finger at me and nodded. 'You've a chip on your shoulder, my lad. You should do something about it.'

A couple of weeks later, the only British Army officer I ever loved was posted to Kuala Lumpur and I never saw her again. The rule, as everybody knew, was 'No fraternisation between ranks'.

One afternoon in the summer a few months before my two years National Service in the Royal Army Medical Corps was due to come to an end, I was ordered to pack my kit and given a travel warrant to Bagshot in Surrey. I only learned why I was going because the corporal from the dental lab was on the same train and told me we were going on a week's Catholic retreat, though he didn't know whether it was intended to be a punishment or not.

It was about a three-mile walk from the station to a beautiful old mansion owned by the Duke of Cornwall, which had been converted into a seminary, and we were met by a silver-haired rubicund Irish priest, the only army chaplain I had ever met who looked more like a priest than a British Army officer.

We were invited to join our fellow guests in a huge drawing room with magnificent furniture and carpets, fine paintings, stone sculptures, and bronze, silver and porcelain ornaments. It was quite disorientating being in a place like this with so many soldiers in uniform taking tea and biscuits from tiny china cups and saucers with their little fingers sticking out; there were men from regiments and corps all over Britain, all of them NCOs; presumably Catholic officers retreated to a castle with a bishop.

'Father Foley', as he asked us to call him, explained that we were here to spiritually renovate ourselves and get in touch with God and he would help us via talks, religious services, prayer and confession whenever we needed it. The whole thing seemed like a good idea, God had maintained a fairly low profile for most of us for quite a while.

I was glad about the title. 'Bless me, Lieutenant Colonel, for I have sinned. It is six weeks since my last confession...' would have jangled a bit; I was sure I wasn't the only Catholic National Serviceman who would never normally confess to a regular army chaplain.

The food was excellent and served in a refectory, and the accommodation which was in individual oak-panelled rooms, was absurdly wonderful. For the first couple of days I was expecting at any time to be ordered to pack my kit and move out, because of a major billeting cock-up, into slightly-modified stables or gun-dog kennels. Outside, where we were allowed to wander at leisure, there were huge and beautiful gardens, woods, and fish ponds.

By no stretch of the imagination could this be considered to be an army camp of any sort. Perhaps it was used as a retreat for civilians also but I didn't think so; 'Father' Lieutenant Colonel Foley seemed altogether too much the man at home, too much the Lord of the Manor. I didn't know about Sandhurst but no army accommodation I had ever been in was situated in an area that wasn't pastorally bleak - flat, treeless and arid, as though nuclearly bulldozed only a century or two ago. This place was like Eden.

It was extraordinary to think that one human being could own all this - wonderfully fertile land for farther than the eye could see, magnificent buildings with lavish furniture and priceless art, fresh water and incredible gardens - and that he almost certainly owned more than this, sufficient for him to let this place and live somewhere else, somewhere even better perhaps.

I had grown up with a few square feet of practically uncultivable earth adjoining our residence on a council estate. Within a couple of miles there was a working-class park, the kind of place that grew tough plants like hawthorn, rhododendron and scutch grass, and had a body of water that was regularly limed to control the newts and tadpoles - ostensibly to prevent children with a bit of their mother's old nylons wired to the end of a stick, from falling into fourteen inches of water, and thus fortuitously allowing the sportsmen with radio-controlled toy motor-boats to take over; that's what happened at Paddy Freeman's.

But anybody who grew up in a place like this wouldn't have bothered either with tadpoles or toy boats, half the time they wouldn't have been here, they'd have been somewhere else, like the Duke was now.

There were no parades and no drill, at least nothing military. We had lectures on Catholic doctrine, theology and philosophy but weren't obliged to attend them all, only the religious services were sort of compulsory. Officially we were 'confined to camp', but this was in the form of a personal undertaking and merely morally binding, not something enforced by any regimental or religious police. Most of us made the long trek into town at least once but it was no Hamburg or Amsterdam and certainly not worth losing a recently acquired plenary indulgence for. A few of us went for a midnight swim in one of the ponds a couple of times and because nobody had any bathing trunks we swam naked, it was cold but spiritually cleansing I thought.

A week was just long enough. It was peaceful, it was idyllic, it was like living in a different world and in a different age. Another week however and I think we would have begun to see a few bald patches where hair was starting to be torn out, and the sound of teeth grinding could have become irritating.

It would have been nicer if the Army had invited us to Bagshot rather than putting us on a kind of religious detail but at least we weren't forced marched here and had to be grateful for that. Nothing anywhere since I had joined the Army twenty-one months previously had prepared me for the shock of being treated decently, let alone as a guest the way I had been throughout that whole week at Bagshot and I could not help but look at it with just a scintilla of cynicism. Was it perhaps a kind of 'softening up' or brainwashing experiment to prepare us for the choice we would be given on Discharge Day: whether to disappear in a puff of smoke back to civvy street, or become a permanent member of Her Majesty's Armed Forces..? Or was it an incalculably more expensive alternative to putting a few grains of barium in the tea?

It could have been that the old duke had made a bequest in favour of a specified number of NCOs from the British Army spending a specified number of days 'in retreat' on his estate, a kind of penance for him perhaps. But why just NCOs..? Why not privates, gunners, sappers and the rest of the cannon fodder?

The day I handed in all my kit and was given my last travel warrant, I was called in to see the Orderly Officer, a captain who had made the Army his career and worked his way up through the ranks, the only kind of officer I ever encountered that I liked.

He hardly raised his weary face to look at me when I marched into his office, turned sharply to the right and slammed my boots down hard on his wooden floorboards. To my left was the Regimental Sergeant-major who had heralded my entry with asinine bawling and was now watching to make sure I didn't move, say or do anything I wasn't supposed to do.

The officer went through the ritual of asking me if I would like to stay on and avail of the opportunities the British Army had to offer and I said 'No. Thank you, sir.'

'You realise you still have a duty to the Army and that you have the option of joining the Territorial Army or the Reserves?'

'Yes, sir.'

'Which is it to be?'

'The Territorial Army, sir.'

'Right. Sign here.'

He pushed a form towards me.

I looked at the document, rapidly scanning it to make sure it wasn't a trick and I wasn't going to be signing anything that might have increased my association with the British Army by as much as a single moment. I signed it carefully and handed it back, only he being allowed to push anything across a table. He didn't shake my hand or wish me the best of luck or anything, he just shoved me my discharge papers which included a few words to the effect that I wasn't a liability to the Army.

The RSM then barked 'Atte-nnn-shun!' By the right! Quick-march!'

I never even considered signing on. I had picked the Territorial option because although it was for three years, it required no more than presenting myself at the barracks behind Leazes Park in Newcastle and declaring I was available for call-up should the British Government decide to try to bully anybody else.

I had made up my mind that when I changed into civvies and left Colchester, having given two years of my life to my country without seeing any benefits and without receiving any thanks, I would never in my life address another human being as 'sir'.

I was glad I had done two years in the Army but would never recommend it to Johnny or any of my brothers. It had little regard for justice and none at all for compassion. It was led by people with the right accents and connections, rather than with ability and character. And in my opinion, it brought out the worst, not the best, in everybody.

VIC, Longbenton

17

Getting out of the British Army is an exquisite experience. In it, aware of the restrictions that affect every part of one's life, it is easy to believe that civvy street offers unrestricted access to every kind of opportunity and delight. I had of course followed time-honoured tradition and got so drunk on my penultimate night that I had to be carried back to camp, spewing and farting all the way, but was stone-cold sober on the last one.

I was going home three inches taller, two stones heavier and physically much stronger than when I left two years earlier; ever since the PT course at Salisbury I had done weightlifting and judo and had been NCO i/c Swimming Baths at Colchester.

I had been a student member of the IMLT before I went into the Army and knew it was a body recognised worldwide but which acknowledged no other; I had an army qualification in medical laboratory technology impressively titled, 'Lab III', which we had been told would be recognised in civvy street but knew of course that it wouldn't. I had worked in two hospital laboratories, albeit military ones, and much preferred medical work to veterinary; it was more exciting, there were infinitely greater career prospects and I had decided I wanted to become a medical microbiologist. The veterinary experience should be of some value and in any case I had to go back to my employers for at least six months in return for their holding my job during my two years in the Army.

So I decided to go back to the VIC, study for the IMLT diploma in bacteriology and then leave; I wanted a good career and I wanted to see something of the world and I wouldn't get either with the Ministry of Agriculture, Fisheries and Food - as it had now become.

When I got home to Newcastle there was no fanfare or anything. My father and Johnny were out at work and the others were at school except for the youngest, Anthony, who was still a toddler. Only my mother was in and she was ill in bed and that's why it took her so long to come to the door.

I assumed she was suffering from some kind of 'woman's complaint' since neither she nor my father subsequently advanced any information beyond the fact that she was going to have to go into hospital for a minor operation. There was no way I would be taken into anybody's confidence, two years in the RAMC notwithstanding; I could have got myself qualified in obstetrics and gynaecology and it wouldn't have made the slightest difference, a motion of no-confidence was permanently in effect where I was concerned. As a consequence of my mother's hospitalisation, a state of exiguity was tacitly declared in the house, which meant minimal meals, minimal laundry, minimal comfort and minimal goodwill all around.

I had saved my twelve days annual leave before recommencing work at the VIC for a period of rehabilitation but spent it doing what my mother would have been doing had she not been poorly: looking after five males aged between three and forty-six, with no taste, yet parky as hell.

Nothing I did was right, especially not the cooking. 'This isn't the Army!' they grumbled. 'It might do you but it's not what we're used to.'

By the end of the week when all the tired and irritable people came home from overworked office or victimising classroom, they were fed up with fried egg, beans and chips. By now I heartily wished I'd gone straight back to work and let an aunt or grandmother come and look after them, as originally mooted.

One day for a treat I suggested to Dad that I make a bilberry tart because I hadn't given them any dessert so far. Bilberries were out of season and fairly expensive but bilberry tart had always been held in high esteem in our household.

'Are you sure you can make one..? You won't mess up your mother's oven for her coming back..? Any mess and you clean it up yourself, mind.'

Ever since I was a child I had seen my mother rolling pastry, sprinkling sugar over chopped apple slices and luscious purple bilberries, seen her flop the top on and make the indentations along the rim with a blunt knife, put three slits in the domed centre and anoint the top with milk via a pastry brush; then in the oven it went. A couple of hours later, shazam! -

perfect bilberry tart - the smell indescribable, the crystalline surface an exquisite shade of brown, and oozing through the three central slits a sticky mouth-watering deep purple juice.

There was nothing to it, just a combination of memory and common sense, and I set to.

I don't know precisely what went wrong: whether the oven had been in need of an overhaul, the gas supply erratic, the milk slightly sour, the pastry too thick or too thin, or even whether they were the right kind of bilberries. By the time my father came in it could be smelt in the yard and probably out in the back lane but he didn't say a word.

After the beans and chips plates had been cleared away I produced the tart, having carved most of the carbon from the sides, and laid it on the table, right in the middle.

'Ugh! Ugh!!'

When the pie was opened, no birds began to sing. The bilberries had been transmuted into little black stones, the juice into a super-glue that would never come off the plate, and, inexplicably, although the pastry was soft and doughy in some parts, it was burnt to a frazzle in others.

All four of my brothers thought the tart a great joke but refused to eat any of it. Dad was furious. He tried a bit but couldn't swallow it.

'I told you, you couldn't do it! But no... Smart Alec wouldn't listen... Well, you made it, you wasted the money, and you can damn well eat it! Every bit of it. And I want it eaten before you leave the table.' With that he went out, followed by everybody else - one big ingrate and four little ones.

I set about the task with determination, if not much enthusiasm. Five minutes later Johnny came back and sat down. 'Here, I'll give you a hand,' he said.

I could hardly believe my luck and cut the tart in two so quickly I almost broke the plate.

'Pity you made such a big'un.'

We laughed and got started.

'Christ, though,' I said, 'even in the Army they didn't ram food down your bloody throat.'

'Don't blaspheme here..! And don't say anything about Dad either.' He had stopped with his first helping a good inch in front of his mouth. 'I'll help you eat it but I'm not sitting listening to any criticism of anybody in this house.'

Nothing had changed. I'd been away for two years and the whole family expected me to slip back into my place and resume life as though the two years had never happened. It was easy for them, the Army had only happened to me. At least there it had been 'them and us', and you could talk as bolshy as you liked with your mates. Here it was 'them and me' and nobody would brook any criticism of the house or anybody in it, especially not of Dad or Mam.

I was twenty-and-a-half years old now but would still have to wait another six months before being given a key to the front door, so like Cinderella I always had to be back before midnight. It was difficult to go out with a girl, take her home and get back before the Westminster clock on the mantelpiece in the living room began to chime; it meant leaving the cinema before the end of the big picture, leaving a party just when things were getting going, and only having girlfriends who lived nearby or on a regular bus route - the Ambassador had long since become too slow for me and I'd sold it.

I must have been the only ex-soldier in Newcastle operating under a curfew in peacetime.

Whenever my mother heard me tapping gently on the front door - and I do mean tapping, I certainly don't mean anything remotely as crass as casting a handful of gravel at my father and mother's bedroom window - she would always come tiptoeing down in the dark and unlock it; but only if my father was asleep.

One night I came back at five minutes past midnight to find the door locked. It was a cold night, I only had a thin snazzy jumper on and I'd nearly bust a gut trying to meet the deadline. I instantly set about sending a Morse-code message to my mother, she was a light sleeper and in any case wouldn't go to sleep until she knew I was safely back indoors. But The Warden must have been awake because she never came down. I could imagine her begging and pleading with him, then turning away on her side, softly weeping and trying not to think of me shivering outside in the street having sought and been denied the sanctuary of my own home. After about twenty minutes I reckoned he must have taken the old bristle hairbrush from the dresser, the one that felt as though it had been designed for grooming wire-haired fox-terriers, and put it in the small of his back to fight off encroaching sleep.

I had no cigarettes left and only a half-crown so I approached the only figure in sight with a view to exchanging it for a florin to use in the machine outside the sweet shop across the road. I had already slept at Tod's twice the last week, lying on the floor of his room without so much as a blanket and his socks putrefying in the dark, so I wasn't going there.

Just as I was about to address him, he broke into a run and absolutely fled up Chillingham Road as though there was a harpie after him.

Quarter of an hour later I was still looking for somebody when a police car drew up, two constables jumped out, grabbed hold of me and bundled me into the car; a vicar doing his constitutional had reported me for 'attacking' him.

I explained what had happened and they seemed to believe me because they let me out, but they wanted to know where I lived and why I wasn't there now so I had to tell them I was locked out.

'What number Simonside is it..? We'll knock them up.'

'I haven't locked myself out. I've been locked out deliberately.'

'Why..? Who by?'

'Look, I'm not long out of the Army and my father hasn't got used to the idea of me coming in late some nights... Don't worry, it'll be okay. I'll go back tomorrow for breakfast. If you went and brayed on the door, what with all the neighbours and everything, he'd never forgive me.'

'What d'ye think, Bill?'

'He's probly tellin' the truth. Let's giv'm the benefit o' the doubt.'

'Right... But don't make a nuisance o' yoursel', mind. Anybody else reports ye and ye'll be spendin' the night in the cells at Pilgrim Street.'

'Right. Thanks... Oh, before you go. You don't happen to have a two-bob bit and a tanner, do you?'

'Wait a bit... Here y'are.'

I gave him the half-crown and he gave me the change and they drove off.

The cigarette-machine was out of order and I lost the two shillings.

Time passed very slowly during the night on Chillingham Road in winter and I wandered backwards and forwards looking in all the shop windows and reading the pathetic advertisements by people trying to make a few bob.

I was looking at the boards advertising forthcoming attractions outside the Scala Cinema (pronounced 'Skaler'), Heaton's famous fleapit cinema with its hard Venus-fly-trap seats and all-pervading smell of working-class humanity, when I saw a luminously white figure emerge from the lane behind, cross the road and disappear through a doorway. It appeared too stocky to belong to the spirit world and I hadn't anything else to do so I stealthily approached the doorway which was open and led to a steep stairway, at the bottom of which was a closed door with a light coming from between the cracks. No sooner had I stepped inside the doorway than the figure grabbed hold of me.

'Wha' d'ye think you're doin?'
'What..? It's flour..!'
'Wha' did ye think it was?'
'I thought you were a ghost.'
'Where are ye from?'
'Simonside Terrace.'
'Why aren't ye in bed this time o' night?'
'I've been locked out.'
'Who by?'
'My father.'

'Did he now..? Well, maybe ye'd better come in. We can always make room for one of the world's outlaws... Hey, Tony!' he shouted down the stairs. 'We've got a visitor...a lad that's been locked out of his house by his old man!'

'Fetch him down and gis a look at him!'

I was pushed down the stairs and through the lower door to find myself in an all-night bakery in the company of two of the bawdiest individuals I ever met. On a huge central table was rolled out what must have been several hundredweight of dough.

'Here, have somethin' to eat to warm ye up. Then ye can kip down on that' said the one who had brought me, nodding towards the dough table and handing me a red hot bun which I straightaway dropped. They laughed, it was obviously one of their party tricks. They then each grabbed a bun straight out of the oven, crushed it in the palm of their hand and looked at me, smiling, and I gave a low whistle of admiration. They grinned and did it again and again until there was a small pile of broken buns steaming on the floor.

They guffawed after everything they said and after I'd eaten they bade me lie down on the table and guffawed again.

'Are you serious?' I asked. 'What about..?'

'Divven't ye worry yoursel' about that. Two married women have laid down on it tonight already. A healthy young feller like you won't make much difference.'

'That's what puts the spice into it. You know when you see the sign, "Watson's Wholesome Wonderbread"..? Well, that's what the "wholesome" bit means. Aaah, ha-ha-ha! Oaah, he-he-he!'

There was a shout from upstairs.

'That'll be Nobby the bobby come for his daily ration. You'd better hide in there,' one of them said, shoving me into a warming cupboard and closing the door.

By the time they'd got rid of him, his arms full of stuff, I was just about passing out with the heat and overpowering smell of yeast, and when they opened the door I practically fell out.

The next morning after a very warm but restless night - I had lain on the table but couldn't go to sleep with those two around - I set off for home laden with freshly baked loaves, bread buns, doughnuts and even a chocolate birthday cake. Although my arms were full as I mounted the stairs into the cold morning air, they had kept piling more and more on to me.

As I approached Simonside Terrace I passed my father standing at the bus stop in his off-white mackintosh with his brown trilby and black attaché case. When he saw me, he never made any sign of acknowledgement, his mouth simply opening slightly and then closing tight. If the Queen Mary had come by on wheels I doubt if he'd have been more surprised; I of course just smiled, hands too full to wave.

My mother was so relieved when she came to the door and absolutely delighted when she saw I was bearing such munificent gifts. She readily accepted my explanation as to how I had come by them but had to be persuaded it wouldn't be bad luck or anything to eat a birthday cake even though with seven of us in the household, there wasn't a birthday in sight. However, when my father came home that night he wouldn't touch a morsel of what he described as 'contraband', though my brothers had had no such inhibitions at all, being already stuffed with it.

    He was like that, for him there was no virtue in certain kinds of opportunity.

18

I had called into the VIC on my first Army leave, mainly I suppose so they could see how much I had changed in just a couple of months, how the willing boy in his threadbare lab coat with jars of sheep faeces in his pockets had been left far behind and a soldier had come back. I hadn't marched down the corridor, arms swinging or anything but I had kept my beret on until they had all seen how tightly it fit the contours of my head and covered my right ear. Flossie the typist had even warbled 'Are you in the paratroopers, Joe?' and I had replied 'Not yet. I have to get basic training out of the way first.' I'd had my boots and gaiters on as well so they would all have known I'd very shortly be in their lab or office and as I'd clomped down the corridor, the word would have been out: 'It's Joe! He's back! You won't believe it when you see him!'

They had all seemed pleased to see me, though needless to say I had more time for Steve than anybody else, he and I having been the only two in the place to have served in the Armed Forces. But I did spend a respectable quarter of an hour with Mr Bailey, he had a right to know so he could start preparing for the changes that would be necessary to accommodate me when I returned in less than two years' time.

Most of the non-senior staff had come to the door to see me off and I wouldn't say I was showing off exactly but I did carefully replace the beret, which at half-time during the visit had been tucked under my epaulettes to show them what a soldier off duty looked like, and I did stamp my boots hard on the concrete step to make the gaiters hang perfectly over the tops of my boots. Then there was the long walk up to Whitley Road which I made much of, never once looking back as I imagined them waving, tears in the eyes of the women, until I had passed out of sight and they had all sighed and gone back inside to their work.

I had called about six months after that, the time I bought the Ambassador from Mr Standish, but it had been a Saturday afternoon and there had been nobody else about.

A few days after I came out of the Army I had telephoned Mr Bailey to let him know I would be starting back at work soon but he hadn't been in so I had just left a message, I expected he would have been informed by the Ministry of Defence anyway. I had been home for less than a fortnight when I turned up on a Monday morning; Mam was out of hospital and all right and I had vowed never again to look after that ungrateful lot, it had been two weeks holiday utterly wasted, a selfless gesture that had netted me only scathing criticism from start to finish.

The VIC had a different quieter and less bustling air about it, largely I surmised because Standish had now gone to Weybridge, the only place big enough to accommodate his ambitiousness. He had been replaced by two AVIOs (Assistant Veterinary Investigation Officers), a burly Scotsman in his mid-forties called McCulloch, and a bespectacled tall skinny corduroy-suited fellow from Cornwall, called Norris. There was also a new cleaner, Lily, who was Albert's wife and worked mornings, and a lab attendant called Sidney who had been discharged from the Army after thirty years because of a heart condition.

Oliver asked me to go back into Parasitology to do the work he and Lawrence had been sharing the past two years because Lawrence wanted to work in Bacteriology.

The Nematodirus research work I had done with Standish hadn't been acknowledged in the scientific paper he had published in the veterinary journal, Lawrence's name was on instead, and because he had been confident about passing his final examination, he had put the initials 'A.I.M.L.T.' after his name. The paper had gone to press by the time it was learned that although Steve had passed, Lawrence had failed and Steve showed me a batch of papers in which he had neatly drawn a line through the erroneous initials.

'I thought you'd appreciate it seeing how he got the credit for all the work you did.'

When I came back from lunch on my first afternoon Mr Norris was waiting to ask me to help him with a ram he was going to dispatch. Anybody else would have killed the ram with a blow on the head and then cut its throat but not Norris, he wanted me to hold it while he used the humane killer on it. It was a .22 pistol with a three-inch retractable bolt that was fired through the skull and he was handling it as though it were a Colt .45; he didn't see me but when I went into his office he was pretending to draw it from an imaginary holster strapped to his thigh.

We went outside and I caught up the ram, put my legs over its back, grabbed its horns and pulled its head between my knees. But a ram will only stay still for so long before it starts struggling to get free and that time had passed and Norris was still messing about with the gun, plainly terrified of it. I offered to do it for him.

'No, no. I want to do it properly. You just hold its head.'

'Okay,' I said, 'but don't fire till I tell you. Use both hands and wait till I've got a good hold... I'll tell you when.'

The ram was withdrawing its head between my legs and Norris was following it with the gun at arm's length, the muzzle slipping off all over the place, and his free hand covering his eyes.

I was trying to yank the ram's head well clear of my private parts and had my head down almost parallel with the ram's, when he fired. I felt the vibration as the bolt just missed my hand and was deafened and for a few moments blinded.

'You bloody fool!' I shouted. 'I told you to wait until I was ready!'

It was a good five minutes after bathing my eyes under the tap before I could see sufficiently to find my way out of the PM house and down to Norris's office.

I knocked on his door but he had locked it and wouldn't come out.

'Come out!' I yelled. 'I want to talk to you!'

'It was an accident... You moved... I'm sure you said "Fire"... You said something very like it... You're not hurt, are you?'

I don't know whether he was more afraid of what he'd done to me or what I might do to him. In the finish he rang through to Mr Bailey to ask him to come and talk to me and calm me down.

The MAFF Veterinary Investigation Service existed for the sake of farmers, it would examine specimens from domestic pets but only as a favour to a vet in general practice and it was a favour rarely asked. It carried out research on diseases that commonly afflicted sheep, pigs, cattle and poultry, the four genera that constituted the livestock industry in Britain, it did specific laboratory investigations at the request of vets, on behalf of the farmers, and it gave farmers advice on husbandry - something they never asked for and largely resented.

The main investigations carried out by our laboratory - which served the whole of Northumbria - were post-mortems on sheep, lambs, calves, pigs and hens and bacteriology on their organs, examinations for parasitic worm eggs in the faeces of farm and domestic animals, the examination of cow faeces for Johne's disease, and the testing of milk for TB. We also did research into deficiency diseases like swayback in sheep but blood samples were sent to the central laboratory at Weybridge. Everything that came in had to be fresh because there were no refrigeration facilities and in the case of post-mortems, that usually meant still alive.

Farmers paid nothing for the service, indeed they behaved as though they were the benevolent ones giving work to a whole lot of civil servants who had no idea what it was like to have to go out and work for a living; they regarded Ministry staff as a bunch of interfering, overpaid, over-holidayed backroom boys who didn't know their arse from their elbow; short shrift we got from these fellows who would sometimes come in just as we were leaving to go home, dump on a polished mahogany bench used only for paperwork, the leaking carcass of a pig that had been dead for three days, was turning green and had been half eaten by crows, and say 'There you go... Something to keep you happy' or 'Here's sommat'll keep ye's off ya behinds.'

Those that had been in the Armed Forces were invariably a superior type who didn't like to be referred to as farmers and retained the rank they had been given as though it were an acceptable title in civilian life, hence there were colonels whose strategies consisted of no more than getting a few score sheep through the fluke season, and squadron-leaders who commanded flocks of flightless permanently-grounded turkeys. There were none however that insisted on being called 'corporal'. Steve reckoned the title was sure proof they had no academic qualifications.

I had been brought up in a strictly urban environment and like most kids had read books about the country and about farm animals and farmers which portrayed the latter as robustly healthy, irrepressibly jolly, wise and kind-hearted to a fault.

The ones that came into the lab or that we visited on their farms tended to be different: loud and ignorant or totally self-preoccupied but all of them tight beyond belief. Steve and I never addressed any of them by anything other than 'mister' and got a real good laugh out of it with some of them.

Albert, almost all of whose waking hours were spent measuring out and dispensing one kind of pellet, and shovelling up and throwing out another, never went anywhere without his wheelbarrow. And as he went from room to room, every wall crammed with cages, the incessant squeaking and squealing of his greedy rodents would have denied him space in his head for a single worthwhile thought. The only thing that would shut the din suddenly and dramatically - but only for a few minutes - was a loud preferably strange noise. If I'd been an animal-house keeper I'd have made myself a large flat holster for each hip in which I would have carried a pair of stainless steel cymbals and I would never have gone anywhere without them.

It wouldn't have cost the Veterinary Investigation Service of the Ministry of Agriculture, Fisheries & Food, a great deal to have called Albert an 'Animal House Keeper', thus conferring a bit of dignity on an occupation without any; after all, they were full of grand titles for everybody else. But it must have best suited their purposes to designate him 'Animal Attendant' and I doubt if anybody lost any sleep over it.

No ordinary woman marries a man who comes home every day of his life stinking of mice, guinea pig pee and rabbit droppings, and Lily's life, even before she met Albert, had been tragic. They were both poor even though they were both hard-working and, strictly speaking, both civil servants. Every Christmas Day, every Good Friday and every other day in the calendar Albert would leave their warm bed to catch whatever bus was running, to go to feed and water, and then pick kale or pluck turnips from the field for the hundreds of small animals he looked after. When the VIC was in Elswick which is where it was when he joined the staff it was relatively easy to get to from Scotswood where he lived, but now it was at Longbenton, at the far end and beyond the city, it took him three buses.

When Lily joined the staff - 'taken on' would be a more appropriate term for her - it was plain she believed Albert to be if not a pillar then at least part of the foundations on which the establishment rested. And if when she was mopping the floor or polishing a bench she were to catch a glimpse of her little man going about his task in the building parallel with the main lab, his domain, she would be so proud that she would flick down her dentures, puff out her cheeks and audibly cluck. And when it was tea-break time and the tea made and already poured out by Bella and then in came the tuneless-whistling, brown-coated figure himself, now bespectacled and with wellingtons replaced by shoes but still retaining his huge flat cap, to join the rest of the staff in the library, she would lean on her mop and almost wee herself with pride.

First the door of the long animal house would be heard to slam shut, then it would be a matter of a few moments before the careful opening and closing of the bottom door of the laboratory suite, the end where the big shots had their offices, would be heard followed by the approaching uneven tramp of uneven legs accompanied by the jingle of a big ring of impressive keys. And then in he would come, her man.

Pretending not to notice her he would have a look on his face that said 'Right, I'm going to show this lot what's what around here'. Her little man was a doer, not a talker, a man prepared to put his boot where his mouth was. When he had warned her in their bed that he had had enough of being treated as though he were a nobody around the place, he meant it.

But Lily never got to actually hear him kicking in the door, flinging his massive keys on the table and scattering cups of tea everywhere, nor did she get to hear him grind his teeth to powder as he slowly and meaningfully said the words, 'I've come in here for one thing and one thing only...to kick somebody's backside!' He'd be stuming right enough but would have decided in the interim to keep it to himself. Oliver would be over in the afternoon to do some mice, he could blow off a bit of steam with him, Oliver wouldn't drop anybody in.

Albert knew the shitty grotty little life he had was all he had a right to expect. He knew he was a one-carat nobody and if he opened his mouth he wouldn't be even that for much longer. Anyway it was Albert's way to be strong and silent, brooding under his huge cap.

But it certainly wasn't hers. Whatever was on Lily's mind, was off the moment she felt the weight of it; Lily was volatile. She didn't have a secure pensionable job with a lot of responsibility, she was just the cleaner and ten-a-penny. She could afford the odd indiscretion, the little swearword when she put a foot in her bucket of filthy slimy water and it spilled all over, and every day the air would be pierced by her shrieking laughter as she told Bella some Chaucerian tale from Scotswood while the two of them had their tea together in the wash-up, and 'For God's sake, woman!' coming up the corridor in an Edinburgh accent would do no more than elicit a brief pause.

She suffered from high blood pressure and either because of it or because of the drugs she took to subdue it, she was always having headaches, getting dizzy and falling all over the place. But if you showed her any sympathy she would drape herself around you and breathe on you and you would very quickly regret it. She would say Bella thought you were 'having it off' with her and then you would really regret it.

Sometimes I would be sitting alone working at my bench in Parasitology when Lily would come in to clean the room. She would bend over double, skirt hitched high, holed stockings stretched to the point of ripping over her huge varicosed legs and her enormous tatty off-white bloomers nearly bursting. She would then make a sound that was impossible to ignore - with her mouth - and when I turned around she would straighten up, give me a playful punch that practically knocked me off my high stool, and cackle 'I saw you peeping, you rude little boy! I wouldn't like to be left alone with you!' Then she would screech with laughter and having regained my seat I would be almost knocked off it again as, with a bucket of dirty water and mop in one hand and her duster and brush in the other, she would lurch at me with her elbow as she went out.

Sidney, the laboratory attendant, had been taken on as permanently temporary while I was away doing my National Service. He had been given a brown coat, making him level pegging with Albert hierarchically speaking, but both would be prepared to argue their claim to superiority to the other to anybody with the time and interest to listen.

Although the nature of his duties were 'lowly but light', everything Sid did, from wrapping a parcel to nailing out a hen, was done the way a soldier would do it - by numbers, memory steps you could almost hear being called out inside his head. His great boast was that he was the only man ever to have been discharged from the Northumberland Fusiliers against his will. Whether this said more for Sid or for the Northumberland Fusiliers, nobody was able to determine. Whilst others lied and connived, going so far as to gently maim themselves in order to get out, Sid after forty-two years seemingly still hadn't had enough. I never saw him salute but if you looked down beyond his long brown coat you would see he was unequivocally standing to attention whenever he was being spoken to by any of the veterinary officers or farmers with conserved titles. His face was purple because of his angina, his weary eyes magnified to twice their size by his army-issue spectacles, his dentures slack, his hearing defective on one side and he had a trench-and-mustard-gas quip for everything that happened at the VIC and the world at large; levity would have been asking too much.

He was an obliging enough chap providing it was well within working hours and was always ready to demonstrate his army-acquired ability to improvise. He would turn one of an odd pair of plastic gloves inside out to create a true pair, steam re-usable labels off brown-paper parcels, reverse paper and recycle string; nothing ingenious but useful enough if there were to be a third world war. There was no doubt about it, Sid felt almost half a century in the British Army had been time well spent.

But Lily was unimpressed. She hated Sid and none of us knew why. We all had our differences from time to time but they were usually just the ordinary mean-spirited, covetous sort of differences that seemed to afflict all Ministry employees.

The kind of vindictiveness that existed between Lily and Sid was something else and I couldn't quite get the idea out of my mind that Albert was somehow involved and that it had to do with something that predated Sid's arrival.

There was one thing the three of them had in common apart from their lowly status and that was that their working day started before the rest of us. What foment went on then was a matter of conjecture but one day when the three of them had the place to themselves Sid escaped by only a hairsbreadth what would surely have been the most inglorious exit ever for an old fusilier.

It began with Sid accidentally or deliberately leaving some official letters addressed to and opened by himself, lying on the bench in the autoclave room overnight. Because he worked in there a lot and had no laboratory or even a drawer he could call his own, Sid considered the autoclave room his base. Be that as it may, the whole place was open season as far as a cleaner was concerned.

Perhaps Lily had only opened the first one to see if it were empty, in which case she probably thought she could safely chuck it in the wastepaper basket. And if it had been left there carelessly, how would Sid have been able to tell that it had been moved a few inches this way or that? How, or indeed why, should he suspect that it had been pried into at all?

Whatever, Sid developed a buff-envelope paranoia and over the next few weeks left on his bench an astonishing range of temptingly large, always opened packages which were subsequently invariably moved. If they hadn't, he would probably have complained that Lily hadn't cleaned the bench properly.

Sid spent such a lot of energy devising ways to prove that his personal letters were being read, without it seemingly ever occurring to him to put his private possessions away like anybody else, even if he just shoved them in the pipette drawer. It was inviting trouble to leave fascinating looking open letters lying around sometimes for nights on end, we told him. Steve, Lawrence and I would suggest putting a wafer-thin mousetrap inside the package, or present him with an elaborate design for a guillotine suspended from the ceiling that would sever her whole arm.

'You're not treating it seriously,' he would retort. 'It could be any of you next.'

But there was nothing you could say, he was as stubborn as he was obsessive.

Every one of us, especially Oliver, had warned him about the apparently long established army practice of checking for gas leaks with a lighted match. He had this idea that if gas were leaking from a pipe and you struck a match close by, a little pilot light would appear to pinpoint it; you would blow it out, mark the spot with a piece of chalk, put a piece of chewing gum over it and some sellotape around it, and Bob was your uncle.

The main reason for the smell of gas was that whenever it was too steamy in the wash-up and Bella had opened the window or forgotten to close it, the gas ring on the Ewing water heater would blow out. But that was too straightforward an explanation for Sid.

Fortunately it was mid afternoon when the bang went off and aid was at hand. The sheet of blue flame that had accompanied it had moved quicker than the kneeling - neck twisted around, head up inside the heater - Sid, and he lost his eyebrows, eyelashes, hairs in his ears and nose, the receding line of his hair was advanced by about five years and the skin on the end of his nose was practically roasted. When we dragged him out, scorched and nonplussed, all he could say was 'Did you see that?'

But it didn't affect by a whit his campaign for the sanctity of the bench in the autoclave room. Lily was now tormenting him by smiling at him, he complained, just because his face was like a hamburger.

One night before going home he planted an open envelope containing an official letter to him, on the back of which were scrawled the words: 'YOU ARE A FAT NOSEY WHOOR'.

The next morning, Lawrence, who had providentially come in early, heard screams coming from the autoclave room. When he rushed in it was to find a crazy Lily pounding the life out of a crumpled gasping Sid who was lying in a heap on the floor; with her mop, she had sloshed him into a corner and seemed to be trying to reduce him to pulp. By the time Lawrence managed to pull her off, Sid couldn't speak and an ambulance had to be sent for.

When Sid recovered enough to come back to work a fortnight later, it was 'Goodbye, subordinate lab attendant' and 'Hello, barrack-room lawyer'. Mr Bailey was a good vet and a gracious boss but totally unequal to the task of dealing with anything like this. The Edinburgh School of Veterinary Science had taught him how to deal with lambing malpresentations and ragwort poisoning, not attempted homicide. Broken spectacles and shattered pride were the least of it, and while Sid was away in hospital Bailey must have been praying he would die peacefully of an unrelated but natural disorder or that his daughter would insist he retire and come to live with her in South Africa.

Throughout the days of acrimonious negotiations which Mr Bailey tried to confine to his office and which eventually came down to who was going to pay for Sid's new glasses, the small unperturbed man in the big cap next door had tended his rodents, the muzak of their incessant squeaking and his mindless whistling providing the perfect backcloth.

Eventually the whole thing settled down, the way the dirty water in a mop bucket always settles, with the scum at the top, sediment at the bottom, and the undrinkable portion between.

19

I don't know why Arnold Dodd asked me to be best man at his wedding, maybe he'd heard I'd recently done it for an old Army friend in South Shields, maybe he'd had too much to drink; because before the night we found ourselves peeing next to each other in the urinal at the Traveller's Rest, we hadn't seen each other since we were thirteen years old. I could even remember the night.

Johnny and I used to go to the Dodds' house every Saturday night to watch their 14" black and white television that virtually put their council house on a par with the Lyric. By the time we arrived just before eight o'clock, Mr Dodd would be out drinking with his mates at the Newton Park Hotel and Mrs Dodd would be at the High Heaton Tenants Association whist drive.

On the fateful night the three of us had been watching Patrick Troughton in an episode from a swashbuckling series and as soon as it ended I had picked up the poker, Arnold had rushed into the kitchen for the carving knife and he and I had begun duelling the sequel. He had lunged at me and I had brought the poker over my head with the intention of disarming him. Unfortunately, on the down-stroke the poker totally shattered what must have been one of the few genuine glass chandeliers in Newcastle and almost certainly the only one on this estate; just as the television represented a lifetime's achievement award for Ernie Dodd, the chandelier was Sadie's.

Nobody who has not beheld a chandelier dispersed by a two-foot long, half-inch thick iron poker with an ornate brass handle, could conceive the devastation; even the atoms split. Uncountable thousands of minute slivers of glass were stuck in the ceiling, the wallpaper, the highly polished wood of the piano and buried in the armchairs, the sofa and the carpet. Even the air was filled with a cloud of glass dust and nobody was daring to think about the damage to the television screen.

Arnold went to his knees, head down, rocking backwards and forwards and emitting a kind of whine like an Aran woman keening at a graveside.

'Sorry, Arnold...'

'Get out and don't ever come back to this house..! Me mother'll go crackers when she sees all this.'

'Have you any glue or anything, Arnold?' Johnny asked. 'Or a brush and shovel?'

'Glue..? You as well, Johnny..! Get out the house..! I never want to see either of you for the rest of my life!'

There was no point in staying, we'd done all we could, Mrs Dodd would be back at any time and Arnold probably wanted to have a damned good cry before that.

Although it was dark and we had kept a very low profile all the way out of the estate, as we turned the corner by the fish-and-chip shop we suddenly bumped right into the big hard bosom of Sadie Dodd.

'Had a good time, me bonny bairns?'

'Yes, thank you, Mrs Dodd,' we answered in unison.

As soon as she was out of sight we ran like hell all the way home.

It had happened eight years ago, longer than either of the world wars, yet the first thing Sadie Dodd said on the morning of the wedding when I arrived at their house to get changed into my hired formal attire and begin my duties as best man and manager of a perfect day for everybody, was, 'You're a proper bad'un, Joe Robinson. The least you could have done was own up and got your mam and dad to pay something towards it. Your dad could easily afford it with his job.'

I was standing on the step from which I had fled with such consternation the last time I was here.

'There's never been one word out of you all these years.'

I obviously didn't want to treat the matter as a joke if she still hadn't got over it but I didn't want to have to plead my case here and now either, I felt I had the right to presume some kind of amnesty would have been operating.

'I'm very sorry, Mrs Dodd. It was an accident.'

'Sorry..? What good's sorry? You can't mend anything with sorry.'

I shrugged in a way I hoped would convey sincere repentance and the best of good faith.

'I suppose you'd better come in, then. Our Arnold never told us until the day before yesterday he was letting you be best man.'

Ernie Dodd then came to the door. He was a big guy with shiny black hair parted down the middle and a tiny black pencil moustache, like a burly Django Rheinhardt.

'Out the way, woman, and let the lad in... How're ye doin', son..? Aal reet, are ye?'

He shook my hand and I could tell nothing good or bad about me frolicked or festered in his brain, any snippets would have long since been flushed out with pint after pint of draught Exhibition.

'Fine, thanks, Mr Dodd. How's yourself?'

'Cannot complain, ye know... Howay in an' see wor lad. An' have somethin' to drink.'

Mrs Dodd had a little scowl as she let me by but nothing that cowed my high spirits and I just winked.

Arnold was marrying a girl called Dorothy Bell who was scatty but good-natured. In her school days she used to be called 'Dirty Dot' and the boys used to shout 'Dottie Bell, she goes like hell!' I think it was probably because she was so well developed.

Arnold worked at the Co-op and was hoping to go to Loughborough College, the Co-op academy, soon; both families were Co-op people through to their marrow.

Dougie Bell, Dorothy's father, a little fellow with crooked teeth and matted hair, believed that his own generation represented the apogee of physical, mental and moral evolution and that after it everything had begun to slip back. He was forever on about the value of broth - 'bread broily broth', whatever that was - and it was impossible to have a conversation with him on any topic from the fitness of Newcastle United players, to the current spate of gallbladder operations, without him finding a way to trumpet the life-enhancing qualities of broth and condemn anybody younger than himself for being degenerate. No matter how bigoted and ignorant you thought he was, and what a clown he was, you couldn't come away from half an hour in his company without feeling jaded. You couldn't ignore him, his voice was too loud.

The marriage ceremony was at St Francis's in Cragside and there were few frills although the bride and groom were as handsome as any.

When we came out and I had crammed the three big Co-op taxis with those I deemed to be principals and those I deemed to be handicapped - amid strident complaints from the excluded - and was about to get in one myself, Arnold asked if I had paid the vicar and organist.

I hadn't been called upon to do anything like this at the wedding in South Shields and thought weddings would have been part of their duties. An uncle of Dot's stuck his head out of a car window and said 'Bugger the vicar. But we know the organist and he's only a working man like the rest of us and Saturday should be his day off. If anybody gets anything, it should be him.'

Arnold pressed a shilling into my hand. 'That's for the vicar. And that,' he said, pressing a sixpence into the other, 'is for the organist. He wasn't all that good but that's by the by.'

I ran back to the empty church and searched all over for the vicar. Eventually I found him out the back, still in his vestments, attending to some plants. I gave him the money, asking him to give the shilling to the organist and keep the sixpence for himself and then hurried off. I'd already kept the taxi waiting for more than five minutes and knew Dougie and Myrtle Bell would be counting.

When I got back to the road, there wasn't a soul, Every taxi, car and guest had gone. Here I was dressed in morning suit and the only group that could give me any credibility were probably miles away.

An old woman limped up. 'What's the matter, son? Have the forgotten ye..? Where've ye to get to?'

'The Crown Hotel.'

'The Crown..? Near the Central..? That's a canny way.'

'Is there a bus I can get?'

'Aye, there is, but ye'll probably have to change at the Haymarket. It'll be along any minute. Just tell the conductor where ye want to gan. He'll keep ye right.'

When the bus came it was packed with Newcastle United football supporters heading for the match at Leazes Park. They were all hyped up and full of aggravation and I was just what they needed, standing in the middle of them in my black jacket, pinstriped trousers and carnation in my buttonhole, and they never let up for an instant.

'Well, well... What have we got here? Who's a bonny lad, then..? Gannin to the match, are we?'

'Whose side are ye on..?'

'The directors, I'll bet. He-heh-heh!'

'He's spent aal e's money on the suit an' e's nowt left fo' the taxi.'

When the conductor got to me which thankfully wasn't until we got to the Haymarket, by which time I realised my wallet was in my other trousers at the Dodds', I was put off and had to half run, half walk, all the way, carnation and all, down Northumberland Street, along Blackett Street and down Grainger Street; what with the match and it being Saturday afternoon, the whole town was packed.

When I got to the Crown the wedding party was well into the drink and it was clear I'd hardly been missed.

'There you are!' exclaimed Dougie Bell, coming up with an empty whisky glass in one hand and an empty pint glass in the other, he certainly wasn't drinking his broth now.

'When are you going to buy the bride's father a drink, then?'

Just then Arnold came to say a number of guests had had too much to drink and would I usher everybody into the dining room before they had any more.

After the meal and the speeches I had just sat down after delivering some witty response to the suggestion that pokers should be licensed, a not too abstruse allusion to my association with that weapon, when the headwaiter, a very tall man with a military bearing, tapped me on the shoulder. By the time I turned around he had already retreated into the doorway of the catering room and was beckoning me by slowly curling his forefinger as though he were winding in a sprat. He was a good four inches taller than me and had a very supercilious air.

'Yes?' I asked.

'Very sorry to trouble you, sir. It's a little matter of delicacy...pertaining to the lady staff, sir.'

'Oh?'

'Well, sir, it's customary for our clients to show their appreciation in some way.'

'We did. We drank a toast of thanks to all the catering staff.'

'Yes, I know, sir...and grateful we are indeed for that token. But you see, sir, I suspect they are thinking in rather more practical terms.'

'Like what?'

'Well, sir, I leave that up to your good selves.'

I stood there, not sure I should be dealing with this.

'By rights, you see, sir, this is their Saturday afternoon off and they have come in specially to make the wedding feast something the handsome groom and his lovely bride will always remember... Everything has been satisfactory, I trust?'

'Yes, as far as I'm aware of... Are you saying the women aren't being paid?'

'Oh no, sir! Of course they receive some small recompense for their work.'

'Do you mean you want them to be paid something extra, then?'

'Well, if you felt... But as I say, I'd leave that up to you.'

I was going to make him squirm. It was the way he was so damned patronising at the same time as he was importuning, that stuck in my craw.

'How much do you want?'

'I couldn't possibly answer that, sir. I leave it entirely up to your own discretion.'

'My discretion has nothing to do with it. It's the bride's father, Mr Bell, who's paying for all this. I'll have to see him.'

'Thank you, sir. So sorry to trouble you.'

When I went back to the table and told Arnold, he was furious. 'The greedy swine..! He's been paid just like the rest of them... Here, give him this.' He pressed a sixpence into the palm of my hand. 'I know Dougie won't give them another penny.'

There were smiles all around as I went into the catering room and the headwaiter came over.

'Ah, sir... Everybody satisfied, I trust?'

'Yep. The groom gave me this. He told me to tell you to share it out.'

I dropped the sixpence into his long, beautifully manicured and waiting hand.

First there was shock and then there was anger. The fawning was all finished.

'For three waitresses and myself...for a whole afternoon's work?'

I threw out my arm and pushed back the cuff on my shirt. It was only ten past three.

'I'd be insulting them if I gave them this.'

We stood there with the women looking on, stock-still; it was stalemate.

'Hang on,' I said and went back to Arnold who was in the middle of an argument with his father-in-law.

'What!' he expostulated. 'Where is it?

'Where's what?'

'The tanner.'

'He's got it.'

'Right!'

Up he got from the table went out into the catering room and strode straight up to the headwaiter.

'You're their agent, are you..? Sixpence not enough for you, is it not..? Right! Open your hand!'

The headwaiter immediately did so, revealing the little coin in the centre of his palm.

'Give's it here, then!'

Arnold swiftly picked up the sixpence and put it in his own pocket.

'That'll teach the lot of you not to be so damned greedy... And forget about going home yet,' he said to the women. 'You can take your hats and coats back off and get in there and see if anybody wants anything...as you've been paid to do. We're not finished yet...not by a long chalk.'

He then stormed out and I followed, smiling a 'Sorry, pal' smile.

Twenty minutes later, during an impassioned debate among the guests about the relative merits of the staff of the Crown and Co-op, Dougie's sister Gladys suddenly rushed in to say the waitresses and 'that long streak of misery' were making their way down the backstairs, loaded to the nines with chicken and ham, huge portions of wedding cake, wine and other goodies Dougie Bell had paid for out of his hard-earned wages and his and Dot's mother's Co-op savings.

All the fit and able women and some who weren't so, from both the Bell and Dodd families, rose up and dashed for the stairs.

Dot went after them in her bridal gown to make sure Aunt Gladys didn't have one of her heart attacks.

Arnold sat down beside me and we chinked glasses. 'It's in Daddy-in-law's hands now. Good old Dougie. He'll give them what for.' He grinned. 'Thanks, mate. Thanks for everything.'

'Don't mention it,' I said. 'It's been a pleasure.'

20

Few creatures are more endearing in their infancy and more exasperating as adults, than sheep. Avian species make incredible attempts to survive disease or injury, even flying or running a considerable distance after death; but if a sheep stumbles and falls, it is liable to remain down and wait for pneumonia to set in.

Before I went into the Army there were those at the VIC who used to think I was some kind of sheepdog. 'Just wait,' they'd say. 'Joe'll get it.' And they'd suck on their pipes as I bounded off, leaping ditches and scrambling over hedges. But not any more, I was still physically capable but no longer so inclined.

One cold wet blustery day in January Norris and I went to a sheep farm in the Cheviots. It took two and a half hours to get there in his old wreck of an Austin; the doors wouldn't close properly, the windows kept rattling open and the iron frame of the seat had dug into my back like a pair of crowbars. To think he would have the nerve to claim ninepence a mile for this when we got back...

By the time we arrived at 'Major' Bennington-Selby's we were at daggers drawn, at least I was; all the time he had this silly grin on his face as though he hadn't the faintest idea what kind of a day we were in for.

We were met by a surly shepherd called Edward who to all intents and purposes was mute - I say 'met by' but the truth was we had to go looking for him. Even though he was continually howking up lumps of phlegm and sluicing it out, Norris was chatting away as though the two of them had a real conversation going.

'It's been a bumper of a year for triplets I hear?'

No answer.

'Maybe not so much around these parts, though.'

Howk and spit.

'It was a pretty mild winter, mind, wasn't it?'

No answer.

'Though not compared with where I come from.'

No answer.

'Have you ever been as far south as Devon or...on holiday or anything, I mean?'

Howk and spit.

'No, I don't suppose you have... Do you go to see Newcastle United..? You're probably more interested in rugby, a big feller like you, he-he-he!'

'You ever played rugby, Joe?'

No answer, just a shake of the head.

'I haven't myself but I believe it's a good game to watch if you've got a telly... Mmmm. Looks like it's coming on to rain. That should make things nice and mucky, he-he-he!'

Howk and spit.

Bennington-Selby was no doubt indoors sticking various farm-animal-shaped drawing pins into a map on the wall. Outside where we were in a pen loosely made with willow branches, the kind of north-easterly that saps strength and exposes nerves was already howling.

In addition to his large Aberdeen Angus herd, breeding stud of hunter horses and goodness knows how many pure breeds of poultry, 'Mr Selby' - which was how I was going to address him because I didn't believe in double-barrelled names either - had six hundred and thirty ewes, about enough for a hobby. This meant that at our normal rate of working, where I'd be going more than twice as fast as Norris, the middle finger of my right hand, my guitar finger, was going to be entering the back-end of upwards of four hundred and twenty sheep.

Standish would look at a herd of cows he was going to bleed, or a flock of sheep he was going to faeces-sample, decide how long it should take and then roll up his sleeves and get on with it. You never got back late when you went with him. Farmers, shepherds and sheepdogs were all bent to his will, the way they would have been with any hurricane. When you went with Norris, you were always late, I think he thought it impressed Mr Bailey.

Norris quickly commandeered Edward so I had to catch, hold and sample my own beasts, and do many on the run, so the air was soon rife with the kind of language I forwent in the Army. Norris kept looking over disapprovingly as though I was showing no regard at all for the sheep's feelings, and occasionally exclaiming 'I say! Steady on there!'

He had brought a new gadget for collecting sheep faeces samples, the prototype of something they had been developing at the veterinary school he'd been at and obviously given up on. It was a conical glass tube with an aperture at the narrow end, like a centrifuge tube with a flaw in it, the kind of thing you might come across in a new box and chuck out; and he was insisting I use it.

The idea was to thrust the narrow end into the rectum, twist it through three hundred and sixty degrees, withdraw it and shake the contents into a glass sample pot. It could only have been designed by somebody who had never been near a sheep, for someone working under perfect field conditions with the sheep sedated and preferably lying down on its side. The drawbacks were legion: first, there was a limited number of tubes so they had to be cleaned out and reused; second, the reason we were sampling the sheep was because they were infested with helminths [intestinal worms] and when they were thus infested, their droppings were no longer the firm, discretely spilled clusters of what pastoral poets call 'dingleberries'; third, thin glass is fragile.

We started off as always with scores of labelled sparklingly-clean glass pots in shallow cardboard boxes separated by tongued and grooved corrugated cardboard, and several sharpened pencils.

Within twenty minutes half the revolutionary tubes were broken, some inside the rectum, some underfoot. The cardboard boxes were rapidly disintegrating in the rain and under hoof, the labels obscured by mud and faeces, and all but two of the tiny pencils had disappeared into the mire. The conditions weren't freakish by any means and none of this would have happened had it been Standish's behind I was looking at instead of Norris's. If anything ever needed changing because of circumstances, Standish would have instantly changed it. But not Norris, and he was using every argument he could think of to insist we continue with the tubes. He was even disingenuous enough to suggest our fingernails might injure their rectums, even though we both knew his were kept permanently bitten so far down that the tips of his fingers were like little pink flaps.

I repeatedly drew his attention to the sticky mucoid nature of the material that was blocking and contaminating the tubes and he kept carping 'How many times have I to tell you it's not "shit". It's "faeces".'

But if he was getting exasperated at my using an increasing number of four-letter words, I was exasperated at having to climb out of the fold every five minutes to find a twig or something to poke down the few tubes I had left, to try to clear the ends.

'Where are you off to?' he would shout after me as though I were playing about.

'I've told you!' I would yell. 'To get something to clear these bloody tubes with... Where do you think?'

'Come back here, man! You're wasting valuable time.'

But I would just ignore him, get a supply of sticks and coarse grass and climb back in.

After a while there was a triumphant shout. 'There's no need to poke them with sticks! Just blow down them!'

'What?' I yelled above the howling wind, unable to believe what I thought he'd said.

'Come here!'

I put my things down and went over to where he and Edward were huddled in a corner.

'Blow down them... Like this.'

He was kneeling down in his thick black Corporation mackintosh and gum boots, bits of wool, bramble and burrs sticking out of his ginger hair, bending over a sheep's dirty back end. With the wide end of a tube to his mouth, cheeks inflated like Dizzy Gillespie's and a specimen pot palmed in his left hand like a miniature mute, he was practically blowing his brains out of his ears. A tiny amount of faecal matter was dribbling out of the end of the tube.

'See!' he gasped.

'Bugger that! I'm not getting sheepshit in my mouth..! Not for Major bloody Bennington-Selby or anybody!'

For the first time Edward was grinning.

'I've done a whole box and nothing's gone in mine!' Norris snorted as he turned to look up at me.

Encircling his mouth and reaching up to the tip of his nose and down into the cleft in his chin, was an unbroken brown ring.

I burst out laughing.

'What's the matter?' he said with a note of hurt in his voice.

'You should see yourself in the mirror. Go back to the car and take a look.'

He rubbed his mouth with the back of his hand, smearing it all over his cheeks. 'How's that?'

'Ask Edward here.'

Edward wouldn't say a word but his face was now wreathed in smiles, he would remember all of this at the Black Bull tonight.

'If this's what it's come down to, that's me finished with the tubes, Mr Norris. Thanks for the demonstration.' I chucked my last two tubes into one of his soggy boxes.

From then I used my finger and there was no further communication between us, nothing intelligent that is. I did once hear him mumble something to Edward about a chip on somebody's shoulder but I didn't catch the name so had no idea who he could have been talking about.

About an hour later, by which time the wind had dropped and a few shafts of pale sunshine were coming through the clouds although they were petering out before they reached the ground, a spanking new jeep pulled up and out stepped the man himself, Bennington-Selby.

'Good day, gentlemen,' he hailed us. 'Is that you, Hunter..? Or is it the new fellah?'

I pointed towards Norris. 'He's the vet... Mr Norris.'

He tramped right around the fold so he could get a better look at Norris and assure himself it wasn't some nincompoop messing about with his animals. He was dressed like an Englishman on safari: thick tweeds, silly crumpled hat, grizzly grey hair curling out at the sides and at the back, briar in mouth and a baton whacking a magnificent pair of knee-length boots with the kind of stroke that would have raised a respectable weal on any coolie's back.

'I say there..! Managing all right..? Edward looking after you..?'

Edward mumbled something sycophantic and Norris clambered to his feet. He had been down on his honkers for about two hours so it couldn't have been easy, he must have been stiff and even a bit dizzy. He tried to steady himself by holding on to a moving sheep and almost fell.

'Fine, thank you, sir. Thank you... I estimate we're about three-quarters of the way through.' His heavily embroidered smile was ingratiating.

'My lady-wife was wondering if you could do with a mug of coffee to fortify the old spirit?'

'Oh, no, sir, thank you very much. We're doing fine. We've got whatever provisions we need in the car. We'll just work away until we're finished, if that's all right with you.'

'Well, don't let me interfere with the good work,' he quickly responded. 'You're probably doing the right thing. It could snow in a bit. What do you think, Edward?'

'It could at that, sir. It's been mizzling on and off this past hour or more.'

So, Edward could in fact speak, he was quite the interlocutor when he got somebody worth interlocuting with.

I don't know how good a look Bennington-Selby got at Norris, or what kind of impression he had formed from their brief exchange, but my guess was that he wouldn't have wanted him mouthing one of his lady-wife's best bone china cups.

By the time we were finished it was dark and we were filthy and tired and Norris and I couldn't have been any more disenchanted with each other. All that mattered to me now was that we got back to Newcastle in time for me to keep the date I had made with a girl I'd been after for ages.

However, on the way back when we reached the outskirts of Gosforth, Norris did the most extraordinary thing. After the day we had spent together, a day best forgotten yet not easy to obliterate entirely, Norris had the temerity to make a wide detour so that we could call at his home in order for me to see his new baby.

'Come in a minute,' he said. 'I've something to show you.'

I was sure it was going to be another device for extracting faeces, a pump of some sort perhaps, he was always on about pumps.

As we entered the living room, an amazingly untidy place with clothes and books and tools scattered all over the place, his wife appeared, a tranquillised-looking woman who was prettier than I would have expected, and pleasant.

'This is Joe, the young man I was telling you about. He wants to see Annabelle.'

'Annabelle?'

'Yes, the baby.'

She looked as surprised as I was.

'Oh... Right... Shall I...or..?'

They took me into their bedroom to see the baby and I was more exasperated with him than I'd been all day because I didn't know what to say. I didn't want to hurt her or him but I never knew what to say when confronted with newborn babies. I always thought they were ugly and looked like nobody. When I was a lad and we lived at Plessey Terrace, the woman next door once had a baby and Johnny and I were sent in to see it. 'Well, boys, what do you think of him? Who do you think he looks like?' the neighbour had asked, and I had quite ingenuously replied 'He looks like a little old man.' The woman, a mature person who had been a nurse during the war and had three other children, burst into tears and shrieked at us to get out of the house. I was made to go in later to apologise and say the baby was beautiful and looked like her. I was only seven but I resented it, realising I was being called to play an adult's game that I didn't like and didn't understand.

Here I was, fourteen years later and no less inept. Because I never took anything valuable with me on farm trips, I had nothing with which to cross its palm with silver, if that was what they did in Devon also.

Following a couple of girls coming out of the pictures or a dance and trying to tap them up with a load of corny patter, with Tod and Jim tagging along taking the mickey, had begun to lose some of its magic; it was invariably only the more bitter fruit that was left, the choicest always having been plucked long since.

I suggested we started going in to dances, rather than hanging about outside until the end, but they would only consider the lowest dives where you weren't expected to 'get up' and could stand around the sides all night with a beer in one hand and a smoke in the other, weighing up the form; this meant somewhere like The Heaton where you were more likely to end up with a glass in your face than a girl you'd want to be seen with in broad daylight.

Respectable dancehalls were the best places to meet nice girls, lots of them; the only problem was that the best ones were always up on the floor dancing. Tod's plan was for me to get one up, dance around a bit, bring her back and hand her over, and then go back and get another one and so on. But it wasn't as easy as that.

The music would be live and really good at places like The Oxford where George Evans played and it was probably the most popular place in Newcastle. There was also the Old Assembly Rooms off Westgate Hill, where the county types went. 'The classy bitches all go there!' Tod would almost spit. But I didn't mind classy bitches and decided to go on my own.

It wasn't enough to get up however; at places like this you couldn't just lurch and teeter with a cigarette in your mouth, doing your own thing, you had to do what the rest were doing. I knew a few basic steps of the foxtrot, quickstep and waltz from a crash course we'd had at school five years ago in preparation for a fifth-years' Christmas dance. Even the word 'basic' was somewhat of an exaggeration but I was determined to challenge Tod's gloomy summation that none of us was the dancing type and that we'd be better off patrolling the Quayside.

One day I was going down Shields Road when I saw an advert for the Silver Swing Dance Studio. They apparently taught Latin American as well as the boring stuff, and that was what I really wanted to do; I had always fancied myself swaying to the mambo and samba, tango and cha-cha-cha. So I enrolled for the Tuesday night session without telling a soul, they'd have been merciless at home if they'd known, and Tod would almost certainly have puked. The first anybody would know would be the next time there was a wedding reception or something when everybody would be there. I would wait until the messers and middle-aged uncles were making idiots of themselves and then unobtrusively take to the floor like Victor Sylvester and wow the whole lot of them. 'Did you see our Joe..? Fantastic, wasn't he! I never knew he could dance. You'd think he was from Argentina. Did you notice how shiny his hair was..?'

'The Silver Swing Studio, Byker' might have sounded a little tacky and the girls weren't great but the teaching wasn't bad: a leisurely tempo and a dance floor not too well lit was just what you wanted when you were learning. The first night it took so long to get underway and because even the girls didn't seem to be able to move in step with the music, I went out to check the poster to make sure it wasn't just for disabled or mentally handicapped people. But after a while I saw they were all right; like me they were fugitives from another world where everybody else could dance. I had always been quick in my reactions and movements and was never clumsy but I had no sense of rhythm and, I suppose, no natural grace.

The anonymity was one of the best things about the place, it was the only time I had ever been on a dance floor anywhere without some geek I knew hooting from the sideline, somebody who couldn't dance a step themselves. Then one night a fellow in a black jumper and trousers with a clerical collar came in and I was sure I knew him; he didn't seem to recognise me and never spoke but I couldn't take my eyes off him. Eventually it clicked.

'Excuse me,' I said to him. 'You wouldn't happen to be Sammy Wilson, by any chance?' Actually, 'Stinkbomb Wilson' was what we used to call him but I could hardly call him that now. 'You're not from Walker...and we were in the same class at school?'

He smiled. 'Why, yes,' he said in this strange voice. 'Joey Robinson, isn't it..? Mind, how you've grown.'

When I last saw him he was a kid nobody would invite to a party and nobody ever voluntarily sat beside; not because he was very poor but because he revelled in the most obnoxious anti-social habits. He was more vulgar than anybody in the class and was always in trouble but he was intelligent and articulate and said things about famous politicians and historical figures that nobody else dare even think; he would start on and there was no stopping him, even the teacher's jaw would sag. There was nothing they could do with him because he was so hard that no amount of punishment made the slightest difference.

We shook hands and he told me he was in his final year of preparation for the Anglican ministry. I could hardly believe it. His short spiky hair which used to be kept short because of the infestations at the infamous Rochester Dwellings where he lived, was long and well groomed; the buck teeth that caused him to splutter whenever he spoke, had been replaced; his coarse and raucous voice had gone, so maybe his vocal chords had been re-tuned. I could only surmise that something had been done to control the abominable flatulence for which he had been so notorious.

The most profound change of all for me, however, was that he had been a devout Catholic; at least I always thought he was. I didn't know him well enough to ask what I was dying to ask, which was why if he wanted to enter the ministry hadn't he become a Catholic priest.

But we were missing the coaching and I never got the chance again because I never saw him any more after that night. I'd hate to think I frightened him away or given the impression I'd seen through a disguise, because what he appeared to have done with himself was remarkable.

Every Tuesday after doing my weight-lifting I went to the Silver Swing Studio and then came home and studied; of the three, the effect of the Silver Swing Studio would have been the hardest to detect. I liked music, I thought I was quick on the uptake, so why, oh why, couldn't I do something as simple as dance? Why couldn't I move my legs at the same time as a girl of no more than average intelligence and turn her around without it seeming as though I were trying to put her down with a judo throw?

In the end I decided dancing wasn't something you could learn, you were either born able to dance or you weren't, and I wasn't. If I was going to get girls, I'd have to go back to the patter.

21

Since coming out of the Army I had never let a day pass without doing some kind of physical training. I always cycled to work and several nights a week on the way home I would do a dozen lengths at Chillingham Road baths. Every night I did weightlifting in the bedroom and sometimes Johnny would join me and we'd have a competition, though more often it would be a laugh and we'd have to pack in before one of us was badly hurt.

At least once a week Steve and I would visit the dump at the RAF camp and come away with something useful. He and his wife now lived in the caretaker's bungalow next to the lab and he would look for bits and pieces he could use for the house. The best thing I ever found was a 56lb cast-iron weight with a space for a hook, into which I could fit my hand, and I devised all kinds of exercises with it.

I had never been one for tea-breaks dominated by somebody with nothing to say that didn't reflect favourably on themselves, especially boasts about the diminutive feats of their youngest children, and in the mornings I used mine to do press-ups between the high stools in my parasitology lab.

Steve was now too heavy to sprint competitively but he threw the hammer for a local athletics club and taught me, and I would spend my afternoon tea-break out in the field going through the motions of throwing without letting it go and having to waste time retrieving it. It called for beautiful circular movements which could be as tight and quick or loose and slow as you wished.

One night he rang to tell me there'd been a slight accident and did I want half a ewe; if so, to come straightaway and bring a haversack. As I came down Whitley Road I could see smoke rising from the incinerator and when I arrived he had already skinned it, divided it into butcher cuts and the fleece and offal was on its way to ash.

'By God, they're stupid buggers, though... And it had to be the best of the lot.'

'It's an ill wind...' I replied.

He was still in his tracksuit but had taken the top off; there wasn't a single speck of blood on his white vest, even his hands were clean.

'The lot of them just stood there and watched it sailing towards them. I was yelling like hell, yet not one of them budged. It came down and she watched it all the way till it hit her between the eyes.'

'Did it kill it outright?'

'Are you kidding?' He laughed. 'I'm letting the whole lot out first thing to tomorrow morning before anybody comes in. That way it'll look as though they've escaped during the night. They won't get far and I'll be heading them back in like the Good Shepherd by the time Bailey gets in.'

'Do you need a hand with this one?'

'No. When you get going with yours, there won't be a trace left. Mine's already in the deep freeze.'

We loaded part of my share into a potato sack and tied it over the crossbar, the rest went into the haversack on my back.

Ever since my first Christmas with the VIC at Elswick Park I'd had meat from time to time and I suppose all veterinary centres were the same. Wages were low, good meat was expensive and there were few other perks. We always kept a lot of rabbits, a pig or two and some fowl, and when we came to Longbenton with its acres of pasture we expanded our stock to include a small flock of sheep and the odd heifer.

At Christmas lots were drawn to see who would get a rabbit and who a hen, skinned or plucked and prepared by none other than our own master butcher, Steve; but nobody touched the guinea pigs or mice, at least not as far as I knew.

The only red meat we took was from healthy animals, whether brought in or from our own stock but not everybody took it when it was offered. Some, like McCulloch, lived in digs; others, like Oliver or Mr Bailey, would have misgivings about the propriety of it; and some, like Lawrence, were a bit squeamish. Hunter and Steve were carnivores, pure and simple, and they relished the whole thing; it was perhaps no coincidence that they were the most vigorous and robust of the staff, though Hunter had gone now.

When we were at Elswick Steve once got a mouthful of the stomach contents of an aborted foetus suspected of being infected with Brucella, because of a faulty pipette. Straightaway he had opened the clip on an aspirator of 10% lysol which stood on a bench above the sink and squirted the mordant liquid straight into his mouth; he kept it in for at least a minute even though it must have been extremely painful, gargled, spat it out and continued working. He didn't rinse his mouth out with water or anything, he just let the disinfectant do its work until tea-time when he had his mug of tea like everybody else, and he never said a word to anybody.

Although I had never been given any laboratory first-aid lessons or special instructions in aseptic techniques, I was never kept away from infected animals or material. Because we were a veterinary investigation centre, diagnosis was our main assignment and the hazard of most of the material that came into the VIC, living or dead, in whole or in part, was an unknown entity; it was only by exposing ourselves to the risks that we learned what they were. Identification of pathogenic bacteria could only be made after culturing them in the laboratory and carrying out tests on the living organisms. We examined tissue from any organ, examined milk and other secretions and excretions from any source, and every day isolated tubercle bacilli, brucellae, salmonellae, staphylococci, streptococci, tetani, botuli and many others, most of which were zoonoses and therefore capable of killing or causing serious disease in us.

Many of the reagents we used were also toxic. We handled concentrated acids - in my first few days I had to be taken to the General Hospital to be treated for sulphuric acid burns to my hands - concentrated alkalis, toxic vaporous fluids and many chemicals in solid and fluid form that were suspected of being carcinogenic or teratogenic.

Reagents had to be prepared in the laboratory by pouring from large, fragile but heavy, glass bottles called winchesters, and because of their viscosity the fluid would frequently run down the outsides of the bottles, attacking the wood of the benches they stood on, the rubber tubing connections and almost everything else they came in contact with; this was how I was burnt. Because the preparation of reagents was considered a lowly task, it was the most junior member of the laboratory, the lab attendant, who usually did the weighing out and pouring and therefore touched or inhaled these substances most.

There were no restrictions regarding the handling of carcasses either. The vets and scientific assistants [technicians] dissected the carcasses with knives and scalpels, opened up skulls and bones with hammer and saw, slit oesophagus, stomach and intestine and sliced and exposed the cores of abscesses, tumours and other lesions. Mostly they recognised pathology when they saw it and were aware of what was dangerous and what was not. But not those that came in their brown coats to clean up after them.

The only time I ever heard the word 'union' mentioned at the VIC was the time Oliver was kicked and slapped by Hunter just after I started at Elswick.

Vets had their own professional bodies to protect them and look after their interests, just as medical doctors had theirs, but veterinary technicians only had the IMLT, most of whose executive committee was composed of medical doctors, and it did nothing like that. At Longbenton, as at Elswick before it, you had to stick up for yourself.

Although a trade union would have concerned itself with our pay and working conditions, with any injury resulting in disability and presumably with being kicked by a superior, I suspect Steve, Lawrence and I had all been brought up to believe that unions were strictly for people like miners and dockers and that they upset the smooth running of the country. We were probably conservative without necessarily voting Conservative, though I hadn't had the opportunity to vote as yet. People were very secretive about it; in our household my mother and father thought it a matter of conscience, like the confessional, and never asked or told each other what they did at the ballot box.

My mother came from a large family, all of whom had to support themselves from an early age. My father came from a poor family on his maternal side, his mother striving to provide for her young children by getting little shops and running little businesses. My father's father had died young but his family were prize-fighters and business people, so my father was brought up to fend for himself. He had joined the Civil Service, served as a soldier in the Second World War and then returned.

I also was a civil servant, albeit a scientific one, and subject to the same pro-Masonic fraternity and anti-Socialist ideology he was, though I suspected our crowd was more subtle about it. Tradesmen and trade unions were seen not so much a necessary evil, as 'common' and a bit of an embarrassment.

Like my father I had to sign in accordance with the Official Secrets Act, a document which didn't interrogate or condemn but merely sought assurance in a very naïve way, that one wasn't related to or acquainted with anybody who was a Communist. I had signed without qualm because it was the truth and because it was regarded as a bit of a joke, like some silly rite of passage, without considering that I was contributing all the way to the House of Un-American Activities.

The crunch with my father came when I was praising Paul Robeson's voice one day and my father shook his head and said he was a Communist. It was then that I saw everything clearly, or at least differently. I would have joined the Communist Party there and then if I had known of a local branch and it would probably have been for the wrong reasons, namely to nark my father.

He and my mother frequently wondered aloud where they had gone wrong with me, how they had managed to bring up a son who could bring three girlfriends for tea at the same time, thus creating, for some reason, great embarrassment for my mother. Neither of them ever suggested I had a chip on a shoulder because it wasn't the sort of thing you said when castigating your own son, it would be like criticising him for being dark-skinned; they blamed all my faults on me and left no doors open to heredity, conditioning or anything like that.

Whatever my father wanted us to be, my mother wanted us to be, pretty much. And he wanted us to be frank but tactful, fair but firm, tough but not cruel, proud but not vain, wise but not cynical, courageous but not foolhardy, respectful without being sycophantic, obedient yet individualistic, confident though not arrogant, provident but not mean, and forgiving after hitting back. He wanted us to be our 'own man' but exactly like him in all that mattered, better than him in fact.

Some of these were pretty tough combinations and a few nigh on impossible. I think that more than anything and practically from birth I had been a 'natural dissenter', if there was such a thing, and nobody had realised it. It was supposed to be a merit to accept things on face value, but I couldn't without being intellectually dishonest. I only had to hear words like 'orthodox', 'established' or 'confirmed', or phrases like 'tried and tested' or 'beyond all reasonable doubt', to feel my ire rising, no matter what the context, and I was absolutely convinced that authority was synonymous with abuse - idiosyncrasies my father thought perverse.

I didn't like mottoes or quotations either, and I distrusted laws of precedence and the impeccability of tradition. I hated privilege and hypocrisy even more than I hated sycophancy and spite, and my father was the same, though not necessarily in the same order; but he wouldn't say so in case I tried to make capital out of it.

He and I argued but we could never usefully discuss or debate anything and at times we fell out bitterly. As a father he thought it beneath him to try to persuade his own son and he would only say what, not why, and then only briefly. My inclination was to be longwinded and dramatic, though just as dogmatic. He didn't see the need to explain himself and he didn't see the need to let me. It seemed tragic that the person in my life I quarrelled and got angry with most was a man I loved very much and whose character I had immense respect for. My mother didn't understand it, my brothers didn't and I'm sure neither my father or I did, but that's the way it was.

Having a 'full set of wheels' made all the difference Steve reckoned when it came to females. You got 'girls' with bikes; with a car you could get 'real women'.

I had told him I was thinking of getting a Matchless 500cc from one of the motor-cycle shops along Scotswood Road.

'Fine, if oil on your pants and somebody to giggle with is what you want.'

'But if its crumpet you want...and I mean la crème de la crème...forget it.'

What I especially needed apparently was something sporty and low slung with leather seats and a natty dashboard. And he happened to know where there was such a vehicle going dead cheap.

'An old mate of mine has a Singer Coupé he only wants £28 for. Black on the outside, red on the inside...like an African shorthand typist... Many a rare old time we've had in that. You couldn't fail with it. Get yourself a county cap and a pair of string-backed gloves to go with that green cord jacket and suedes you've got, and you'll need a pitchfork to keep them out.'

I had enough for the car but not for tax and insurance.

'Forget the tax... That's not important. And just get yourself a couple of months' insurance. Norwich Union'll fix you up for a few quid. I could ring Chris tonight if you want. He'd bring it round for you to have a look at tomorrow night. You could get your insurance on Saturday morning and be motoring on Saturday night. A good-looking bloke like you with a Singer Coupé could take this town by storm. Wear the gold tie pin your Grandma got you and you could pass for Beau Brummel.'

Nobody could have passed up an opportunity like that and the following night I was being driven along the Coast Road by Steve's old buddy.

'Why don't you ever turn left?' I asked suspiciously, having noticed the lengths he was going to avoid such a manoeuvre.

'Glad you noticed. You're sharp. You'll have your licence in no time... It's the kingpins on the right wheel. I was just about to mention it. I'd arranged to change them tomorrow but Steve said you were in a hurry.'

But it was a beautiful car and I really didn't want to know if there was anything else wrong with it so I didn't ask and he didn't tell. He had replaced the kingpins by seven o'clock the next night, and by quarter-past the car was mine. It wasn't until the next night I found the brakes didn't work properly and not until the night after when I got Jim, who had been a car mechanic in the Fusiliers and had a full driving licence, to look at it, that I learned all the brake cylinders were faulty. There were others things as well, he said but I said we'd talk about them some other time. Right now I wanted to get going and see some action.

After a couple of weeks, because we couldn't get proper washers for the brake cylinders, it was costing me more for brake fluid than it was for petrol; I had to take several cans with me whenever I went for a drive, plus a bleeding kit, plus Jim, and the girls got fed up waiting two hours while we overhauled the whole braking system. Many a night I would get dressed up: green cord jacket, cap, string-backed gloves and suedes, and sit in the car in the back lane outside our house; I'd sit there with my hands on the big steering wheel, sometimes for two hours fantasising, then come in, watch a bit of television and go to bed.

One night Dot arranged a blind date for me with a girl in her office that she and Arnold had been telling me about for a long time, a girl who was seemingly mad about old sports cars.

The meeting place was outside a fashion model studio above Thorne's bookstore in the Haymarket where this girl Judy was doing an evening course.

It was a pain in the neck having Jim in the back. I'd have gladly taken a chance with the provisional licence but I needed him to bleed the brakes when we got to where we were going, which was Whitley Bay; I never had the petrol for anything further and that was the maximum distance the car would go before all the brake fluid had drained out and I'd have to use the handbrake every time I wanted to slow down and the reverse gear in an emergency.

I had to deliver non-stop patter while I was driving beside her and nobody knew better than Jim how well it had served him in the past, so he should have sat back and enjoyed the ride instead of sitting there with his blond crew cut touching the ceiling, laughing at practically everything I said.

One thing shut him up though. We were going past Wills Woodbine Factory when I overtook a bus and was driving alongside it with no more than ten or twelve inches between us when I leaned back to tell him to 'Wrap up!' and the steering wheel came clean out of the column, I was talking away and the steering wheel was waving about in the air in my hands.

'Shit!' he expostulated and Judy's jaw dropped.

I pushed the wheel back into the column, continued overtaking the bus and then drew in front of it once we were past.

The whole thing had only taken a few seconds but it was a long time to go without a heartbeat and Jim kept his mouth shut for the rest of the journey - and so did Judy I must say.

The remainder of the night was uneventful except for losing the keys in the sand amongst the dunes, going back for them in the dark and miraculously finding them. And there was one other thing. I had parked the car on the cliff top as part of the initial male courtship display, and because the handbrake was a much abused accessory the car had rolled so far backwards that it was within a yard of the edge of the cliff. Jim not only wouldn't get in, not only wouldn't get behind and push and double as a chock, but he had the neck to suggest we abandon the Singer altogether.

'Better still, push it over for a laugh.'

I couldn't believe it.

'It's a heap of crap, man. What do you expect for £28..? Leave it. We'll get the train.'

'Like hell we will!'

Neither Jim nor Judy could dissuade me from getting in, at which point the car moved back about six inches and they both - late Northumberland Fusilier notwithstanding - screamed.

But the best thing I had ever owned wasn't that bad, and neither was my driving, and I coaxed it to safety, pulling up about fifty yards further on so they would both have to walk, if they wanted a lift, to find me grinning in the driving seat.

'She's a beauty, isn't she?' I said proudly patting the wheel with my string-backed gloves and adjusting the peak of my cap in the mirror.

The Singer was supposed to be taking Jim, Johnny and I to Munich so I could meet up with the German pen girlfriend I'd been writing to in the Army, plus her younger sister and a friend, and although it was a canny way from Newcastle I never for a moment doubted that we would have managed it.

My father thought I had too many girlfriends and if I wanted any more, a German one was about the last thing the household needed. It was maybe easy enough for certain politicians and some well-meaning schoolteachers to exhort others to 'Forgive and forget' but some people needed more time, perhaps the rest of their lives.

Having a German girlfriend, whilst seeming insensitive considering he had lost his brother Joe at Dunkirk, certainly wasn't to defy or upset my father; really it was because it seemed a challenge. She had turned out to be a very intelligent and highly cultured girl, much more so than any English girl I'd ever met, and I had communicated with her for three years. The culmination was to be meeting her face to face for the first time in Munich and when the car came along I decided to drive to Germany instead of hitching. However, Rosemarie seemed to think I had 'other interests' and had written in confidence to my father, asking whether he thought I was serious about her or not. Without telling me he had received the letter, he had replied to the effect that she would be better off getting on with her life and leaving me out of it because I was too fickle. She had abruptly stopped writing to me and it wasn't until some time later that my mother told me what had happened. My mother had agreed with my father's maintaining that because the letter was sent to him in confidence he was obliged not to say anything at all to me. But I was really miffed at what I though was a piece of high-handedness.

My father was so much against nepotism and boasting about oneself and one's family, that he would sooner understate his sons' achievements than state them at all. He would tell his mother or his brother Edmund if any of us had done particularly well in something, but never anybody else. And if asked to recommend his own son for an appointment, as happened with Michael when in a few years' time he would also join the

Civil Service, he would refuse, saying he wasn't in a position to do it. The problem for us, and ultimately for my father, was that he spoke a language nobody appreciated; nobody I had ever met had scruples like his and none of them would have accepted that anybody that scrupulous existed.

He believed that sooner or later virtue would always be recognised and rewarded. Already, at twenty years of age, I was absolutely certain that this was not so, certainly not both. But I couldn't persuade my father that he was wrong and didn't try. When I came out of the Army I had tried to argue the ineptitude of the British Army and the pointlessness of the Second World War but he had replied that he would entertain no contention that would render the tiniest drop of his brother's blood wasted, let alone his whole life.

I felt it was always scruple over sense with my father, certainly over imagination, and Johnny was exactly the same. Sometimes it was magnificent and sometimes it was excruciating, depending where you stood, but it was something I was never other than proud of them for; it was something that no matter where they went, no silver-tongued hypocrite, loud-mouthed bully or self-appointed leader would ever budge them from, not by so much as an inch, not if they talked from then until Kingdom come - by which time they would have walked off.

The price of principle is sometimes high, especially somebody else's, and I never got to see my fraulein pen-pal.

One Sunday afternoon I was driving from Judy's house in Walker to our house in Heaton, with Anthony who was six years old, in the back, when Judy suddenly remembered something she needed to go back for. We were in a street in the posher part of Walkergate and I had accomplished the first two parts of a classic three-point turn, when the brakes failed and instead of stopping at the kerb as it was intended to do, the Singer mounted the kerb, slowly crashed through a wooden front gate, flattened the hedge on either side, knocked down a young lilac tree in the garden and only came to a halt when it had ascended the steps and met the front door of the house.

Nobody came out so we pushed the car, with Judy attending to Anthony who had fainted inside, back onto the street. By then there were a number of people already outside their doors with pencils and notebooks.

We had previously dropped Jim off at his home so I went to fetch him and he and I pushed the car from there to Walkergate Scout Club which

Jim, an ex-scoutmaster, assured us would be a perfectly safe place to keep it until we had fixed it. The car itself had sustained minimal damage, so formidable was its big bumper and thick metal body.

Lamp posts and other redoubtable immovable objects are one thing, scouts are something else. In three days the car was utterly vandalised and I was lucky to be able to salvage the twelve-volt battery which I carried away in a haversack on my back, and the wheels which I bowled two at a time up the Fossway to Les Eagleton's, the scrap dealer, where I got ten shillings for the lot.

With my German girlfriend out of the picture and the Singer likewise, I persuaded Judy to go halfers and we bought a four-year-old AJS 500cc which apart from an inclination for its timing to advance, something I soon learned to reset, was terrific. Judy absolutely loved it; I never in my life met a girl who had once been on the pillion of a motor-bike, who didn't. 'The women' would have to wait a while yet.

22

I had been successful in the intermediate examination of the IMLT and decided to take my final examination in bacteriology, this would give me Associate-membership of the Institute and allow me to make a medical career. I wanted to get out of the Veterinary Investigation Service but knew I couldn't hope to enter the Hospital Service at my age unless I had a medical qualification. All branches of laboratory science were more highly developed and demanding where they applied to human disorders and there were infinitely greater prospects, in England or abroad.

I was taking evening classes at the Royal Victoria Infirmary and was studying and competing with men and women from different parts of Tyneside, all of whom worked in bacteriology departments in the Hospital Service.

Bacteriology was the biggest department at the VIC and although it dealt with veterinary diseases, much of the methodology was similar to that used in medical laboratories, so I asked Mr Bailey if I could be moved from Parasitology to Bacteriology; all the time I had worked at the VIC I had never worked so much as a day in Bacteriology. Mr Bailey said he didn't feel 'able to accede because Lawrence hasn't got his finals yet' - the more explicit, 'Lawrence failed his finals', was never used by anybody except Steve. Leading up to the time he and Steve had taken their finals for the first time, they had alternated in Bacteriology: one day Steve, the next day Lawrence.

I didn't see why Lawrence and I shouldn't do the same. He wasn't yet thirty and if he took until he was fifty to pass, which was still less than it had taken Oliver, I could be in my forties before he'd move over and I could have a go. Not the least of it was that with the massive strides being made in medical technology, the differential between experience in a medical laboratory and a veterinary one was going to increase every year.

'What about sharing like he and Steve did..? He could go in one week and I could go in the next. Or alternative days... Anything so I can get some work experience?'

He hummed and hawed but kept his gaze fixed on the floor and shuffled his feet.

'Fair's fair, you know, Joe. He's quite a bit older than you and it's only right that he be given all the help we can give.'

'Well, let me say this... When I did my Intermediate I had to do bacteriology as well as all the other subjects. And I wasn't given any bacteriology experience then either. And I didn't ask for it. Now it's essential. I go to evening classes for the theory but I need the practical experience.'

'I appreciate that. But you're young and ambitious. And although that's not necessarily a bad thing, you should remember "All good things come to he who bides his time".'

I didn't know where he'd got that but I hadn't been brought up to live my life by platitudes.

'Couldn't you just ask him..? What if I did one week out of every month? Or only one day a week?'

'You're making things very difficult for me, Joe. I can tell you now that he won't agree. He's already made that very clear.'

'But you're the head of department. Could you not insist I be given some time in Bacteriology..? Any time at all?'

'I may be head of department but that doesn't give me the right to do anything I want. I have to consult my colleagues on important matters, you know.'

'Mr McCulloch and Mr Norris, you mean?'

He nodded with a grimace.

'Well, ask them, would you? It's important to me. Surely somebody has to see it as fair.'

'I think Steve worked very hard in addition to his experience in Bacteriology,' he said sort of reprovingly.

'So would I,' I said exasperatedly.

'Look how long it took Oliver.' He was gently wagging his finger.

'Yes, but if he'd worked thirty years in Bacteriology instead of Histology, he might have got it quicker... Anyway, I'm not Oliver.'

'You know, Joe, some people think you might have a teeny weeny little chip on your shoulder.'

I knew what this meant. It meant I'd had it.

'All the same, would you please put it to them? That's all I'm asking.'

'Of course, old chap. Of course. I'll let you know.'

'I'm sorry, it's quite impossible,' he said a few days later when I went to see him. 'Both my colleagues agree it's only fair we give Lawrence the full support of the department. I also had a word with Lawrence...and he was adamant.'

If only Standish had been here with his 'merit is all'...or Eugene Hunter with his brutal survival-of-the-fittest philosophy. But they were both gone now and when I carried a tray of viscera from the PM house into Bacteriology where Lawrence would be sitting humming, he would flare his nostrils like some kind of male territorial insect. I'd never get to work in Bacteriology at this rate, I'd be counting worm eggs in sheepshit till Doomsday and at the same time having to pray for Lawrence's success.

But I wasn't going to leave it at that. I would stay behind after work every night of the week when I didn't have a class, and one by one I would take every method, test and technique in the bacteriology syllabus, prepare every reagent and aspect of it myself, obtain biological samples from myself or from friends I'd made at evening classes, time myself with an alarm clock and do everything as many times as necessary until I could do it right and do it in double-quick time. This way my programme would be more comprehensive than any because I would do the obscure, the tedious and the time-consuming tests that were ignored or given only superficial attention at evening classes.

And I wouldn't say a thing to anybody.

More than anyone in the department, I think Oliver regretted my going into the Army. 'What happened to the sweet obliging lad we used to have?' he would sometimes muse after I had said something cynical. 'He was killed by the first encounter with the realities of life,' I would reply laughing, and he would walk away shaking his head.

There were plenty who said he was nothing but a senile and useless old crawler, but as far as the VIC was concerned I think he had more integrity than anybody; only Bailey would have been in the same category. He might have been a bit of an old woman and he was definitely no scientist but he wasn't a total idiot either, he had considerable knowledge of birds, his one and only hobby. Occasionally he would bring photographs he had taken into the library at tea-break, mainly to show me because he knew I would show some interest but it was very hard to maintain a serious expression amid the loud derisive laughter when the others came in.

'Which way up is this one supposed to be, then?' somebody would say, picking up a print. 'Is it sitting on a nest or has it crash-landed?'

Afterwards when they had all gone, still laughing and leaving him to pick up his prints, he would sort them out, wipe off the ring of tea left by a mug carelessly placed, and put them back into their envelopes with a resigned smile. There was no vindictiveness in him; for instance, nobody but Oliver would have tolerated being sheep-dipped.

He, Steve and I, were dipping the VIC's sheep one afternoon and Steve was furious because he reckoned Albert should have somehow done the job by himself. Albert had made some excuse for not even helping, which Oliver had accepted; as a consequence, Steve was roped in; I had already been roped in.

The dip was a concrete 3' x 3' x 3' tank sunk into the ground with a ramp at each end and filled with a liquid noxious not only to blowflies and Scab but to all forms of life. Oliver's task was to trick, coax or bully the sheep into the tank. Steve's job was to stand at the side with a rake and make sure they were completely submerged. And my job was to yank them out the other end and send them on their way into the field.

We had done about half and Steve was getting madder and madder with Oliver's slowness and clumsiness, as well as with his patience and smiling stoicism; sheep are loath to dive into a sheep dip, they are loath to do anything you want them to do.

Single-handedly Oliver wrestled with ram, wether, hogget and ewe, straddling their shoulders and grabbing their ears or horns, trying to get them to do what their instincts told them not to do, until finally he went in on the back of a particularly recalcitrant ewe. As ewe and rider plunged in, Steve thrust both of them down beneath the surface all the way to the bottom so that every square centimetre of skin would be drenched and acquire six months' protection against the predation of maggot and mite. Not a fold, not a cranny, not a wrinkle would be missed. Ears, eyes, nose, mouth, anus and genitals would all be done by the time the two beasts came back up.

'Oops! Sorry, old chap,' Steve quoted Oliver's own oft-repeated words at him as he emerged, saturated, red raw, and, with his heavy black plastic coat, looking like a Farne Island seal.

'Are you okay..? I didn't see you at first. As soon as something goes in, I'm at it with the old prodder.' He turned to me with a wink and a grin of feigned helplessness. 'My reactions are so quick.'

As I hauled poor Oliver out, slavering corrosive sheep dip, he was too well brought up even to spit. His wire-rimmed spectacles were hanging from one ear, his eyes bloodshot, his wellingtons full to the brim and he had such a look of benign suffering on his face; he was probably thinking 'Forgive them, Father, for they know not what they do.'

Quarter of an hour later when we had finished, by which time his skin must have been in torment, he couldn't get into the PM house quick enough. Having declined Steve's offer to hose him down with cold water, he locked himself in, stripped off and was washing himself and surely employing all his resources to resist yelling out with the agony and indignity of it all when Mr McCulloch came to the door with a couple of country vets and a sackful of piglets with query swine fever.

'Open up... Who's in there?'

'Me.'

'Who?'

'Me. Oliver. I - '

'Open the blasted door!' stormed McCulloch.

Instead of replying 'Get lost, you Scotch get!' or something very like it, Oliver opened the door in bare feet with an apron around his waist.

McCulloch and his two companions stared at him, aghast.

'What the hell do you think you're doing..! Make yourself respectable at once!' bawled McCulloch. With that he tipped the sack on the floor and five squeaking piglets shot out and began running around the room. Oliver never said a word, he hadn't the kind of wit or nerve that might have turned his plight into a triumph.

McCulloch slammed the door and the three of them went to have tea in his office.

When I went for the practical part of the Bacteriology Final, the performance of a Rideal-Walker phenol-coefficient test was required. Because this test was rarely carried out in a hospital laboratory and was very time-consuming, it had never been demonstrated during the course I had taken and probably hadn't been at any of the courses my fellow candidates had taken and some of them complained of it. But because I had worked through everything in the syllabus on my own, tedious or otherwise during my lonely nights at the VIC, I knew how to do it and was fairly confident about the results of the exam.

I had decided that when I passed my Bacteriology Final I would move down to London, get a job in a good hospital and study virology with a view to gaining Fellow-membership of the IMLT; Judy and I would then get married, get a job abroad and see a bit of the world. Things at home were steadily getting worse and it had come to the point where neither my father nor I could have compromised even had we wanted to.

A vacancy was advertised in the bacteriology department of Enfield Hospital in Middlesex and I applied for it, was called for interview and informed I would be appointed subject to success in my recent examination. As soon as I came out of the interview I telephoned the secretary of the IMLT in Harley Street and was told the results wouldn't be announced for several weeks but could assume they would 'not be an impediment'.

On the strength of this I handed in my notice at the VIC and told Mr Bailey I was finished with the Veterinary Service because medical laboratory technology was more sophisticated, more satisfying and there were far more opportunities for advancement. I laid it on but it was perfectly true and I felt he deserved it. I am sure that, as he said, he was genuinely sorry to lose me and although his colleagues were insinuating events had shown they were right to keep me out of Bacteriology, especially since being there hadn't done the trick for Lawrence, I suspected he wasn't so sure.

Judy worked for Tullis Hunter, a branch of the Inveresk Paper Company on the Quayside. She would stay at home with her father and mother and young brother until I had sussed things out down South.

Enfield Hospital

23

A couple of minutes after nine o'clock, one sunny Saturday morning early in September, I threw my leg over the AJS, kicked the engine into action, and with all my necessaries in a haversack, waved goodbye to the family standing in the doorway of 41 Simonside Terrace. I shot off with my customary roar, up towards Heaton Road, down Shields Road and along Newbridge Street, down Pilgrim Street, across the Tyne Bridge and on to the Great North Road.

This time I knew I was leaving home for good. I was twenty-two years old and had never settled in after coming out of the Army. Newcastle, the VIC and the house in Simonside which had never really seemed like home, weren't big enough to contain me any more; I couldn't unlearn what I had learnt in the Army, not for the sake of my family or my colleagues.

I stopped only once by the side of the A1 for a sandwich, a drink of orange juice and a cigarette, before pulling up outside a prim semi-detached house in Parsonage Lane in North London. I don't know whether the name of the street had anything to do with the vocation of the residents but it seemed a very genteel area with well-kept shrubby gardens and no evidence of privet, leeks or pigeons.

When the hospital secretary had written to confirm my appointment he had given me the address of Mrs Mabel Timms and I had briefly corresponded with her. This was the first time I had ever been in 'digs' and I was interested to see what advantages and disadvantages there would be over living at home. I imagined it would be better. I would be paying £4 per week which was a bit less than the half salary I had always paid at home, and apart from my every needs being catered to by what I imagined would be a homely buxom mother-like figure, I would be entirely my own man. It would be like a small cosy hotel, a guesthouse with an all-night key, and that had considerable appeal.

When I switched off the engine after verifying the number on the house, took off my gauntlets and helmet with the skull and crossbones on the front, shut off the petrol, re-set the levers on the handlebars and stepped off the bike, it was to see the lace curtains at the front windows of the house that was to be my homely hotel, drawn aside and three faces huddled together watching me.

Had I done this in the North, the front door would have been open as soon as the bike stopped and the woman of the house would have been down the path. Here I had to walk up the path, leathers creaking and boots clomping towards a front door that remained resolutely closed. I guessed this was how they would have responded to an invasion from Germany or Mars, remaining behind the curtains of their front rooms until they were taken away.

I knocked on the door twice before a thin woman with a 1940 hairdo, large pale blue spectacles on a big pinched nose, no lips and no sign of any breasts, opened it with caution.

'Yes?' she said, looking over my shoulder as though I had just landed a plane on the lawn.

'Are you Mrs Timms?'

'I am,' she said challengingly.

'I'm Joseph Robinson. I've been writing to you about digs.'

'Digs?'

'I thought that's what they called them down here.'

'Not in this house, we don't. But that's by the by... When you said in your letter that you would be coming on your "bike", we naturally presumed you meant "bicycle".' She had that high-pitched timbre of outrage that English women manage so well. 'My husband and I will have to reconsider the whole question of you staying with us now,' she said, withdrawing and shutting the door in my face.

When it opened nearly ten minutes later, by which time I had gone back to the bike and was just sitting on it having a smoke, there was a bald-headed man with small features and tortoise-shell spectacles standing beside Mrs Timms.

'This is Mr Timms.'

'So, you're the young chap who's come to work at the hospital?' he said in a querulous tone, as though the matter had not yet been finally decided.

'Yes.'

He had obviously said his piece and established his authority so Mrs Timms now took over. She stood there with her big bony arms folded, eyes huge behind her spectacles, thick pink nostrils immobile and airtight, the lobes of her soft shapeless ears hanging like blobs, and behind her the most awful smell of cooking.

'Well, Maurice and I have discussed the matter and because you've obviously come from quite a long way away, we've decided to give you the benefit of the doubt for the time being and allow you in until we've had more time to think about what to do.'

'Right. Thanks.'

As I stepped into the hall she said 'We would never have agreed to one of those going backwards and forwards to the house every day with all that dreadful noise and smoke.' She nodded towards the bike. 'Would we, Maurice?'

Maurice shook his head as he lit up a filthy pipe.

I was told to leave my things in the hall and shown into the small front room which had a dining table in the centre. A sideboard with crockery displayed was on one wall, a bookcase with a few drab books along another, the other two walls each had a small wishy-washy picture of a country scene.

A very nervous wire-bespectacled boy of about sixteen in a grammar school pullover came in, who Mr Timms introduced as their son Aynsley. As I reached over to shake his hand, something he appeared never to have been called on to do before, I felt a wave of revulsion at the thought of Mabel and Maurice Timms having coupled even once.

Mrs Timms, in the clattering way of those still possessing examples of the first wave of NHS full uppers-and-lowers, announced she might make tea, and Maurice, with a clatter, said that would be very nice and everybody nodded and the motion was carried. Back home they would have just made it, poured it out and passed it around.

After the tea ceremony which consisted of a gentle grilling, was over, I was shown my room. It was, like the rest of the house, clean and tidy. I don't know why it gave me the impression that somebody had recently died in the bed; maybe it was because the bedclothes were white and the bed-ends old fashioned; maybe it was the queer smell; maybe it was because there were no pictures or anything on the walls, nothing to engage your attention or cause you to linger. It was clearly just a place to sleep, especially if you were terminally ill.

Meals were at strict times and there were no snacks between because the Timms didn't 'believe in it', though whether it was for religious or dietary reasons, they didn't say. I would be allowed an apple a day from the tree in the back garden, or rather from the 'windfall' on the ground beneath the tree, and one biscuit with a cup of cocoa if I came in after supper had been served.

There were napkins at the table which were patently used a number of times before being washed and I was relieved I had never used a napkin in my life and that it was too late to start learning now. Mr Timms was forever wiping himself and I suspect regurgitating bits he didn't like, so sooner or later every napkin-user was going to find one that he'd used folded up with its dried tomato seeds and traces of other perhaps unidentifiable matter in front of them; not that Aynsley's or Mrs Timms' would have been any less repulsive.

Maurice Timms was very proud of the fact that he worked at the Royal Mint but didn't talk about his work, as though it were very hush-hush; maybe they were working on some new super-coin that never lost its milled edge, or perhaps employees who came into contact with the product were forever being importuned by relatives and friends. So apart from a question-and-answer session about 'The North' which preceded almost all conversations, topics were almost entirely to do with Aynsley and his school.

By the time I went to bed on the Sunday night I had only seen four rooms: the tiny hall, the dining room, the kitchen and my bedroom, all of them lacking in human warmth; they were like sets from a BBC children's programme about a family of neat and tidy depressives. So far I hadn't seen the slightest trace of endearment between the three of them at any time, they might just as well have been made out of the hard colourless plasticine we used to get during the war.

For a while I lay wondering about the morrow, how I was going to get on at the hospital and if Enfield would be full of people like the Timms. In the end, feeling as though I had already been laid out, I went to sleep thanking God for the mother and father he had given me.

On the Monday morning I started my bike as quietly as I could, aware that there were probably dozens of people behind lace curtains with half-written letters in their hands, counting the decibels. Then I rode up the hill to Enfield Hospital, parked my bike, and twenty minutes later was working in Bacteriology.

I immediately liked it: the bacteriology laboratory, the pathology department and the hospital. It was a small general hospital with a feeling of humanity and liberal conviviality about it and very different from the military hospitals I had worked in. There were two young women in the laboratory, Chloë who was very upper class and Sandra who wasn't quite, and about twenty men and women of various ages in the other labs.

I was something of a curiosity in a place like this which I doubted had ever encountered anybody as exotic as a Shieldsman, though I must say I was well received by the majority. I don't think the initial difficulty they had was so much with the accent, as with the personality, but they probably put it down more to birthplace than birthright. To have one's vices attributed to a geographical pedigree, in my case the collective original sin that a Northerner inherits, was most convenient; it meant I could get away with being blunt, tactless, ignorant and maybe a few other quaint regional foibles.

Mind, I had some shuffling to do, the accommodation wasn't entirely one-sided. Something I was totally unprepared for was working with some very intelligent, attractive and strong minded women. In the home I was brought up, my mother was the only woman; in the Army I had never worked with any woman, and in the vet lab 'female' was synonymous with limited responsibility.

On my third day I was standing at the sink washing my hands, when I was suddenly grabbed and embraced from behind by a very strong pair of arms. When I turned around it was to be met by a big toothy smile on a bronzed muscular face framed by receding blond hair that looked as though it had been electrified. Even inside the white laboratory coat with its pockets stuffed with pens and forceps I could feel the body of an Amazon.

'Ooh, I think I'll come back to Bacteriology.' She still had me in her grasp and kissed me hard, though of course without any passion. She was looking me in the eyes, presumably searching to see how much nerve or humour there was, and all the while pressing her hard and undulating body against me.

I had never met anyone like her. All the girls I'd ever come to grips with, I'd been the one doing the gripping. Any adult women had been relatives and their hugs had been brief and non-threatening, never head-on like this with their knees touching mine and their crotches thrust at me like an American football. My embarrassment and confusion seemed to delight and urge her on and the only way I could have perhaps broken free would have been to have gone into judo mode and thrown her. But not only would that have been inappropriate, I could easily imagine her being a third or fourth dan and my landing on the lino with my arm twisted up my back, whacking the floor with my free hand to signal submission.

With Chloë and Sandra looking on she at last released me. 'I'll be back,' she said and went out.

'Who was that?' I gasped, straightening my clothing.

'That was Pru,' Chloë declared.

'Does she usually..?'

They both laughed. 'Depends on how soon your novelty wears off.'

Just before lunch-time Pru came into the lab to invite me to a play by Arthur Miller that she was in. I had never been to a play before and had always thought theatre people cissies but she wouldn't brook a refusal and I had nothing else to do.

That night I was sitting in the audience of a theatre listening to the most outlandish American accents from people in baggy trousers, golfing pullovers and huge Buster Keaton caps; I thought it must be a farce of some kind and couldn't stop cringing. Nevertheless at the end after rapturous applause from an audience I assumed must have been friends and relatives, I was invited back stage.

Of course I had never been in such company before. Some of them were in theatrical dress and make-up, all of it overdone, the women talked like men and the men talked like women and they all talked all of the time; they were so excited and so full of themselves. I didn't know adult people could behave like this and I didn't know whether it was supposed to be a party or what. Pru was plainly in her element but she didn't forget about me and made sure I was never without a drink and introduced me to umpteen people with names I couldn't believe they had been baptised with.

When she introduced me to somebody who looked like Liberace, he asked me what I thought of the play and I told him.

'Hold it, everybody!' he shrilled. 'Stop what you're doing this instant and listen to them...the vowels. They're incredible..! Now, Joseph,' he said to me. 'Repeat what you just said... Go on... Exactly, now... Word for word.'

I thought he wanted me to repeat my opinion of the play so they could lynch me.

'Well, I...'

There was dead silence.

'Don't worry about the...er...critique.' He rolled the word around in his mouth and winked at everybody so they would all know whether I was an 'aye' or a 'nay'.

'It's not what you say that's important. It's how you say it. Now... Listen to this heavenly voice, children.'

I sat, the power of speech gone completely. 'Ah, er...'

They were all staring, all waiting for a laugh I was certain.

'Give us your Bardolph!'

'What about Rabbie Burns..?'

'No, you silly bitch! That's Scotland..! Wordsworth's his countryman.'

'I bet he'd be perfect as the gardener when somebody gets around to adapting Chatterley!'

'I'm sorry, I cannot think of anything to say,' was the best I could muster. I had never been so bereft of speech in my life. Nonetheless they applauded and I realised crucifixion can take different forms.

I was heading back to Parsonage Lane one night when I saw Aynsley walking home with his schoolbag on his back and I slowed down to see if he wanted a lift.

'My mother would go mad if she knew,' he stammered. But I could see he was dying for a ride.

'She won't know unless you tell her. I'll drop you off at the top of the street.'

'What if she's out shopping and sees?'

'The back of this bike's the last place in the world she'd look... Howay, hop on.'

He was trembling as he climbed on and grabbed the sides of my jacket. I only took him half a mile and he clung to me like a leech but by the look in his eyes when I let him off I could see it had probably been the greatest thrill of his life.

'Good, eh?' I laughed.

'Smashing..! Gee whizz!' Tears were streaming down his face.

From then on Aynsley looked on me as if I had been party to his deflowering and he would grin salaciously at me when no one was around.

The following Sunday I took him for a run that culminated in a visit to the hospital outdoor swimming pool. It was October so although it was a sunny day the water would have been cold. I had pulled my bike on its stand and was switching off the petrol, when out of nowhere there was a hell of a splash and a torpedo-like form moving through the water towards where Aynsley and I were. Suddenly the surface broke and the shining athletic face of Pru thrust itself out.

'Come on in! The water's lovely.'

'My trunks are in Newcastle.'

'Come in naggy-shaggy, then. You're not scared of little old me, are you?' She powered her way to the far end in a back crawl. 'I thought you Northerners were supposed to be tough..? Wait till I tell them all at work tomorrow.'

To Aynsley's horror, I stripped down to my underpants and dived in. Immediately she was at me like some kind of shark, grabbing a hold of me and trying to pull my pants down with her foot. I had to wrestle to get free, she was so strong. From then on it was like predator and prey, with me swimming as fast as I could and she tearing after me and making deep-throated 'ooargh!' sounds as if she'd taken leave of her senses... Eventually I got out and lay down on my back to dry off. Aynsley had witnessed everything and was shaking like a leaf, maybe he thought he was next.

'Hadn't we better be getting back for tea?' he suggested.

Just at that I was aware of the sun being blotted out and a second later a hard round wet body slapped down on me.

'Pru..! What about Aynsley?'

'Never mind Aynsley! Concentrate on me! He might learn something... You wouldn't tell anybody, would you, Aynsley?' she said menacingly.

'Oh no! But I really think I'd better be going. I've got some homework to finish off and...'

'Give over!' I said to Pru, forcing myself to the sitting position. 'We can't let him go by himself. If he's late for tea, his mother'll have the police out looking for him.'

Aynsley nodded.

Virology was a new and exciting science and more and more infectious diseases were being attributed to viruses - the common cold, flu', hepatitis, poliomyelitis - at least as many if not more than bacteria. It was a different branch of microbiology, still dealing with living micro-organisms but requiring completely new techniques of cultivation and identification. I had to travel to the Public Health Laboratory in Colindale two nights a week for the IMLT virology course but it was good exercise for the bike and the wind and wet never bothered me after working in a hot and stuffy laboratory all day.

Chloë was studying for her Intermediate IMLT examination and I would occasionally go to her house to give her some tuition. She lived in Winchmore Hill and took it upon herself to teach me to speak 'properly'. Her parents weren't impressed by me at all - not where I came from, how I spoke, that I rode a motor-bike and had a helmet with skull and crossbones, that I was a Catholic, nothing.

But when the spoilt Chloë borrowed Daddy's beautiful big Rover, his tangible pride and joy, it was me - not 'I' - who drove it as soon as we had got to the bottom of the street and turned the corner. And it was me singing 'Cushie Butterfield' and 'Keep Your Feet Still Geordie, Hinny' that they heard when they turned on their new tape recorder to play some chamber music. Sometimes I wished Tod had been down here, I would dearly have loved to have taken him around one night. Whatever they thought about me, a couple of hours with Tod would have disabused them once and for all of any notion they might have still entertained about the latent charm of the industrial beast.

Although the Timms hadn't introduced me to their next-door neighbours, the Morleys, nor ever referred to them, even though it was their daughter Janet who had put Mrs Timms in touch with me, I very soon got to know them.

Janet worked in the pathology office at the hospital so I saw her every day and when I came back to the Timms' after being out at night, as soon as Bill Morley heard the sound of the bike he would come out into his garden to have a few words.

Bill was short and burly with a thin moustache that sometimes looked as though it were there and sometimes looked as though it wasn't, thin hair, small eyes and a slight speech impediment caused by a few missing teeth. He was an engineer with the GPO and married to Elsie, a woman with white hair, slightly protruding teeth and a slight stoop, and they were as different from their neighbours as any neighbours could be. They were cheerful, they were kind-hearted, good-humoured, broad-minded and couldn't have been nicer to me.

When Judy came to London for a weekend, it was with the Morleys that she stayed, and because of it there was a right 'row upon the stairs' at the Timms'.

'And who might I ask was the young lady we saw you taking next door with her suitcase last night?' Mrs Timms called up, hands on hips, as I began to descend the stairs for breakfast the following morning.

'My girlfriend Judy.'

'Is that the one from the North?'

'Yes, it is.'

'And how long might I ask will she be staying down here for?'

'Just the weekend.'

'Then why might I ask didn't you bring her here?'

'There's no room. Anyway she wanted to stay there.'

'How could she know she would want to stay there and not here, unless you said something to her..? Both Maurice and I are deeply offended that you should do such a wicked thing after all we have done... Maurice!'

Mr Timms, who had obviously been waiting behind the door for his cue, came in.

'You've been very sly about this,' he said, wagging his finger. 'You've led us right up the garden path. Nobody could have treated you better than her good self, Mrs Timms, and, I might say, myself... Coming here with that great big motor-cycle of yours, the way you did... And then you go and do such a thing as this.'

I was halfway down the stairs when he came out with: 'We don't want people like you in our house'.

I came down quite fast and he almost ran back down into the kitchen. I reckoned they would both be hoping I would choke on my cornflakes so I decided to skip breakfast and go straight in to see Judy.

'You've got a chip on your shoulder, my lad,' Maurice shouted as I closed the front door.

I collected Judy and we went into town for the day, returning to the Morleys for tea.

When I told them what had happened, they were over the moon.

'Great! Great! You can come here! We wanted to ask you ages ago but couldn't say anything because they were our neighbours... Get your things. You can move in right away.'

I went next door, packed my suitcase and was coming down the stairs when my passage was blocked by both of the Timms, Mr Timms in front like a shield.

'Where do you think you're going, may I ask?' Mrs Timms demanded.

'I'm leaving.'

'You have to give a fortnight's notice. That's the law,' said Mr Timms.

'You've already told me you don't want me here.'

'That was meant to be notice... Anyway Mabel and I have thought it over and are prepared to consider giving you another chance.'

'I've got somewhere else now. I'll be back later for the balance of rent I paid yesterday.'

'We'll see about that..! I'll have to make out a proper bill,' sniffed Mrs Timms.

As I was going down they were retreating a step at a time before me as though trying to delay my departure.

When I went for my money the next day they had made out a bill and charged for every sock reputedly darned and every handkerchief washed and ironed, and I ended up getting two shillings and seven pence back. I could have said more but I was glad to get out of the place. Anyway what could you say to a woman who counted the number of biscuits in the tin first thing every morning and would hold an inquiry if there was one less than she had anticipated, to a woman who woke you up every Sunday morning to ask if you were going to Methodist Chapel, knowing you were a Catholic, especially to a woman who never mentioned a daughter who had got pregnant at sixteen, had been put out and had ceased to exist as far as her mother and the rest of her family were concerned.

Judy went back to Newcastle the next day and I took over her room. Bill and Elsie were wonderful to me and so was Janet. I never met better people.

Bill was crazy about electronic gadgets and the room they made up for me was wired so that he could contact me at any hour of the night. Sometimes it would be 3am when my headphones would buzz and I would hear 'I've got the short-wave on and can tune you into a fight in Piccadilly with three of them in the fountain. Or an indecent exposure in Russell Square... Which one do you want..? You'll just love the prattle of the police at Russell Square!'

24

The pathologist at the hospital was Dr Hans Blüchner and he had apparently escaped from Austria before the war, though you could be forgiven for thinking it was only the day before yesterday. He had more hair in his ears and nose than on his head, enormous ears, a huge drooping nose, thick wet lips, no chin and no neck, and he walked like a turtle on its hind legs. He never moved his head but his bulging eyes served him well enough and if you hailed him they would turn towards you and his lips would move but nothing intelligible, at least not in English, would come out. You could have a conversation with him and not understand a single word he said and not know whether he had understood a single word you had said either; in my case he probably thought I had some kind of speech impediment.

The only time I ever saw him approach anything like animation was the time I had post-mortemed four guinea pigs that had been injected four weeks previously with suspected tuberculous material, and had died from Pasteurella pseudo-TB, a common enough pathogen for the guinea pig and rabbit but not for man. The livers and spleens had the typical Pasteurella nodules that were similar to those produced by tuberculosis but different in their profusion, colour and shape. I had seen many cases of Pasteurella during my time with the VIC and was so certain of my finding that I hadn't bothered doing the microscopic examination that would have confirmed it beyond doubt.

I told Dr Blüchner that I had done the pigs and left them for him to look at.

A couple of hours later the Pathology chief technician came in to tell me I'd made a serious mistake with the guinea pigs and they were all tuberculous.

'How do you mean?'

'Dr Blüchner says every one of them is positive for TB and he's sending the report. He said you'd better take a good look at them so you don't ever make the same mistake again. He says I've to check them over with you in future.'

'He's wrong. All four are Pasteurella. That's why it's called "pseudo-TB"...because they superficially resemble TB. I've seen hundreds of them, hundreds of TBs as well.'

He was a very self-effacing little man called David Green; everybody called him 'Davy' and he was so soft everybody took liberties with him, especially the women.

He went off to tell Blüchner what I'd said and came back very discomfited ten minutes later.

'I'm afraid he's adamant. He says what you say is' - he hesitated - '"rubbish"...and he's never heard of any kind of Pasteurella like you're talking about.'

'You have though, haven't you?'

'To tell the truth, no, I haven't... Sorry.'

It was standard procedure to use guinea pigs in cases of patients strongly suspected of having TB who had given negative results for other TB tests. Sputum or biopsy material would be injected into two guinea pigs - the guinea pig being very sensitive to the human form of TB - one of which would be killed at four weeks and post-mortemed, and the other at six weeks. If the first four-week pig was positive for TB, the other pig would be killed also and checked. If the four-week and subsequent six-week pig were negative, the report would go out as negative.

These were all six-week pigs so there were no others to confirm or otherwise.

'You can't let those reports go out positive, Davy. Otherwise four people are going to be put in a sanatorium and given massive doses of dangerous drugs for nothing. If they don't have TB when they go in, they'll more than likely have it when they come out... Come on. I'll show you.'

'I've already seen them.'

'Well?'

'I must say they look like TB to me.'

'Right. There's a very simple proof... I'll get some microscope slides and we'll take scrapings. I'll stain one batch by Gram's method which will show if they're Pasteurella, and one by Ziehl Neelson which will show if they're TB. I bet you anything, they all show Pasteurella and none show TB.'

He pulled a face and glanced at Blüchner's closed door.

'It'll only take five minutes and I want you to check everything I do.'

He was still hesitating.

'You've no choice. You've got to, Davy. You put me in charge of bacteriology and I have a right to expect your support.'

He bit his lip and nodded. 'Okay.'

Furtively he followed me out to the animal hut where I swiftly took the samples and together we checked the identity of the pigs. Then we came back to the lab where I stained one lot by Gram's method and the other by Ziehl Neelson's and examined them under the microscope. They were all Pasteurella, no doubt about it and there was no evidence of TB.

'Shit,' Davy said softly as he looked down the microscope. 'He isn't going to like this.'

'Neither will the poor buggers who end up in a sanatorium because of our mistake.'

'Do you mind if I check them myself?'

'Course not. Do whatever you want. I'll just leave you to get on with it.'

An hour later, after taking umpteen slides and staining them and examining every one of them microscopically and discussing the matter with Bart, the senior technician who had done the TB work before I came, Davy came up to where I was working on the bench.

'I've never seen anything like it.'

'Do you want me to tell him?'

'Oh, no. I'll have to do it.'

He then went to Blüchner's office and closed the door behind him. I couldn't hear what either of them said but I could hear the guttural tones of Blüchner.

Finally Davy came out looking very chastened, followed by Blüchner. Neither of them spoke a word to me as they went through the lab and out to the animal hut. They were in there a long time before Blüchner came out and a while later Davy carrying a tray with microscope slides on it. He came into the lab, winked at me and stained the slides himself and then took them into Blüchner's office.

'Well?' I said to him when he came out half an hour later. He just grimaced and walked on and I knew they both knew old Hans had made a mistake and they were wondering how many others there had been over the years.

Although I had kept frogs and tadpoles as a boy, I had never encountered them in a laboratory. Here toads were used to diagnose pregnancies in humans and it was an easier, more reliable and humane test than that using mice which had to be sacrificed and dissected at the end; toads were just let go afterwards.

Toads didn't keep well and once a week a consignment would come in from some kind of poacher who caught half a dozen at night and brought them to Davy.

For the test, the toad was first examined for the presence of spermatozoa and if negative injected with urine from a possibly pregnant human female, usually a girl or 'not straightforward' adult. If she was pregnant the accompanying hormones in her urine would stimulate the production of sperm in the toad. It was so neat and bizarre a test that I wished there were many such more in medical laboratory technology. It would have been interesting to test Catholic doctrine on the procedure, somehow I felt sure it would have been a sin.

An old friend of Chloë's who was a sales representative for Pfizer, a big American pharmaceutical company, often came into the lab. He would always be beautifully dressed, smelling of expensive after-shave and pass handmade Russian cigarettes around as he entertained us with tales of the rich and famous that he'd heard on his travels; just outside the window his annually-replaced company car would be waiting gleaming.

He and I became friendly and whenever he called we would talk about repping, about the £750 per annum salary, the bonuses and competitions with prizes of refrigerators, television sets and holidays abroad for two.

'You're just the kind of guy the big companies are looking for. The market's ready to explode... Your veterinary experience would be an extra asset and you could still do your virology final if you wanted to. It'd be no harder than it is now. You make your own time in this job... With all the perks you'd be more than twice as well off as you are now. I couldn't afford to go back to a lab now.'

He would toss a couple of science magazines on the bench.

'Look in the back. There's at least half a dozen good vacancies in each one... Why not go for a couple of interviews and see what you think? You could do two in a morning and be back at your bench for the afternoon.'

I'd only been at the hospital a short time and I liked it. My job was interesting and neither Davy or Blückner ever bothered me, I think that after the guinea pig affair Blückner had quickly forgotten I existed. And it was great staying at the Morleys and being only half an hour from the centre of London.

But the situation with Judy living in Newcastle and me living in London wasn't working out very well and she didn't want to give up her job unless we were definitely going to get married. It was going to be hard to save enough on £12 per week gross. If I had a job that paid £3 more, especially one that provided free transport, it would make all the difference. I could take on such a job, save enough to get married and then resume my career in medical microbiology.

There were those who said the life of a medical rep was an easy one and there were those who said they wouldn't do it for love nor money, but they all agreed it paid far better than any laboratory.

Most of my friends and colleagues in the pathology department who felt they knew me sufficiently said they doubted very much that repping would suit me, or I it, and I was rather peeved. 'How do you mean?' I would say. 'Well, you know...' they'd reply. They knew about 'commercial travellers', about how seedy and disreputable they were supposed to be, always away from home, scraping a living. But a pharmaceutical rep was a different genus altogether. The ones I had seen visiting the hospital - there were many more than just the Pfizer rep, every pharmaceutical company had them - all had smart suits, new cars and a comparatively luxurious lifestyle compared with anybody who worked for the MAFF or the NHS. Even Davy Green who was in his fifties, well qualified and at the top of the laboratory promotion ladder, came to work by bus and always wore the same clothes; he didn't have a big family yet only had haircuts at long intervals and his watch was always stopping.

At the end of October I went up to Newcastle for Johnny's twenty-first and while I was there I did the shittiest thing I'd ever done in my life.

Whenever I visited home, even though it would only be for a day or two on the odd weekend and most of the time I would be out, my father and I would invariably be at loggerheads. I suppose we were both at fault, he was always certain he was right and I was every bit as certain I was. I was resigned to the likelihood that this was the way things would always be and that long after the provocation had been forgotten the bitterness would be preserved to warn us not to engage in anything, however tempting or apparently safe, for fear of irreparable injury.

I arrived about 2.30pm on the Saturday afternoon and bounced into the house. It was already the big day and everybody would be fleeing about getting things organised for the party.

The back door was open but nobody appeared to be in so I went through the scullery and kitchen into the passage, calling out; but there was no answer. I looked into the sitting room and it was empty and so was the front room. Then I noticed the front door was ajar as though my mother had just slipped out for something, and was about to turn around to go back into the kitchen when something made me look up. Halfway up the staircase, kneeling, sleeves rolled up, taking out and polishing each stair rod, one by one, was my father. Nobody outside this family would have thought him capable of it and he would never have told anybody, but every weekend the Higher Executive Officer of the National Assistance Board swept and scrubbed, scraped and cleaned, dusted and polished, working every bit as hard as my mother; he had done it for as long as I could remember and had always insisted we boys did our share also.

He looked at me, his mouth half open, and I could see he had been on the point of calling out to answer me. It would have been so easy to have put my arm through the bars of the banister and shaken his strong white hand with the few dark hairs on the fingers and the worn-smooth signet ring. But I didn't. We looked at each other and I could see he was waiting. I was sure, despite all the years of discord, that he loved me and wanted my love in return. But this time I wouldn't give in, I had always been the one who had to yield as the prelude to our making up. He could just as easily have put his arm through but didn't, so I didn't; if the price was too high for him, it was too high for me. I couldn't resist hurting him, I couldn't resist punishing him for all the unflinching years of discipline.

'Oh, I thought it was...' was all I said, and it was out before I could stop it, before I turned and walked out.

By evening, by about eleven o'clock when the party was in full swing, it was too late to recant. I had got myself into the position where I could do nothing but persist. By now, he the stronger, tougher man, had regained his composure and would make no further offer. He would acquiesce readily enough if I did, as he always did, immediately and unconditionally, but anything now would have to come unequivocally from me. I thought about it and reckoned I could last out the night, I'd be in Enfield this time tomorrow. And because I didn't make the gesture, and he wouldn't, couldn't or felt he shouldn't, we let the moment pass a dozen times: standing by after a nod of the head to let the other go through the passage first, coming out of the toilet adjusting our pants to find the other waiting, going into the pantry to get another bottle and silently pouring out glasses side by side with nobody else around, or simultaneously starting up with the same song from different ends of the sitting room.

We both did our bit, did our own repertoires, danced, carried on and everything else; and nobody knew what had happened. He wouldn't tell my mother about the incident on the stairs until everybody had gone, until everything had been washed up and put away and they were lying in their bed, he reflecting on the day with his hands behind his head, the way he always did.

The following night I was sitting upstairs on the bus on the way to the Central Station and I couldn't stop the tears running down my face. I remembered some of the times I had said to my mother or to Johnny, in my father's hearing, that Bill Morley was like a father to me, and I knew I couldn't have put my hand on my heart and pleaded it was merely giving somebody else his due, innocent praise from a man who always spoke his mind. Right now I couldn't imagine anything more hurtful to a father than that. I resolved to write to him as soon as I got back, and on the train to London I composed the opening lines in my head.

I wrote the next day and posted it in time to catch the evening post in Enfield. He of course, prompt in everything, wrote back immediately. Three weeks later when he and a colleague came down for a conference in London they came to see me and had tea at the Morleys. My father made no fuss, not in front of the Morleys, not in front of his colleague, because he never made a fuss about anything in front of anybody. But when we parted and he shook my hand, I could feel all the years and more, much more.

My father and I never afterwards tried to rationalise our differences, we both knew what they were and that they were likely to increase and become more diverse and that we'd both have to accept that. I didn't want to be exactly like him and I think he had given up trying to achieve it. He had always said he wanted all of us to do better than he had but hadn't intended it to mean in a different way. And it fell to my lot, as the eldest of the brood, to prove that different didn't necessarily mean perverse.

By the beginning of December I had applied to five pharmaceutical companies advertising for sales representatives and been invited by interviews to four of them, all in the London area. The first was like no interview I had ever attended.

I was sitting in a dingy little office opposite a balding fat man in his late thirties in a shapeless bluish black suit burnished by overuse, and could see Kings Cross station through the filthy window behind him. He had traces of something at the corners of his mouth and there was a half cigar, wet and still smoking, sticking up out of an ashtray like a small dog's turd. Piles of pharmaceutical journals, files, letters and accounts cluttered his desk.

'Look, he said vexedly, getting up, 'do you want some really good advice..? Free advice that will save you a lot of heartache..? Do you think you could take it?'

I nodded tentatively. What else could I do?

'Forget about repping. You're just not cut out for it. You're neither brash enough or tough enough. You're too sensitive.' He waved a fat finger. 'I can see it in your eyes right now as I'm speaking. I've sat and listened to you talking for nearly quarter of an hour of my valuable time and I can tell you you wouldn't last six months selling anything...let alone in the hardest field of all. Selling pharmaceuticals isn't what you think it is... It's a jungle full of leeches, snakes and man-eating tigers.'

His eyes narrowed and he paused as though waiting for me to fill my pants.

'Go back to your pretty nurses and bunsen burners and leave this sort of thing alone... Now I'm not going to pay you subsistence and a whole lot of expenses, because I know you've only come from the other side of town, and I've given you advice that's worth a lot more.'

Was that it..? I began to rise. I proffered my hand but he waved it away.

'No need for that.'

'I'd have preferred a slap in the mouth to somebody declining to grasp my hand when it was already out.

'Right. Thank you,' I said in a voice unknown to me that was supposed to be conveying *sang froid* or something like it. But he had already turned away and a finger was poking in his ear as he rummaged through a drawer and sniffed.

It was a bad start but I had an interview that afternoon with BioMed Pharmaceuticals in Aldwych and it couldn't be any worse than the one I'd just had. I took the Underground to Aldwych, found a nice pub and sat down in a quiet corner with a Cornish pasty and shandy to marshal my resources.

I had held an inquest on the first interview on the way over on the train and decided the honest-to-goodness 'Hullo, everyone, as you can see I'm a clean-cut, dead honest, personable young fellow from the North and a lot sharper than I look' approach had been no use at all. What I needed was to come over as hard-nosed, brass-necked and pushy. I wasn't going to take any of the codswallop I'd taken from Horst & Klein's, from anybody else. If at any time I felt inclined to be modest, polite or deferential, I'd do the opposite. Next time I wouldn't sit with my hands clasped in my lap and let myself be talked off my chair and down through a crack in the floorboards. In fact I might yet give Horst & Klein a ring and ask them what kind of schmuck did they think they'd been talking to.

Whatever, I must have done it right this time because BioMed Pharmaceuticals offered me the job. Mind, the three people who interviewed me in the plush office at BioMed House, with its red-carpeted floors, subtropical plants and chic magazines, were of a different order altogether from your man at Horst & Klein's.

The conditions of employment required attendance at a four-weeks training course at BioMed House beginning on the second of January, provision of accommodation and sustenance at the Dosdorf Hotel throughout the period and a brand new Hillman Minx at the end of it, my own 'territory' in North Kent, and a salary of £750 per annum plus generous expenses and bonuses.

I accepted immediately. I had already forgotten the morning's debacle. Horst & Klein..? You mean the horse dealers..?

I gave in my notice at Enfield, worked until Christmas and went up to Newcastle.

The Morleys were sad to see me go and I was sorry to leave them, and the hospital were rather piqued at my departure after such a short time, though few of the staff in Pathology were surprised. But I had to move on, I was impatient to see new places and experience new things and BioMed Pharmaceuticals sounded like the door to Sesame.

Nobody at Simonside Terrace was surprised to hear I had been seduced by a high salary, generous expenses and a new car, though nobody there would have used such an obscene word as that. Judy of course was delighted and during the holidays we became engaged. We decided that she should hand in her notice after the holidays, come down to London for the last week of the course and stay at the Dosdorf. Then we would go to live in Kent until the wedding which would be on the 2nd July, my twenty-third birthday - though we only told our families the bit about the wedding.

Johnny bought the AJS and took on the remaining hire-purchase payments. I was going to be a four-wheel man again.

BioMed Pharmaceuticals

25

'Good morning and welcome to BioMed Pharmaceuticals, gentlemen. Believe me when I say you have never begun a new year more auspiciously.

'As employees of the best pharmaceutical company in the world you have the right to congratulate yourselves. Learn fast and work hard and the outer edge of the known universe is the only limit. Everybody in this Company, all the way up to the president, started from where you are right now. Initiative, ability and hard work equals results, and results are rewarded with bonuses and promotion.

'A BioMed man is no ordinary man. He is energetic, he is resourceful and he is successful. He is a man who goes and gets and he is fiercely proud of the Company for whom he works.

'A BioMed man is not born, he is made. He undergoes a process of metamorphosis as dramatic as anything in nature. He changes from an unexciting nine-to-five nobody, into a dynamic twenty-five-hours-a-day somebody. How..? Because he eats, thinks, talks and sleeps BioMed Pharmaceuticals.

'The BioMed man never says "I" or "we". He always says "BioMed Pharmaceuticals". Working for BioMed Pharmaceuticals is not a job. It is a vocation.'

There were about thirty of us, all males in our early twenties, each seated at a different desk in a plush conference room.

The man who was addressing us and never for a moment pausing in his delivery or stride as he paced backwards and forwards using every foot of the floor like a stage, couldn't have been more than twenty-seven years old. He wasn't very tall but gave an impression of size because his hands and fingers, nose, mouth and ears were all disproportionately large.

He had a disarming smile which could disappear and reappear rapidly, and an upper lip that was bigger and thicker than the lower, over which it curled, giving an almost sensual cast to his face. He looked tough and sure of himself and I'd have wagered anything he'd once been a sergeant prodigy at some army basic training camp. His name was Briggs and he was making sure we wouldn't forget it. More than anything however he was making certain we would have no illusions about selling pharmaceuticals being any kind of lark.

A lanky floppy fair-haired fellow called Godfrey, who I'd been chatting with before we came in, winked at me and Briggs immediately picked it up. He glanced at a paper on his desk.

'Mr Godfrey Igo, I believe it is... Since, as of 9am this morning your time is being paid for by BioMed Pharmaceuticals, perhaps you can tell us why we are not getting your full attention. Before this Company invests six weeks of its valuable resources training you, keeping you in relative luxury at one of the best hotels in London, feeding you in a manner to which you are likewise no doubt unaccustomed, and paying you a higher salary than you have ever earned in your life, it requires some kind of bona fide... Stand up!'

Godfrey quickly stood up.

'It was nothing, sir. I thought you were joking.' He was beautifully spoken.

'About what?'

'About sacrificing ourselves to BioMed Pharmaceuticals, I suppose.'

'First, what you refer to as "sacrifice", this Company calls "commitment". And that commitment has to be total and unequivocal... Second, when I am talking about BioMed Pharmaceuticals, I never joke.'

He turned from Godfrey and looked at every one of us.

'If there is anyone in this room who cannot here and now give this Company the kind of commitment it deserves...and demands...from its staff, I want him to get up and walk out of that door. And this Company wants never to see or hear from him again...'

He waited a full minute without moving or speaking. There wasn't a sound.

'Well, Mr Igo?'

'I'm sorry, sir.'

'Then sit down and from now on show us only what qualities you might have.'

He turned to the rest of us.

'By the end of this week you will have learnt everything you need to know about every BioMed Pharmaceuticals product. You will know every condition they are prescribed for and you will know the scientific evidence that supports it. You will know the price per drop, tablet and milligram of injection, of every product. Nobody is going to waste precious BioMed Pharmaceuticals time teaching you these things because you will learn them in your own time by reading and learning off my heart every word and illustration in your PK [product knowledge] manual.

'However, it isn't enough to know everything about BioMed Pharmaceuticals. We work in a very competitive market and there are people who want to steal our share of that market. Knowledge is strength and we and you need to know everything we can about them. So you must learn about their products as well as our own. You must learn their limitations and side effects...their higher prices... And you must feed that information back here.

'During the course you will be taught how to sell the best pharmaceutical products in the world to the doctors who will prescribe them and the pharmacists who will dispense them. Both are our customers. Both are equally important

'As you will see from the chart and from the books on your desk, BioMed Pharmaceuticals researches, develops and produces an excellent range of medication, all of which is available only by prescription. It produces them in various forms, depending on the chemical nature of the ingredients and the needs of the patients. Capsules, tablets, syrup and injectables.

'It produces medication for a wide variety of conditions from ear infections to epilepsy, from anxiety to malnutrition. Beware of the consultant or GP who tells you he is already using a product with the same or similar generic name and is having good results with it. Our products are not the same as anybody else's. They are better. They are more effective and they have less side effects.

'When you "detail" a customer...which means enlightening them about the superiority of our products...you must be totally prepared before you go in to see them. You will see from your card file what each one is like...what his habits and preferences are. Learn these profiles and keep them up to date.

'To the doctor you will talk not cure or miracle, but effectiveness and tolerance. For him you will produce graphs, colour slides and abstracts from the scientific literature... However, never underestimate the influence of the local pharmacist who might try to persuade the doctor to use another company's product for reasons of his own. You must make sure the doctor prescribes BioMedetic and not just any diuretic. If he prescribes generically, then all you will have done is sold your competitor's products for him. Remember...a generic sale is probably a lost sale.

'To the pharmacist, you will talk ease of dispensation and acceptability to the patient. You will speak of BioMedpen, BioMed Pharmaceuticals' sweet, strawberry-flavoured pediatric penicillin suspension that sick infants will sit up and beg for...as opposed to a competitor's sour lemon product that requires their practically being strapped to a chair so the vile stuff can be forced down their tender little throats. You will talk of our smooth, soft, vitamin capsules that glide down any throat...compared to the hard dry tablets of a competitor that stick in old people's gullets and well nigh choke them.

'You will never be so unethical as to criticise another company's products by name of course. But you will make damned sure they know exactly who you are talking about. And if you find yourself in the glorious position of listening to some old griffin ranting on about one of our competitors, you will not interrupt him. You will merely sympathise and gently stoke away.'

After the induction speech which lasted exactly an hour, we had various other speakers talking about the history of BioMed Pharmaceuticals, how new products were researched and developed, how pharmaceutical products were manufactured, and about the various medical conditions appropriate to BioMed Pharmaceuticals products. But nobody, not even the ones from the America, matched Briggs, neither for sheer power or anything else.

At the end of the day when we retreated to the Dosdorf for dinner, there were four of us, including Godfrey, sitting at the same table, and reactions were mixed.

Godfrey was impressed so far and prepared to believe BioMed

Pharmaceuticals' boast that it was the best pharmaceutical company in Britain, if not the world.

'The big ones are all American,' he said. 'And if they're not now, they soon will be... Anyway, if you believe they're the best, it'll make selling their products a lot easier.'

Eric Norton was tall, like a vicar in his looks and rather mincing in the way he spoke. 'Oh, come on..! I could never see the likes of Boots or Beechams going under the hammer. Certainly not to the Yanks.'

'We're working for them now. So we're hardly in a position to criticise them, are we?' volunteered Herbert Reilly, a little Liverpudlian with wavy hair.

Nobody seemed too impressed with that.

'You all seem to be taking the whole thing very seriously,' I ventured.

'Why shouldn't we?' Godfrey asked with a serious face.

'Because it's a load of crap.'

Godfrey laughed.

'How can you say that already?' Eric said with a note of reproof in his voice.

'How can you not?'

'Give it a chance, for goodness sake!'

'I'm going to... We are just talking about first impressions, aren't we?'

'Why do you think that already?' asked Herbert with a frown.

'Because I know some of it is bullshit. For instance, what they were saying about laboratory tests proving BioMedcycline being better than any other tetracycline... It isn't. It's exactly the same in all that matters.'

'How do you mean?' Herbert persisted.

'Well, all that really matters is that the antibiotic in it kills the germs, the bacteria. Not what it tastes like. And all tetracyclines...as they well know...have the same range of antibacterial activity.'

They looked at each other.

'Where did you work before you came here?' Herbert asked.

I told him.

'Bloody hell! I know nowt about things like that. I'm an insurance salesman... What about you, Godfrey?'

Godfrey smiled. 'Headmaster of a private girls' school.'

'Shit..! What did you give that up for?'

Godfrey winked.

'What about you, Eric?'

'Latterly in an estate agency. But I did two years pharmacology before that.'

It then transpired that all of us had come to BioMed Pharmaceuticals for the money and the car but Godfrey and I had also come for the freedom and excitement.

We had a beer in the lounge and first Eric and then Herbert decided to retire to their rooms to read up on BioMed Pharmaceuticals from the considerable literature we had been given during the day.

Godfrey had been born in Monmouthshire to a Welsh father and English mother - 'equivocally Welsh' was how he described himself - had read English literature and modern languages at Oxford, played rugby for Monmouth and gone to the same elocution master as King George VI. From the way he trotted it out, as though read straight off the inside cover of a book, I suspected everybody he thought might be somebody would get to know all this within the first five minutes. He was sarcastic as hell but very funny and had obviously been around. Like Steve back at the VIC he seemed to have the talent of being able to quickly divine the essentials of a situation, what and who was important and what and who wasn't. And like Steve I think he was probably born self-sufficient.

I was twenty-two years old and until the previous night had never stayed in a hotel and never had a meal in a real restaurant. I didn't know who to tip, when to tip, and most important of all, how much to tip; nor whether a subsequent tip on another occasion would have to be the same value or could be a bit less; and when you tipped, should you do it in private in case the others in your party started sneering at your generosity or cracking up at your stinginess, or in case other waiters came running over and started hanging about or tugging at your trouser leg. If you tipped the wine-waiter today, what about the ordinary waiter tomorrow, the cook, receptionist, chambermaid, pageboy, doorman, barman, washroom attendant, Uncle Tom Cobley and everybody else? And what about Miss

Hero de Ramboiné, the portly dowager who was playing the piano and apparently played every night? Were you supposed to go up and drop a coin into her lap while she played 'We'll Gather Lilacs in the Spring Again'?

When I had arrived the previous night, a gaunt and stooped man in a braided dress suit that was several sizes too big for him, had grabbed my suitcase when I was going up the steps and kept giving it a tug to try and break my grip.

'It's all right, thanks,' I kept saying. 'I can manage.'

But he took not the slightest notice and in the finish I let go because the two of us must have looked ridiculous and it was an old case and the handle might have come off. But as soon as he put it down beside the reception counter, another one picked it up and a few minutes later after I'd been checked in, I found myself in the ludicrous position of having to follow very slowly behind a little old man dragging my suitcase, gasping and wheezing and possibly damaging the valves of his heart. I'd thought all these people were supposed to do as they were told.

'No tips at this table. Not yet, anyhow,' was Godfrey's opinion. 'We've been booked in by BioMed. They'll be paying any service charges.'

My room was dowdily luxurious, I could imagine the decor having remained unchanged since the First World War, and in the top drawer of the bedside cabinet was a bible which I presumed had been left behind by the previous occupant. There was a dressing table which doubled as a writing bureau on which was some writing paper and envelopes with the Dosdorf Hotel insignia at the top. I immediately wrote: *Dear Mam and Dad, It's not home but it certainly beats the all-night bakery, Love, Your prodigal son*.

To think that less than two years ago I was sleeping in a barrack-room.

At breakfast, the most telling as well as crucial meal of the day, Herbie was last to come to the table, eyes red, face white. Godfrey and I were finishing our coffee, the shining-faced, bright-eyed, red-eared, sleek-haired and smiling Eric had already left to give his teeth a quick brush over and freshen up a teeny-weeny bit more.

'You're not having your periods, are you, old son?' Godfrey asked as Herbie sat down.

Apparently he was always a bit groggy first thing in the morning but we managed to persuade him to have a few sips of the orange juice, it was too late for anything else.

'I don't think I'm going to make it,' he said. 'I'm out of my depth with people like you. I should have stayed with the "Norwich". Doreen, my missus, always said so and she was right.'

'Bollocks, man. It'll be a doddle,' Godfrey assured him. 'Don't let a few wankers put you off.'

Having a few minutes spare before the morning session began, Godfrey, Herbie and I had a brief look around the various suites at BioMed House. They were luxurious by the standards of any kind of office I had ever seen: every inch of floor was carpeted including the washroom, there was subtle lighting along the walls and little mahogany tables with their own little lamp around every corner, and comfortable modern furniture. Like everywhere else, the lecture room was spacious and air-conditioned, the desks were set well apart with comfortable chairs, and there was a window which ran the full length of one side and overlooked the Strand; you couldn't have asked for better conditions to study anything.

There were eighteen of us, most of whom I would never get to know on a first-name basis, although by the end of the first day we all knew each other's surnames. We came from all over Britain including Scotland and Northern Ireland. Everybody was well dressed but none as immaculately as the man who sat all of the time at the front by the window, observing, making notes, sometimes smiling at something that was said but never saying a word himself. Sometimes there would be a meaningful exchange of glances between him and Briggs, as sometimes there was between Briggs and the big bald American at the back of the room who never moved, never said anything and looked as though he was convalescing from something serious.

First thing every morning we were given a PK test. Then we had Briggs teaching selling techniques until lunch-time. In the afternoon we had lectures on the technical side of the business. BioMed's chief accountant, chief clerk, transport manager, chief pharmacist and medical director all spoke to us but none like Briggs whom Godfrey reckoned must have been a prodigy. 'He'd have been selling before he could walk, closing deals in his cot. They'd have had to gag him to stop him.'

The medical and pharmacological films were slickly done though almost criminally biased, but the films on selling were something else. In black and white, set and filmed in 1940s America with an American newsreel narrator, they were crass beyond belief. The approach was to reduce to half a dozen Commandments and hammer home with the subtlety of a baseball bat, the virtues of The Good Salesman.

To illustrate the importance of perseverance coupled with initiative, there was a film entitled 'Blast Your Way in With Visual Dynamite'. In this, the always lean and hungry salesman in trilby and overcoat who looked like a little Fred McMurray, would be seen carrying a case containing either the parts of an easy-to-assemble vacuum cleaner or a huge pad of blank life-insurance policy forms. Repeatedly he would try to gain an interview with the boss of a big office who sat behind a huge desk looking like Mussolini, but every time, either the salesman would fail with the secretary or she would fail with the boss.

Eventually the salesman would come in with a bundle of what looked like large altar candles under his arm; these he would place at the foot of the boss's door, in full view of the amazingly unperturbed secretary who presumably saw this kind of thing every day of the week. Next he would take out a box of matches and light what turned out to be not just a long wick, dive under the secretary's desk, obviously getting a butler's eye view while he waited for it to burn, which wasn't very long.

In the explosion, the door, best part of the walls on either side of the door, and part of the ceiling over the secretary's desk, would be blown to smithereens. As the smoke cleared and the secretary would be seen still typing, the salesman would be standing victorious atop the rubble. The boss, previously shown only with a surly expression, would now be looking absolutely delighted, the assumption being that the salesman's faint-heart-ne'er-won-fair-lady approach had really impressed him. There was no front view of the salesman at this point, so you couldn't be absolutely certain he wasn't indecently exposing himself.

The films were shown over and over again and some of us always laughed, but afterwards when the lights came on we would muster as grave expressions as we could and try to look as though we were digesting the message.

'If you tried that with our GP, he'd take a stick of the dynamite and shove it straight up your arse,' Godfrey said one night when a few of us were having a few beers and reviewing the films.

On the Thursday night at dinner he announced he'd had enough of studying BioMed Pharmaceuticals and everybody else's PK, and was going to spend a night on the town. 'Three nights in a row swotting the price per drop of gooseberry-flavoured, versus raspberry-flavoured enemas is enough for me. When are the buggers going to produce "Supercock, the revolutionary tumescent for the all-night stand"? That's what I want to know. I don't care if it tastes like shit.'

'The elocution master you went to that failed so abysmally with poor King George, didn't specialise in niceties, I gather?' I said.

'I'll tell you what though. He had a notice on his door that said "Sorry, No Geordies".'

'I'll have you know that before I came down to London I bought a book on "Teach Yourself Elocution".'

'Don't tell me... You lost it before you ever got the chance to open it?'

'Do you want to hear the end of this tale, or not?'

'Go on, you sensitive Geordie bugger.'

'Well, I had the book out on my bench at work...I'd been reading it during my tea-breaks before I left. And this plumber comes in to do something with the radiators. He sees the book and says "What the hell's 'elocution'?" So I told him... You know what he said?'

'No. What?'

'Wha' d'ye want wi' that? Tords divvent faal oot o' my mooth when I taalk, di' the'?'

'What the fuck does that mean?'

'"Turds don't fall out of my mouth when I talk, do they?"'

Godfrey roared with laughter. 'Good for him, you second-class twit. Serves you right for leaving it lying around.'

He stood up. 'Well, what's it to be, gentlemen..? Piccadilly or PK?'

It was PK for the other two but Piccadilly for me.

Godfrey took me on a tour of Soho, showed me where the jazz clubs were, the posh restaurants, the best night clubs and pubs and places where the prostitutes and pimps hung out. Coming from Newcastle whose red light district was only a few yards in length and appropriately called 'Pink Lane' - a name nevertheless used to instil terror into young hearts - places like Greek Street were like series of dens of fascinating evil.

26

I had three stiff white collars and two white shirts which I had reckoned would last me a week. Two of the collars were size 15" and one was 16" and I had bought them specially, without knowing that my size was in fact 15½". I had worn each of the 15s for two days and was hoping to last out the week on them because the 16 was far too large. But the trouble with wearing a stiff collar that's too small is that the collar-stud gets caught on your Adam's apple and when you swallow or say certain words, the collar rides up and down, taking your tie knot with it.

By now, Friday morning, there was a sore on the front of my neck that was red and painful to the touch and I couldn't get any of the 15s on, not with my father's hard collar-stud; I had got up late and with a hangover and the last thing I needed was a garrotte around my neck.

However when I put the 16 on it looked like a horse-collar and the stud still chafed my throat. So I took out the stud and from the inside, after puncturing my neck several times, managed to fasten the two shirt-button holes to the two collar holes with a safety pin. But the pin, small though it was, allowed so much slack that I could get my whole hand inside my collar. Unfortunately I only had the one pin, which had come from the bookmark in the bible, and when I bent it to try to take up the slack it wouldn't fasten properly. This meant that in certain positions the point could stick in my neck and, what was worse, in others the collar was forced open wider than ever. At its widest the collar was slack enough for my chin to slip in if I lowered my head too far. But I had no time left to mess about with it any more.

When I got down to the restaurant Godfrey and Eric were just giving themselves the final dab with their napkins, both looking so suave and debonair.

'I was just saying to Eric when we saw you coming in the door that you look like a bag of shit.'

I sat down. As I raised my arm to attract the attention of the waiter I felt my neck being pierced.

Godfrey looked at me, deadpan.

'On a neck diet, are we?'

When we got over to BioMed House it was to find we had a new lecturer, the man who had sat by the window all week observing.

Up until now, before I'd had a really good look at the way this man was dressed, I had been using the word 'immaculate' to describe anyone who was well dressed. Now I knew what the word really meant.

He was pacing about waiting for us to come in and settle down. There was none of the consummate self assurance there had been with Briggs. He looked to be in his early forties but I was sure he wasn't that old. His eyes were large and round and slightly protruding, otherwise he was quite handsome. He was the kind who would daily trim his eyebrows and the hairs in his ears and nostrils, and check his nails every time he combed his hair.

'Good morning, gentlemen. My name is Ralph Tyler and I'm one of BioMed Pharmaceuticals' five district managers. When this course is finished, some of those who come through it will become part of my team. Not all of you will survive the six weeks, however, and BioMed Pharmaceuticals has allowed for a fifteen percent wastage. Of those who last long enough to enter the field, twenty percent will not survive the first six months. Of those who do, thirty percent will not survive the first year. Some of the misfits will leave of their own accord. Those that don't will be swiftly weeded out.'

He paused and looked around. Papers were being shuffled, chairs moved and there was a low murmur: just the degree of apprehensiveness he wanted, I reckoned.

'I see you are smiling with confidence, Mr Harrison,' he said to poor Herbie whose smile could only have been precipitated by nerves.

Turning to the rest of the class, he said 'By now you will all have committed to memory the contents of your PK file, so we can now move on. You will see there is a new file in front of you. Inside is a questionnaire with thirty-three questions. Take it out and look at it.'

It was an assessment of an anonymous salesman's selling techniques and had such things as,

1. How good was his entry? Was it bold, courteous, timid?

Tick where appropriate.

2. Was his appearance satisfactory? Was it flamboyant, tidy, dishevelled?

Tick where appropriate.

3. What were his first words? Did they include "BioMed Pharmaceuticals"?

Cross out "Yes" or "No".

4. Did he use the terms, "I" or "we"? If so, how many times?

Tick appropriate box.

'Most important of all,' Tyler interjected, 'is the very last question, Question 33.'

Pages could be heard turning as everybody looked for it.

Tyler read the words loudly and slowly: *'Was the client positively committed to prescribe or buy?'*

He then paused to let their profound significance sink deep into every skull. Then he read the line once more, almost in a whisper, the way Olivier might have delivered it, and you could have heard a pin drop.

'This is a "DAF", a Detailing Assessment Form. Every one of you will be given the opportunity to demonstrate your detailing skills in front of everybody else. And when you have finished...using this form....everybody, including you yourself, will assess your performance with special regard to the last and all important question, "Was the client positively committed to prescribe or buy?"

'Now, who will be our first doctor? We already have our first BioMed Pharmaceuticals sales representative, don't we, Mr Harrison..? No volunteers..? Right... Out here, if you please, Mr Igo... And Mr Harrison.'

Godfrey and Herbie got up and went out to the front.

'Now, Dr Igo sits there. And Mr Harrison...complete with bag, literature and samples...goes outside where he will remain until called.'

As Herbie went out the door Tyler addressed the rest of us with an air of conspiracy.

'From the instant the door opens you will start taking notes. Observe everything. His dress, his demeanour, his approach. And keep on observing and recording until the moment he departs and the door has closed behind him.'

'Knock when you're ready, Mr Harrison!' Tyler called towards the door.

A few moments later there was a very timid knock.

'Come!' called Godfrey, quickly entering into the spirit of things.

The door remained shut.

Tyler motioned to Godfrey to call again, louder this time.

'Come in!' Godfrey shouted.

The door still remained closed so Tyler opened it and went out.

We could hear every word. 'We haven't got all day, Mr Harrison. Next time you are called, come in and do your stuff. We don't want shrinking violets out here. We want bold warriors in there. Remember the films you have been shown.'

Tyler came back in and closed the door.

'Now, Dr Igo. Call him in.'

In loud commanding tones Godfrey called out, 'Come in!'

Nothing happened. Tyler was pacing backwards and forwards between the sitting Godfrey and the closed door. Suddenly he yelled 'For pity's sake, get yourself in here, Harrison!'

The door immediately opened and Herbie tottered in.

'I feel dizzy, sir. I'm afraid I can't go on with this.'

'Don't worry. You've come to the right place!' I called out. 'There's a doctor in the house.'

Everybody except Tyler laughed.

'So, you think this is some kind of game we are playing, Mr Robinson..? A comedy perhaps..? You think BioMed Pharmaceuticals plucked you out of your tedious, unrewarding job and gave you this once-in-a-lifetime chance to forge a brilliant career for yourself, so that you can come here and act the clown?

'Look at the state that man is in! He isn't fit to buy a box of matches from a blind man...let alone persuade a cynical and clever medical man to prescribe a pharmaceutical product he has never heard of...worse still, has reservations about.

'Sit down, Mr Igo. Sit down, Mr Harrison... Now, Mr Robinson... If you will be good enough to gather your appurtenances together and position yourself outside that door, you can demonstrate to everybody how consummate your detailing skills are.'

I put my things in my leather detailing bag, got up and went out. Tyler then came out and pulled the door shut behind him. 'You had better be good, boyo,' he said in a low voice, 'damned good... You might not know it but that's the UK General Manager by the fire exit. And if you haven't guessed it already, that gentleman at the back is from America. If either one of them so much as sniffs, you're career with this Company is over.'

'I wasn't - '

'Don't you ever...not ever...try to make a fool of me!'

He opened the door to go back in, then turned, hand on knob. 'And for Christ's sake get rid of that collar! If you're still with this Company at lunch-time, go to the Brompton Oratory's graveyard and bury it... That's if they'll allow you to bury such a monstrosity in sanctified soil.'

Then he went out.

I could imagine what it would be like when I went back in there, all eyes riveted on my neck. I had clean forgotten about it. 'How was his appearance?' and all hands simultaneously writing 'Collar too big. Neck scrawny.'

I went in to find Tyler sitting in the doctor's seat.

'Good morning, Doctor,' I began. 'I'm from BioMed Pharmaceuticals.'

'What..! Not another rep! You're the fifth this morning!'

I pressed on. 'BioMed Pharmaceuticals are introducing a new product in the broad-spectrum antibiotic range, a new tetracycline - '

'Not interested... Out!'

At no time during any of the lectures had provision been made for a client who wasn't prepared to listen once you had successfully blasted your way into his presence.

'What do you mean exactly, Doctor?'

'I mean, I don't want to hear about any more tetracyclines.'

'Why not?'

That threw him.

'Because...I...don't,' he rejoined exasperatedly. Then resuming his GP persona he snapped 'There's enough already!'

'Yes but ours...I mean BioMed Pharmaceuticals'...isn't just another version of the same old tetracycline. Ours...BioMed Pharmaceuticals', I mean...is a different kind of tetracycline, a new and more palatable form... Longer acting and less toxic...'

Tyler's eyes gleamed. 'Less toxic but nevertheless still toxic, eh?'

'No, not toxic - '

'Then why mention the word..? To me, "less toxic" means "still toxic".'

'Ah, well...not necessarily.'

This was getting nowhere.

'Er, could I perhaps show you some slides?'

Without waiting for a reply I reached into my bag for my battery-driven projector and box of before-and-after-treatment slides.

'What's this going to be..? Holidaying with your family at Butlins?'

'No. Medical trial material.'

'No, you can't. I'm too busy... But I could do with another one of your lighters. The gold ones. Somebody walked off with my other one.'

I just ignored this and proceeded to set up the viewer and insert some slides into the magazine.

'If you would just look through here...'

'What am I supposed to be looking at?' he snorted. 'Everything's upside down.'

'Oh, I'm sorry. They should be the other way up.' As I reached over to take the magazine from him, he deliberately let it fall to the floor.

'Now look what you've done!' he shouted. 'The blooming things are all over my floor... Hurry up and get them out of the way! I've got sick patients to see.'

I had to fight down the urge to tell him that on my way out I'd recommend they go somewhere else.

'We' - a huge sigh went up from everybody and they all began writing - 'BioMed Pharmaceuticals, that is, have also produced a new multivitamin for geriatric patients, called BioMedvit - '

'I don't believe in giving vitamins willy-nilly.'

'Nobody's suggesting you give them willy-nilly,' I snarled. 'I have the literature here in my bag...somewhere... Trials have proved...' I was groping in my bag for the file of abstracts... 'that...' I found the file and was rummaging through, looking for the particular papers... 'Muhamwan and Al-Enrahile - '

'Muhamwan and who?'

'"Al-Enrahile", I think it is... Anyway, in Cairo they found that... Just a minute if you don't mind. I know it's here...'

'Come on, man! I haven't all day!'

'Give me a chance, will you?' I said to him through gritted teeth.

'You'd better get a grip of yourself, boyo!' he hissed back. 'Or you won't live to see the end of this session!'

As I leant back to collect myself I realised the pain had gone from my neck. That could only mean one thing. I put my hand to my collar... It was slacker than ever! The safety pin had come right out, it must be loose and open somewhere inside my shirt, which meant only my tie knot was keeping the collar from springing ajar.

In desperation I whispered to Tyler, 'What do you want me to do now..? Go on, or what?'

'You're the BioMed man. Do what a BioMed man would do,' Tyler answered loudly in his non-doctor voice.

'Well, Doctor,' I spoke aloud for the benefit of the audience, 'thank you for seeing me. I'll just leave you a sample of our new pediatric suspension, Biopen, if I may. It's for strep throats. And please accept this pad and biro with the compliments of BioMed Pharmaceuticals. We don't have lighters any more.'

He didn't say a word but just sat looking at me, arms folded.

'Shall I go back out or go back to my place?' I whispered.

'Do what a BioMed man would do,' he answered in full ringing tones.

'Right. Thank you, Doctor... Good-day to you... See you next month.'

He looked straight at me, unsmiling. 'Back to your seat, Mr Robinson.'

He turned to the class. 'You have five minutes to complete your assessments of Mr Harrison and Mr Robinson.'

Somebody raised their hand. 'Sir...presumably that of Mr Harrison relates only to his entrance?'

'It relates to everything.'

'What about "Was the client positively committed to prescribe or buy?"'

'If you do not know the answer to that by now, you shouldn't be sitting in this room.'

At lunch-time I was combing my hair in the washroom when I heard a voice behind me say 'Buy yourself a new shirt.'

As I turned I caught a glimpse of a dark-suited figure going out. It could have been anybody, somebody on the course or a member of staff. The last time anybody had spoken to me like that was when I was in the Army, when 'Get your hair cut!' could be a curt command from an NCO or a friendly greeting from a comrade. I turned the sentence over and over in my head, trying to match the voice with various people; I tried to recall on which word or words the emphasis had been, anything that would give a clue to the identity of the speaker.

'Buy yourself a new shirt!' just like that, as though buying a shirt were like buying a packet of cigarettes. When I came to think about it I didn't think I'd ever bought a new shirt, my mother had always done it. I wouldn't have the faintest idea how to go about it. I knew nothing about the shops down here. You couldn't just walk into a shirt-shop or wherever they sold them, in a place like London, a complete stranger. Something like buying a new shirt could only be carried out somewhere like in Newcastle where one knew one's way around. I could be laying out a lot of money on a new shirt thinking it was an investment in a career with BioMed Pharmaceuticals, and it could be redundant by the end of the afternoon, me as well, the way things were going.

I was damned if I was going to be stampeded into buying a new shirt. I'd go back to the Dosdorf, bathe my neck and rest it over the lunch break and then wear a 15 for the afternoon even if it felt like an iron-maiden. That night I'd cut the bottom button off my two shirts and sew one at each end of a half-inch piece of string, thus creating what was probably going to be the first truly flexible, non-chafing collar stud.

That night when Godfrey, Eric, Herbie and I were having dinner and discussing the day's events, Eric and Godfrey having performed superbly both as doctors and as salesmen, Herbie was in despair.

Godfrey slapped him on the back.

'It's only a bit of fun, old son. You take life too seriously... What do you think, Eric?'

'If you can sell insurance, you can sell anything,' Eric said kindly and unconvincingly.

'If I thought I was going to be put through an experience like Joe was with Tyler, I'd jump straight out that window and end it all.' Herbie pointed to the window with his fork.

The rest of us laughed but he wasn't meaning to be funny.

'I'm not cut out for this.'

'What about me?' I said. 'Do you think I am?'

'I don't know...but I know you've got all the technical knowledge. These two have all the flair and patter but you know more about the technical side than anybody on the course. That's what saved you today, I reckon. That talk Tyler made you give this afternoon on testing antibiotics in the laboratory, was really something.'

Godfrey and Eric nodded.

'You think I was that close to..?' I drew my finger across my throat.

They nodded again.

'Tyler was working on the principle of "Give him an extra few inches of collar and he'll hang himself",' said Godfrey.

And even Herb laughed at that.

27

By the end of the second week everybody on the course had been sent outside the door, come back in, and done their rep stint, some of us questionable ones several times. Everybody that is, except Herb. Sometimes he took heart from this and would ask if we thought they had forgotten him and Eric and I would try to reassure him by saying yes, that could well be the case, or maybe they thought he had sufficient talent to not need testing.

'Maybe they're not testing me because they've already decided to get rid of me,' he wailed.

'If that were the case, they wouldn't be feeding you and putting you up here and all the rest of it, now would they?' I said.

'No, you may be right there.' He obviously took a bit heart from it.

But Godfrey couldn't resist teasing him. 'I reckon they're saving you for the end, Herb. You're the *pièce de résistance*.' Bravely Herb would smile, allowing the rest of us to belly laugh and get the pent-up humour of it out of our systems, there was little enough opportunity for it once the increasingly depressed Herb joined the company; whenever there was laughter coming from a group of BioMed trainees at another table Herb would always sneak a glance towards them as though expecting to catch them out. Relentlessly he turned every meal and drinking session into a tutorial, when the rest of us wanted to forget about BioMed Pharmaceuticals, PK and Ralph Tyler who had now taken over entirely from Briggs.

On the Friday morning of the third week Tyler announced there was one person who had not yet been tested. Did everyone know who that was? Would that person now stand up and show he was willing to enter the crucible?

Godfrey was right. BioMed's Beau Brummel, whose one ambition in life according to Godfrey who had got on chatting to him one lunch-time about rugby, was to get into the Atheneum gentleman's club, was going to lay on a show for the UK and USA general managers. He, the ex-fourth year medical student, was going to exercise his wit on a little Scouse from the wrong side of the Mersey whose wife had already spelled out his limitations in an effort to spare him such tribulation as this was going to be.

Pluckily Herb rose, he didn't need anybody to grab him by the scruff and yank him to his feet. But he certainly didn't leap up; rather, he lurched to his feet like a magic bean and swayed and we all thought he was going to fall over but eventually he achieved the perpendicular. Then without any further prompting, detailing bag already packed, he made his way to the front, leadenly like a man just about managing to walk unaided to the scaffold. On he went, all the way to the door, and there surely couldn't have been many watching who weren't with him every inch of the way.

Without turning around he opened it and went out.

I don't know whether the sigh just came out of me or whether it was a collective thing; there were one or two looking on with glee and practically salivating but no more than you always get when somebody is being publicly humiliated or hurt.

'Let's hope he can get a bit more bounce into his act when he comes back in,' I was thinking.

But Herb never came back in. The mock doctor called until he was blue in the face but there was no response. Tyler eventually went out and closed the door behind him. He was away for about twenty minutes and when he came back he was alone and looking very grave.

At lunch-time I was in the washroom when Godfrey came in.

'You'll never guess what happened to poor Herb!'

'Gone back to the Hotel?'

'The poor bastard shat himself!'

'Shit..!'

'Shit indeed! Shit's the operative word, buddy. Now you're getting the full picture!'

'What..? How do you mean?'

'How do you think..? His anal sphincter opened up and all the crap came gushing out.'

'Shhhh... Where is he?'

'Apparently he came along here, cleaned himself up and buggered off back to Birkenhead. That's it. Finished.'

'Bloody hell fire...'

'God help anybody sitting in his compartment on the train. Let's hope they haven't got the heating turned up.' Godfrey was creased up laughing, tears running down his cheeks.

'When did it happen?'

'Who knows precisely when he did it. All that really matters is that he did it. Maybe he did it while he was sitting at his desk in his usual state of suspense. You saw the way he walked out... To think all these years I thought it was just a cliché... He should have been wearing cycle clips.'

Poor Herbie. But if he hadn't gone of his own accord I'm sure they would have made him. I hoped he was able to get his old job back in Birkenhead, or a satisfactory alternative, and that his wife would still have some faith left in him.

By the beginning of the fourth week there were only eleven of us left but the empty places were filled up by the rest of us moving that much nearer to the front - 'closing ranks' is how the Army would have described it. If the course had gone on for another three weeks there wouldn't have been anybody left.

Judy had been staying at the Dosdorf for the last five days and having her meals on my account, she and I having alternate courses: one of us would have the hors d'ouvre and the other the entree, one the dessert and the other the coffee and biscuits; yet the bill was still horrific. That night she moved to a modest guest house in Russell Square, the kind of place frequented by commercial travellers. Had she moved in with me there were a number of fellow trainees who would have turned informer.

The front line could hardly be worse than the basic training and the last week was the best of all. We were allocated our territories and district managers - mine were North Kent and the newly-promoted Ralph Tyler - and given enough supplies to get started. I wondered if Tyler had had anything to do with my being on his team. 'You must be joking!' Godfrey had said. 'He wants to succeed, man. He'd never get into the Atheneum with you on his back. He'd be better off with a hump.'

At three o'clock on the Friday, with BioMed House and the Dosdorf and Russell hotels behind us and practically the whole of London in front of us, Judy and I began to inch our way from the Strand towards Sevenoaks in the middle of Kent, in a brand new Hillman Minx.

The journey was a nightmare. I hadn't driven a car since the days of the Singer, with the exception of a couple of lessons in an Austin 35 at the BSM School of Motoring in Newcastle before I took the test, and Friday afternoon in London, in a new car that belonged to a new employer, wasn't the place to encounter a great deal of consideration. One-way traffic was a new experience for me and the taxi drivers in particular, who plainly knew exactly where they were and where they were going, stretched even a phlegmatic northern temper to the limits. Judy kept saying 'It's no good losing your rag. It'll only make matters worse.' But not losing it wasn't achieving anything; if there really were such a thing as 'knights of the road', none of them were in cabs and none came anywhere near us.

How I got the car unscathed through London was testimony to the value of having brake cylinders that didn't leak and to one of the last flings St Christopher must have had before he was decanonised, Judy had fastened his icon to the interior wing mirror during our first serious joust which had taken place at the end of the Strand; but near-miraculous driving skills must have contributed.

Once through Bromley the traffic eased up and we were able to savour the lush verdure of Kent and glimpse the wealth and style of its landowners; we couldn't help wondering if this part of England had been at war twice in the last half-century, as ours had; everything looked so charmed and permanent.

We booked in at the cheapest hotel we could find in Sevenoaks, which was still expensive but 'enchanting', as it said in the foyer - a word I couldn't ever recall having heard on Tyneside - and then went to Le Chanticleer for the first meal I had ever had in a proper restaurant, something Judy had been trying to get me to do ever since we met.

On the Saturday night we were invited to meet my district manager and the most experienced rep in his team, and his wife, at the Bromley Court Hotel.

When we arrived it was to find ourselves welcomed by the most winsome of hosts - 'Please call me Ralph', a different entity completely to the churlish Welsh git I had unwittingly portrayed to Judy, and she was quite entranced. He was superbly dressed and beautifully mannered and I might have been bewitched myself had I not already been acquainted with his Hyde. He took us over to a very smart, radiantly-healthy looking couple.

'Ed, this is Joe who I have been telling you about. And this lovely young woman is his fiancée, Judith.'

The Knights had lived in Vancouver for eighteen months prior to coming back to Sussex and Ed's joining BioMed two years ago, but to hear him you would think he'd been born and raised there. Petite kittenish Paula was so proud of her big quasi-Canadian hulk that she hung tightly onto his arm, constantly looking up at him with wonderment. He could hardly have been more than 'five eleven', as they say in Canada, but with his short-cropped hair, fairly broad shoulders, country-and-western jaw and fancy paperweight of a wife, he looked bigger.

In a googoo voice Paula told us how her man just loved the canoin', fishin', shootin', scalpin' life out there.

He was 'Big Boy' and she was 'Baby Doll' - as if they couldn't have suspended the sex-games terminology for at least a couple of hours - and Big Boy had been manager of a chemical plant out there and broken a strike by some 'lazy, good-for-nothing Eskimo half-breeds'; she cuddled closer, strike-breakers evidently turned her on.

Ed just grinned.

'He's too modest to tell you himself, aren't you, Big Boy?' If you had an erotic little mouthpiece like Paula, you wouldn't need to boast.

'Joe, I've been thinking,' Tyler said, smiling affably, 'it might be a good idea for you to spend your first few weeks under Ed's tutelary wing...just going around with him...observing and asking questions. I think it'd prove invaluable. Nothing can equal experience in the field.' He was using his hands to drive home the message as though there was any way I couldn't have got it already.

Big Boy Ed had his eyebrow raised as though it was news to him but he was analysing it as it was coming in.

Without any devices I was sure my feelings registered plainly enough. 'Would we be working his territory or mine?'

'Ed's of course.'

'What about the BioMedbalm competition?'

BioMedbalm was a new tranquilliser which was being introduced onto the market for the first time next week and there was to be a competition throughout the whole of the UK sales force. The rep who sold the most over a three-month period would win a weekend in Paris; there were other delights to be won also, like a television set, an automatic washing machine and a domestic refrigerator.

Tyler laughed good-humouredly.

'Good to see you thinking competitively already... Isn't it, Ed? But you've got to get to know your territory...get to know your doctors and pharmacists...familiarise yourself with the various order forms, daily reports, monthly reports... Don't worry. There'll be plenty other competitions to demonstrate your prowess... Is that all right with you then, Ed?'

'Yeah, sure, Ralph. Be glad to help anyway I can.'

'Course he will,' Paula cooed as she snuggled in. 'My Eddie would help anybody, wouldn't you, darling?'

It might seem a tad ungracious, considering it was a canny meal, but I couldn't help hoping the three of them would get food poisoning.

As we drove back to Sevenoaks, all Judy could think about was the 'lovely' meal we'd had and how friendly everybody had been. All I could think about was missing out on the BioMedbalm competition.

'A chance to get to Paris at last, and I get stuck with that phoney Canadian palooka and his little Lolita of a wife. When I was fourteen I was all set to go with the school but because of a French railway strike we never got out of Newcastle... Pity they didn't have 'strike-breaking Big-Boy Knight' there... As for Tyler, he's nothing but a slimy Welsh toad.'

'Joe! How could you..! He was absolutely charming...and considerate. They were only trying to help you. As Mr Tyler said, there'll be plenty more competitions.'

But I was inconsolable. 'Aye, but not to Paris I'll bet. Next year it'll probably be bloody Clacton or Scarborough. Just you watch!'

The first week on the road, or rather, 'in the field' as we pharmaceutical reps put it, was really exciting. As much as anything it was because it was so different to anything I had ever done and anywhere I had ever worked. When you were in a department your efforts tended to be subsumed in the overall output but when you were on your own, you got the credit for what went right and the blame for what went wrong. And if you were a rep you could choose when to start your day and when to finish, when to take a break, where to go, who to see and what to do. But that five minutes when you were on stage performing was vital. You had to come on, strut your stuff fast and flawlessly, get him to 'positively prescribe or buy', and get out.

The greatest difference of all for me however was that instead of dealing with blind, deaf and dumb bacteria with unlimited patience and very small egos, I was having to confront another human being, a human being with a large ego, a human being who was often antagonistic to the Company, if not the product, and antagonistic to me for taking up his valuable time. Patients could be awkward or unpleasant to deal with yet be untouchable, but there were no Hippocratic strictures to protect reps, a doctor could easily kick one in the metaphorical groin and get away with it. Patients had their charter to protect them, doctors their defence union, but the rep had nothing but the thickness of his skin.

In a laboratory you could dress casually, be antisocial or eccentric, speak in a dialect or not speak at all, have dandruff, a nervous tic, a speech impediment, a toothache or hangover, you could sometimes make a mistake and rectify it without anybody being any the wiser and be as miserable as sin into the bargain; and none of these things need affect the quality of your work. Any single one would seriously reduce your effectiveness as a rep.

Ed had an easy relaxed style and people seemed to like and respect him. He obviously liked the work, liked working for BioMed Pharmaceuticals and had considerable faith in its products. But he was a fatalist and I wasn't. I liked to balk for the sake of it, flex my muscles, test the safety net; he didn't. If anything seemed to work, his policy was to leave it be. I supposed he was unimaginative, he probably thought I was asking for trouble.

By the end of my first week Ed must have been satisfied with my ability to detail because he suggested I do his doctors from now on and he would do the pharmacists. This way he would be covering the maximum ground and shifting the maximum quantity of BioMedbalm, though he didn't give this as a reason. He introduced the proposal by lamenting that having me around all of the time and having to explain every move, answer every question, psychoanalyse every detail, was slowing him down and he was concerned he might start falling behind in his budget.

A budget was the quantity of any given preparation, from BioMedbalm at the top of our list of products, to BioMedvit at the bottom - about fifty products in all - that Head Office set a month in advance to be sold; and every rep's budget was different. I never saw Ed's or any of his figures but was pretty sure he was on target, he would surely have oversold last month and carried over in order to give himself as much time as possible to detail BioMedbalm.

So from now on we would both be 'working our butts off' to make sure Ed and Paula got to 'Paree', as he called it.

There are good guys and there are bad guys among doctors, as there are among pharmacists, and Ed must have known who was what on his patch and that it wouldn't be in his interests to send me into one of his 'real bastards'. But because things were going so well and he wanted to mop up every GP in his territory, and because he obviously didn't like dealing with real bastards even though they were his and not mine, he couldn't resist sending me into Dr Butler.

At first before going in to see every doctor and pharmacist he had given me a little potted biog of them in the car, but now with Paris clearly in his sights, we were too busy hauling in the nets and there was no time for lifejackets.

While I was sitting in Dr Butler's waiting room I could hear his bellicose voice in the surgery, everybody could hear every word, and whenever he shouted 'Next!', for a few moments everybody was stunned. I was still waiting when Ed came in.

'Not been in yet?' He looked at his watch.

'No. And to tell the truth, I don't think there's any point. He's bawled at everybody who's gone in there. He's likely to go berserk when we go in.'

'Don't let that bother you. It's just his manner. He's the hale and hearty type.'

'Next!' the voice roared down the corridor.

'That's you... Go on in,' Ed said impatiently. 'I want to do the general hospital before lunch.'

'Let's go then, and skip this bugger,' I said, getting up.

'You've got to be joking, buddy.'

I had warned him but he wouldn't listen. He was so greedy for BioMedbalm business, what with Baby Doll back home nearly dying for the want of going to Paree and getting something from the latest fashion, he just had to net Butler as well. Even an unsporting man like me realised some fish have to be played on a line for hours and some have to be harpooned. But there are some you just let get away - and ol' huntin', shootin', strike-breakin' Ed should have known that.

As soon as we went in and I saw all the framed photographs of rugby teams around the walls and the trophies on his cabinet and even on his desk, I knew that I at least had come to the wrong place; he was a big sod and from the moment we set foot inside the door I knew it was going to end in disaster.

Afterwards, back in the car, Ed was so angry he forgot his Canadian accent.

'What in God's name did you have to go and say that for? There's going to be one hell of a stink about this and I'm the one who's going to be getting it in the neck. I told you, you'd have to tread lightly with him. I thought he might act up a bit seeing as you were new... That's why I came in with you.'

'Why didn't you detail him yourself, then..? After all, he is one of yours, not one of mine.'

'Look, buddy, that's not the attitude to take! I didn't ask to have you slung around my neck like some dead albatross. All I want to do is get out and sell BioMedbalm. I need incidents like this like I need holes in the head.'

'He was in a bad temper before we went in. Anybody could see that. And whatever gripe he's got with BioMed Pharmaceuticals or anybody else has nothing to do with me.'

'It's got everything to do with you! We are BioMed's field representatives, their ambassadors. If you can't get that into your head, you won't last any time at all with this Company.'

'As soon as I opened my mouth and said we were from BioMed Pharmaceuticals, he swore... Are you going to dispute that?'

'No, but - '

'I don't know what you're prepared to put up with down here. But where I come from, if anybody treats you like a bit of dirt, you tell them to get knotted.'

'You what..? "Get knotted"..? What kind of language is that, for Christ's sake..? Where you come from it might be in order to talk to your doctors as though they were navvies, but down here we are more civilised. And if a client...whoever he is...feels aggrieved about anything, we do our level best to smooth things out...not give him a stroke! That man we have just left is in a paroxysm of rage and he could well put the bubble in for both of us... I love this job and want to keep it!'

'Do you never get your back up, then?'

He started up the car and we accelerated away.

'No, of course not!' he said after a while. 'Never... Never so much that it shows, anyhow. Any insults I get, I let them go straight over my head. As far as I'm concerned, they're directed at the Company and not at me personally.'

'I see.'

'I'm not sure that you do.'

We drove on in silence until we came to where my car was parked. He pulled up.

'Look, Joe. I think I've shown you just about all I can. From now on, you're just going to have to get out there on your own territory and learn the rest from experience. I'm prepared to tell Ralph I think you're able to go it alone. You've detailed a couple of dozen GPs now...and a few pharmacists... What do you say..? Ready to give it a whirl?'

'Fine... Okay... Right... Thanks for everything.'

We shook hands.

'Good luck. Keep in touch.'

'I will. And good luck, yourself.'

He drove off and I never saw him again.

Judy and I were now living in a bedsitter in Bromley that we'd found within a few days of going to Sevenoaks, and she'd started work as secretary to the manager of an engineering works in Beckenham. By the time I went to meet her coming out of work - something I didn't normally do because I was usually out burning the 5pm oil to make sure Ed and Paula got to Paris - I had already etched a couple of notches on my own gun.

When she saw me waiting in the car, she looked surprised, then pleased, then alarmed, all before I had a chance to open my mouth.

'What's happened?' she said, quickly getting in the car. 'You haven't fallen out with Ed, have you?'

'Nah. Not really.'

'You have, haven't you? Something's wrong. I can tell.'

'It was just time for the division of the waters, that's all. He wants to go his way and I want to go mine.'

'Are you sure that's all it is?'

'I'm positive. Listen to this... Already I've got four orders of my own. I've sold two thousand, two hundred and fifty milligrams of BioMedbalm to two pharmacies. And I've got three GPs who've promised to prescribe it. I've only seen three and every one agreed to try it..! Gay Paree, here we come! Yip-eee! Ed's going to have to settle for the brush and shovel!'

'That's fantastic! Do you really think you have a chance..? What will Mr Tyler say? Will he mind that you've broken off from Ed, do you think..? You won't be in trouble, will you?'

'Why should I? It was Ed's suggestion.'

'He's got a good start on you, though, hasn't he?'

'Well, yes and no. I really buggered one of his up this morning so there's not going to be much business coming that from quarter.'

'Not deliberately..?'

'Course not. It just happened. That's just the way the cookie crumbles, as Ed would say. Though it's not a bad idea now you come to mention it. Whenever I'm in a bad mood I just veer off into Ed's territory and blow my top in a few of his GPs' surgeries.'

28

Sevenoaks had been a nice little country town, totally different to any town in the hard grey stony North. It was quiet and wealthy and recognisable from the books we had read as children about Farmer Giles and his coterie. It was also the first time we had seen twerps from a private school poncing along in twos and threes, with straw boaters, tailored blazers and long trousers - even the tots. Their hats wouldn't have lasted five minutes in a real town. And whatever Sevenoaks was, it wasn't what I would call a real town with real people. It was a town with self-preoccupied people, most of whom got out of new estate cars and didn't greet people in the street, a town with more estate agents than pubs. It was a town where the young citizens wore silly hats and walked with their noses in the air, spoke as though they were mimicking somebody affected and didn't blend or consort with anybody but themselves. You could feel the aura of superiority that surrounded them even from across the road and I found it hard not to lean out of the car window and shout something ignorant, like a yob.

'These twerps will be governing our lives in twenty years,' I remarked to Judy. 'They'll be making laws down here that will affect our families up there. And most of them will never visit the place.'

But all good things must come to an end and that was why we'd had to move to Bromley; there at least we could afford the rent for a grotty attic, the big money hadn't started to roll in yet.

The fat sleazy landlady and her tall skinny daughter were as miserable as sin and the only tenants they got on with were a couple from Yorkshire. He was always in the small back garden, which was surrounded by rhododendrons growing through the rusty skeletons of mangles, bicycles and prams, practising with a single golf club and ball. We knew he only had the one ball because every time he lost it in the bushes or amongst the scrap, he would go and fetch his wife and the two of them would spend ages looking for it, him with a haircut done with a razor and she with her hair in rollers and feet in slippers with battered bunny-rabbit heads.

There was only enough room to drive the ball about eight feet before it would be off the lawn and into the junk, and he would stand for nearly five minutes in his frayed woollen jumper, flat-arsed trousers and sandshoes, concentrating before making a series of ghost strokes to the side of the ball; he probably wanted to get the action right before chafing both club and ball and wearing them away that little bit more. He didn't seem to have a job or any other interests so I can only assume he was preparing to become a professional.

I had already joined the public library and the Penge and Beckenham judo club and enrolled for an evening class in woodcarving at Bromley Technical college; Judy was doing German twice a week but I was having a job keeping her there. We were intending to do a tour of the Continent in a year or so and I had assumed responsibility for the French and Spanish.

I quickly got into the swing of things, repping for BioMed, and enjoyed the freedom of going more or less where I wanted each day, though I soon learned not to do all the good calls at the beginning of the week and leave all the bad ones till the end. They all had to be done sooner or later so wherever possible I would do one or two bad ones in the afternoon of each day; this way I would have made a good start and would be in a better frame of mind to deal with somebody euphemistically referred to in the card file as, 'can be difficult'.

I hadn't been selling pharmaceuticals very long before I realised that although England was supposed to be a nation of shopkeepers, it certainly didn't care much for salesmen. Anybody who sold goods outside of a shop, and that would include commercial travellers and stall-owners, besides reps, were 'midnight flitters' as far as the shopkeeper and general public were concerned; we were shady, seedy, heavy drinkers, womanisers, bumptious and never went to church.

Although the pharmacists didn't care a damn who manufactured the pharmaceuticals they dispensed as long as they were making a good profit on them, there was a disingenuousness about the attitude of many of the medical profession, who particularly disliked American companies. The medical profession couldn't have functioned without medicine and medicine was no longer made in their kitchens or in the back of chemists' shops; neither of them had the skills or resources to manufacture the kind of medicine they both depended on, let alone to research and produce new ones.

The thing that rankled with me most about pharmacists was that they were businessmen first and last and not chemists who could compound medicine, and not the poor man's doctor any more. They were dispensers, like the Durex machines in barber shops and gents lavatories, but with the human touch that added so much more to the price. All they had to do was tear a label off a pharmaceutical pack and put on their own, the only skill needed was to be able to occasionally count out a specific number of pills if the number on the prescription did not conveniently match the number in the pack; even then, they used plastic counting devices provided free by the pharmaceutical companies.

Nevertheless they still sought to preserve the myth of the apothecary, the illusion that when the nice attractive girl disappeared with the little scrap of paper through the doorway, wonders would be worked by a Merlin with spectacles. Many of them never came out into the shop to see their customers, leaving that to the sales assistants, so now they didn't even need to have a genial personality any more, they could afford to be sociopaths and still be successful. The respectful English public, always willing to be awed by authority, never knew that the silent scholar inside was a hard-nosed, brass-necked wheeler-dealer, as tough as any Covent Garden barrow boy but without his redeeming sense of humour.

With doctors who on the face of it weren't concerned about the dirty business of money but only with the dastard disease, you had to be bubbling over with enthusiasm and show absolute faith in the product because although they were cynical about any form of enthusiasm, they still expected it, and you had to launch into your spiel with the kind of exuberance and pride appropriate to the discovery of a cure for cancer. At least that's the way Head Office reckoned it and every day they bombarded us with literature to substantiate it.

As for scientific evidence, no doctor was interested in trials carried out by foreign scientists in foreign journals, they only wanted to hear what people with the kind of names they could trust had to say, English names, Scottish names, Welsh even, and they wanted them in the *Lancet* or *British Medical Journal*.

They would rarely give you the time to deliver the BioMed minimum of a three-product spiel, nor would they clear a space on their desk so you could rig up your film show with a handheld projector that took ages to set up, that showed an American pharmaceutical-company-engendered miracle and shone a bright light into their eyes.

Who did Head Office think they were kidding? These people didn't want to listen to earnest fresh-faced young men coming in one after another who didn't know the first thing about medicine. So they were impatient, testy and rude; sometimes they were insulting and sometimes they were really nasty.

In our daily report we were supposed to recount every conversation we had engaged in or overheard that referred to BioMed Pharmaceuticals products or personnel, and to that of our competitors. This was the most onerous chore of all. The obvious thing would have been to write a load of bullshit about how wonderful everybody was going around saying BioMed Pharmaceuticals products were, and how brilliant its personnel, plus what a load of bastards our competitors all were and how they should be locked up for hawking their toxic alternatives. But all of them at Head Office had been on the road themselves, so although they told us to say this and do that, they knew reality was far different; so fantasy had to be used with discretion.

While the tenor of my reportage was unquestionably salutary - I knew the daily report could serve as a death warrant - if I were really pissed off with the Company I would insert some abuse of my own inside a pair of inverted commas and indicate that it came from some highly irascible but influential consultant. Then I would balance it with fulsome praise from a doubtful source, so by the time whoever read my stuff had finished it they wouldn't know whether to laugh or cry.

With the BioMed mail came daily updates of the BioMedbalm competition and a table giving the name, position, territory and amount of BioMedbalm capsules, tablets, syrups and injectables sold, and the total expressed in grams, of every rep in the UK force.

One day I would be 100 capsules behind Ed Knight, the next a mere 500cc of pediatric syrup ahead, but every day both of us were rising higher and higher. Once I was seventh; only six in the whole of England, Scotland, Wales and Northern Ireland were above me but one of them was Ed and another was Godfrey. 'I must have done him far more good than harm,' I complained to Judy.

I didn't like any of the north Kent towns. If there really was a difference between the people in the north and south of England, it was here. Although I never drank from either, not directly anyway, I was convinced the waters of Tyne and Medway were of entirely different and mutually repellent composition.

Worst of all was Chatham where things always seemed to go wrong for me. One day I had parked the car on a patch of waste ground, of which there were many in Chatham - war scars I think - to eat my lunch. I never went to restaurants or hotels because this way I could get it over and done with quickly and make on expenses, plus I could take off my jacket, loosen my tie, sit back and relax; Judy and I had bought one of the new Bush transistor portable radios and I could listen to it in the car.

I had finished all my sandwiches and foolishly drank a pint of cold milk on an already full bladder - Chatham was desperate for public conveniences - and suddenly found myself in a most uncomfortable situation which rapidly became critical.

There was absolutely nowhere to go here. There was plenty of space and piles of rubbish to go behind had it been after dark but it wasn't yet one o'clock on a bright afternoon and there were people everywhere. Every time I made to open the door and dart out, some idiot would decide to come by: kids, a lame old woman with a dog, somebody on a bike. I could just imagine the headlines if I were caught standing peeing behind the car and two schoolgirls came by. 'MAN FROM THE NORTH EXPOSES HIMSELF IN FRONT OF LOCAL THIRTEEN-YEAR-OLD VIRGINS'.

The exasperation was making it worse and I could barely move or take a breath without putting an extra strain on my bladder, while with every second my kidneys pumped in more regardlessly. 'COMMERCIAL TRAVELLER DROWNS IN URINE-FILLED HILLMAN MINX'.

Thinking about it made it worse but I couldn't think about anything else, all my philosophies had been turned on their heads as I realised nothing in the world was more important than having a pee: not BioMed, not socialism, not the Catholic Church, sex, art, Judy or my family hundreds of miles away. I thought how wonderful it would be to be a dog and pee without drawing attention to yourself: piddle pee piss, piddle piss pee, pee piddle piss - lamp-posts, trees, car wheels, gates, bare legs, anywhere in the known universe practically.

Suddenly I had a brain wave. The empty milk bottle..! I grabbed it, manoeuvred it into position and started, sitting there in the front seat smiling at passers-by.

'Ahhhhhhh..!' It's quite absurd that the orgasm should be the most highly exalted of human sensations. It was bland, almost tedious, compared with this...

Already the bottle was nearly full. Why was it that whenever I drank a pint of anything, within ten minutes I needed to pee two?

It was only with the greatest effort and after an infinitesimally small spillage that I managed to arrest the flow. But the urine in me was no longer confined to the bladder, it was right up to the tip and I was bursting worse than ever. And then I remembered. In the last batch of lemon-flavoured 500ml BioMedvit I'd been sent, two bottles had been completely empty and I had the box in the back of the car. Oh, heaven-sent error! Oh, ill wind that never blows without... They were still there.

'Come out, you beauties. Let's have you. Oh, glorious litre of space... Oh... Ah... Ahhhhhh... Thank you, God. Thank you, BioMed.'

But after that it was a pure Chatham afternoon.

'A terrible thing happened today,' I said when Judy got in the car at 5.05pm outside work.

'What?'

'You wouldn't believe it. I can scarcely believe it myself.'

'You haven't lost your temper and punched somebody, have you? Don't tell me you...'

'Worse. Far worse.'

'What!'

'Don't say anything. I know it was stupid...damned stupid. And the last thing I need is for you to get hysterical - '

'Hysterical..! What do you mean, "hysterical"? What should I not be getting hysterical about? How bad is it? Tell me..! I can't bear it!'

'You're getting hysterical already and I haven't even begun.'

'No, I'm not... I won't.' Her voice was a little calmer.

'You know how I hate Chatham. If anything's going to go wrong anywhere, it'll be in Chatham. I don't like the place and I've never liked the place. I don't like the people, I don't like the way the town is laid out, I don't like the weather... There is nothing I like about Chatham.'

'No, I know. But what happened?'

'Well, I was parked on a patch of waste ground at lunch-time and the bottle of milk I'd bought was ice cold. And by the time I had finished it, I was bursting for a pee. But there was nowhere to go... Nowhere... Every time I was about to get out of the car, somebody would come by. Eventually I started doing it in the milk bottle with a view to emptying it out later on. But the milk bottle wasn't enough to hold it and once I'd begun I couldn't stop. Then I filled up two empty bottles of BioMedvit.'

She looked around the car and began to sniff. 'Don't tell me. You forgot about them and they've spilled all over the seats?'

'I only wish they had. Because the damned BioMedvit is a lemon-flavoured suspension, it looks just like pee and - '

'Oh, no! No, no, no! Don't say it.'

'I was at Chatham Hospital this afternoon seeing a real swine of a surgeon who got me in a right fluster. And then I had to go to see their pain-in-the-neck of a pharmacist and I was rushing back and forth to the car... And what did he want..? He wanted two bottles of BioMedvit. No antibiotics, no steroids...nothing. And of course no BioMedbalm, which is the only reason I went to the damn place.'

Judy gave a little shriek.

'So I went back to the car, grabbed two bottles quickly...and you know which two I'm talking about...and took them in.'

'Oh, my God! Are you absolutely certain?'

'I'm certain all right. I've checked all the rest.'

'Oh, my God... This is unbelievable.'

'They're probably forcing some old lady to take a spoonful right now.'

'Surely the nurse or whoever's giving it will find out, think it's just gone off and throw it out or something?'

'Vitamin preparations never go off... Not so they smell and taste like horse's piss.'

'It wouldn't do them any real harm though, would it? You sometimes hear of people in the desert drinking their own.'

'If it was me, I'd rather die of thirst.'

'But yours isn't all that bad, surely? You're in good health and all that. If you say nothing, it'll probably never be noticed. Whereas if you go and ask for it back...'

'I know, I know. And because they had need of it urgently, chances are at least one of them will already have been broken into. Tyler told me if I had any problems to go to Ed Knight. Anything special and I was supposed to go to him direct... Imagine trying to explain how my urine happened to get in one of BioMed Pharmaceuticals' beautifully labelled bottles of medication.'

'Even if the worse comes to the worst, it's hardly going to kill anybody though, is it? It's not as if it was arsenic. Goodness me, it's only human fluid. They'll probably drink it and never know the difference... Come on, cheer up. Look how well you're doing in the BioMedbalm competition.'

But I couldn't think of Paris right now. I could only think of litigation...of how much BioMed Pharmaceuticals could be sued for causing an old woman to drink a spoonful of rep pee...and whether they in turn would sue me.

Kent was a luxuriant county and we liked the Sevenoaks area so much, despite a formidable proportion of its inhabitants, that we were always calling into the estate agents in the area to see if they had anything, and eventually we found somewhere near Borough Green. Within two days, before even moving in, Judy got a job at Reeds Paper Company in Larkfield which was only eight miles away. Neither of us were sorry to leave Bromley, an unbeautiful place with airs and graces but no substance.

Borough Green was hop country and the furnished house we moved into was a converted oasthouse adjoining a mediaeval farmhouse owned by the landlady, a tiny old lady who told us her name was 'Miss Turfel' - though it was down in the contract as Miss L.A. Turfel-Soames - and that got her off to a good start as far as we were concerned.

The oasthouse was a kind of two-storey cottage, lime-washed inside and out, with a living room, dining room and kitchen downstairs, and a bathroom and toilet and two small bedrooms at the top of the staircase which spiralled up inside the cone that give the oasthouse its distinctive appearance. To get to the house you came down a drive which led off from a secondary road between Borough Green and Claygate, past several horse chestnut trees and around a lawn surrounded by rose bushes, lupins and other tall perennials, and a high stone wall. This was the first time Judy or I had lived in the country and we loved it.

Miss Turfel spent nearly all of her time in her glorious flower garden and never bothered us. She was intelligent, wealthy, had a very affected voice and a London barrister son who made me want to puke and I wished I could have said the same about her but I couldn't. She was kind, she was tolerant, she was polite, and apart from when she initially showed us around, she never came to our door. She couldn't have been quite as frail as she looked because she was very independent and had a gardener handyman to run her errands and provide some muscle. He hated us right from the start, I think he thought we were heathens, and we didn't care much for him either; he was a sly one and we could well imagine him telling tales about us nonstop to Miss Turfel and all the willing listeners in the district. The Red Lion was nothing but a gossip shop, I don't think they realised that pubs can be friendly places.

He must have been ecstatic the time he found out about the pears.

Within a few days of occupying the house I had discovered a pear-like fruit vine growing wild, just like ivy, covering the wall at the bottom of the lawn. Without a second thought I shinned up and picked the lot, and there were hundreds. Whooping with delight I tossed them onto the lawn below and filled half a dozen boxes which I took into the house where, in less than two days, they all went rotten. It would be many years before I would hear the word 'espalier', Miss Turfel would certainly have been too polite to explain, but only a matter of time before I would realise that throwing fruit a distance of twelve feet or more causes them to bruise and they don't recover.

Miss Turfel hosted the local flower-club meeting on her own front lawn which looked as though it had once been used for croquet, and held garden parties for the local Conservative Ladies' Club but if she ever told them what a pair of ignoramuses from the North she had living in the oasthouse, who had stolen and destroyed the full crop of carefully cultivated pears on the west wing of her property, she did it very discreetly.

In all fairness to myself however I must point out that I never reproached her about the Sunday afternoon when Barrister Son and his wife brought their friends down from the big city to celebrate their new house which was about twenty yards from ours, even though only the foundations had been laid. In addition to the architect's plans which they wandered around with, they had brought a champagne lunch and borrowed a table and chairs from Miss Turfel which they set up on a patch of grass they called 'the dining room'. Talking loudly and unselfconsciously and acting as though the walls were all up, the roof on and they were in the privacy of their own home, they were saying things like, 'Do come into the drawing room, darling,' and 'I've just been into the library, Edward. It's positively charming.'

We played games like that when we were kids but it was in a tent with Tizer and the adults never joined in... Nevertheless it was compulsive viewing.

'I'm waiting to see what happens when one of them wants to go upstairs for a lie down or a wee,' I said to Judy.

'Leave them alone, man. They're not doing any harm.'

They stayed and played out their little charade until the heavens opened up in answer to my prayers and it absolutely bucketed down. They made a mad dash for Rover and Rolls and Judy said 'Ah, what a shame!' and meant it.

Meanwhile I thought of Tod, my old brontosaurus mate.

29

One Monday morning Judy and I were sitting having breakfast and I was going through the mail.

'Look at all this bumf! Every day the same thing... Exhortations to improve on our reporting of what people say... If we wrote down everything they said about BioMed and its products, that lot at Head Office would be jumping out of their five-storey windows.'

'What about other reps? Do they have the same sort of thing?'

'Substitute praise for slander, is what most of them do... Hey, look at this! I came overall fourth in the competition! And because I was the highest of all in the new intake, I'm to get a prize! Yippee!'

'Not Paris?'

'Brighton, more like it...'

I read eagerly. 'Haha, Ed Knight came nowhere...fourteenth or fifteenth. Practically out of sight. Eat dirt, bruin... Now, where's Godfrey Igo..? Hmmph, the old bugger came overall seventh. Not bad, Godfrey, old son...not bad for a novice.'

'Come on! What did you get..? Where are we going..? I'm going crazy with the suspense!'

'Oh, no..! Bloody hell..! You won't believe this.'

'What?'

'An evening in the company of Ralph Tyler, damn his soul, blast his arse.'

'What do you mean?'

'Tyler's coming here to take us out to dinner.'

'What a let-down.'

'Let down..? That's a punishment, not a reward. Imagine having to sit and listen to him all night preaching the gospel according to Dale Carnegie... Buggeration!'

'What?'

'He's going to combine it with a tour of my territory and 'monitor' my skills!'

'Can I have a look.'

She pondered for a while. 'It might be quite nice. He might even be presenting you with a cheque. Companies often do things like that.'

'I've a good mind to write in and tell them I've been trafficking my own waste products and have myself disqualified... Let's have a look at that letter again. When does it say he's coming..? Bloody Hell! The twelfth! That's this Thursday.'

At 9.20am on Thursday, Tyler and I were at Chatham General Hospital.

Before going in to see the Chief Pharmacist I had parked the car in the only space left, the space reserved for the Matron. Tyler had whistled under his breath but said nothing. When we came back it was to find a Ford Prefect with all the trappings of maidenhood parked right behind me; I was hemmed in on three sides and directly in front was the kerb that bordered the lawn and a 'Keep Off The Grass' sign.

'That's what comes of parking in the spot reserved for the Matron of the hospital. You've had it, boyo. There's no way for it but to go to her with an excuse she might be prepared to forgive, and apologise profusely and obsequiously. In other words, slaver all over her with your North Country charm but keep the Company right out of it.'

'To hell with that,' I said, taking off my jacket. I studied the space between the car on either side of my Hillman. There was marginally more space on the left, the passenger side, but it was going to be a tight squeeze.

I took off my shirt and tie.

'Hold these a minute, will you,' I said, handing them to Tyler.

'What are you doing, man? You're not going to strip off, are you?'

'I'm going to climb over her car, reach into mine, try to get the window down and climb in. Then I'm going to mount their lawn, drive around the flower bed and meet you over there by that opening. Once I get started we're going to have to get out of here pretty damn quick.'

'You must be crazy. You'll never do it. You'll get yourself stuck halfway and do yourself a serious injury. And don't expect BioMed Pharmaceuticals to bail you out. If anybody comes by, I don't know you.'

As I clambered over the Ford, there was a yelp from behind.

'Jesus! Come down, man, before somebody sees you! The one next to you is a consultant's car for bloody certain!'

I waved a hand at him to be quiet and pressed on. Slithering into the Hillman was more difficult than I had anticipated but I did it. Once in, I realised I hadn't pulled up the 'Keep Off' sign and had no alternative but to drive over it and gently flatten it so it wouldn't damage my tyres.

A couple of minutes later I had done it, driven across the lawn and around the large crescental flowerbed back onto the roadway, and was holding the door open for Tyler. He rushed up with the shirt, jacket and tie and detailing bag and got in, grinning.

'That was the neatest piece of prestidigitation I've seen in a long time,' he chuckled. 'Let's get moving!'

I drove out onto the main road and shot away. A couple of miles later I pulled up and put on my tie and jacket, Tyler was writing something in a small notebook.

'Impressed?' I asked him.

'Very. However, you do realise it's my duty to report the incident.'

I laughed. 'Who to..? The Matron?'

'Head Office.'

'Head Office..? You're joking?'

'I'm not.'

'What for?'

'It's all part of the job, boyo. Nothing personal, you understand. Just supposing somebody saw what went on back there and decided to report it to the Company..? I'm only covering myself.'

'You mean anything I say or do while you're with me might be taken down and used in evidence against me, sort of thing?'

'Will be taken down, boyo. Will be taken down. Including the fact that you were driving at ninety in a thirty-mile-an-hour zone.'

'Shit!'

I drove to Chatham in silence and he sat writing in his book, closing it and then opening it again and adding something. I was now driving within the limit and not saying or doing anything to give him reason to write anything else.

Half an hour later we were sitting in the restaurant of the Chatham Station Hotel, having ordered lunch. Tyler was leaning forward, elbows on the table, head on one side looking at me. I was waiting for him to come out with something. I wished they would hurry up with the soup.

'Tell me... If this is the hotel where you claim on your expenses sheet to have lunch every time you're in Chatham, how come you didn't know where the dining room was?'

'Couldn't I have simply made a mistake..? You know...been panicked by the awesomeness of the occasion and all that?'

'Flippancy will get you nowhere... You wouldn't descend to the mean and grubby swindle of that feckless creature, the commercial traveller who eats cheese and tomato sandwiches out of yesterday's newspaper, drinks stewed tea out of a thermos flask, and then puts in a claim for lunch at a four-star hotel, would you?'

'Does nobody who works for BioMed Pharmaceuticals ever sink to those depths?'

'Nobody.'

'What about you when you were a rep?'

'Never. I'd sooner be put up against a wall and shot.'

'And no doubt reject the benefit of a blindfold?'

'Correct.'

I clinked glasses. 'Then I'm honoured to be in such good company.'

He smiled and shook his head slowly.

'You were saying before about the competition?'

'Ah, yes... So when they authorised me to take you and your charming wife out to dinner, I thought I'd couple it with a two-day visit to see if I could discern the secret of your success.'

'I bet the initiative of that impressed them?'

'I'd watch out for that little chip on the shoulder, if I were you. It could be an obstacle to progress. Let me tell you a little parable from which I hope you will distil some moral.

'Once upon a time...just a year ago in fact...there was a very successful pharmaceutical representative called Ernie, known to his peers as 'Dead Eye Ernie' because whenever he set his beady eye on a woman, that woman was his for the taking...so runs the legend. Whether this eye of his worked the oracle with doctors and pharmacists as well, I don't know. What I do know is that Ernie was far and away the most successful rep BioMed Pharmaceuticals ever had...at least on this side of the Atlantic.

'But at a dinner to celebrate one of his many sales victories, Ernie drank rather too much and...flushed with success...was standing holding forth, glass in hand, keeping the audience spellbound as he convulsed them with joke after joke about Englishmen, Scotsmen, Irishmen and Welshmen. But when he came to the one about the Jew...although everybody laughed...word went out from the Godfather. As you probably know, only Jews can tell jokes about Jews...and even then only to a Jewish audience... Ernie was allowed to finish his dinner and collect his prize, somebody had a quiet word in his ear, and he was never seen again.'

'Sounds just like the Mafia... And the moral?'

'Any true BioMed man would perceive it.'

'Ernie evidently didn't.'

'That, my dear chap, is why Ernie is no more. In this life you can be world champion one minute. The next, you can be flat on your back and counted out.'

He sat back, arms folded, looking around the room, clearly relishing himself. He then placed his folded arms on the table and said in a very low voice, 'How observant are you, I wonder? How quickly do you perceive the little quirks and foibles that make human nature what it is? For these are the strings on which you should be playing your melodies.'

'What? Like the Shostakovich Shortcomings Symphony, you mean? Or Franz Lizst's Failure in F?'

He raised an eyebrow and looked at me with an eye that looked as though it had seen all there was to see, an eye that had suffered many assaults and although might no longer be able to undress a woman with the same clarity, it could still show devastating contempt for both sexes if need be. There was something of St Augustine about him, something of the reprobate who'd had a great time sinning his soul, but now, like many a recanter, narrower and more censorious than any who had always done the right thing and missed out on all the turpitude.

'See the fellow sitting at that table over there..? You can't hear him but he's whistling... Why is he whistling..? He is whistling to try to give an air of self confidence when in fact he is very ill at ease.'

'Maybe it's because he knows you're trying to see into his soul.' I began to whistle softly and tunelessly.

'The eternal clown, eh? You simply cannot resist it, can you..? Listen carefully while your Uncle Ralph gives you some friendly and very valuable advice. Sail only so close. No vessel has ever been made that cannot be capsized. Forget not the Titanic... Now, let's discuss your programme for this afternoon. Where are we going first?'

'Mainly to GPs, starting with a Dr Rowse whose place isn't far from here.'

Three quarters of an hour later, after a mediocre meal and a surfeit of Welsh irony, we were standing outside Dr Rowse's front door, or what according to my cards should have been Dr Rowse's front door. It was odd the door was closed, his surgery hours were supposed to be from 2pm until 3pm and it was now a quarter past two. It was even odder that there was no response to my persistent ringing of the doorbell.

'He must be on holiday.'

'When did you last call on him?'

I was humming and hawing when the door suddenly opened and a woman with her head tied in a turban and wearing a smock appeared.

'Yes?'

'Is there no surgery today?'

'No, and there won't be until the end of July at the very earliest.'

'Why's that..? Dr Rowse hasn't left the district, has he?'

'More or less... He's dead.'

'He's what..! Oh, I'm terribly sorry to hear that. Well... Please accept our condolences.'

'It's not me. Mrs Rowse is away. I'm just the housekeeper.'

'Well, all the same we're sorry to hear it. He'll be a terrible miss. Could you give us the name of whoever it is that will be taking over the practice?'

'I think it's Dr Winters or something like that.'

'Dr Winters... Right, thank you. Sorry to have bothered you. Thank you very much. Cheerio.' I had already retreated down the steps, unable to get away fast enough.

She was just about to close the door when Tyler said 'Excuse me. I wonder if you could tell us when Dr Rowse became deceased. Just for our records.'

'When he died..? Oh, it must be over a year now.'

'A year?' repeated Tyler, dragging it out so it sounded even longer.

'At least that.'

'Are you sure?' I asked.

'Of course I'm sure. I should be. I've been his housekeeper for more than ten years.'

'Right, thank you. Thank you very much. Again, sorry to have troubled you.'

Tyler and I walked down the path in silence. What a start to the afternoon.

You could never see everybody on your list. Some surgeries were always packed and although that meant they were doing a lot of business and therefore you should see them, like as not they'd have too little time to let you do a proper detail; you would be following them around while they were putting their pens in their pockets, putting their files away and locking their drawers, and paying hardly any attention at all; and because you always had to wait till the very end, it would have taken a big chunk out of your morning.

There were those who lived in places you could never park near to, or could never find, I had at least half a dozen I'd never been able to locate. Some doctors had a rule that they would never see you and their receptionists would either shrug their shoulders if they were pleasant, or tell you to get lost if they weren't; usually it was because the doctor didn't like the Company or because he didn't like reps. Then there were those whose voices you could hear and they sounded such bastards you didn't feel like waiting, especially if you'd just come from one.

Wherever we went Tyler had something critical to say. Most doctors cannot be bothered with one rep, especially one after the other, let alone two at a time. Yet not once did he sell so much as a single capsule or tablet, not once did he show how it should be done, not once did he help me out when he saw I was in difficulties. He wasn't concerned with selling the products, he was more concerned with me. Before we went in and after we came out, he couldn't keep his mouth shut, gloating whenever he detected any sign of human frailty, mine or anybody else's; he couldn't see a woman with a twitch without drawing some moral from it, even some poor sod whistling was revealing a mental condition that could be exploited.

That night when Judy and I arrived at the Chatham Hotel Tyler was sitting in the foyer reading the Spectator and I have to say he looked superb. I don't know what the rules of admission to the Atheneum were but surely he deserved to get in. To Judy he was a perfect gentleman. 'Like Stewart Grainger,' she said later.

'Michael Medwin, more like it,' I'd retorted. If she'd seen the other face, the one I'd been looking at all day, she wouldn't have been so rapturous.

'How do you like living in the Garden County then, Judith?' he asked when we had sat down and he'd ordered the drinks.

'It's nice. There's some lovely scenery around here...and it's a lot warmer than Northumberland.'

'The people leave a lot to be desired though,' I volunteered.

Tyler flicked an imaginary crumb off his thigh and rearranged his eyebrows.

'Well, to be serious for a moment and recall the reason for this little celebration... On behalf of BioMed Pharmaceuticals may I wish you both every happiness. Joe, your sales figures for the new product, BioMedbalm, were truly outstanding. What you need do now is concentrate on getting your other products up to scratch. You can't afford to give the impression you've been neglecting your folic acid tabs. Get your medical men to think pregnancy, think BioMedfolic. Get them to couple the two in their minds so they become indivisible...'

He suddenly stopped himself. 'Please accept my humble and most sincere apologies, Judith. We pharmaceutical people are inclined to forget there are other things in heaven and earth apart from antibiotics, anticoagulants and nutritional supplements.'

We all laughed.

I have to admit it was a very pleasant evening. Judy, who loved dancing, had the opportunity to dance with somebody who could dance, rather than with somebody who told everybody he could dance but always had an excuse when crunch-time came around. Tyler was also well-read, a very entertaining conversationalist and an excellent host, and it was almost midnight when we left the cosy intimacy of the hotel lounge to go home.

The next morning I entered the foyer of the Bromley Towers Hotel to find Tyler having coffee and reading the Financial Times.

I greeted him breezily. 'Morning, Ralph. Stocks and shares doing all right?'

'Pop over to the mail-rack and see if there's anything for me, will you?' he replied. 'There's a good chap. It's number twenty-three.'

The geniality of the night before was already consigned to history.

I went over to the pigeon-holed cabinet and looked in No. 23. Empty. Up above it, several huge envelopes were stuffed into No. 6, the kind of packages I received from BioMed, except that they had the red and black insignia of Honneker & Schlering Pharmaceuticals.

I went back. 'Nothing.'

'See anything of interest when you were over?' he asked without raising his eyes from his paper.

'No. Why..? Except that somebody from Schlering's obviously staying here.'

'The enemy in our midst.'

'Have you seen them?'

He didn't reply, he just looked at me with a steely eye.

'What's the matter?'

'I'm waiting for some initiative.'

'What kind of initiative?'

'Wouldn't you like to know what our competitors are up to..? Wouldn't the Company like to know what our competitors are up to?'

'Of course, but...you're surely not suggesting..?'

'I'm not suggesting anything, old chap,' he said as he folded his paper under his arm and got up. 'I'm merely assessing...among other things...your initiative.'

'Well my initiative doesn't stretch that far.'

'How far?'

'As far as what you're implying.'

'Implication and inference are often very different.'

As we were walking towards the car he said 'Supposing you had a forty-eight-year-old paediatrician on your territory. There's bound to be at least one. A woman with a geriatric wart on her upper lip from which grows a long and winding ginger whisker. The hair on her head is grey and unkempt. Her bosom is hanging around her knees and her legs are varicosed... Like every other professional woman she desperately wants to bite on forbidden fruit but it has never been handed to her on a plate. As a consequence she has become crusty, she smells of old tabby cat and has bequeathed her teeth to plaque. But what makes this woman least appealing of all is that she never prescribes BioMed Pharmaceuticals products.

'Now, this is what you have to ask yourself... "Would I, a"...presumably..."virile young man, be prepared to give this woman what she needs, thus relieving that awful incessant ache in her loins..? And, more importantly, opening the gates to a veritable flood of BioMed pharmaceuticals?".'

'You mean, would I seduce her?'

In a loud whisper he said 'I mean, would you fuck her? Would you stick it into her for the sake of the Company?'

'No, I damn-well wouldn't.'

'What if every goose-pimple on her body was crying out for it, wouldn't the good Samaritan in you at least be moved to compassion? Wouldn't you be concerned about the fact that the ailing in your territory were being deprived of the benefit of BioMed pharmaceuticals..? In other words, what would you do about it?'

'Detail her extra hard.'

'But we have already established that it isn't hard detailing that the woman wants...whatever her needs. Again, two very different things.'

I started the car. 'It's all hyperbole.'

'No, it isn't. These things happen and I need to know what you would do?'

'I'd send for you...Puck.'

He burst out laughing.

'You've got something to you, boyo...and that's for sure. I haven't quite made up my mind what it is and whether it's likely to be of any value to the Company...but you've certainly got something...'

'Well, where to first? Somebody still of this world, I trust?'

'That was just a fluke yesterday. I still haven't got all my cards up to date after the state my predecessor left them in.'

'It's a bad rep who blames his predecessor.'

'I thought it was a bad rep who blames his products?'

'No. That's a dead rep.'

'Maybe that's what happened to him. Vaporised while being handed a cheque. Like poor Ernie.'

Half an hour later we were sitting in our first doctor's waiting room of the day, it was a cold and blustery day so the room was packed with gloomy snivelling faces. Tyler had his notebook out and was giving me a PK test and people were straining hard to hear what it was that we were so intensely whispering about.

'And how much does Vita-Boehring's CNS depressant work out. Their injectable, that is?'

'Look, Ralph. I cannot answer test questions under these conditions. Give over, will you?'

He ignored me.

'Who...in what trial...found the side effects from BioMedpen were less than with any comparable drug?'

I folded my arms and sat back.

He continued his loud whispering. 'This is no game, boyo. This is deadly earnest. You must remain composed and fully in command in any situation. Answer!'

'Grafton, Lee and Mawani in Toronto,' I angrily whispered. 'But they also found BioMedpen to be less effective than at least three of the others.'

'Careful. That's treachery, no less.'

He picked something off his trousers and held it up between his forefinger and thumb. 'What's this?'

'It looks like a hair.'

'Well it's certainly not one of mine.' He screwed up his eyes and looked at my hair. 'And it doesn't look like one of yours. I'd say it was a dog's. Guess where I picked it up..? In your car. I know I must have because I can remember seeing others that were just like this one. It looks as though it belongs to a Sealyham Terrier.'

I immediately took the bait. 'It's an Alsation, not a bloody Sealyham Terrier!'

'You mean one of those huge German shepherd dogs..? Pray, what would a vicious unpredictable beast like that be doing in a BioMed Pharmaceuticals car?'

'Don't ask unless you really want to know.'

'What on earth do you mean..? Tell me. I demand to know.'

I drew very close to him and began whispering out of the side of my mouth conspiratorially. 'Well, I have this massive Alsation which I've trained to attack doctors. It can bite their nuts off in one snap, clean as a whistle.'

'I won't ask how you managed to accomplish this feat,' he said with a little smile. 'Spare me the details. But to what purpose..? Is it so that when BioMed Pharmaceuticals eventually shrugs off your mortal coil, you intend savaging its clients with this Baskerville brute of yours?'

'On the contrary. The dog cracks nuts in the service of the Company.'

Tyler started chuckling.

'The dog is trained to go into action when it hears the word "No" as in "No, I don't want any more of your crappy pharmaceuticals..."'

At this point I knew he was already ahead of me. He had his monogrammed handkerchief to his face and was trying to stifle his laughter.

I continued. 'After my spiel I say - '

'Shush! No! Please don't say it!' Tears were running down his cheeks.

'I say "Will you promise to prescribe BioMed Pharmaceuticals products and only BioMed Pharmaceuticals products from now on and well into eternity?"'

'"Well into eternity"..! Oh Jesus... Oh! Stop, will you..!'

'By this time, "Bite"...that's the name of the dog - '

'"Bite"..! Jesus, Mary and Joseph!' he shrieked, snot coming out of his nose. 'No more, I beg you! I'm serious..! No more!'

I continued. 'Bite, who is never fed until the end of the day when we've done all our calls - '

'"We" did you say..? When "we've" done all "our" calls..?'

I nodded.

'By now Bite is getting a hard-on with excitement. This usually transfixes the would-be non-prescriber who for a moment is thrown by the size of the dog's erect dick.'

Something seemed to snap in Tyler who was now folded over, hands over his ears but with his fingers spread so he could still hear.

'I command you to stop..!'

But by this time we were both laughing aloud and the melancholy semi-circle of patients were looking very disconcerted.

'Last week I sent away to Spain - '

'No more, you Geordie twat!' he shouted. 'I can't take any more..!'

Just then the surgery door tore open and a very angry doctor came out.

'What on earth is going on here!' His eyes alighted on Tyler and me. 'You two..! Are you reps..? I might have known. Get to hell out of here this minute!'

'Good job you haven't got Bite here with you today,' Tyler almost shrieked as the two of us tottered out of the door, hanging on to each other for support, no doubt the only human beings ever to cross that threshold laughing.

Halfway down the steps he turned, his hand gripping my tie. 'There's something I've got to know...before I take another step... What is it you have coming from Spain?'

'A jar of live Rabies virus to inject the dog with.'

When we finally got to the car, on which we hung like drunken fools debilitated by laughter, we could see the miserable faces of the patients and the puffed-up enraged face of the doctor, the decorum of whose dingy waiting room we had for a few brief moments violated.

Once in the car Tyler regained possession of himself and was soon writing in his little book. I'd have given anything to see how he reported incidents like this. Would they be general comments such as, 'inclined to be frivolous', or something stronger like, 'Robinson is a maniac and deserves to be certified'?

Tyler strove all of the time to give the impression that BioMed Pharmaceuticals was his life. Even when we were in a hotel having a pee in the urinal and he would be standing next to a smartly dressed young man, he would be looking over the top of the column; not so much to see if the fellow had a nice cock, as to identify which company he worked for by the colour of his pee - all reps dosed themselves with their own vitamin products.

The oasthouse tenancy agreement's 'No animals or children' clause really meant, I had assured Judy, 'No badly behaved animals or children', and we had bought an Alsation pup, and a few days later, a young Indian Hill Mynah.

Coming from a council estate - terrier-land - I had always wanted a decent-sized dog and now that we lived in the country it seemed too good an opportunity to waste. And it was ages since I'd had a bird.

I had read the Wehrmacht Colonel Konrad Most's book on training 'The German Shepherd' and was looking forward to producing what the British Army was always trying to turn out: a strong obedient animal with no will of its own. Most used strict methods and his dogs never begged for titbits nor did they ever shake anybody's hand with their paw.

Notwithstanding my loose interpretation of the Agreement we tried to give the dog a low profile, hoping that by the time Ned Yule had seen it and gone to his mistress with his cap off, Sheba - its real name - would be seen as a welcome addition to our little rustic community.

Ideally an Alsation should be eighteen months old before serious training begins; until then and especially for the first eight months, until the first brain cell appears, it does nothing but wantonly shit, pee and vandalise.

We couldn't leave it in the house while we were both out, so Judy took it to the office she worked in at Reed's and kept it in a box under her desk until the day it bit the boss's leg - actually, 'snacked' was the word we would have used in the North for a nip barely sufficient to break the skin, but he hadn't been acquainted with the word.

From then on I took the dog with me and Judy kept the Indian Hill Mynah under her desk. The bird would never bite anybody - only what we would call a 'bit of a peck' - but being a superb mimic, as mynahs are, it occasionally gave a kind of shriek which Judy had to try to explain. However, because of the insectivorous food it had to be fed every hour, it stank, and she was very relieved when it was old enough to be left at home in its cage. The dog and the bird were the source of more arguments between us in the early days of our marriage, than anything.

One day I had been in with a GP when there was the most awful ruckus outside. We had both gone to his window to see Sheba barking like mad in the car which I had parked outside.

'What the..?'

'Sorry, Doctor,' I said. 'It's my dog. I had to have her with me today. Somebody must have upset her.'

'What!'

I had just shrugged, put my stuff back in my bag and rushed out.

Although she hadn't damaged the car, she had ripped open all of my boxes of samples and there was strawberry-flavoured (and coloured) antibiotic syrup, liver-brown tablets and capsules, plus my order-books and scientific literature, chewed up and vomitted out all over the place. It took Judy and I a whole weekend to get the car cleaned up.

We had had to hide the dog when Tyler came. I just knew that if the dog ever really had the impulse to bite anybody's nuts off, they would have been his.

30

On the 2nd July, my twenty-third birthday, Judy and I were married at St Dominic's Friary in Newbridge Street, Newcastle, and Johnny was best man. We had driven up in the Hillman because we had a lot of running around to do and because we wanted to go for a motoring honeymoon in the Lake District.

Todd was the only invited guest who failed to appear, I don't think he could face all the shmaltz. He must have realised that things would never be the same and I never heard from him again.

My younger brothers claimed not to be impressed at all by the Hillman, my 'salesman job', living 'down south', or any of it.

'Urrgh! Our Joe thinks he's a big man because he's getting married. Thinks people will call him 'Mister' now. Tries to talk posh. "Parse the shoogar, there's a good chep". Calls everybody else "pathetic" when he's the one who's pathetic.'

But the morning after we came back from our honeymoon in the Lake District and Michael and Peter came into the spare bedroom at Anthony's bidding, to see me in bed with Judy, they were so appalled they were speechless. Nothing, no physical flaw or petty vanity of mine could compare with this and they still hadn't recovered when we left next day to go back to Kent.

A couple of weeks after the wedding I was called back to BioMed House for a three-day refresher course and booked into the Charing Cross Hotel along with all those still surviving from the January intake, and on the Friday night we met in the bar.

The difference was amazing, I was reminded of the change in my old squad at Crookham Barracks when I returned from the PT course to find them all looking and behaving like veterans. They were now very sure of themselves, most had taken some knocks, some of them hard, and they had all had some success, however fleeting.

As we sometimes talked seriously and other times laughed, we boasted, slandered and pontificated, we told and heard of outrageous doctors, some of whom should have been wearing straitjackets, others who should have been wearing pyjamas with arrows on them, of shyster pharmacists and of crazy reps who worked for other companies, some of them great guys, some of them rogues.

Once inside the BioMed Pharmaceuticals suite on the Monday morning, separated from each other by the rarefied air of wide aisles and dear friends departed, it was cold turkey all over again, especially when Briggs came striding in, and the six months just fell away.

He walked up and down the aisles, looking from left to right, from the front and from the back, his eyes engaging our souls.

'Well, well... So here are the fledged of January fifty-nine...the hardcore who haven't had enough and are raring for their first refresher course.'

He was back at his desk. 'Right, then.' He picked up a pile of folders.

'In these files I have details of every one of you... Every sale...every missed sale...every transgression. Copies of all reports...daily, weekly, monthly... Budget targets and budget achievements. District managers' reports...and the occasional communication from a dissatisfied customer.

'And I can say with total conviction that none of you have any reason to feel complacent. None of you has the right to rest easy in his bed at night or to go to church on Sunday and give thanks for a job well done. None of your positions is secure.

'The reason you are here today...some of you by less than the skin of your teeth...is for one reason only. BioMed Pharmaceuticals has invested a great deal of money in each and every one of you...and it wants something back!

'It wants commitment! It wants energy! It wants sales..! Not just a once-off effort because of a competition...but repeated, continuing, increasing, sales. Not just of excellent products like BioMedbalm which are so good they sell themselves...but of vitamins, of sulphonamides, of enzymes like BioMedase, the forgotten wonder...products that deserve dedication.

'You people aren't pedlars hawking vinyl carpets or vacuum cleaners. You are privileged to be purveying the best answer to the illnesses that afflict mankind, that science has to offer. Not nostrums, not poultices...but highly sophisticated medicines that have been researched and developed by the very cream of the pharmaceutical industry... And manufactured to the very highest of standards.

'You should all get down on your knees and thank somebody that you are here today..!

'Now, let's start with you, Mr Benjamin. Please come out here and explain to your colleagues how you managed to consistently achieve your BioMedanin budget whilst consistently failing to sell any BioMedaflin. Zero is the exact number of sales of BioMedaflin in your four months in the field. Cynics might regard that as some kind of achievement in itself, considering the reputation of this peerless product. Perhaps you can explain to us how it is that in West Devon no child ever seems to suffer from sore throats?'

And that is the way the 'course' went; there was no let up; it was a 'shake-up'. The best thing about it was the night Godfrey and I went to 'Heaven and Hell', a club Godfrey used to be a member of, and the first one of any kind that I had ever been in.

Godfrey was doing well as a hospital rep in London; the things that bothered me about selling pharmaceuticals didn't seem to bother him at all, and the gratification he got was something I'd experienced only momentarily.

We ended up back in the bar of the Charing Cross Hotel, making plans for Judy and I to visit him and his wife Carol at Carol's family home in Norfolk.

He was surprised and not just a little hurt when I told him that Judy and I were now married and he realised he hadn't been invited to the wedding. Really I should have liked to have invited him; Bill and Elsie Morley had been invited, but I had lived with them and they were much older, and even then we didn't invite their daughter Janet who was a couple of years older than I was, because of the no-children rule. Silly it was to have to ask every last relative whether you liked them or not, but to be able to ask only 'one or two' friends and then only longstanding ones. But that was the way we did it in the North.

Until the day I crashed into an old Ford Popular, cutting it in two halves, telescoping the front of the Hillman and causing seven other vehicles to crash including a lorry laden with gravel that brought down a telegraph pole which flattened a bread van, I had not put so much as a scratch on the Hillman. I would gladly have had the whole lot of them from the transport department at Head Office go over it inch by inch with a magnifying glass and defied any of them to have found the teeniest weeniest little scratch; even the wafer-thin coat of enamel varnish I'd sealed the bumpers, headlights and chrome trim with had been perfectly intact; there were no tiny dents in any hub cap from driving too close to the kerb, no minute crazes on the windscreen from grit; nothing... But it was too late now.

It had been very foggy when I dropped Judy off at work and she had pleaded with me to go back and wait until the fog lifted before going to Tonbridge.

Impatient with an old Morris that was being driven with excruciating care, I had pulled out and drawn alongside with a view to overtaking it, only to discover it was being towed; and I was weighing up whether to go on or drop back, when out of the gloom appeared a Ford Popular right in front of me. It immediately slewed to its left, more or less obliging me to ram it broadside before ramming the big Humber that was right behind it, which stopped me from hitting anybody else but didn't stop the Austin behind the Humber from hitting the Humber, nor the one behind the Austin from hitting the Austin and so on. Even the pole-axed bread van which, due to the skill of its driver on a day not memorable for great drivers, had managed not to hit anything itself, would most likely be chalked up to me.

It was only later when I had climbed out of my own back door, checked on the Ford Popular, the front half of which was in a ditch with the driver and his wife both still sitting with their hats on in the front seat, alive and apparently well but unhappy, had staggered along the line of wreckage and returned to stand by my own vehicle and await arrest, that I realised I was the architect of nothing less than a disaster. This was my first ever accident and I had immediately apologised to the Popular couple, thereby incriminating myself. Every driver on the road couldn't have been in a state of shock, so they were presumably following their insurance policy instructions, because nobody said anything to me, certainly nothing that could be interpreted as contrition. However, when the police arrived they found their tongues all right: 'He was driving like a maniac! Somebody said he's a commercial traveller. He should be locked up!'

Miraculously, and this was surely no abuse of the word, nobody was seriously hurt and it could only have been because everybody was driving so slowly. After I had made a provisional statement - the police were considerate enough to offer to send someone around to my house that evening to take a full one - I telephoned Head Office and broke the news. They put me on to Mr Fynes, the new transport manager, who said nothing while I totted up the total, giving one driver plus make of vehicle plus registration number plus insurance company, after another. There weren't eight vehicles as I had originally thought, there were only seven. But that didn't include the Hillman. The worst of it was that I had taken a detour and the accident had occurred in East Sussex, strictly outside of my territory, which seemingly created all kinds of legal problems.

'If they shunted one after another into the back ends of each other, surely that implies they weren't keeping a safe stopping distance apart from each other?'

Mr Fynes said it wasn't funny but I didn't intend it to be funny, I was pleading mitigation for the Company's liability, trying to help them out. He didn't say 'Don't worry, old chap, we're right behind you. Nobody's going to pin a rap on any of our lads. You just get yourself on home and promise me you'll have a nice mulled rum and take it easy for the rest of the day. You must have had quiet a shock. Accidents will happen, it's part of life. And the weather is such a nusiance, isn't it? We here at Head Office will just offer up a prayer of thanks that you're not hurt'. He said nothing remotely like it.

At the end of the conversation I said 'I'm very sorry...really, really sorry.' There didn't seem to be anything else I could say that he wanted to hear except perhaps 'April Fool!'. I knew how woefully inadequate the word 'sorry' can be but surely they weren't expecting 'God, I wish I were dead. Take it out of my next thousand pay packets'.

By the time evening came and the policeman called at the house, I had prepared and rejected one defence after another; self righteousness was hard to sustain under the circumstances. I had ventured the cynicism to Judy that I seriously suspected some of them at the end of the line were opportunists: 'Great! What a mess. Now I'll be able to get a new wing. Under cover of this fog I'll just ease into the back of him... Easy does it so nobody gets hurt...' Bang! 'Whoopsadaisy!'

But she hadn't been impressed. 'Don't even think about it,' she said. 'It sounds absolutely ridiculous!'

When the policeman came in and we saw he was a big thick Geordie, we could hardly believe it. He was patient, plodding, open to a bribe of one cup of tea after another with three sugars, and it was all we could do to refrain from softly singing 'Oh, me lads, ye shudda seen us gannin'' as we followed him down the stairs to see him out.

He had been in the house for over two hours and we were glad to get rid of him at the end but he told us not to worry and that everything would be all right - though we knew he meant relatively speaking.

Head Office weren't stress counsellors but they were otherwise very efficient. At the time of reporting the accident they had instructed me to contact the nearest Rootes dealer who came immediately and towed away my Hillman; the very next day I had an almost new one, this time a column gear change rather than the floor change type I prefer; however I didn't insist Rootes change it and hadn't the heart to bother Fynes and the transport department again.

Hospital consultants were regarded by all pharmaceutical companies as the most important of all 'customers' because of their influence on the prescribing habits of the GPs in their area, so there was considerable pressure to detail every one of them. But they were hard chowder.

One morning a surgeon at Rochester General, who I had never managed to get an interview with, granted me five minutes. At first I thought it must have been an act of courtesy because of all the times I had called and had left my card along with generous samples of some very expensive drugs. When I answered the command, 'Come!' which I knew meant 'Enter at your peril!', he was seated in a leather swivel chair surrounded by his registrar and five students. I wasn't invited to sit, so had to deliver my spiel standing holding my bag between my clasped hands in front of me like a girl with a toy handbag.

'Now, let me see if I've got it right,' he said, swivelling. 'You're telling us that if I prescribe Bio-whatsit my patients are going to be so relaxed they're going to be looking forward to having their chests opened. Is that it?'

Several of the students forced appreciative laughs.

'Well, the Company claims - '

'Oh, I see... This is just a claim...to be taken with a pinch of salt, no doubt?'

'A dessertspoonful, I suspect, sir,' volunteered a student with a tooth brace.

They all laughed.

'Can you explain to us the mode of action of this wonderful new drug?'

'Well, it... I... Like all anodynes it has a depressive action on the higher centres of the brain.'

'Does it now..? And, pray, where might those be? Would you be kind enough to point them out with your finger on this chap's head - ' He was tapping the nearest student on the head with his pencil.

'We shall presume...for the purposes of this demonstration...that he has some "higher centres".'

There was more laughter, one of the students heehawing like a donkey.

'Now, Johnson. Lower your head so our friend can get a good look.'

I was looking at the top of a round head, its dandruff-peppered hair beginning to thin at the crown.

'No, I cannot,' I said, very embarrassed. 'I'm not sure anybody can. No more than I can point to where his conscience is, even though I'm sure he has one.'

The smile left his face.

'So your Company thinks that if my patients come into the theatre feeling depressed, rather than just anxious, they'll be better off?'

'Don't their pre-meds have pretty much the same effect?'

'No, they do not! Because very soon they'll be under the umbrella of a general anaesthetic!'

'I didn't mean to give the impression that BioMedbalm causes depression. I meant to say - '

'Oh, we know exactly what you meant..! You were trying to tell us that you haven't the foggiest idea what you're talking about. You people who come from God-knows-where, do a weekend course in high-pressure selling and then have the audacity to presume you can influence the prescribing habits of highly trained doctors with a lifetime's experience behind them... 'What part of the Empire do you say you come from..? Shouldn't you be wearing a tartan skirt or something?'

'I'm from Tyneside. We're the ones who wear big caps and howk.'

'Eh..? Oh... I suppose that explains it... Well now, we've just about had enough of you and your sales chatter, sonny boy. So you can skedaddle. Go on, be off with you! Go back to your firm and tell them to stop sending us ill-informed salesmen who are still wet behind the ears and bring us the same old drugs under new American brand names. Tell them to get off their behinds and do something useful like finding a cure for cancer. Then they might have our attention.'

'You don't want a sample..?'

'I most assuredly do not! Nor do I ever again want you in here wasting my valuable time!'

As I left, I heard him say 'Young upstart!'

Somebody else said 'Is it worth writing to his Company and complaining, sir?'

When I got back to the car, I lit up a cigarette. At least I had seen the great man, so I could now write a little playlet and give us both some good dialogue, classic stuff, the kind the Company fantasised about, but I'd retain the bit about American brand names.

I thought how it would be if all the pharmaceutical companies got together and withheld all products until every consultant and GP had signed an undertaking to treat reps like decent human beings. A week would do it, probably even a day.

I stuffed some products and abstracts in my bag and went to call on the hospital pharmacist to tell him who I had just seen and that I thought I might have convinced him to try some BioMedbalm.

'You got an interview with him and he agreed to try BioMedbalm..? I'll believe that when I see his name on a prescription.'

'He didn't make any promises but he's definitely thinking about it.'

'Well, we don't use any of your psychotropic drugs. All our stuff goes out to tender and only last month the Rochester & Chatham group gave the contract to Waterhouse & Thurber. But I'll tell you what I could use... Have you any of those gold pens left? Not that they're real gold I know... My wife took a fancy to mine.'

'I'll see if I've got any in the car. Is there something else you might need..? What about sulphonamides...diuretics...tetracyclines?'

'As I told you, it's all tendered. It's not up to me. I'm just a humble pharmacist who does as he's told. Anyway, if ever we need anything in a hurry, we can always get it from the wholesalers. I just need to pick up the phone and it's here the same day.'

'Is there anything at all you need of ours..? Not even some vitamins..? What about folic acid for the ante-natal clinic?'

He shook his head. 'No, no. All I need is a couple of those pens. One for me and one each for my two kids. Then there'll be no fighting.' He chuckled and waited for me to do the same but I couldn't manage it.

'I'll go and have a look,' I said.

I was just going out of the door when he called me back. 'There is something. Pam's just passed these to me. Can you change them for us? There's a good chap.'

He handed me some packets of long-expired penicillin and cortisone. One of the penicillin bottles was leaking.

'But these are samples,' I protested - damned expensive samples at that.

'Well, we can still use samples, can't we? That's the general idea, isn't it?' he smirked.

'But we don't do this cortisone any more. It's three years old.'

'Well, give me something else instead.'

'But I thought you weren't using our...'

'Well,' he winked, 'we can all bend the rules a little from time to time. Anyway, you wanted to do a little business, didn't you?'

Giving things away hardly constituted doing business.

I had only seven pens in the car. I took him three, plus some new penicillin pediatric and some of the very expensive cortisone tablets. It was one of the assistants who took them from me, Mr Edge was busy, he'd given enough of his valuable time already.

'Mr Edge wants me to ask if you could do him a very special favour and see if you have just one more pen. He says that with his luck, his wife's will be sure to run out soon and then there'll be a rumpus'. She pulled a wry face.

I went back and gave the mean sod an extra pen. Why not? I'd given him everything else. But I came away with nothing, no sales and no prospects of any. We reps gave these stingy blighters free samples, some of which were worth a lot of money and then they used them and charged for them and it was pure profit. Those in the retail trade especially, those who called themselves 'chemists' when they were only dispensing pharmacists, made a great deal out of all the free samples they got from all the various pharmaceutical companies. They were so mean, some of them, that I'd several times been in their dispensary when somebody had come into the shop for a bottle of distilled water, and they'd filled the bottle straight from the tap and then charged sixpence for it. 'That'll do for a car battery,' they'd wink.

From Rochester Hospital I went to the biggest pharmacy in town, a huge shop modelled on Boots, who likewise sold a lot of items that had little or nothing to do with pharmacology. I don't know why I resented retail pharmacists selling other goods, I suppose it struck me as grubbing. If they had declared themselves to be just businessmen out to make a fat profit, like any other, customers would at least have known where they stood. But they used the mantle of medical professionalism to get the best of both worlds; nobody would dream of haggling over anything with a 'chemist'; if a 'chemist' stocked it, whatever it was had to be both good quality and at the proper price; everything in a 'chemist's shop' was invisibly stamped with integrity, especially the 'chemist' himself.

In this shop, as was usually the case, the dispensary was at the far end of the shop and to get to it you had to pass everything from glass-covered counters displaying gold wristwatches, to cabinets packed with cameras and photographic equipment, shelves of books, racks of cosmetics and many other things that had nothing at all to do with health, let alone pharmacology.

When I arrived in front of the little archway that led into the dispensary and introduced myself, a pretty young thing looking after beauty-care made a twittering sound and fluttered inside. Moments later she came back and told me her boss wasn't able to see me today and that I was to come back tomorrow. I'd already called twice this week and I told her 'Okay, thanks, but I won't be back in Rochester for at least two weeks'.

I was halfway towards the exit when I heard a voice behind me shouting 'Hey! You! Come back here a minute! I want a word with you.'

I turned.

'Yes, you! The rep from BioMed Pharmaceuticals! The one who is too busy to look after his customers properly!'

As I walked back through his crowded bazaar, he began to unleash a stream of abuse. It was polite abuse, if that's what abuse without obscenity constitutes, nevertheless it was abuse: BioMed Pharmaceuticals was American, profit was its only motive and those who worked for it were no better than a 'bunch of nignogs' and so on. Everybody was looking.

As I drew close I could see how badly his over-compensating nut-brown hairpiece was made.

I leaned over his counter and asked him to keep his voice down; if he had anything to say, I would appreciate it if we could talk somewhere in private, perhaps in his office or dispensary.

'We most certainly will not! I'll say what I like wherever I like on my own premises! Now you listen to me, you young whippersnapper - '

But I'd heard enough. I took hold of his thick hairy hand in a handshake and squeezed it, I squeezed it like I squeezed the powerful German spring handgrip which I kept in the dashboard of my car, I squeezed it until first the hand and then the face went white.

'Don't say another word until I'm out of this shop,' I said and picked up my bag and went out. As I was going out of the door he shouted 'I'm going to report you for this!'

I got into my car and drove out of the town. I hated Chatham and I hated Rochester. I needed a break.

31

The last time I saw Godfrey, at the refresher course, he had tried to persuade me to come up to Norwich with Judy and meet his wife Carol at her family home and spend a few days. Norwich seemed an interesting place with some historic buildings as well as the Broads. The problem was I had no holidays left and we were short of money after the wedding.

'Work twice as hard the week before and share out the orders for the week you're away.'

'What about the daily reports?'

'Write them out ahead and get somebody reliable to post one each day.'

It had sounded hairy to me but Godfrey said that's what everybody did. So Judy and I decided to go. We'd buy a tent, which we were intending to do anyway, leave for Norfolk on the Friday night, have the weekend and take three days of the following week and camp there and back.

On the Friday, after working extra hard the previous two weeks to get well ahead with my budget, I wrote out three daily reports with orders and dialogues for the Monday, Tuesday and Wednesday, put them in envelopes, pencilled on them the days they had to be posted on, and asked Miss Turfel to post them, a thing she said she'd be more than happy to do.

It was the last Friday in July and a beautifully sunny day when we set off with our drip-dry tent and various bits of camping equipment, in the direction of Norfolk.

It was great to see Godfrey again. But Carol... She regarded Judy as though she were a primitive and me as though I were an out-and-out barbarian. I don't know who disliked the other first or most but I must say ours was pretty much instantaneous. It was very hard under the circumstances not to lay on thick the northern chauvinism she had clearly made her mind up about long before meeting us, and I must confess to rather wallowing in it. I'd be telling them of my experiences 'in the field' and although Godfrey laughed uproariously, his lady was not amused at all. I nearly always told Judy what happened to me but I think Godfrey must have been very careful about what he told Carol.

On one occasion when he and I were having a drink at the bar while the two women were at the table, he said he 'would give anything to have Carol strapped into harness in one of your collier families. A year as a slattern scrubbing the front steps with rubbing stone in full view of the whole street... Possing the stinking, steaming washing in a tub... Having a leather belt thrashed across her lily white buttocks. And then humped by a drunken brute of a father... By God, it would do her the world of good.'

'Bloody hell, Godfrey!' I said. 'Her father..? What do you think we're like up there, man?'

'That's the sort of thing, though, isn't it?' he grinned, 'give or take a metaphor?'

We spent much less time with Godfrey than we had intended. He had a wonderful sense of humour and was a brilliant raconteur but he and Carol got more and more ratty with each other each time we met, and I think we had something to do with it. She unquestionably considered Godfrey and herself to be superior to us and despised what she called my 'rebellious attitude to everything'. After a tale about a doctor I'd detailed, she scoffed 'You know what you've got, don't you?' and I had replied 'Give me a clue... Is it on my shoulder?' She nodded and I said 'I know..! A succubus!' 'What?' she said. Godfrey had howled with laughter and she was more annoyed than ever because she obviously didn't know what the word meant, she probably thought it was some kind of parrot.

It left us more time to look around Norwich and have a drink of awful beer in every old pub we came across. Norfolk was hardly spectacular, Kent was prettier. And Northumberland was wilder and infinitely more beautiful than the two of them put together.

By the Wednesday we weren't sorry to depart and leave Norfolk to Carol and her kin. I felt sorry for Godfrey when we shook hands and said our farewells, although he had always seemed the last person to require or desire sympathy.

As we began to head south I began to wonder aloud about the daily reports being sent in on time, about Miss Turfel's reliability - her integrity was beyond doubt. What about her memory, for instance..? Or her eyesight..? She was in her late seventies and had to start going senile sometime, what if she had taken the first few faltering steps downhill this week?

'She's as bright as a button,' Judy retorted. 'Look how quickly she comprehended what we asked her to do.'

'Maybe she only seemed to comprehend. What if one of the pencilled dates was obliterated by her thumb? With all that gardening, the skin on her fingers must be like coarse grade sandpaper. I deliberately only wrote them lightly.'

'They're as soft as mine. She always wears an old pair of gloves. Anyway, even if she sent them in the wrong order, they'd only think you'd made a mistake with the date, that's all. They can hardly sack you for that.'

'Whoa! That's a nasty big word you just used.'

'What?'

'"Sack".' I winced as I repeated it.

'I didn't say they would sack you. I said they were hardly likely to sack you.'

'Stop saying it then, will you?'

'You're worrying too much. They're not going to get rid of you - '

'"Get rid of" is even worse. It sounds like a cement-boot job and a drop into the Thames. Or should I say "Medway"?'

'They're hardly going to do that. Not after they spent all that money training you and everything. Not after you came nearly top in the competition. If they were going to do anything, they'd have done it when you wrecked all those vehicles in Sussex.'

'Bloody hell..! I didn't wreck them all..! I only wrecked a couple. I just started the ball rolling.'

At that moment a van we were overtaking suddenly turned right without any warning.

Bang!

Neither of us were hurt. The van had crashed into the front of the Hillman, near the wheel.

We quickly got out and checked the damage. There was only one occupant of the van, a man in overalls and he was already inspecting his damage. A dent in the bumper and a smashed side light was all I could see wrong with his old, already battered, plumber's van.

But the Hillman, the new Hillman I had been given because my original one had to be written off, was in a real mess. The left wing was folded into the wheel, making it impossible to move the car, and all of the near side lights were smashed.

It was time to start the dialogue and establish liability.

'You bloody fool!' I yelled at him. 'Why didn't you look where you were going! You must have seen us coming up behind you? I had my indicator to signal I was overtaking!'

He shook his head. 'I'm ever so sorry. I didn't see you. I was just - '

'I want my car fixed immediately! I'm on urgent business and I have to get back to Kent.'

He looked blank. Godfrey was the man we needed now, he would know the local garages and whatnot.

'Watch him,' I told Judy. 'I'm going to see if I can get hold of Godfrey... If he tries to drive off, stop him. His bloody van is practically unmarked compared with ours.'

'How am I going to stop him if he - '

'Scream blue murder if you have to.'

With that, I broke into a run, back the way we had come.

It must have been all of three miles before I reached a telephone kiosk and it was Carol who answered, Godfrey was up at Cromer playing golf. I didn't tell her anything, only that I needed to contact him urgently. She probably guessed we were in some kind of trouble but didn't bother to enquire. However, she gave me the golf house telephone number and I rang it. Godfrey was out on the course but someone promised to get the message to him without delay.

By the time I got back to Judy and the Hillman which was still slewed across the road and looking worse than it did before, it was to see the plumber's van neatly parked on the side of the road with a little Austin in front, and a dapper little busybody with a little handlebar moustache strutting about, notepad in hand, pointing here and pointing there.

'Who's that?' I asked Judy.

'I don't know but he obviously knows the other one well. Did you manage to get hold of Godfrey?'

'No. Er, yes, I think so. I hope so... Where did he come from?'

'The fellow in the van must have rang him.'

'What! You didn't let him go?'

'I didn't have any choice. He didn't ask. I was watching you disappearing up the road, when he took off to that house up there.'

When I went over, the two of them had a tape measure out and were measuring the road.

'Who are you?'.

'Move back a bit there,' the busybody said without looking up.

I called to the van-driver. 'I want you to send for a garage immediately and instruct them to repair my car as soon as possible at your expense. And I want you to sign this bit of paper to say you're entirely responsible. Otherwise I'm getting the police.'

'Hey, hey... Hold on,' said the busybody.

I had my BioMed Pharmaceuticals pad out and was writing 'This is to say that I - '

'He'll do no such thing.'

'Oh, and who might you be?'

'I'm the traffic manager of the firm this man works for. And we are paying for nothing.'

'What..! He's already admitted it was his fault and - '

'He's admitting nothing.' He turned to the plumber who was standing back, looking rather sheepish. 'Now remember what I told you, Ken. Not one word!'

I was taken aback. 'This is ridiculous!' I said, trying to regain ground with some bombast. 'Look at the damage to my car! His is hardly touched! That's because he hit us broadside with his bumper. It's obvious to anybody what's happened.'

'Don't waste your breath. Put it down on your insurance form, like we're doing. Then maybe we can get your car out of the way.'

The road was very quiet, hardly more than two or three cars had passed.

'I'm not going through the insurance. I want him to pay.'

'What do you think we pay insurance premiums for..? Out of the goodness of our hearts..? Just give us the name of your insurance company and we'll give you ours. Let them sort it out... You are insured, aren't you..? You'd better be.'

'Of course I am.'

'Well, then. Who is it?'

'I'm not giving you it.'

'Right, then. We'll get the police.'

'Get them, then.'

He went to get into his car and I made the mistake of throwing myself on his mercy, as it were, by appealing to his sense of decency.

'It's a company car and I'm outside my normal territory.'

'That's too bad. There's only one way out of it. And that's for you to pay out of your own pocket.'

'Pay for what?'

'Everything.'

'What do you mean..."everything"?'

'I mean everything. As long as you pay for all the damage to our vehicle, you can do what you like with yours.'

'What..!! I'd rather lose my job!'

'That's up to you, sonny Jim. Here's the name and address of our insurance company.'

He tore a page from his little note book and handed it to me. In scrawling, childish writing, with capital letters in the wrong places, was written 'Norwich Union' and the full address.

'Now you give me yours or I'm calling the police.'

I couldn't believe it. I thought I was pretty shrewd after six months selling pharmaceuticals for a hardboiled American pharmaceutical company but I obviously still had a few things to learn.

I then heard voices behind me and turned to see Godfrey talking earnestly to Judy, his perfectly intact Hillman perfectly parked a little way off. I was so glad to see him.

'Godfrey! Good man! Thanks for coming.' I went over and patted him on the shoulder. It was two against two now. I told him what had transpired between myself and the traffic manager.

'It doesn't look rosy, old son,' he said. 'If it was me, I'd be inclined to pay for the damage to both cars, get the repairs under way as quickly as possible and keep my mouth shut.'

'What..! And let these sods away with it..? I - '

He held his hand up. 'That's what I'd do. But it's your decision... Look, let's try a long shot. What if I ring Head Office, say I'm a consultant at Norwich General, tell them Judy's been spending a few days in Norfolk and been taken ill with a gynaecological complaint, and that you were rushing up to see her when you had this accident.'

'Why gynaecological?'

'Gynaecological, abdominal, renal... What does it matter?' he said impatiently. 'I'll tell them she has a suspected brain tumour, if you like. Only if you say its a gyne problem, they're less likely to ask for details, that's all.'

'What about today's report going in?'

'You'll have to see if your jalopy can be patched up quick enough to hightail it back before the old lady posts it.'

'She gives it to the postman.'

'What if the postman doesn't call today? He surely doesn't call every day?'

'He does ours because of all the BioMed bullshit.'

'She might miss him. In which case she'll have to get ready and tootle off into the village herself.'

'Fat chance of all that.'

'I said it was a long shot. You can't afford not to be optimistic. It would be rather a shame if you paid for both cars and then got the chop.'

'I know one thing. I'm certainly not paying for any damage to his.'

'Would you be prepared to pay for the damage to your own, then?'

'Depends how much it's going to cost... If it meant not losing my job.'

'Well, go and ask them. The damage to theirs is negligible. It's not worth having their premiums increased over. I'm sure they'll see the sense of it.'

But they didn't, or rather wouldn't. It was all or nothing, as far as they were concerned and the plumber was already giving a completely different account of how the accident happened.

It would have to be nothing.

'Look, old son,' Godfrey appealed. 'If you're going to pay for all the damage to yours...and that could be substantial...you're going to need an entire new wing for a start...theirs is only going to be a few quid more.'

'No! On principle, most definitely not!' I shouted so the other two could be in no doubt.

'Even though it might mean curtains for you?'

'Yes.'

'Why don't we do what Godfrey suggests, Joe? It's not going to be much extra and it might make all the difference to whether...you know what.'

I shook my head. There was no way I was going to spend a halfpenny of my own money on their grotty van.

It was back to the long shot. Godfrey and I got in his car, drove to the nearest call box and he rang Head Office using his classic stuff-of-monarchs' diction. I couldn't help wincing he was so far over the top but they probably knew his voice anyway by now.

There was surprisingly little reaction at the other end, they just took down the details and then I spoke to Mr Fynes telling him I'd been involved in a 'comparatively' trifling accident. He was quite insouciant, didn't shout or bawl or anything, just took down the details and said goodbye when I said cheerio.

All five of us then bounced and bumped the Hillman to the side of the road. Godfrey got a local garage to come out and tow us in, replace the wheel with a second-hand mismatch, bash the wing off the wheel and bash the bonnet so it was flat enough to be wired down. All the parts they bashed would have to be replaced in any case, so there was no point in being timid with the mallet, they told us.

I don't know why, maybe it was because we were silly English people, but before we left the accident scene, without thinking we had bidden the plumber and his traffic manager goodbye and I even noticed my arm up waving to them as they drove away.

Like a bat out of hell we drove to Kent, stopping only once for petrol and not at all for toilets. I raved and swore and Judy cried and resigned herself to not getting back alive; it was nothing like the outward trip had been, reminiscing and singing the old songs. One minute I was cursing the plumber, then BioMed Pharmaceuticals, then poor Miss Turfel, all with equal rancour.

When we got back to the oasthouse there was a telegram to say Tyler would be coming yesterday at 10am. We had just finished reading it for the fifth or sixth time, trying to read some hope in it, when Miss Turfel cheerily came to the door.

'I just wanted to assure you I sent everything off, just as you told me to.'

'Thank you, Miss Turfel. We're indebted to you.'

I could have screamed with exasperation.

Next morning at 9.43am in the lounge of the Maidstone Hotel, Ralph Tyler, on behalf of BioMed Pharmaceuticals, extended to me with some panache I must say, the customary 'gentleman's benefit'. This was where they gave you ten seconds to resign with dignity, or...

I was sure this was the first time Tyler had ever had the privilege of counting a man out and he couldn't have realised how much his eyes were shining. I should have thought that because he knew I did judo - which he, like most other people, thought was the same as karate - he would have been just a tiny bit apprehensive in case I might have gone berserk and chopped the place up into small cubes with the edge of my hand. If he was, he didn't show it.

As he counted, I sat there completely immobile, angry and humiliated but cool, playing his game. I thought of waiting until 'nine' and then yelling out the word, 'Resign!' so loudly that glasses would shatter and wood might even splinter. But when the time came, I salvaged a tiny bit of dignity and just said it quietly. We both knew, as in the legend of Dead-Eye Ernie of Stoke, that all good reps die young. I promised him he would have my resignation in writing by Monday; in return, he would allow me to keep the car until the next Tuesday when I would deliver it to Head Office, along with spare samples and anything else belonging to the Company.

We stood up and shook hands.

'I'm sure it's for the best,' he said not unkindly. 'You really weren't cut out for this. Will you go back into the hospital service now?'

'I don't know. Probably.'

'Give my regards to your charming wife?'

'Right.'

He pulled his coat collar up, went out through the swing doors and into the rain.

It was lashing down but he could hardly have hung back now, not after what he had just done.

I had been with BioMed Pharmaceuticals for six months, three weeks, and five days. Who said I wouldn't last six months in the selling game!

Labouring in Kent

32

That afternoon while I still had the car, I went looking for work. The oasthouse was a great place to live but so isolated that without transport Judy wouldn't be able to get to work and I wouldn't be able to look for any.

I was sick of sitting in a car most of the day or sitting in waiting rooms and smoking too many cigarettes, and fancied a labouring job if I could find one, so I drove down to the unemployment office in Maidstone to see what they had.

There was a vacancy in a breeze-block factory near Tunbridge Wells but they didn't think I'd be suitable.

'It's mainly labouring work,' the woman said, looking at my suit and then at my hands.

'That's what I want,' I replied and took the name and address from her.

Half an hour later I was being interviewed by a man in his sixties sitting in a little hut, at a tiny table with a racing paper spread over it. He had a mug of tea in his hand and a pipe in his mouth and continuously supped from the one and sucked at the other as we talked.

'What does somebody like you want here?' He could barely conceal his contempt as he looked at the Hillman. 'What are you..? A salesman?'

'I was,' I said.

'You won't be looking for a permanent job, then?'

'Well, not forever exactly...but...'

'It's hard work. Only labouring. The pay's very little. You won't be able to work in those clothes.'

'When can I start?'

'If you can get yourself here at seven o'clock tomorrow, I'll give you a go. If not...'

I only had the car for a couple of days so if the job was all right I'd have to see about buses or hitching lifts.

Judy wasn't too happy about it, she didn't think I'd be up to heavy labouring and was worried in case I'd have a heart attack from changing jobs so drastically. But I wasn't bothered at all, it would get me fit and bring in some money until I could get a job back in the hospital service.

I was there at seven o'clock sharp the next morning. There were three of us in the 'factory' which consisted of a large yard with a shed at one end under which the breeze-blocks were stacked to harden, a machine press which had a conveyor belt with buckets leading up to a hopper into which was poured the cement and aggregate, and an area for stacking the hardened blocks ready for delivery.

The two lads who worked the machine that produced the blocks, were on piece-work. They were rough, they were in-laws and they were constantly bickering. One was married with a baby and he was pushing all the time to go faster, the other was only working for beer money and had a lackadaisical attitude. The married one on the ladder at the top of the machine depended on his brother-in-law down below to mix the concrete and shovel it into the moving buckets. My job was to load the newly minted blocks onto a trolley, pull them into the shed and stack them; then draw those that had been in the shed longest, outside, and stack them; and when the lorries came I had to load them up.

In no time my hands were cut to ribbons and by the end of the first day I had very little skin left on my palms or the undersides and in between my fingers. But I certainly surprised the other two and the foreman who I'd heard laughing and betting I wouldn't last till lunch-time. Everything they put out, I carried away, and I kept up the supply in the yard and on the lorries. I'm not saying their work wasn't hard - mixing wet concrete and shovelling it and lifting buckets of it up and down - but nobody worked harder than I did.

When we left to go home, nobody said cheerio but there was no jeering either. By now I knew the 'Men of Kent' and 'Kentishmen', as they variously called themselves, and whatever distinguished the one from the other certainly wasn't friendliness; in Kent you were more likely to encounter hens with teeth.

When Judy saw my hands she wanted me to quit, but so did my colleagues, so the next day I went back with a pair of old gloves that didn't last five minutes; there were bits of glove and bloodstains on a good many of the blocks that stood in the high walls I built in the yard and I was rather proud of it.

There was no light in the shed except from the rust holes in the corrugated roof and when the sky was overcast, as it frequently was, it was impossible not to bump my head on the five-feet high roof. But this wasn't the kind of injury to be proud of so I tried not to do it when any of the others were around; and if I did, I made sure not to yelp.

On the evening of my second day, when Judy and I were out at the Red Lion, Johnny called at the oasthouse. He was doing a round-England trip on the AJS, which he had begun with a friend who had quit after three days and gone home because the weather was so bad. Johnny, being Johnny, had continued alone and when he came to the house, had gone to Miss Turfel's door by mistake. Even though he was a complete stranger and on a motor-bike, in a terrible mess because of the rain and the oil from the bike, she invited him in, gave him a cup of tea and made something hot for him to eat while she was letting him have a bath. When he heard us come back from the pub, he emerged all smiles, ruddy-complexioned with his normally ungovernable hair plastered down.

He could only stay two days because the weather had severely delayed him and he had to get back to his job at Parsons.

'You keep the bike,' he said without hesitation. 'You're going to need it now.'

The two of us drove up in convoy to Head Office the next day and I handed over the car, my detailing bag and whatever else I had belonging to BioMed Pharmaceuticals and collected my salary, and then rode back to Kent on the bike. It was a fine day, I drove, and we had a great time. Once I went straight over the top of a roundabout because I'd been turning around to hear what Johnny was saying and taken my eye off the road; up the kerb we went, across the grass between the shrubs, past an appalled Kenter who was doing something with the rhododendrons, and back on to the road before I'd had time to de-throttle.

By the time we got back to the oasthouse we had made another of our lifelong pacts, this time to eventually go into business together, breeding and selling the full range of domestic pets.

The next day I took him up to London where he got the train to Newcastle.

The job at the breeze-block factory lasted three weeks and then I was made redundant. The other two had had a fight one lunch-time and the married one had set about the other with a shovel, inflicting injuries that required medical attention and would prevent him working for some time. Because they both had to be sacked, there would be no work for me 'for the indefinite future', the foreman said without a note of regret.

The day after I finished we got a letter from my father and mother saying they were on their way down to see us and would be arriving at Borough Green station at ten o'clock in the evening of the following day and could I pick them up in the car.

My father hadn't been impressed when I went to work as a 'salesman' because he thought all salesmen were what everybody else thought they were, and he'd have been even less so if he knew I'd been a labourer, but he had no time at all for people who were unemployed. I hadn't said anything in my letters home because I didn't want to upset them and was confident I'd soon get something better.

A Rolls-Royce had been advertised for sale at £12 in a local shop window for some time; obviously it wouldn't be in great condition but if it only lasted for the week my father and mother were down, it would be worth it. However when we went to see it, in the middle of a field, it wouldn't budge, either under its own steam or ours, and even when the price came down to £10 because 'All it needs is a new set of plugs', we had to decline.

By the time the train arrived at the station it was already dark but we had the place to ourselves and I was able to explain the essence of what had come to pass before leading my mother and father to the only vehicle in the car park, the AJS.

They were so shocked by what I had to tell them, that I was on my way out of the station with my mother on the pillion, clinging on to me, before the full weight of it would have entirely and leadenly sunk in. Within quarter of an hour I had delivered her to Judy who was waiting, arms outstretched, under the beautiful horse-chestnut tree at the top of the oasthouse drive, and was on my way back for my father who would have by now pondered my career and be ready to deliver an opinion.

It was the first time my mother had ever been on a motor-bike so it was understandable that she would hang on tight, especially with my having to drive fast so as not to keep my father waiting too long. He however would never hang on, not even had he been riding pillion on a Tiger Moth, most certainly not if one of his sons were driving, so with hands in mackintosh pockets, trilby firmly in place and bespectacled eyes penetrating my back and on into infinity, he sat there and you would never have known he was there had you not felt a slight tremor as he nimbly climbed on, hands in pockets, and heard him quietly clearing his throat.

I like to think my mother and father's holiday in Kent was enjoyable, although we did a lot of walking for people who had never made a hobby of it. In every town we visited, my mother and father scrutinised in minute detail every card in every post office or shop advertising vacancies for milk roundsmen, caretakers, chauffeurs or anything. It proved the point that my father thought employment of any kind to be incomparably better than unemployment. It was futile trying to persuade them that sooner or later I would be able to get a good job in microbiology somewhere and that they should enjoy the week instead of worrying about my being unemployed for a few days or labouring for a few weeks. I was totally confident about being able to get a good position and although they could have regarded that as an asset, my father didn't and my sureness bothered and annoyed him and he construed it as recklessness tainted with vanity.

On their last day I got an interview for a job as 'temporary farm labourer'.

'Temporary's better than casual, isn't it?' my mother surmised.

'We-ell,' my father cautioned... 'Do you think you could do it though?' he asked me.

I laughed. 'A farm labourer..? Why aye, man!'

'Don't be funny with me, lad! This is a very serious matter. I've never seen my insurance cards in my life. Let alone been kept by my own wife.'

He shook his head. He must at least have been a little relieved that it wasn't happening on Tyneside.

My mother, soft and affectionate to all of her sons and full of respect and loyalty to their father, would never take our side against him; not mine, not Johnny's, not all of us put together. His principles were her principles, though not necessarily in the same order. She was always ready to forgive, even without an apology. He took much longer, even after one.

She was slow, thorough and artistic in everything she did. He was rapid and thorough but 'more practical'. She could be merely stubborn where he could be absolutely inflexible. She could never keep a secret. He kept them all. 'If it's a secret, why do you want to tell anybody?' he would say, exasperated as she confessed to having given gross hints about the nature of a 21st birthday present where only the price remained a mystery. He said she was unpunctual and fussy yet he never gave her the chance to be, so I suppose really she wasn't, whatever her natural inclination. They were both beautiful writers, in their handwriting and their style; hers would be gentle, sentimental and solicitous with infinite detail; his eloquent and direct yet considerate.

Both were respectful of any authority, and of all laws, rules and regulations that included anything from not stepping on the grass, to playing a game properly. And even though the Catholic Church didn't make things easy for them, they went along with it or confessed.

They were provident when it came to money, being savers not squanderers, though in another life I could imagine my mother preferring a little indulgence. But they never instilled in us a desire to make money; a livelihood, yes but no more than that, and this was maybe an oversight. The real handicap however was that my father believed if you were honest, conscientious and good at your job, it would be acknowledged eventually; somehow I didn't think that was the case. He was intolerant of weakness, physical, mental or spiritual, and he hated stupidity, clumsiness and slowness whatever their cause. He also believed many illnesses could be cured, and all ameliorated, by refusing to acknowledge their existence; and I already knew this wasn't the case.

I never heard my father promise to do anything. He would have considered it beneath him to reinforce anything he said with the word. If he said he would do something, he would do it without fail even if the circumstances changed. There was never any gossip in the house and I never heard my father complain about any treatment meted out to him, to us or to anybody; he never complained about pain, disappointment, frustration or anything; not ever. He had the strongest character of anybody I had ever known, read or heard about and I was proud to be his son. But living with a very strong character can be tough.

Yet in spite of all that, like his own father who was a boxing champion, and in whom the trait was considered a drawback, my father wasn't a punisher or a finisher. As far as he was concerned, once you had somebody on his knees, you put out your hand and pulled them up.

Johnny would be needing the AJS in Newcastle and Judy and I needed transport of our own so we went to a motor-cycle shop in Rochester, bought a Triumph Tiger 110 650cc Twin and arranged to have it fitted with a front-end faring, windscreen and panniers, and sent to Borough Green Station.

It arrived in three days. I had sent the AJS up to Newcastle by train that day so we walked to the station.

We took off the cardboard wraps and there it was in all its splendour: a beautiful machine, immaculately glossy black except for the white trim on the petrol tank.

I had brought petrol because I knew the tank would be empty, and very carefully filled it up. I then kicked the starter and the engine thundered into life but it was only whirring when we climbed on. I twisted the throttle and we were instantly thrust away, as though astride a rocket. Any other vehicle I had driven always had a perceptible time lapse between instruction and response, if only a fraction of a second. But not this one; I had never been aware of being in control of anything so powerful, so dangerous, so fast and exciting.

33

The farmer I went to work for was called Geo. Hawthorpe. He was tall and erect and could easily have been an ex-RAF officer. His main crop was hops, though he also had apple and pear orchards and sundry livestock.

There were only three farmhands: a forty-odd-year-old man and his son and a sullen wiry little fellow with a paratrooper's beret. They didn't like 'foreigners', they didn't like salesman past or present and they didn't like anybody with any education. They were so damned contrary, they didn't even like the bike. Here everybody had a chip on their shoulder. I could understand what Mr Hawthorpe said because he clearly wanted me to, but I hardly ever saw him, so I had to be content with following, observing and copying my three colleagues. They never told me when and where they were going or why, so a couple of times I ended up behind a barn watching, or rather waiting, while the three of them emptied their bladders.

They wouldn't tell me when it was tea-break and never invited me to join them. And when at the end of the day I leapt on my dream-machine and blasted away, leaving them trudging along the road, more than likely stroking rabbit's paws in their pockets, willing me to break my neck on the A20 so my soul could go straight to hell.

Hawthorpe himself was rather taciturn and I think he would have been better for a course of BioMedjoy, had my former employers produced anything of the kind. He had a superior air about him, more aloof then affected, and he always looked as though he had something hard rammed up his back end. I had looked for the farm on my Shell map and wasn't at all surprised to find it was virtually dead centre of Kent - 'at the heart', one might have said had it been another county.

At first I did chores that required no skill - only a certain amount of strength and balance - such as carrying sacks of grain from a loft, down a ladder and onto a trailer. My companions were sure I would fail, sure I would topple off a plank, fall to the ground and break my fragile legs or sink to my knees and be driven like a fence-post into the ground under the pressure of a hundredweight of one of their products. And when I not only carried as many as quickly as they did but began to trot, I could nearly hear the ex-paratrooper's teeth grinding - 'bruxism' it's called but BioMed had nothing for that either.

If ever I spoke, they always pretended they couldn't understand a word of it; but instead of asking me to repeat myself, they would turn away and walk off. In all fairness, I don't think it was just the accent, I think my soft skin and neat crew-cut bothered them just as much and they couldn't cope with it. They probably thought your hair had to be matted with chaff, your teeth vile and your fingernails packed with manure for you to be of any use on a farm.

One day Mr Hawthorpe set me on picking apples on a piece-work basis with more than a dozen casual workers. The apples were put in crates with each picker's name tag on them but weren't tallied until the next day, by which time any bruising caused by apples that had been shaken down or otherwise badly handled, would show and the individual penalised. At first I chucked apples into my crates to save time but not after I realised what it did to them. However, no matter how carefully you picked and stacked your apples, anybody with a grudge could easily have come along during the night and whacked them with a hammer.

After that fortnight when I made practically nothing, I was put back on wages picking apples from the big trees with the lad, and the other two were put to some entirely different task somewhere else.

He was about seventeen, looked as though he could do with a bit of fun, and I was sure he would speak now that he was out of earshot of his father and uncle.

We were standing with big shoulder bags slung around our necks, at the tops of twenty-foot ladders, in adjacent rows of trees, when I saw his gloomy young face looking straight at me. Instinctively I took one of the huge hard cooking apples and threw it at him. It was only at the very last moment that he saw it and ducked, and through the branches I could see him looking in astonishment as the twigs broke noisily around him. Judging by his gaping mouth, being pelted by one of his employer's apples on his employer's land, must have been an entirely new experience for him. I threw a couple more that made him duck and dodge and it wasn't long before he was tossing them back. Soon it was like a battle with green cannonballs going back and forth and the loud cracking of next year's fruit-bearing twigs. He continually made appeals to the effect that we would get the sack if the 'master' came by but he was wasting time and I kept up the bombardment till he returned my fire.

We were in the midst of a particularly violent exchange when a big one hit him square between the eyes and must have stunned him because he remained on the ladder, making no attempt to grab anything, whilst the ladder slowly went over backwards. As they went down together, his pitiful cry of fear mingling with the quite terrifying sound of splitting branches, I had no doubt that his concern was for breaking the limbs of his master's apple tree rather than for any of his own.

I descended my own ladder immediately, expecting to find him spastic on the ground with blood trickling from his ears. To his credit he was lying there laughing and apparently uninjured. But it put a stop to the apple-throwing.

The next task, and the most important on this farm, was harvesting the hops.

Hops grew hanging down from a network of cords suspended from poles about fifteen feet high, and were picked by dragging the long descending vines with their small dry brown fruit and leaves down and loading them onto the back of a trailer pulled by a tractor.

It was great fun at first because dozens of gypsies had come down from London for the hop-picking and their rough talk and good humour was a new experience for me; some of the younger ones would ride with me on the trailer and we would pull the vines down on top of each other.

The vines were coarse and would have been harder on my hands had I not been doing labouring work for some time now. At the end of the day, looking as though I'd been steeped in betel juice and by now so used to the cloying smell that I didn't notice it, I would go to pick Judy up from Larkfield. It was a good job we weren't in the car.

'What a stink..! Have you seen yourself?' she would say every day. But I carried the stains and smell everywhere I went and there was nothing I could do about it.

After several days of getting increasingly vexed with the man in the red beret - 'red berry', as we would say in the North - who, whenever he drove the tractor drawing the trailer I was on, would deliberately accelerate or brake when I was reaching up or bending over to bring hops on board, I was put to work in the hop shed.

I was the only 'local' in there, the rest were all part of the 'London gang', as the regular hands called them, all of them women. They were as rough as any I had ever encountered. When they were at their various positions at different points along the unlovely cumbersome machine that shook off the hops and was constantly getting fouled up by vines, they were like the enemy encamped and behaved as if the shed and everything in it was theirs. They had come, the way they came every year, to take over the harvesting of the hops by sheer force of numbers and verbal bullying, and not even Redberry could do anything about it; this was something he and his little bevy would have to suffer until every last hop had been picked and every member of the occupying force had been paid their pennies, packed their rags and bags and retreated as suddenly and completely as they had appeared.

When Redberry brought in his trailer-load he put it exactly where the big forewoman wanted it, not one inch further back or forward, nor to this side or that; like a policeman on point duty with a foul mouth she would wave her huge arms this way and that and thrust out hands like shovels, directing him.

After a week of unloading trailers, feeding hops into the machine and picking out pieces it had missed or rejected and feeding them back in, and having to listen to yelling, singing and cursing all day, I went to see the 'master' about changing my job. It was driving a tractor I had in mind and when he asked me if I had ever driven one, I told him I even had a licence for one.

'All right,' he said. 'Get the old Massey out of the shed and I'll give you a trial.'

I took my time getting it out, having a few practice runs in the shed first. He was waiting and pulled a face at my coming out in reverse.

'All right. Take it out to the hop fields. You know the drill out there. Don't forget when you get to the junction by the pond, you take the right lane.'

'Rightio.'

This was great I thought as I headed out to the field, bloody great!

I got there without mishap but knocked down one of the poles as soon as I arrived. From the yells you would think I had knocked the lot down, instead of one that was probably due for replacement anyway. To hear them, you would think everybody knew how to drive a tractor, except me; no matter which way I went, in whatever gear, however fast or slow, somebody or other was disgusted. Nevertheless I eventually got my first load and returned with it to the hop shed.

A huge trailer piled so high you cannot see over or around it presents problems when reversing, and notwithstanding my earlier demonstration to Mr Hawthorpe, things were a lot different now. The doorway was ridiculously narrow, the area in which to turn around absurdly limited and sooner or later somebody was going to clip the crates of apples stacked so ludicrously high outside the entrance; it was an accident begging to happen. It was just too bad it had to be me, and all it took was the gentlest of nudges.

Not only do wood crates smash to smithereens when they hit the ground from a height of twelve or more feet but the fruit inside is instantly turned to mush; if any of it survives and they're apples, they can roll farther than tennis balls.

I immediately jumped off the tractor and made a gesture towards putting back what crates I could but there were hundreds of apples scattered about, no sign of Mr 'H' or any of his snitches, and the women in the shed were baying for more hops. So I got back on the tractor and continued into the shed. Once inside I had to make a sharp right turn, a partial left and then straighten up and reverse along the loading side of the machine. Even though all of them in there must have realised this was my first time, no quarter was given and the big forewoman was the worst of the lot. She shouted and cursed at me nonstop as the tractor went one way and the trailer the other - which is always the way when you're reversing - until I got it within a foot of the machine at the side, and the same distance in front of where she was standing on her platform.

But this wasn't good enough, it had to be virtually making contact with her huge belly.

The problem was that I couldn't see her, I could only hear her and even then only understand half of what she was saying. 'Come back! Back! Back, you useless ——!'

'I cannot go any further back or I'll bump into you,' I called back.

'You'll put it where I tell you! I...aaghhhh!' she gasped as the trailer pressed her against the wall, shut her up, and stopped. Immediately women were running from all over and yelling that I was crushing their boss. As is often the way, I found reverse before I found forward, and as I jerked back, the screams were more poignant. Fortunately I then located the right gear and jerked a yard in the right direction and stopped. She was all right, just badly winded and it was a great, if only temporary, cure for bad language.

The trailer was unloaded in five minutes but it was a very long five minutes during which I concluded that not all rough diamonds were priceless.

'Right! Get it away!!'

As I went out the door, which I had to do in reverse, I misjudged the distance between the huge wheels of the trailer and the row of bags containing the women's lunch and other belongings. The mess was incredible: a streak about twenty feet long and six feet wide of mashed tomato, black lettuce, slimy pastry and finely ground eggshell mixed in with coffee and tea, newspaper, tampax, and the shattered remains of plastic thermoflasks, crockery, glass and, I imagine, pretty basic cosmetics.

A number of them came after me, howling and unreasonable, and I was sure their intention was to lynch me. I slammed into top gear and shot off. Quicker than I anticipated, I reached the junction where the path forked around the pear orchard. The left track bordered the pond and the right went around the far side of the orchard. Both paths were wide enough for only one tractor and that is why there was a highway code in operation, but with all the malice still buzzing in my ears and the worry about what was going to happen when I went back into the shed with the next load, I couldn't remember whether I was supposed to take the left or the right.

I fancied he'd said right and that that was the way I'd gone last time, but it seemed more natural to take the left, given that's the way it was everywhere else in the British Isles, so I took the left and took it at a fair lick in the hope of getting around before anybody met me.

Halfway around, with the pond on my left and the orchard on my right, who should be heading straight towards me but the little paratrooper with his beret pulled down and face like hell. He was shouting and yelling and waving his arms but still kept coming, and I kept going. At the very last moment he swerved into the pond and I went into the pear trees.

Things happened quickly after that. Mr Hawthorpe was called and summed up the situation without the need of testimony which he got anyway. He had already heard from the ladies in the hop shed, and his employee, with what looked like a small freshly-voided cowpat on his head, up to his waist in muddy water and wrestling with an almost completely submerged tractor, looked as though he would be ready to testify as soon as he got ashore. I was told to leave my tractor where it was, get on my motor-bike and get off the farm as soon as possible.

I went back the next week, by which time the tractor was out of the pond and back into commission and the hop-picking finished, to collect my insurance cards and what little remained of my wages which turned out to be nothing.

The London Eye Hospital

34

For the last couple of months I had been writing after vacancies in bacteriology or virology in London and had had several offers already, though not what I wanted. I intended to continue the studies I had started at Colindale when I was in Enfield, and had enrolled for evening classes at Bromley Technical College.

The course had already been under way two weeks when the chief lecturer asked us to complete a questionnaire about our background. Mine in no way resembled that of any of the others whom he persisted in calling candidates rather than students, as though a place on the course still needed some endorsement even after we had paid our fees. Every other candidate had been at the same steady job in the Hospital Service or Medical Research Council since starting work.

The fact that I had been a rep produced gasps of horror when the various questionnaires were for some unexplained reason read out. Reps, who had deserted the hospital service to seek their fortunes and live the 'high life', were regarded at best as adventurers and at worst as turncoats, by those who remained behind to 'man the fort'. So when he got to the bit about BioMed Pharmaceuticals and every head turned to the back where I was sitting in the corner like a dog in the manger, I gave a little bow. When he came to 'current employment' and read the words, 'farm labourer', he stopped. 'This looks like "farm labourer". Surely it can't be correct?'

'Yes,' I said. 'It is.'

A balding ginger fellow that came with a group from The Royal Free Hospital asked the lecturer what right could I possibly have to be on the course, given he knew somebody who worked at Guy's who had been turned down.

'I have a diploma in bacteriology and hope to be working in a virology unit shortly,' I said. 'Why, like? What have you got?'

He didn't answer but when his questionnaire was read out it was to inform those to whom it might concern that he expected to get his bacteriology diploma very soon; by the age of him he must have failed the annual final examination several times. Later on when we were asked to define our role as laboratory technicians in microbiology, he expressed the opinion that we were the instruments of doctors and scientists and that it was our duty to make ourselves as useful as possible. 'A surgeon cannot do his work properly if his scalpel is rusty or blunt. We must keep ourselves keen and sharp.'

I hadn't liked him even before he said that and when at tea-break I overhead him saying several of them should get together and make a complaint about my being allowed on the course, I decided I should have a word with him after class.

Ten minutes before the end he asked to be excused because he had to catch a bus, and the lecturer gave permission. As he went out the door I got up, excused myself for a few minutes and in my haste to catch him, didn't quite close the door after me.

I caught hold of him in the corridor and told him that if I heard him making trouble for me, I was going to give him a good hiding. 'So if that's your intention, tell me right now and I'll give you something to be going on with.'

'Are you threatening me?' he said in a shrill voice.

'Definitely,' I said. 'For two pins I'd throw you down those stairs.'

'If you touch me, I'll go to the police. I'm warning you.'

'By the time I've finished, it won't be the police you'll need.' I had him by the collar and up against the wall. 'Now beat it!'

He ran down the stairs and I straightened myself up and went back to the classroom to find dead silence and all eyes on me.

The lecturer smiled and said 'I think we've had enough excitement for one night, everybody. See you all next week.'

Later on when I was having a drink with a fellow I'd become friendly with, I said 'Did anything happen when I popped out the room at the end?'

'You bet..! We could hear everything that went on between you and that idiot with the ginger hair. Dr Synge put his finger to his lips and said "It seems to be more interesting outside," and we all listened. You probably don't know, but they work in the same department and apparently nobody can stick him.'

In October I got a job in a new virology department that was being set up at Euston Eye Hospital and Judy and I very reluctantly moved from the oasthouse; Borough Green was so far from London that I was having to leave too soon in the morning to take Judy to work and returning too late at night to pick her up. There was no way we could keep the dog now.

The day we moved into a bed-sitter back in Bromley, a truly grotty little place, we carried the dog between Judy and me on the first removal trip and sent it up to Newcastle by train from St Pancras. On the second we carried the next biggest item, the stereogram, with the mynah in its cage on top of it, the same way. The panniers were packed both times and the back piled high with things wrapped in the tent groundsheet and held on with elastic spiders. Two trips did it, we didn't have much in the way of belongings.

It was easy to get from Bromley to Euston on a motor-bike, weaving in and out of the traffic and getting up the noses of car drivers who resented motor-cyclists for no reason other than that we could always make much swifter progress than they could.

The back yard of the hospital was shared by the Traffic Department of the Metropolitan Police and was where they kept their Triumph Thunderbirds which were almost identical to the Tiger 110 but not quite as fast. The police who rode the bikes were more bikers than policemen and a great camaraderie existed between us; many a time they would be down there, sleeves rolled up, tuning their bikes, and so would I and a fellow called Tom Fairlie from the photography department of the hospital, who had a BSA Shooting Star.

My job had appeared from the advertisement and subsequent interview to be much more interesting and fulfilling than it in fact was, the department having 'far more chiefs than Indians', as current parlance had it. The chiefs, who were doing post-graduate medical or related science degrees, were full of unpractical ideas that the Indians tried to turn into results that would benefit the careers of the chiefs but make very little difference to those of the Indians.

My duties were to do the routine bacteriology - which wasn't a big task as it mainly consisted of testing simple eye swabs - prepare tissue-culture media for the Pathologist, Dr Colm Floret who was studying a form of cancer that attacked the eye, and cultivate Trachoma-like viruses for Mr Peter McEwan, the Principal Eye Surgeon who was interested in the correlation between a group of viruses which infect the eye and the vagina.

Dr Floret was half Irish, half French, in his mid-fifties, small and not very robust. He was self-effacing, especially in his humour, obliging, gentle, generous and highly cultured. Yet despite his considerable intellect he was very much the poor relation when it came to the chiefs and he was very frustrated in his work. He got little support in terms of equipment or material and technical help and nobody took him or his work seriously; as far as everybody else was concerned, he was 'just pottering about'.

Colm Floret was content to be called by his first name, but the egalitarian New Zealander, Mr McEwan, had to be properly addressed. Both men were clever but McEwan was much more ambitious and very impatient. He professed repugnance for the superior airs of the British and he knew I didn't care for them either, and on this rather insubstantial foundation our rapport was based; but whereas I was blunter and more pejorative where the upper circles of medicine and the Establishment were concerned, he tended not to commit himself beyond eye-rolling, grimacing and an almost imperceptible shaking of the head. He had a nice face, a charming smile and a very soft voice and most people liked him immediately.

The Head of Department was Professor Cecil Gwynn-Forsythe (pronounced 'foresight'), a man who looked and talked like Noel Coward. When he had returned from the Second World War he had brought his batman technician with him, a man of proven sycophancy called Tripp. Tripp's skin was so tightly drawn over his cheekbones that his face looked mummified, his teeth were grooved like little sticks of celery and serrated at the edge and his hair so tightly curled it's a wonder it didn't give him a permanent headache.

Mr Tripp was the Head Technician and he was very grateful to the Professor who he always loudly called 'Sir!' in the manner of an NCO; he even liked to be called 'sir' himself. Although I was always polite and addressed people by their proper title, 'sir' was of course out; that was my rule and the way it had been for some time now.

Gwynn-Forsythe and various colleagues of his, both in our department and elsewhere, considered themselves superior in an entirely different way to the way officers in the Army had. In the Army they knew they were despised by the rank and file and that they were paid respect only because it was rigidly enforced and it was to the uniform they wore rather than to the creature within. Gwynn-Forsythe and his compeers, on the other hand, believed we recognised, understood and therefore accepted our inferiority and that it would have been a self-evident truth even in the bath.

I told Mr Tripp he could either call me 'Joe' or 'Mr Robinson' but not just 'Robinson' because I had never been addressed in that way wherever I had worked. Even in the Army, I reminded him, the lowest ranks were addressed as 'Private', 'Gunner', 'Sapper' or whatever. He had just looked at me in surprise. The next time I saw him I was working at the bacteriology bench and demonstrating something to the other technicians.

'Morning, Robinson,' he said loudly and curtly as he went through the lab.

'Morning, Tripp,' I called back cheerily.

He turned, face white, but didn't say a word. Those around me were absolutely delighted and patted my shoulder as soon as he went out.

'You're for it now. He'll never forget that.'

From this very small incident my rating shot up with the technical staff and those who hadn't been there made it their business to come to express their admiration and tell me of a few more things that needed addressing, more cannonballs for my cannon, other cannons evidently being in short supply. But it was a small victory, if indeed it was a victory at all, because Tripp was never called anything but 'Tripp' by all the chiefs, even by my Kiwi mate.

Because, unlike bacteria, viruses need living material to reproduce themselves, animals were used in their propagation, initially monkeys which were prohibitively expensive and difficult to keep in an animal house. The hospital had only a small animal house with a few rabbits, guinea pigs and mice, so we mainly used the embryos of hens' eggs. I would 'candle' the eggs with a very powerful light which would show up the various membranes, cut windows through the shells with a dental drill, inject the virus and then seal the shells up with cellotape and continue incubation until the end of their term at which time the eggs would be 'post-mortemed'.

Colm used only tissue culture for his work. Certain animal and human cells will proliferate outside the body - 'in vitro' - if provided with an appropriate complex substrate in fluid form, and produce a tissue of cells. Colm used 'HeLa Cells', which were originally isolated from a tumour in the womb of an American woman called Helen Lane and by now used all over the world although the woman herself, the unwitting donor, had died. Theoretically, because medicine was based on treating the part that was diseased, if you could grow skin cells, you could treat dermatological problems; the same with heart cells, brain, liver, the eye and everything else. However because every type of cell had different requirements - different substrates, atmospheric and other conditions - the first task was to identify these.

By virtue of being a pathologist, Colm had access to an almost unlimited supply of cells but he didn't have unlimited resources to experiment with the substrates; he only had me. The preparation of sterile complex chemical compounds is a long, expensive and tedious business and although Colm was better than anybody to work for because he was such a nice guy, being his part-time technician wasn't very appealing. Apart from anything else McEwan was very demanding and by the time I'd done what he wanted, there was never much time left to help Floret. He was rather bitter about the way he was treated but there was no glamour in pathology and no clout came with a gentle introspective personality, especially when coupled with a small and unimposing physical presence.

McEwan was probably the top eye surgeon in the country and would have been called in if ever the Queen had got a fly in her eye. He had a sotto voice, an appealing way of hunching his shoulders and was good-looking into the bargain. Add that to his size and loud laugh when necessary and he invariably got what he wanted.

He sent me to a research colleague's laboratory in Bayswater for training in the technique of preparing certain virological material for microscopy but for some reason we could never get it to work at the hospital. Whether the material we were working on wasn't infected with the viruses he thought it should be, whether our equipment was inadequate or my experience insufficient, I don't know and neither did he. It was a most unsatisfactory situation because I had three totally different jobs to do and no help whatsoever. As a consequence, all three of us - Floret, McEwan and myself - were frustrated.

The system in research labs was for bonded pairs - vertical not lateral -

and none of them produced anything that changed the face of science, not even that confined to the human eye. The technicians were disgruntled servants unable to work miracles, and their masters, 'the scientists', considered them incompetent because they failed to produce the results that would enable the masters to walk on water while the servants went on treading it, or if fate decreed it, sank like a stone.

I had never experienced anything like this before. 'I am so-and-so's technician,' was the way my colleagues, the technicians, introduced themselves, proudly or otherwise according to the status of their masters. In their own way, they were fearfully loyal and would do everything they could to please and keep them off their backs. During tea-break I would ask them why they did things they thought unreasonable; surely it was enough that they worked hard and conscientiously to advance somebody else's career, without putting up with being talked to as though they were nothing. This wasn't the Army where they could punish you by making you run around the premises all night in a greatcoat or lock you up. They couldn't even sack you unless you did something criminal. But no matter what I said they would never stand up for themselves, not one tried.

In the wash-up, where we technicians went for our tea-breaks, the washer-upper, a tall gaunt man with an undershot jaw who looked as though he might have been the leader of a second-rate dance band in the 1940s, talked insubordination aplenty; Ted even talked of vengeance but he was only a talker. Despite the fact that he had been a POW under the Japs and had suffered the sort of humiliation that could only have been devised by treating it as both an art and a science, he seemed incapable of making the distinction between Japanese captor in wartime and young English science graduate in the age of Aquarius. I think he thought the whole of mankind was intrinsically bad and that anything posing as kindness was only lighthearted relief. He would accept whatever burden of work was put upon him, making all kinds of promises about how it would be accomplished quickly and done exactly as requested, and then moan like hell to whoever came in next.

'If Mr Tripp comes in once more today to give me something else to do, I'm going to bend over and show him a little hole which I'm going to cut out over my arsehole, and I'm going to say "Give's a broom and I'll shove the handle up and sweep the room at the same time."'

Although there were times you felt he was on the brink of violence, he could still be extremely funny. If you gave him a lot of glassware to clean and he was already snowed under, he would start fiddling with his fly as though he was going to bring his penis out, and then stop just in time and say 'You don't mind if I pull my cock out, do you, old chap? I might as well look like a horse if I'm expected to work like one.'

On other occasions he was funny without realising it. No matter how much work he had to do, he would spend nearly all afternoon doing a newspaper crossword, and if you went in the wash-up there'd be a mad scramble to hide it in a cupboard in case you were Mr Tripp. When he saw it was only you, he would get it out and ask about a word he was stuck for.

Philip Morris was the technician attached to the biochemist, a big overbearing man who was more interested in building racing cars than anything in the department, and the stocky heavily-bespectacled and mild-mannered Philip was genuinely devoted to him. Philip was friendly with everybody and would come into my little virology laboratory to tell me the latest gossip. He was the one who told me that when the Duke of Edinburgh visited the department, his equerry, or whoever organised such things, had gold fittings put on the lavatory in case the duke wanted to go, and none of the staff were allowed to use it until he'd gone and the gold gone with him. I suggested the shaft of the huge central lift would have been an excellent place for them to have made a point.

I had made my point by taking the day off as part of my annual leave, hoping Professor Gwynn-Forsythe would have explained it by saying something like, 'Sorry we haven't the full complement, today, Your Highness, but Mr Robinson...a Northerner we have working here...said he wasn't too keen on watching you strutting about while the rest of us were bowing and scraping for all we were worth.'

There was an American brand of cigarette called 'Philip Morris' and although Philip didn't smoke, he collected the packets from pubs and other places and everything from his blazer pocket to the crossbar on his bike would be labelled with one. He was good friends with Ted and would come to me and say 'He's coming to ask you the word for a South African novel that has seven letters. He's obviously got a couple of them wrong but the first is "w", the second is "b" and the last is "e".

A few minutes later Ted would come in and ask, and I'd say 'Let me think... There's "wbwre"...an old Zulu word for armour.'

'How do you spell it?'

I'd spell it out for him and he would write it in.

'That's it! That's it!' he'd say delightedly. 'Don't tell Philip I got it off you, will you not?'

'No, don't worry.'

He wouldn't be gone two minutes before Philip would come back, shut the door and crease up with laughter.

This would happen two or three times every week and Ted never copped on because when the answers were published in the next day's paper, he would see where his answers had been wrong and that he had therefore fed me the wrong information and consequently my erudition would remain unimpugned.

35

Judy was working at the Board of Trade in Bromley and quite liked it apart from the supervisor of the typing pool who told any of the women she caught going to the toilet before morning tea-break that in future they would have to 'settle' themselves before coming to work; she had her desk situated so she could see whoever was going into the toilet, time them and reprimand them if necessary.

Because Judy and I loved grand opera, I would get tickets for Covent Garden or Sadler's Wells at least once a week on nights I wasn't going to night classes, and at one time or another we saw and heard all the great opera singers of the day. Judy would get the train up from Bromley and I would meet her on the bike, take her to the opera house and park up a back lane nearby, having fastened our motor-cycle gear on to the bike with an elastic spider. We would sit in the cheapest seats in the upper circle, eating liquorice pipes, have a drink in the pub at the interval and then ride back together through night-time London which was a totally different experience from rush hour during the day.

The place we were living in was awful and the old and slovenly landlady was so mean that if she saw Judy had three pans on the stove, she would stack them one on top of the other and then turn the other two rings off, with the result that the contents of the top pan were underdone, the bottom burnt, and the middle somewhere in between, like cooking for the Three Bears. We had to share the ordinary-sized kitchen with three other couples.

We were careful with the gas-fire yet it gobbled up the sixpences and shillings even though the room was never warm enough. We asked her if she had the meter set high and was emptying it herself but she denied it so I got some gentian violet powder from the lab and sprinkled it liberally around the part of the meter that would have to be touched to empty it. The powder is dullish black when dry but becomes intensely purple when moistened and because it is a biological dye it is very difficult to remove.

One night we came home and there were purple handprints everywhere:

over the meter, the carpet, chairs, door and even the telephone out in the hall. It made the point but we were given notice to leave immediately. Fortunately we found another bed-sitter in Bromley where the much younger landlady had a thing about cleanliness that almost amounted to an obsessive compulsive disorder, so we were more than happy. However there was no conveying to her that the mynah wouldn't attract mice, so I had to take it to work where I kept it on a shelf in my lab, draped with a cloth to keep it quiet during working hours.

I had trained it to wolf-whistle, to say 'Wa' cheor, Geordie!' and 'You stu-pid bu-gger!' in broad Tyneside. And now I rued it. The Greater Indian Hill Mynah isn't like a budgie or a parrot whose vocalisations usually have to be interpreted by the owner, a mynah can mimic almost perfectly any sound repeated often enough.

One day a group of scientists from Italy came to see around the department and Professor Gwynn-Forsythe brought them into Virology.

There were seven of them in all, including Mr Tripp in tow, crowding into my small lab and I was having to continually move myself as they shuffled past. One or two nodded or smiled when they were so close they couldn't do anything else but none of them spoke and the Professor never introduced or acknowledged me; it was as though I were just a piece of unremarkable apparatus.

Mr Tripp was there to open and close doors and record any comments the Professor made, not to speak. If the Professor wanted to say something to a technician, he would never speak to him or her directly; he would say it to 'Tripp!' and Tripp would repeat it, beginning, 'The Professor says that...' If a reply was required the technician would give it to Tripp who would then render it in a form acceptable to the Professor; the technician would never address the Professor directly and would keep his or her eyes averted at all times.

On this occasion the Professor had shown his guests around and delivered his spiel and was on the way out when he noticed a stainless steel bucket on the floor under the incubator table. He waved a finger at it and Tripp leapt forward, crawled under the table and raised the lid to reveal the contents which consisted of eggs that had been opened and were waiting to be disposed of. I only had two of these buckets and the other was in the autoclave in wash-up so I had to continue with this one until the other was sterilised and cleaned.

'What is the meaning of this disgusting mess?' the Professor snapped at Tripp.

'Why haven't these been discarded?' Tripp snapped at me.

'Because I've only got two buckets. The other's away being sterilised and I need - '

'Rubbish!' shouted the Professor as he led the way out. Some of them raised an eyebrow, others slowly shook their heads.

'No, it's not!' I shouted angrily.

'Do something about that immediately!' growled Tripp as he went out, closing the door behind them. Then he poked his head back around it. 'You'd better learn to hold that tongue of yours or you're for the high jump.'

He had only just shut the door when there was an ear-splitting whistle.

He whipped open the door again. 'What in God's name was that?'

'What?'

'Tripp! Get yourself here!' yelled the Professor from along the corridor, and Tripp hurried off.

When the guests had left the building and gone to lunch with the Professor, I went to see Tripp in his office.

'I'm busy right now,' he said, knowing what I was going to say.

But I said it all the same. 'Why didn't you tell them I've been asking you for an extra bucket for weeks?'

'We've only a limited budget and stainless steel costs the earth.'

'Then why didn't you tell him?'

'You don't tell the Professor. You say things to him in a respectful manner. I'll have to wait till I can catch him in the right mood now.'

'Meanwhile all those people he was showing around think I'm sloppy.'

'You should have put the bucket somewhere else.'

'Where..? It's biological material. There's nowhere else it can go until it's sterilised. And I can't do that yet because I've more eggs coming out this afternoon.'

'Why have the bucket half full then?'

'Because I was going to finish them this morning. Until he came in. Nobody told me he was bringing a tour around.'

'You're a good technician but you're going to have to get rid of that chip on your shoulder. I don't know how they go on up north in Newcastle, but down here you've got to learn to do as you're told.'

'I'm not going to have anybody shout "Rubbish!" at me when I'm giving an honest explanation. Especially not in front of a whole lot of people I don't even know. And I'm going to tell him that.'

'You'll do no such thing..! Now go on out of here. I've more to do than listen to you and your bolshy talk.'

That afternoon when the Professor came back at about three o'clock I told his secretary I wanted to see him urgently. I doubt if any technician had ever done this before so the chances were that neither his secretary nor he knew how to handle it. When she came out and started trying to find the words for 'No', I just thanked her and went straight in.

He was sitting at his desk in his office surrounded by things that testified to his expertise and established his authority. By the way he invited me to sit down, I was sure he knew what I had come about; he wasn't what you could call 'penitent' but he was gracious; maybe it was the good lunch he'd had, maybe he was suffering from hunger pains last time I saw him.

'Yes?'

I told him I wouldn't have anybody speak to me the way he had spoken to me that morning, that I disliked people who shouted 'Rubbish!' or 'Nonsense!' when somebody was trying to give a sincere explanation, and that I wanted an apology. I told him the situation about the buckets and how it hadn't been my fault.

'You should learn to accept a rebuke without taking it too much to heart.'

'Not when I don't deserve it.'

'Mr Tripp tells me he thinks you have a chip on your shoulder.'

'Whereabouts?'

He looked at me but didn't say anything and there was a few moments' silence. I knew he wasn't going to apologise and I didn't want to be going out of here empty-handed and with some parting chastening platitude ringing in my ears, so I said 'That's not a bad painting there,' referring to a large oil painting on the wall, depicting a microscope with a sandwich beside it.

'It's one of mine,' he said, surprisingly smiling with pride. 'It's to show I earn my livelihood from science.'

'It's quite well done but I think the sandwich is a bit heavy-handed. A sandwich would hardly be on the bench in a pathology lab.'

'Well,' he said, turning back to his desk. 'I don't think there's need to say anything further.'

I came away, I must confess, liking him a shade more than I had done. Somehow he seemed more genuine than McEwan.

I liked Colm Floret very much and Judy and I became very friendly with him. Instead of going into medicine like his father had done, when he left school he had joined a jazz boat going from Paris to New Orleans and played clarinet with the band for a couple of years. When eventually he went to medical school he had already seen something of life, including a lot of poverty, and had a different attitude to many of his fellow students.

His lungs had been damaged by an infection contracted while skin-diving in Ceylon, which left him permanently short of breath and he now studied the guitar under Julian Bream. He lived in Kensington and Judy and I sometimes went to his house and sang while he played piano. He also played judo with a view to learning how to protect himself, but with rather less accomplishment; he had been coming home from a jazz club in Piccadilly one night when he had been set upon and taken quite a beating. Judo requires a lot of strength and fitness as well as rapid reactions and Colm wasn't really up to it, he'd have been better off learning how to use a police whistle.

I also made friends with Ben Horton, the department printer, a lean and angular fellow with a lantern jaw and army haircut, who originally came from Middlesborough. One day I went to see him to find he'd been arm wrestling one of the mechanics in the workshop and broken the mechanic's arm. It was such a bad injury they all had to devise a story as to how it had happened, otherwise both of them would have been sacked.

'I was just beginning to put on the pressure,' he said to me later, 'when there was an awful crack and his forearm snapped right in the middle. And because I was leaning on it, the bone came right through the skin.'

Ben had a big Vauxhall that was his pride and joy and one night on the way home, when he was in the Vauxhall and I was on the Triumph, we were drawing up to some traffic lights when he reached out and tried to knock me off. As a consequence he lost control of his car and jammed me between his car and a car on the other side of me. When the lights changed, my bike and I were lifted clean off the ground and carried three or four yards before Ben turned off, laughing, and disappeared among the traffic.

The next day I took a piece of chalk and wrote 'FOR SALE' and other notices all over his car, things like, 'THIS CAR IS STOLEN. £5 ONO FOR QUICK SALE', 'JUNK. OFFERS CONSIDERED FOR SPARE PARTS. WHEELS CAN BE SOLD SEPARATELY'.

When he saw it, he wiped the chalk off but the pressure of the chalk had gone right through the paintwork and he had to drive it through London twice every day before he could afford to get it completely re-sprayed. All he said was, 'You bloody twit'.

Although the department had its own photography laboratory with two photographers, it also had a full-time artist who worked in watercolours. He was a very effeminate unfriendly and unobliging man of about twenty-five but his work was superb. He used to attend operations and then render beautifully delicate illustrations of the eye and its lesions, painting in all the capillary blood vessels. They were works of art.

There was a senior technician in the lab next to mine, called Alan Worrel, who was extremely bitter about being assistant to a young Irish doctor who was working for his MD but was hopeless as a researcher and hated the English, especially the ones he had as colleagues at the hospital who gave him very short shrift.

Alan had been the youngest Englishman ever to earn a first dan black belt in judo and was now in his thirties, strong and sturdily built, though very thin skinned.

Because he knew I was interested in judo, he invited Judy and I to spend a weekend at his home, along with the Professor's secretary, a voluptuous young woman called Sandra. Alan knew I liked her and that she liked me, and being rather self-righteous and protective of Sandra, he had clearly decided to demonstrate the force that anybody who fancied Sandra would have to contend with; it was okay for Alan to like her because his affection was of the purest, most avuncular kind.

After lunch on the Saturday he put chairs out for his wife, Sandra and

Judy, at the foot of the lawn, and handed me a judogi to put on. I was taken completely by surprise, not least because the hard lawn was too uneven to serve as a mat; judo consists more of throws than arm-holds and the throws are fast and hard and, in the case of abdominal or shoulder throws, from a height.

I was an orange belt so we would never have been matched in any judo club, but instead of doing holds, of which there are many that can be carried out while standing, Alan set about throwing me to the ground in earnest and I would no sooner rise to my feet than he would throw me again - forwards, backwards and sideways - and then leap on me and apply a stranglehold or arm-lock, quickly and hard, so I had to stifle a wince.

Here he was, not an attractive man by any means but perfectly built for judo, in his element showing off to three women who laughed every time I went down, as though it was a clown act and I was the fall guy. I could see his eyes bulging when he came in, his club-like fingers and square palms reaching out to grab my tunic so he could fling me through the air, or grab my arm or wrist so he could twist it as far as the joints would allow before dislocating. I was hurt, I was humbled and I was close to punching his leering face but I resisted and kept on smiling, as I'm sure he knew I would; to have retaliated would have put me beyond the pale for him and for the women.

The next time he invited us and asked if I wanted to 'do some Judo', I told him: 'Thanks, but I couldn't really be bothered having to get changed and comb my hair again and all that. Anyway I prefer a really hard base to work on.'

At Christmas the department had a dinner on the premises for the staff. The lower class, which consisted of technicians, mechanics and office staff, but not ex-POWs with a fondness for difficult crosswords, sat down whilst the upper class of scientists and doctors waited on them. Mr Peter McEwan, Dr Kit Pedlar and Dr Colm Floret were among the waiters, though if the 'maitre-de' himself was there he was so inconspicuous he couldn't be seen, and the divide was as clear-cut as if they had been sitting and we standing.

It would seem like carping to suggest the whole thing smacked of patronage but there was too much deference towards the waiters to make the thing work. None of us, the seated, knew what to expect so it came as a real surprise to see our bosses dressed as pirates with a plate of turkey, potatoes and peas in each hand. It might have been better, if they thought it necessary to touch hands across the Great Divide, to sit down among us and chat, joke or sing; better still to have drawn individual lots to see who'd be waiters and who diners and have us mixed. But that would have constituted fraternisation which the Army had taught was a crime against nature. What we were taking part in was more like the managing director of Ford UK getting dressed up as Santa Claus for the factory-workers' kids.

Fortunately I had come to work armed because it was the last day before the holidays and I had a few scores to settle, and on me I had a huge water pistol which was guaranteed to squirt a maximum of a hundred and fifty jets a distance of ten feet, more than adequate for my needs here.

My fellow diners at first looked on in horror as I blasted one waiter after another, causing their make-up to run like Pagliacci's clown and the immunologist to drop one of his plates. Any protest from anybody loyal to their waiter was met with a treble squirt in the face and a double at their dinner. It was with the greatest effort that the waiters managed to carry on with a smile or a grimace and it probably identified those who would have protested at the waiter idea when it had first been mooted at the November Scientific Staff Meeting. But they couldn't give the whole thing up for the sake of one anarchist from the North, so they bravely carried out their duties without complaint and when I finally got up after the Christmas pudding, there wasn't a dry eye, shirt or blouse anywhere.

One morning I was surprised by Professor Gwynn-Forsythe coming in unannounced with several visitors, and in the rush to draw the curtain over the mynah's cage I failed to cover the front completely, enough light was thus admitted to stimulate the bird and it went into its routine of 'Wha' cheor, Geordie! You stu-pid bu-gger!'

I'd had the bird on the shelf for weeks but it had been covered up and nobody had noticed it, and nobody would believe the bird's prodigious power of mimicry unless they saw and heard it at the same time.

Gwynn-Forsythe was clearly shocked beyond belief that I should address him in such a manner and appalled that I should blame a bird, let alone one he had never seen before and couldn't believe was actually there now.

I was thus in the preposterous position of having to try to get the bird to repeat itself for the benefit of Professor Gwynn-Forsythe and his guests, to prove I was speaking the truth; and the only way I could do it was to say the two phrases over and over ad nauseam until he could stand it no longer. Naturally, as always happens in situations like this, the bird let me down badly, remaining totally mute.

Even after he and his visitors had gone and I had removed the bird that night, I don't think the Professor ever quite believed what had happened, but every time he came into the lab after that, the first thing he would do was glance up at the shelf where the bird had been.

In preparation for a motor-cycle tour of the Continent in summer, Judy and I decided to do a practice run at Easter, touring the south west of England to see how the bike would perform with all the camping gear loaded; but it turned out to be more of a trial for Judy than anything else.

I had asked Colm to give her a smallpox vaccination in readiness for our European trip and the ever-thoughtful Colm had suggested doing it on her ankle rather than her upper arm, the usual place, to avoid disfigurement; the risk of developing complications was higher with the ankle than the arm but it was so negligible that we decided to go ahead.

We were in a tent in South Devon when Judy became febrile and developed generalised vaccinia viraemia and her whole body, face, arms, hands, legs and feet were covered in pocks. It wasn't smallpox, it was cowpox, the species that was used to vaccinate humans because of its diminished infectivity. She had been a bit headachy since first thing that morning but had nevertheless ridden pillion all day and, covered by her motor-cycling outfit, hadn't noticed anything until we had stopped, pitched tent, had our meal and she had got undressed.

I knew there wasn't a great deal to be done except rest, so she got into her sleeping bag and I went into town to find a doctor. I waited an hour only to be told there was no such thing as 'vaccinia viraemia' and in any case he didn't make calls to tents, if my wife was ill I should take her to the nearest hospital which was many miles away.

I thanked him for his concern and valuable advice and went back to the tent. By the next morning Judy was rather better so we packed up and moved on, heading back towards London. By the time we got back two days later after some hard riding, the pocks had all but disappeared, leaving virtually no scarring except on the ankle.

The job I had at the eye hospital was unfulfilling and unsatisfactory; my duties were never adequately defined, my responsibilities therefore not properly circumscribed, and it was impossible to serve two masters. Ocular microbiology was limited; the microbiology I did in the Army with all its constraints was more interesting than anything I was doing here. The likes of McEwan thought they only needed to have an idea and any competent technician should be able to prove it for them; they never contemplated failure even for practical reasons, let alone that they could have been barking up the wrong tree.

The system was deplorable for the technician because if you were put with somebody you didn't like, or more importantly if he didn't like you, your working days would be unrelieved misery. There was constant rivalry and jealousy between the 'scientists', and their technicians were expected to reflect their relationships and likes and dislikes, indulge them in their pettiness, scheme with them, comfort them in their frustrations and praise them for anything that hadn't gone too badly wrong; like squires and their knights, I imagine.

However, scientist and technician liaisons notwithstanding, when it came down to sheer effort, unrelenting taskmasters, frustrations, tedium and humiliation, it didn't bear comparison with selling pharmaceuticals; neither did Geo Hawthorpe's hop farm or the breeze-block factory. The people my heart went out to were those who got up every morning, loaded their cars with samples and screeds of useless literature, packed their bags with lists of names - some with warnings of obnoxiousness - and drove off towards a city where they would have to find a convenient place to park, sit in smoky traffic jams and remain smart and fresh, queue up for hours to take abuse from some of the most arrogant people on earth, and deal with others who were sly and greedy; then come back home and write about it - not in the way it deserved to be reported but in a 'positive' way. It was soul-destroying in a way people like Edward Gwynn-Forsythe and Peter Keith McEwan could never have imagined. To them, having to depend on a technician with less natural gifts and inherited advantage than they themselves had, was soul-destroying. Living in a world that wasn't just the way they wanted it to be, was soul-destroying.

36

In June, after I had taken the Virology Final, I handed in my notice at the eye hospital and Judy did the same at the Board of Trade; we were going to do a two-months camping tour of the Continent before going back to the North East for a spell and then emigrating, probably to New Zealand. I already had a job in the laboratory of a disinfectant firm in Newcastle, starting in September.

Tom Fairlie from the photography department, the fellow with the BSA Shooting Star, had asked if he could come with us on our European trip and we'd said yes if he brought a girlfriend along. He and Mandy only had four weeks' annual leave so they would only be coming part of the way, Judy and I were between jobs so we had longer.

We left Dover after work on a Friday night, crossed on the Boulogne ferry and reached Abbeville in the early hours of Saturday morning. There was a shindy going on in the back of the bar we had stopped at and after a little refreshment I went in to see what it was. I still had my leathers on so wasn't dressed for dancing but was nevertheless invited to join in a dance called 'Donnez Moi Chapeau' where someone stood in the middle of a ring of dancers holding hands, pointed to a member of the opposite sex in the circle and then he or she kissed him and took his or her place; it was the kind of dance I could do.

I was having a great time when Judy and Tom came to see where I was. Judy joined in but neither Tom nor Mandy would because they were both very tired, Mandy had stomach cramp and Tom had a migraine, and they weren't used to long hauls. This was pretty much the pattern from then on. They would want to lie in and make a late start, stop soon and go to bed early. Judy and I were the very opposite. We liked to be on our way by 6am, not 11am, and we didn't like frequent stops for smokes, toilets and giving the bike a thorough examination; at least I didn't, though Judy might have been able to adapt to their routine had her arm been twisted up her back at a sufficiently obtuse angle.

The Shooting Star was a good bike and Tom kept it in excellent condition, so he certainly had the power; but neither he nor Mandy had the will or the stamina to keep up with Judy and me. I loved going to new places, meeting new people and taking on new challenges and had never had to consider anybody with physical limitations or inhibitions of any kind. I had warned Tom that if he came along he would have to be prepared to 'really motor' and he had laughed, probably thinking he was pretty tough and I was exaggerating.

For all its celebrated liberté, the first French campsite we called at refused to admit Tom and Mandy because according to their passports they weren't married and it really shook them up. Neither of them spoke a word of French even though both were well educated, and they were so embarrassed and exasperated, they were nearly in tears. They called France all the names under the sun, which everybody around more or less seemed to understand without any translation and might even have agreed with, but there was no way Judy and I were going to get back on our bike and drive across the nearest border that night, even had it been possible.

After a confab the four of us walked down the road to a parade of tourist shops, found one that sold cheap jewellery, bought an 'engagement' ring for Mandy and had no more bother when we went back to the campsite.

The next night we camped in the Bois de Boulogne.

We'd had a hard time coming through Paris on what had been a hot and humid day and as soon as we found a spot to erect our tents, all Mandy could do was collapse onto the grass, still in her leathers, while Tom sat under some trees to let his migraine subside. Judy and I unpacked our things and put up our tent and then did the same for them. Then after standing for over an hour in a long queue at the camp shop, Judy made a meal for everybody, which as it turned out didn't cater for Mandy's special dietary foibles, while I checked the bikes.

Next morning, when they failed to get up even though we'd called them umpteen times and were packed and mounted by the time Tom poked his head out of their tent, we said 'See you in Marseilles in two weeks,' and away we went. They wanted to go no further south than Andorra, the mecca for duty-free, and said Spain, where Judy and I particularly wanted to go, was too far and too dangerous. Besides, Judy and I had to take a detour to Bordeaux where I was to be best man at an old school friend's wedding and if we allowed Tom and Mandy to slow us down any more, we'd be too late for it.

The wedding turned out to be the best either of us had ever been to, a veritable banquet that lasted for hours with everybody singing at the table, and afterwards dancing to a Latin American band right through to the following morning. We stayed at the splendid home of the bride Jacqueline's uncle and aunt and had a great time there, any longer and I would never have been able to get Judy back onto a bike, let alone into a sleeping bag.

After that we went to Lourdes, a legendarily holy place I had heard about practically every day when at St Teresa's primary school, but I was very unimpressed. I couldn't understand how anybody could make an annual pilgrimage to it. It was one of those spectacles you heartily wish you had never seen.

From there we went across the Pyrenees where they were blasting to make new roads, and down to Madrid where we went to a bullfight and Judy, being blonde and good-looking, created nearly as much excitement as the bulls.

From there we headed towards the coast and Valencia and on the plain it was so hot and tedious riding pillion that Judy kept falling asleep and almost off the bike and I had to tie my belt around both of us so she could sleep in safety. Just outside Barcelona we had a bit of bother with three civil guards, one of whom climbed on my bike at a petrol station, where I had left it to cool for twenty minutes whilst we took some refreshment in the cafe, started the engine up and was revving it like mad. I came out, shouting and yelling, grabbed the guard and pulled him off, and the other two took their pistols out. I think it was because they were so taken aback by my fury and by seeing a young woman in a motor-cycling outfit, that they stood there and did nothing. I yelled a lot in bad Spanish and flung my arms up in the air and I think they were nonplussed. But we learned a lesson.

We caught up with Tom and Mandy in Marseilles but we were off to Nice the next day and they were thinking of heading home, so we parted ways and never saw them again. When we left, not only were they not yet out of their sleeping bags, but the hundreds of duty-free cigarettes they had bought in Andorra, which had got drenched in torrential rain and were in a terrible mess, were still drying out on the ground; there were rows and rows of them neatly laid out but utterly ruined. I think the cigarettes were the final straw and they were both aggrieved that I should have given such a glowing picture of a motor-cycling tour of the Continent that Tom had found it impossible not to ask to come along and thus be obligated to bring poor Mandy.

Just outside Pisa the primary chain snapped and we camped with the leaning tower in view for four days until a replacement came from Milan. Otherwise the bike gave us no trouble and we tore through Austria, Switzerland, Luxembourg, Germany and Holland, ending up in a campsite near Brussels where the rain was so unremitting we couldn't move for three days. Time was now running out for us because we had to get back to Newcastle for my mother and father's Silver Wedding anniversary in two days, and I was due to start my new job two days after.

Beginning the journey drenched and with everything saturated and the rain still falling heavily, we drove a total of 762 miles, resting only on the ferry and stopping only to collect the mynah from an Irish porter at the hospital who'd been looking after it for us. It was well past midnight when we got there but he had the bird ready, and after a quick coffee we fastened the cage on the back behind Judy, and away we went.

I had spent four of the last five years away but still very much regarded Tyneside as home. However, now that I was fully qualified I wanted to see something of the world.

Both Judy's parents and mine were still in their fifties and in good health and both fathers in secure employment, so Judy and I should be able to go overseas and work in several different countries and then return to Tyneside before they got old. And this was the reason we were returning to Tyneside now, to be with them for a year while deciding where to emigrate to and if possible find employment there. Australia, New Zealand, Canada and Africa were all possibilities.

Almost any job in microbiology on Tyneside would have done to fill the gap but it would have to be microbiology because I wanted to advance my career as well as travelling, and any more breaks could harm it now.

Our parents were glad we were returning, they weren't looking as far ahead as the next move, they thought when we came back to Tyneside we'd easily be seduced into staying.

Before going on our trip I had arranged with my brothers, headed by Johnny and Michael, for a surprise Silver Wedding Anniversary treat for

Mam and Dad on the 12th September. At 7pm in the evening a taxi was going to call at Simonside Terrace to pick them up and take them to the Pineapple Grill, a well-known restaurant near Grey's Monument in Newcastle, where they would be served an 'expensive' meal, find a little gift each lying on the table, some of their favourite music would be played and they would be toasted by the MC. After the meal and a dance or two, a taxi would bring them back home where their five sons - we had unanimously voted to exclude Judy - would be waiting to play the Wedding March from Midsummer Night's Dream from a record bought especially for the occasion. We would be waiting in different disguises, with sandwiches and cakes, a crate of Brown Ale and one of Amber, a bottle of whiskey and sherry and a couple of bottles of Tizer, and we'd have a party amongst ourselves. At least, that was the plan.

What actually happened was that when Dad came home from work that night, by which time Judy and I had been back several hours and I had taken her over to her folks in Walker, he refused to go. He wouldn't accept being treated by his own sons, certainly not for his own wedding anniversary. If there was 'any taking out to be done', he would do it and he would pay for it. Mam was his wife and the wedding anniversary had nothing at all to do with us. Furthermore, he wouldn't get into a taxi from Simonside Terrace to go anywhere; it was profligate and pure swank and he'd have nothing to do with it, any of it.

I got vexed, Dad got vexed, Johnny and Peter got annoyed, and Mam and Anthony who was only eight, cried bitter tears as Dad insisted on eating the meal Mam had prepared for him, which he said he had earned and paid for. 'Your mother's cooking's good enough for me,' he said, and other things like it. Meanwhile Michael was on the telephone to the Pineapple Grill to see if we could get our money back. We couldn't, so Johnny suggested Judy and I go instead.

There was uproar from the other three.

'We're not paying for him to go and stuff himself! Or Judy! She's not part of our family!'

'I'd rather pay for Judy than our Joe.'

'So would I. But that's not the point.'

In the finish Dad agreed to go - 'but not for your sake, only for your mother's' - and when the taxi came they were dressed and ready to leave.

We then set about decorating the front room where the 'welcome home' party was to be held, making the sandwiches, getting the drink in and setting the gramophone up ready with the little EP ready to drop on at the turn of a knob.

In the face of a great deal of self-righteous opposition from Johnny, Michael and Peter, I went to work in Mam and Dad's bedroom with the things I had brought up with me from London. On the dressing table I put a copy of *'Lolita'* and *'Lady Chatterley's Lover'* and on the bedside table a Catholic birth control chart which had a little cardboard wheel you turned to line up the dates. To the springs of the mattress under the bed I hung so many tin cans and bottles I'd got from the shed in the yard, that merely opening the door and stepping into the room set them all off jingling and jangling.

My brothers were horrified when one by one they each came to witness what I considered to be a bit of adult humour quite beyond their puerile minds, and I had to threaten to ploat anybody who interfered with them.

After all the preparations, decent and indecent, were completed, we then set about getting dressed up: Johnny as a nigger minstrel with hands and face blackened with soot from the chimney, Michael as a Jesuit priest, Peter as a cowboy, Anthony as a flapper from the 'roaring twenties' and I as a Chicago hitman.

'Urgh! Trust our Joe..! Can't be an ordinary robber baddie. He has to be a killer.'

Then we all got our musical instruments. I had my guitar, Johnny, his banjo, Michael, his mouth organ, Peter, Dad's violin and Anthony sat at the piano. It would be hard to imagine so many instruments in the same place at the same time and nobody able to play more than a few badly fingered chords on any of them, but that's the way it was in our house; mind, I'm being a little modest when I lump myself in with the rest of them, seeing as how I had taken some instruction for the guitar.

By half past nine when the folks were due back, we were all getting a little edgy. We had had nothing to eat or drink and had maintained ourselves in a state of readiness for an hour and a half, waiting for the doorbell to ring whereupon the record would drop on the turntable, the music begin and we would all cheer and sing. But they didn't come. There were plenty of false alarms, people walking down the street and that sort of thing, but no Mam and Dad.

Another half hour went by and then another and by now there was quibbling. There was considerable griping about my desire to start on the brown ale for instance, the sandwiches were going dry and Dad's violin had to be wrested from Peter and Anthony who were rolling over the floor fighting for it.

Eventually Michael telephoned the Pineapple Grill to learn that they had left ages ago. We were all in agreement that Dad would probably have refused the taxi back, even though it had been paid for, and insisted on getting the bus. But even then, they should have been back long ago.

It was only when Peter, who always teased Anthony, asked him for a kiss that it clicked with Anthony that he was the only 'woman' amongst us and he now wanted to be something else but we wouldn't let him. Michael had steadfastly remained the only one not to partake in either food or drink, but not with good grace and he bleated nonstop about how I was more like the bad fairy than the eldest son and that I was the one who had caused everything to go wrong.

'Because he was in the Army, he thinks he's tough,' Peter added. 'And then he goes and gets married and thinks that makes him a man... Well, not to us, it doesn't. Nobody knows him like we do!'

'Unfortunately.'

'Aye, unfortunately.'

'If Judy knew what he was really like, she wouldn't have married him.'

'Now he's the big drinker. Thinks because he's got a bottle of Newcastle Brown Ale in his hand, he's a big deal... We saw you trying to flick the top off like a cowboy. But you couldn't do it, could you..? Did you see him before, everybody..? He cut his thumb and it started to bleed and then he had to get the opener and got his filthy blood all over it... Pathetic, that's what he is.'

'Our Joe, face like a poe. Smells like one an' all.'

As always, I consoled myself with the altruism about powerful wild animals being born to be baited.

It was nearly midnight when Dad and Mam at last came home, and although jaded, we all leapt to our posts and titivated our disguises.

They were delighted when they came in, thinking that by now we'd have all gone to bed. They had been so chuffed with the Pineapple Grill, the Anniversary Waltz, and all the rest, that they had taken the bus to

Walker to tell Judy's Mam and Dad about it and Judy's folks had tried not to delay them because they knew what was waiting for them at home. But they couldn't exactly push them out, so out had come the drinks and they had all had a good laugh as Dad and Mam told them about the meal and everything. Eventually they got up to leave and Judy's dad insisted on driving them home, on strict instructions from Judy not to accept any invitation to pop in...

We were now all sitting around having a drink when Dad said 'Well, you make your mother and I very proud. All of you. You're five fine sons.'

'Yes,' I said, adding to the sentiments without choosing my words very carefully, 'and at least three of them could knock the pants off you.'

'What did you say?' he said, eyes narrowed.

'I said "At least three of us could knock the pants off you."'

'You what..! Who..? Which three?'

His jacket was off and he was standing in his braces, shirt sleeves rolled up, fists clenched in the style of his pugilist forbears.

'Get up all three of you who think they can knock the pants off me!'

My brothers were all looking daggers at me.

'I was only kidding, man.'

'Take it back, then!'

'Come on... You're over fifty... We're in our prime, as you're always saying.'

'Even so, none of you are good enough.' He turned around and looked every one of us who dare look up, right in the eye, his fists hard and his knuckles white.

'I hope I'm not supposed to be one of the three,' Michael said with disgust.

'Well, I'm certainly not,' said Peter.

'Don't look at me, anybody. Because I'm not either,' Anthony said, slight and pale and not even looking his eight years.

Eventually my father sat down but he was still annoyed and drank his drink but left his cake and lit up a cigarette instead.

'Don't ever...say that to me again. Not any of you.'

I was lounging back in my chair with my glass in one hand, cigarette in the other, really only wanting to enjoy the party but not quite able to let it go at that.

'You know, it's only reasonable to say we're stronger than you now. Johnny and me do weight lifting and - '

'Get up!'

I was getting really niggled at what I saw to be his intransigence so I stubbed out my cigarette, put down my glass and stood up.

'Right!' he said, instantaneously on his feet. 'Put 'em up! I can still show you a thing or two.'

He was already advancing so I reluctantly put my fists up to defend myself and my pride. We all knew how he and my mother felt about sons or daughters striking their parents, it mightn't have been specifically covered by the fourth commandment but we all knew they regarded it as a mortal sin.

But he'd left me no choice.

The always reasonable and respectful Johnny now got to his feet and stood between my father and me. 'I'll hit the first man to strike a blow,' he said quietly.

Dad turned towards him, shocked and obviously hurt but more angry than anything else. 'You too, eh, Johnny..? Right! Put them up!'

'Don't look at me!' Michael said, sitting even further back in his chair.

'Me neither!' said Peter.

'Right, then. There's just you two... How do you want it..? One at a time, or both together? It's all the same to me.'

The three of us were now standing in boxing positions on the little rug in front of the fireplace whose mantelpiece was covered with large expensive cards with lots of silvery ornamentation, in a room decked out with 'Happy Anniversary' and 'Good Old Mam and Dad!' banners, with food and drink aplenty nicely set out and musical instruments standing in corners on sheets of music with simplified chords written in, waiting to be played.

Mam and Anthony were now on their knees on the hearth rug that represented the centre of the ring, their arms clamped around each of Dad's legs, pleading with him.

'No, Jack! No!' Mam was sobbing.

'We know you could easy knock those two out, Dad,' came Anthony's shrill little voice. 'But please don't. Not on your anniversary. It's supposed to be a party.'

'Sit down, our Joe,' said Michael. 'You started all this.'

'Yeah,' said Peter in his deep voice. 'It's always him. Ever since he came out the Army he's been trying to play the big man.'

'We all know he deserves a hiding,' Michael went on. 'But not now. Please, Dad... Come on, John. Sit down, for goodness sake, everybody.'

'He needs a good hiding all right and our Johnny could easily give him one.'

Mam was now up and had her arms around Dad, preventing any blows from being struck. 'Please, please, Jack! Not tonight of all nights... Joe, please... And Johnny... Sit down both of you. Then your Dad will.'

We did and then, very slowly like a spring being compressed, Dad sat down.

A few minutes later we all stood up and embraced and sang 'Bless This House' and cried our eyes out.

An hour later I was in bed with Johnny and Peter, Peter moaning because he was being squashed in the middle, when there was the most terrific clatter from Dad and Mam's bedroom.

'What the..?' Dad shouted out.

Then we remembered.

'He's going to come in here and this time you've had it. And I'm not getting in the way,' Peter said, clambering over me to get out of the bed.

But even in the dark I could tell my father was smiling when he came around the door.

'You're a bugger, our Joe,' he said. 'I suppose God must have had his reasons for making you the way you are. But your mother and I've never been able to work it out.'

The Disinfectants & Detergents Business

37

While Judy and I had been racing over the Continent, two weeks before I was due to start at the disinfectant firm, the 'manager' of the laboratory, as they called the chief technician in industrial labs, had come to the house asking for me. My mother said he was a burly man with a purple complexion, a stubby nose, large blubbery lips and straight black hair which even though it glistened with Brylcream, wouldn't stay down. His name was Walter Chubb and I'd met him at the interview. He knew I was going to have a holiday before beginning my new post so I didn't know why he'd come to the door when he knew I'd be away.

There were so many positions opening up in microbiology that it was easy to get work as a laboratory technician in 1961, just as it had been ever since I started working in 1954, and I soon found out that it had been very hard to fill the post of Senior Technician in the bacteriology department of the firm I had come to work for, the main reason being Walter Chubb. Nobody on Tyneside who knew him or knew of him would apply, and that was why he had been so anxious to make sure I was coming that he had taken the very unusual step, but not for him apparently, of calling at my parents' home.

The laboratory consisted of two rooms separated by a glass partition. The first and smaller was divided by a long table down the centre and had a bench running down each side. The second was the wash-up with the usual big sinks, hot air ovens, autoclaves and storage space for glassware. Beyond the large window at the far end was the corrugated iron roof of the factory where they bottled disinfectants and detergents for domestic use.

There was a large chemistry laboratory above ours which tested new compounds at various strengths to measure their cleaning capacity. The bacteriology laboratory's job was to test their antibacterial effectiveness and to carry out daily quality control on all products coming off the line to make sure customers were buying only a limited number of acceptable species of bacteria with their washing-up liquids, and none at all with the disinfectants.

A pale thin man of about thirty, called Paul Dean, was the other senior bacteriologist in the department. Walter Chubb, whose qualifications were similar to ours, called himself an 'executive bacteriologist', meaning he never did any technical work now.

In the wash-up was Hilda, a thirty-odd-year-old, robust good-humoured woman, Nora, an Irish woman of about twenty-two who had something wrong with her nerves, and a nineteen-year-old lad called Brian Nairns from Ashington who was crazy about motor-bikes, especially trials.

Walter Chubb and Paul Dean had come from the Public Health Laboratory in Newcastle, Walter leaving first and then Paul following after Walter had got settled in. The attraction of a job in private industry was its higher salary and faster promotion, plus the possibility of research projects, with none of the grind and unpaid overtime of a hospital laboratory.

Once Paul had left the NHS, which had been very secure employment that had suited his rather timid nature, he had become entirely dependent on the goodwill of the more ambitious and less temperate Walter and I suspect they were so close that they became friends and enemies at the same time. Paul depended on Walter to get him his salary rises and other benefits, and Walter depended on Paul for considerable emotional support as well as his skills as a bacteriologist.

As soon as Walter had moved up from technician colleague in a large NHS laboratory where everybody spoke of sedition and socialism, to manager of a laboratory in a firm that was being taken over by a huge American conglomerate, he no longer talked like the scion of a Catholic Irish family with very working-class roots, whereas Paul proudly never forgot his English Protestant ones.

All this I had learned by the end of the second day in the laboratory when Walter was away in Birmingham meeting important people. Paul was a socialist and a real humanist with a good sense of humour and had played clarinet in a local jazz band, 'The Louisianas', and we immediately became friends.

My main assignment was to try to prove the superior antibacterial activity of the firm's products compared with those of rival manufacturers and this meant using tests designed for the purpose and interpreting results favourably. I didn't like this but the test procedures had been clearly and emphatically laid down and the position of the firm was that since we, like everybody else, only had the resources to carry out a limited number of tests, we were hardly going to select those that implied our products were in any way inferior.

Right from the first morning when Chubb said 'You can call me "Walter" in the lab but I expect you to call me "Mr Chubb" in front of anybody upstairs', he circumscribed the relationship in a way such a provision never failed to do with me.

Quickly and quite unnecessarily for my needs he told me of his major likes and dislikes regarding bacteriologists, personalities in the firm and human nature in general, and I knew I would now have no excuse for saying or doing anything that might conflict with any of the official preferences and aversions of the bacteriology department. They could include such things as affection for a singer who apparently deserved to have his vocal cords cut, respect for a union leader who should be put up against a wall and shot, unwitting tolerance of modern art and 'too much freedom'.

'I think I can say by and large we're a happy bunch of people who get along well together and have never had any real trouble so far, touch wood...except for the odd little niggle you get wherever you go...or when one of the women are having one of their googlies, if you know what I mean, ha ha.'

Chubb would never admit to the possibility that he could be wrong about anything, would never listen to advice - certainly not from Paul or me - and he was always on our backs. I had never experienced this before and although he would have been astonished if you accused him of harassment, this was what it amounted to.

He would sit at the top of the table and would watch you minutely for ten or fifteen minutes, and then get up and come over and tell you that whatever you were doing should be done differently, even though it might only be the way you held a pipette, something you had done a thousand times before. He wanted everything done, said or written, exactly the way he did it.

He was paranoid about his prospects with the firm because although he was a Fellow of the IMLT and held two diplomas, all the other managers had a university degree and the word was that when the Americans came they would sooner or later replace everyone without one, no matter what else they had. His big round hands would clench a pencil he was using to jot down ideas for the managing director in the office next door, ideas that the managing director could use to convince 'the Yanks' that Chubb was not disposable, and he would sometimes have a look of vacant terror.

'I'm going up like a rocket,' he had told Paul many times before take-overs were a twinkle in anybody's eye. 'Hang on to my tail and I'll take you to the stars.'

'What can you say about anybody who says that to you, I ask you?' Paul would shake his head and smile in the funny cockeyed way he had that tried to conceal a missing eyetooth.

'He says he's going up like a rocket...and he's cacking himself at the same time... Let him talk long enough about how great things are going to be and he'll burst into tears... Some rocket. Squib floating in the Tyne, more like it... I'm so glad you're here, Joe. I cannot stand much more. He and I've been like two people in a prison cell. Not bosom pals but knowing everything about each other, knowing too much. I'm suffocated but I can't break away. Nobody knows how I hate this job... Hate it!'

Judy had got a job at Kenton Bar with Civil Defence. She was a shorthand typist in a department headed by a brigadier-general who'd retired of old age from an Army that had never fired a single nuclear weapon or been engaged in so much as a nuclear scuffle, and immediately been given a supposedly vital position in charge of organising civilian defence against a major nuclear missile bombardment of Tyneside.

I'd spent two years observing the British Army at close range, and of its many shortcomings the inability to organise so much as a 'piss-up in a brewery', as the simple lucid testimony of so many fellow witnesses went, was paramount.

This old man was not only responsible for planning the design and construction of nuclear shelters but was also in charge of the mass evacuation of the populace. At a time when anti-nuclear protestors in America were demonstrating on film the utter ineffectiveness of any kind of shelter, let alone one for ordinary civilians, this antediluvian, instead of recalling the devastation and human misery caused by any war and using what few neurons he had left to argue against it while enjoying a comfortable pension, participated in the criminal farce of adequate protection, while continuing to draw a huge salary. For a few more years until senility, like Red China, finally had to be acknowledged, he would have everybody running around after him and treating him the way he had always been treated, as a superior being; not because of his abilities which were unexceptional but because he was born into the class the British cherish as exemplars, the 'Upper Middle'.

If the three of us were sitting reading at tea-break, Walter Chubb with his *Financial Times*, Paul with his *Daily Mirror*, and me with a book, Chubb would constantly interrupt. 'Listen to this, lads.' After chuckling for a couple of minutes so we'd know how to respond, he would begin reading aloud.

One day he said 'Put your book and paper down a minute, both of you...you Joe and you Paul. I've something important I want to ask your opinion about. It's a new method I've worked out for sampling the No 3 tank...to get over the viscosity problem.'

'Don't ask me, Walter,' I said. 'Your mind's made up already and you know it. You just want to be able to go upstairs and tell them you've discussed it with us and we agree with you.'

'You know what you've got, don't you?' he said, puckering up like a little girl about to say something nasty.

'I could probably guess what you think I've got.'

'Right..! A bloody big chip on your shoulder... You don't like being part of a team. You don't like the Queen, you don't like the Government, Newcastle corporation, the BBC, the Pope...anything. The trouble is you don't like authority, full stop.'

'That's about it in a nutshell,' I said without looking up from my book.

'In fact, there's nothing you like, is there?'

'Oh, I think there's a few things left between heaven and hell other than what you've just mentioned,' I said.

After a few minutes he said 'Look, Joe. I'm asking you, please. Let me lay this idea out and then you and Paul can say what you like about it and I'll listen.'

I lowered my book. 'Go on, then. Let's have it.'

'Tell me if you have any ideas,' he said in a voice of such sweet reasonableness. 'This little unit of ours is a far more democratic set-up than you think... Right, Paul..? Paul can tell you of the many tussles we've had over the years sweating things out together when I...with help from Paul...created this department from nothing. This place was just a space in a yard when I came. So what I'm saying is, although you can chip in, you must remember that in the final analysis I am judge and jury!' His voice had risen to a crescendo, just like Hitler's used to.

We both looked at him. I began to laugh and Paul grinned.

'Thank you, Paul,' he said in a pained voice, 'after all I've done for you.'

He then got up, walked over to where Paul was sitting, thrust his face into Paul's and kept it there for a few moments so Paul could be in no doubt about who had been offended, and then went out, the way he always eventually did when he was hurt.

It was hard not to feel sorry for him. He conducted his relationships with everybody in the department in the manner of teenage love affairs and they all laughed at him upstairs. There was no denying he was conscientious and enthusiastic where the firm was concerned, he was convinced its products heralded the dawn of a new era in the science of washing and cleaning; and there was nobody else like that in the whole place. He was quite a good mimic and could be very funny when he was taking somebody off that he had met on the train or at some meeting. But he was so obsessive, so self-centred and so vain that you couldn't like him for long.

Nobody in the lab had ever challenged him and when I came and wouldn't do some of the things the others had done without a qualm, he couldn't cope with it; he became infuriated and complained to the Managing Director and I'd be hauled up to give an account of myself.

There was something done in the bacteriology laboratory which was very bad practice and I had never seen it done anywhere, and that was to scrape the culture medium with its colonies of live bacteria, out of the petri-dishes and into a bucket before sterilisation, thus putting not only the person who was doing it at considerable risk of infection, but anybody in the vicinity then and for sometime afterwards. The first time I saw it being done by Hilda, who had no bacteriological training whatsoever and no idea what she was handling, I protested to Chubb.

'These aren't pathogens,' he said. 'They're just commensals. Aerial contaminants.'

But this wasn't true. Every day we used some common pathogens as test organisms and, in any case, some aerial contaminants can be pathogenic.

I had told him I didn't approve and would never do it myself and one day when he must have decided it was time to make me eat humble pie in front of everybody, he walked over to me with his head held back so that his eyes were looking down at me - so theatrically that I was sure he had practised it in front of a mirror - and said 'Tell Nora to empty those plates.'

'Which ones..? The ones that haven't been sterilised, you mean?'

'You know what I mean.'

'These?'

He nodded.

'No, I won't because I don't think it's right. She wouldn't have a clue what she'd be handling.'

'But you do.'

'Yes.'

'Then you do it.'

'No. I know what's in there and that's why I won't do it. You never did it that way at the Public Health Laboratory and I'm certain you've never seen it done in any bacteriology laboratory anywhere.'

'So you're refusing a direct order?'

'Yes, if that's what it is.'

'Right. I want you to come with me.'

'Where to?'

'To see the Managing Director.'

The whole thing had been staged and the MD was waiting for me. He read the firm's riot act and told me I had to defer to my manager. I said I was at least as well qualified as my manager and didn't regard him as my superior except in terms of his authority within the firm, and that the firm had an obligation to seek advice on this matter and I suggested the two biggest bacteriology departments in Newcastle - the Royal Victoria Infirmary and the public health laboratory at the General Hospital.

The Managing Director wouldn't agree to this - or said he wouldn't - and ordered Chubb and I to each submit a dissertation justifying our position. I never saw Chubb's but know he saw mine because I heard him discussing it with Paul before submitting his own. I never heard any more about it and the objectionable practice continued, though I was never asked to participate again.

There was another thing I refused to do but on less technical grounds.

The firm produced a lavatory cleaner in the form of a bleach powder that was shaken over the faecal stains that are sometimes left in the pan after a bowel movement or two. To test the efficacy of this and rival products, Chubb had had the brilliant idea - as he described it - of having one of the lavatory pedestal manufacturers in Stoke-on-Trent manufacture four minute lavatories scaled down to one eighth normal size. 'An eighth the size and eight times the price,' was how Paul described them.

They were perfect replicas, quite beautiful *objets d'art*, and were Chubb's pride and joy. Whenever the laboratory had visitors from America, or anywhere important, out would come the little lavatories which Chubb kept locked away in his private drawer. The expressions on the faces of the tycoons and chemists when, with a face shining with joy, Chubb would set them out side by side on the table, was something I could never forget.

One afternoon he told me he wanted me to work with them. Up until now he had only entrusted them to Paul, but it was essential, he said, that I learned the technique.

'You've got to soil them first,' he said with a gleam in his eye, probably guessing that the chip on my shoulder was going to reveal itself at any minute.

'How?'

'Put some of yours in.'

'Some of my what in?'

'You know!'

'You're kidding, aren't you?'

'No, I'm not. Get yourself up to the doings. You only need a little bit.'

'What do you expect me to do..? Roll it into one-eighth-sized turds and drop them from one eighth the normal height?'

'There's no need to be facetious. And it wouldn't work... Take a jar up with you and smear the insides with a swab stick when you come back.'

I could see Hilda and them grinning in the wash-up; if I so much as left the room they would know what I was doing, and when I came back they would know I had finally submitted to the will of Walter Chubb.

It wouldn't have been so bad if the test had been carried out in tubes or petri dishes, but little lavatories made the whole thing look so crude. And how would it look to the rest of the staff if they peered in during the cleaning period or afterwards and none of the test products were equal to the task..? Would they be appalled by the smell, shocked by its tenacity, or perhaps disgusted by the colour?

'No. Definitely not.'

He argued with me but I still refused.

'Would you like to do mine, then?' he sneered.

'You must be joking!'

He then went around the lab asking everybody in turn and they all had excuses for not donating, so he went down into the factory. I don't know whether he paid a fee or what but quarter of an hour later he came back with a piece of heavily soiled toilet paper inside a glass jar.

I could hardly refuse to do the test then, especially after he'd soiled the first two with a little stick, as a demonstration.

It was a totally useless test for all kinds of reasons but the little lavatories would have made wonderful ornaments, egg cups, mustard pots, salt cellars or ashtrays.

Every Monday morning I had to go into the factory to take samples from the huge tanks of concentrated detergent under the floor, which were accessed by manhole covers. I would lower a bottle with a piece of string tied around its neck and let it sink to about two feet and then draw it up. There were six tanks in all. The sampling was easy, the hard part was getting by the hard-cased women who worked there and didn't give a damn about a young man's dignity. Whatever you did in the factory, you always had to keep one eye out for somebody behind you.

One morning when I went down there was a lot of activity because of a conveyor-belt problem and I made the one mistake everybody was warned about - I didn't put the manhole cover back on properly. I had completed the sampling and gone back to the lab when a woman carrying a couple of boxes in front of her, fell into the tank of concentrated washing-up liquid. They got her out but there were ructions on and I only survived because the ensuing investigation revealed that sundry other persons had left manhole covers off in the past, only nobody had ever taken a dive as far as they could tell. Another reason I survived was because Chubb knew that no matter how many chips I had jutting out of my shoulders, I was indispensable.

He knew I was shaken by the accident which everybody else in the place was laughing about but which I knew could have ended horrifically, and he hounded me all week for one thing or another.

By the Friday lunch-time I'd had enough. I'd done something very silly which I would never forget and I had apologised for it upstairs, downstairs and wherever else it was required and I had listened to sermons and harangues from people who every day did things I didn't do.

I came back after lunch and didn't bother putting my white coat on, I just waited until Chubb came in. He was rather taken aback when he saw me standing in my outdoor clothes and must have realised I was going to do something he wouldn't like.

'What's up, Joe?' he said affably, hanging his overcoat up.

'I want a word with you in the library,' I said. 'And I want Paul to come along as a witness.'

'Witness to what?' he said, looking alarmed.

'Witness to what I'm going to say to you.'

Paul shrugged towards Chubb and followed me as I went out.

The library was the one place on the premises which was quiet and private and it was used for important confidential conversations or for when one of the women from the office or the laboratories needed to have a bit of a cry.

When we got there I told Chubb what I thought of him and that if he harassed me any more I would hit him and of course leave, but hit him damned hard.

'I didn't realise you hated me so much,' he said with tears in his eyes, more upset at now knowing for certain that he was disliked, than at the prospects of maybe having his nose broken.

'All right, if that's the way you feel. But I must say I'm very surprised and sorry you feel like that. Paul can tell you I'm a very fair man and have always been good to my staff. I'd throw myself off Byker Bridge if I thought everybody felt the same way you do about me. I always buy a little present for them at Christmas...the females, that is... Don't I, Paul..? And when Hilda was sick that time, I went around to her house - '

'Shut up, will you, Walter. I've said what I had to say. Now, what are you going to do?'

'Are you not going to hit me?' he said pathetically.

All of a sudden I felt so embarrassed and so like a bully. I shook my head.

'Of course I want you to stay here,' he said enthusiastically, a smile coming on his face. 'You're a good bacteriologist. I want us to be friends. Like me and Paul here.' He put his arm around Paul's shoulders to show me.

For the rest of the afternoon he couldn't have been more solicitous for my welfare, but on the following Monday he got a hiding anyway.

He had picked Paul up at Four Lane Ends, as he did every morning, and crossed into Benton Road in front of a little van which sounded its horn in anger.

Walter wound his window down, stuck up two chubby fingers and grinned at Paul. 'Stupid get!'

But the van had pursued them all the way to Shields Road where it overtook them, stopped, and the driver got out and come over to Walter's window.

'Open up!' he shouted and Walter immediately obliged. 'Don't give me two fingers, you prick!' the man shouted, and smashed his fist into Walter's face, bloodying his nose and breaking his glasses.

Walter had gone straight to Byker police station to register a charge of assault; he had the make of car, registration number and everything. But the desk sergeant said 'Serves you right.' And that was that.

Paul was ecstatic when they came into the lab and Chubb had gone to the washroom.

'I've been a slave to him for ten bloody years. I've listened to all his troubles, sorted umpteen upsets he's had with people in the lab and outside of it...and he's treated me like shit. I never had the guts to smack him in the mouth myself and was so glad when I thought you were going to do it on Friday. Then today, like an answer to all my prayers, some sod built like a docker comes up and does it right in front of me and the snot from his nose hit me in the ear... "Wham! Bam!" he went and Walter never said a word. His glasses fell off and he turned to me and I thought he was going to start bubbling. The stupid bugger didn't think it was possible for such a big bloke to get out of such a little van. Then he insisted we go to Headlam Street. And what does the desk sergeant say..? He says "Fuck off, you daft twit" or words to that effect...

'I tell you, this is the happiest day of my life. I daresn't go back home with him tonight because if he starts on about the belt he got, I'm not going to be able to stop from peeing myself laughing.'

38

Judy and I had had enough of 'Great Britain' which was now calling itself the 'United Kingdom', presumably because most of its component parts wanted to detach themselves. We wanted to get as far away as possible from a society where a hierarchical system based not on merit, and most certainly not on integrity, prevailed. We hated hypocrisy and we hated injustice and we wanted to leave behind the appalling national history of which we had always been instructed, under pain of punishment, to be so inordinately proud.

We had been living in a bed-sitter in Cavendish Place in Jesmond and although it was a comfortable place in a nice area, the landlady was a pain. She was forever complaining about the slightest noise and objected to our having visitors. We never had any parties or anything, just occasional friends for tea, and the day we had my parents around and she shouted up the stairs and embarrassed them, we gave in our notice as soon as they left.

From there we went to an attic in Rothbury Terrace which was only a short distance from Simonside Terrace. The landlady, who was a widow, was a canny soul, but the attic was grotty and over-run with mice. The toilet and bathroom were in the one room and when the landlady's daughter was in, she was in for so long listening to her portable radio, that Judy sometimes had to go to Simonside to use the family toilet.

Because I couldn't afford to go to university I had started work at sixteen and studied at nights for eight years without a single afternoon off from any job I'd ever had. I was an F.I.M.L.T. with diagnostic and research experience in veterinary, medical and industrial microbiology, and had a wife who was a qualified secretary, yet we lived in an attic, unable to afford the rent for a decent flat, never mind the mortgage for a house. We couldn't afford a car, couldn't afford the books I wanted to read or the recordings of music we wanted to listen to. A night out was to the pictures, and it, holidays, clothes, gifts, food, everything, was always done on the cheap.

My father was a civil servant and he was little better off, my brother was an engineer at Parsons and he was just the same.

I was hardworking, keen to get on and prepared to continue studying but there were no prospects of getting a fulfilling job that would pay a really good salary.

Merit wasn't rewarded the way my father always said it would be, neither was industry or conscientiousness. It seemed to me that unless you were born in the right place or knew somebody who was, you'd have to wait until somebody retired or died, to move up a place. And even then you'd have to kowtow for years, never rock the boat and prove you were just like them, meaning among other things that your shoulders would have to be unhindered at all times.

Yet every day we had to listen to being told that Britain was the best place in the world, with the best judicial system, best police, doctors, teachers, cricketers, footballers, topiarists, scissor-sharpeners and God knows what else.

We were twenty-four years old and sick of the whole damned lot of them and had an application in to New Zealand House in the Strand.

Paul and I had become very good friends and now that I was here he wasn't going to take any more of Walter's bullying. 'I got too close to him for my own good. He lost his first wife tragically and was in an awful state. But because he didn't have any friends, I became like a brother to him. When he got pulled around and got married again and had somebody else's shoulder to cry on, I was back where I was before. Any time he thought I might be going to stand against him, he would put his arm around my shoulder and talk about us being buddies...and that would put the kibosh on it. He can shout abuse one minute and be bubbling his head off, the next.

'He's not bad in the sense of being wicked or anything. It's just that he's a megalomaniac and I cannot live my own life properly while I'm under his shadow. He affects my life more than my own wife and daughter. All day I can feel his eyes boring into my back. If I get a haircut or new pair of shoes, straightaway there's a comment. Either he's got a better pair, seen the same ones cheaper somewhere else, or they don't suit me.

'He reads a book he likes or thinks is useful and as soon as he finishes it, he brings it in for me...and he's nagging on every day asking me about it, so I have to read the bloody thing even if I don't like it. He thinks he's doing you a favour by passing on some bit of information he's got from somewhere, or some philosophy he's heard about. All these years I've been dying to tell him, "Read it if you want, Walter. And then shove it up your arse when you're finished, because I don't want it."'

When I had told Paul that Judy and I were going to New Zealand, he confessed he had always wanted to go to Australia but didn't have the nerve. We talked about emigration all the time when Chubb was out and eventually he decided to go. He wrote after a post at Melbourne University that was advertised in the IMLT gazette and was accepted straightaway. It was a shock to him but I gave him the support he needed to see it through.

'The one thing I'm terrified of, is telling Walter,' he said. 'He'll go crackers. He'll break down.'

I laughed.

'I'm not kidding you, Joe. He's my Svengali. He'll never let me go.'

'I'll tell him for you, if you like.'

'Oh no, no. I've got to pluck up the courage to tell him myself and make up for all the years I've been under his heel. I owe this to myself, not to him. He'll do every damned thing to stop me so I'm not telling him until the last minute...until I've signed all the documents, had my medical and everything, and cannot go back on it... Then I'll tell him and watch him shrivel. Without me all these years, he'd have been nothing. But he always tells it the other way on... No, this is one pleasure I'm not going to deny myself.'

I wasn't there when Paul did tell him - perhaps after all the years he felt he wanted to break it quietly - and for three days Chubb wouldn't say a word to him. Then he changed his tack and began pointing out the advantages of staying in Newcastle and enjoying the patronage of somebody who always had his interests at heart. Besides, Walter had heard Australia wasn't all it was cracked up to be. They were hostile to English people and there was a lot of skin cancer about. You couldn't get the BBC out there and there were no Marks & Spencers or the kind of old pubs Paul liked.

This went on until the day Paul left, on a Friday. On the Monday when Chubb came in he said 'Have you seen Paul?'

'Not since he got on the train at Central Station.'

'You mean to tell me he's really gone?'

'Yes.'

'The bastard! The rotten, ungrateful bastard and traitor..! If you know what I'd done for him all these years and then he goes and does this to me. I suppose you gave him the idea, did you?'

'Look, what I say or don't say to anybody has nothing to do with you. He's thirty-one years old, for Christ's sake. Don't you think he's old enough to make up his own mind..? Good luck to him, I say. And if you were the bosom pal you say you were, why couldn't you have the decency to shake his hand and wish him the best of luck in his new life, like everybody else did?'

'I tried but I couldn't,' he said, his eyes filling up. 'I couldn't bring myself to... He's destroyed me by going. He's wrecked my career, my life, everything. I'll never be able to get over this.'

He went out and when he came back we said nothing more on the subject.

A few days later something came up and I said 'That was Paul's, wasn't it?'

'Whose?'

'Paul's.'

'Paul who?'

'Our Paul. Paul Dean.'

'I don't know anybody by that name.'

'What do you mean?'

'I mean, I haven't the faintest idea who you're talking about.'

'Don't talk such tripe. He was supposed to be your friend.'

'Look, Joe. Don't ever mention his name to me again. I don't want that name spoken in this department ever. As far as I'm concerned, the person you are referring to never existed.'

'He did for me. And if I want to talk about him, I will.'

'Not to me, you won't.'

And from then until the time I left, he never referred to Paul Dean and he removed all traces of his ever having been there - all books or anything with his name on and bits and pieces with his initials.

One afternoon not long before I left we were expecting some important visitors and Chubb had got his little lavatories out and gone to the washroom to smarten himself up.

I was kidding on with Hilda and Brian in the wash-up and was demonstrating how Jackie Milburn scored a goal, when my slip-on shoe came off and shot through the open window and onto the factory roof.

'How did you manage that?' they laughed.

'Just like this,' I said, kicking the other one off in the same direction.

'You've had it with that spud,' Brian said, pointing to a hole in my socks.

'Nip out on the roof and get them, will you?'

'What if the big nobs come in and want to see me?'

'Nobody'll want to see you, you daft bugger! Get out and bring my shoes back before they come in.'

He had just gone through the window when the door opened and in came Chubb and the visitors.

I went into the lab in my stockinged feet whilst Hilda called to Brian who was hanging on to the drain pipe outside the window, to warn him.

It was a devil of a job keeping my end up without shoes, it could hardly have been worse if my fly had been open. It's amazing how your confidence goes when you've got no shoes, you're that much shorter and scared to move in case you stand on something or somebody stands on you.

Chubb, who never missed a trick, knew there was something wrong and kept frowning at me, and I was walking on tiptoe to give me the extra height I would have had with the shoes, whilst keeping the centre table between me and everybody else.

When they went out to the wash-up Chubb told Hilda to close the window. 'Where's young Nairns?' he asked.

'He's outside somewhere,' Hilda said, nodding towards the factory.

At that point the party moved on upstairs and Chubb went out with them. A few minutes later he was back.

'Where the hell's your shoes?'

'On my feet... Where do you think?' I said, nodding down.

Two months after Paul left I was offered the job of Chief Bacteriologist at a hospital in the North Island of New Zealand. Chubb wasn't surprised, angry, disappointed or anything. He just took it like a man due to be executed in the morning takes it when he discovers a tiny cavity in one of his back teeth. On my last day he was significantly absent, having arranged to take a day's leave and told none of us.

It was me who really wanted to go to New Zealand and if it hadn't been there it would have been somewhere else - somewhere sunny, somewhere where I felt my skills and experience would be appreciated, somewhere where I felt Judy and I could have a good life. I had always wanted to see the world and had been denied it in the Army due to sheer cussedness, and had missed out on the Middle East a year previously because of a revolution in Lebanon a few weeks before I was due to join an American team investigating infectious diseases among the nomads. Maybe these faraway places weren't all they were cracked up to be but I wanted to see for myself. A lot of people our age were emigrating and although there were tales of a few disenchanted returning to Britain, there were many more who were never heard of again who must have made it.

We didn't look upon it in terms of forever, we would go and travel around as many countries as we could and come back and then decide whether to stay put or go back. Judy was the only daughter in her family but there was a younger son. Her parents were upset about her going but knew I would look after her. 'I only wish we'd done it when we were young,' was a sentiment we heard from many older couples.

In my case I had a father and mother who I knew loved me, and Judy very much also, but would never interfere, never put pressure on us to remain for their sakes. In addition I had three younger brothers to whom I was very close and one who had always been closer than anybody. Later on I would think I was selfish in respect to Johnny. I had gone into the Army, gone to live in London and then got married, and never asked him what he thought; I had cut him out of so much of my life. I hadn't thought of it at the time because he never mentioned it, like my parents he never made any demands on my life at all, and I just took him for granted.

'You'll come out when you're qualified, won't you?' I said to him.

'I'll see,' was all he said, smiling. 'You can tell me all about it.'

If I had known then that apart from a brief reunion in Canada several years later, we would hardly ever see each other again, I couldn't have gone. But I didn't, and I went.

We had several going-away parties, and for the biggest, which was for all our relatives, we hired the large upstairs room at the Chillingham Hotel, near Heaton Station. At this do, which was only two days before we left Newcastle for Tilbury, every single relative of mine was up from South Shields where they all lived, on my father's side and my mother's, and Judy's comparatively few from Newcastle.

My father did something which very few people, except those that knew him well, understood; yet it was something so typical of him and so full of character, that I loved as well as respected him for it.

My mother's eldest brother was one of the last of the major speechmakers and after his customary emotional speech, where the embarrassingly sentimental words would nearly choke in his selfish throat, the man who had made a right skivvy out of his canny little wife, said there was still time for Judy and I to change our minds and everybody present would be glad if we decided not to go to New Zealand after all.

My father then stood up and said that he, for one, would not be glad if after we had gone this far we changed our minds and reneged on our promises to the immigration people in London, to the people in New Zealand who had promised me a good job and had arranged accommodation, and to ourselves. He wished us Godspeed, good health and good luck, hoped we would work hard and give a good account of ourselves and that one day they would see us again. He said he had given his opinion when asked for it by us, and that we were fully aware of his and my mother's wishes, but that we had decided nonetheless to go. And so be it, he would put us on the ship himself if necessary.

A loud groan went up and many people were shocked; but all of us from Simonside Terrace smiled, even Mam, as she dabbed her eyes with her handkerchief.

On 16th October, 1962 we sailed to New Zealand on the SS Stratheden.